T0364177

SEMANTIC *Ambiguity*
AND UNDERSPECIFICATION

CSLI
Lecture Notes
No. 55

SEMANTIC *Ambiguity*
AND UNDERSPECIFICATION

edited by
Kees van Deemter and
Stanley Peters

CSLI *Publications*

CENTER FOR THE STUDY OF
LANGUAGE AND INFORMATION
STANFORD, CALIFORNIA

Copyright ©1996
CSLI Publications
Center for the Study of Language and Information
Leland Stanford Junior University
Printed in the United States
99 98 97 96   5 4 3 2 1

Library of Congress Cataloging-in-Publication Data

Semantic ambiguity and underspecification / Kees van Deemter & Stanley Peters, editors.
p.   cm.
Includes bibliographical references.
Contents: Ambiguity resolution and discourse interpretation / Georgia M. Green — Quantification and predication / Jaap van der Does and Henk Verkuyl — Monotone decreasing quantifiers in a scope-free logical form / Jerry R. Hobbs — Situated disambiguation with properly specified representation / Hideyuki Nakashima and Yasunari Harada — Resolving lexical ambiguity using a formal theory of context / Sasa Buvac — A compositional treatment of polysemous arguments in categorial grammar / Anne-Marie Mineur and Paul Buitelaar — Underspecified first order logics / Hiyan Alshawi — Semantic ambiguity and perceived ambiguity / Massimo Poesio — Towards a logic of ambiguous expressions / Kees van Deemter — Co-indexing labeled DRSs to represent and reason with ambiguities / Uwe Reyle.

ISBN 1-57586-029-5
ISBN 1-57586-028-7 (pbk.)

1. Semantics. 2. Ambiguity. 3. Computational linguistics. 4. Categorial Grammar.
I. Deemter, Kees van. II. Peters, Stanley, 1941– .

P325.5.A46S46 1996
401'.43 — dc20   95-49881
                                                                         CIP

Cover design by Gerome Vizmanos and Tony Gee

CSLI was founded early in 1983 by researchers from Stanford University, SRI International, and Xerox PARC to further research and development of integrated theories of language, information, and computation. CSLI headquarters and CSLI Publications are located on the campus of Stanford University.

CSLI Lecture Notes report new developments in the study of language, information, and computation. In addition to lecture notes, the series includes monographs, working papers, and conference proceedings. Our aim is to make new results, ideas, and approaches available as quickly as possible.

The painting on the cover of the paperback edition of this book is Salvador Dali's *The Great Paranoiac*, 1936 from the collection of the Museum Boymans – van Beuningen, Rotterdam.

Contents

Contributors

HIYAN ALSHAWI worked on computational aspects of natural language semantics at Cambridge University Computer Laboratory and SRI International, Cambridge. He is currently conducting research on speech translation at AT&T Bell Laboratories.

PAUL BUITELAAR is currently a Ph.D. candidate in Computer Science at Brandeis University. His interests are in lexical semantics, knowledge representation and knowledge acquisition from text.

SAŠA BUVAČ is working on a Ph.D. at the Computer Science Department of Stanford University. His area of reseach is in formalizing context using the methodologies of logical AI, knowledge representation, and common sense reasoning.

KEES VAN DEEMTER works as a researcher at the Institute for Perception Research (IPO) in Eindhoven, The Netherlands, which is jointly governed by Philips Research Laboratories and the Technical University of Eindhoven. His interests include the logic of indeterminate information, and more recently the use of semantic information for the improvement of the prosodic quality of synthetic speech.

JAAP VAN DER DOES received his Ph.D. in philosophy at the University of Amsterdam. Currently he is taking part in the PIONIER-project 'Reasoning with Uncertainty' funded by the Netherlands Organization for Scientific Research (NWO), located at the Department of Mathematics. His main interests are the logical and linguistic aspects of generalized quantifier theory. This includes: proof systems for quantifiers and their dependency structure, qualitative approaches to probabilistic quantifiers, mental models for quantifiers, quantifiers and anaphora, quantifiers and collectives.

GEORGIA M. GREEN is Professor of Linguistics at the University of Illinois at Urbana-Champaign, and a member of the Cognitive Science group at the Beckman Institute for Advanced Science and Technology. Her research areas are pragmatics and natural language syntax.

YASUNARI HARADA is Professor at the School of Law and the Institute of Language Teaching, Waseda University, Tokyo, Japan. He is currently Associate Director of the Centre for Informatics, responsible for the entire university's academic networking and computer literacy education. His main research interests as a computational linguist revolve around where language, cognition and formal systems meet.

JERRY R. HOBBS is program manager and principal scientist in the natural language group of the Artificial Intelligence Center, SRI International. His main research interests are discourse interpretation, knowledge representation, encoding commonsense knowledge, and intelligent text processing.

ANNE-MARIE MINEUR is currently working on a Ph.D. in computational linguistics at Saarbruecken University. Her research areas are categorial grammar, feature grammars and lexical semantics.

HIDEYUKI NAKASHIMA received his Ph.D. in computer science from the University of Tokyo. He is a researcher at the Electrotechnical Laboratory in Tsukuba, Japan. His research areas are mainly in AI, including knowledge representation and reasoning.

STANLEY PETERS is Professor of Linguistics and a member of the Center for the Study of Language and Information at Stanford University. His research centers on applications of situated inference to the development of cooperative software, and on theoretical and computational semantics. He has been a Guggenheim Fellow, a member of the Institute for Advanced Study, and a fellow at the Center for Advanced Study in the Behavioral Sciences.

MASSIMO POESIO received his Ph.D. in Computer Science from the University of Rochester. His research interests include reasoning processes in conversations and natural language semantics.

UWE REYLE teaches linguistics at the University of Stuttgart. He is co-author of the book *From Discourse to Logic*. His research interests include the semantics of natural language, computational semantics and automated deduction.

HENK J. VERKUYL is Professor of Linguistics in the Research Institute for Language and Speech (OTS) at the University of Utrecht. His research interests include the semantics of natural language, in particular aspectuality and generalized quantification, as well as lexical semantics.

Preface

In the winter of 1993-1994, the editors of the present volume distributed a *call for papers* on the topic of ambiguity and underspecification, knowing that some interesting ideas were emerging in this area, and planning to combine these into a book. All papers that we received were subjected to a thorough review process. The present volume, consisting of ten self-contained papers and an introductory chapter, is the result of our joint efforts.

The editors want to extend their gratitude to a rather large number of people for their help. We thank Dikran Karagueuzian of CSLI Publications, who asked 'Do I smell a book?' after attending an informal workshop on the topic of this volume in September 1993 and thus, arguably, became the first cause of its existence. We thank a long series of reviewers, for doing an essential and notoriously undersalaried job: Hiyan Alshawi, Robbert-Jan Beun, Tijn Borghuis, Saša Buvač, Ann Copestake, Dick Crouch, Tony Davis, Jan van Eijck, Tim Fernando, Mark Gawron, Greg O'Hare, Eric Jackson, Leen Kievit, Jan Landsbergen, Alex Lascarides, Larry Moss, Reinhard Muskens, Remko Scha, Dag Westerståhl, Gert Veldhuijzen van Zanten, and Ede Zimmermann. The first editor thanks the Institute for Perception Research (IPO) for giving him the opportunity to work on this project, and expresses his indebtedness to the Netherlands Organization for Scientific Research (NWO) for the grant that made possible his stay in Stanford from September 1992 until October 1993, during which much of the groundwork for this book was laid.

Kees van Deemter and Stanley Peters,
Editors.

Introduction

Natural language is known for the ambiguity of its expressions. Whereas artificial forms of communication tend to be designed in such a way that ambiguity is reduced to a minimum, natural language is ambiguous at various 'levels' of interpretation. At a low (e.g., speech recognition) level, a signal can be ambiguous between various utterances; at a higher (semantic) level, a fully recognized utterance can be used to express various different propositions; and at an even higher (pragmatic) level, a proposition may be used for various different purposes. The present volume focuses on ambiguities of the second kind, which are sometimes called *semantic ambiguities*, or mostly just *ambiguities*, when there is no likelihood of confusion.

Semantic ambiguity can arise from various different sources. For example, the source of an ambiguity may be lexical (as in cases of lexical homonymy and polysemy), syntactic (when an expression has more than one possible syntactic derivation), or contextual (as in anaphoric ambiguities). Combinations of such different sources occur as well.

The most obvious problem in the area of ambiguity is disambiguation: choosing the intended interpretation from a plurality of possible ones. But the notion of ambiguity is also intimately connected with a number of fundamental problems of semantic theory. For example, disambiguation presupposes an ability to determine what the different interpretations of a given expression are, and this is not always easy, as we will see presently. Perhaps the most vexing question involving the notion of ambiguity is the following. In formal accounts of meaning, innocent-looking sentences are often attributed many different interpretations. How is this proliferation of interpretations compatible with the relative ease with which *human* interpreters seem to deal with ambiguous expressions? People seem surprisingly adept at dealing with linguistic information that a linguist would consider as ambiguous and, consequently, in need of clarification. Of course, it has always been vaguely understood that contextually available information comes to the aid of the human interpreter, and it has also been acknowledged that the situation of the interpreter does not always require complete disambiguation. But the exact mechanisms that take such factors into account have always been a mystery. By contrast, natural language processing machines have great trouble dealing with ambiguous input, and it is probably fair to say that ambiguity is one of the most daunting problems for automatic analysis of natural language (see, e.g., Bar-Hillel 1960 and Carbonell and Hayes 1987 for some very outspoken statements of this claim).

Recent developments in computational semantics have rekindled slumbering questions about ambiguity. Mainly to avoid the need for separate storage of all possible interpretations, computational semanticists now use levels of semantic interpretation that contain ambiguous representations. The oldest instance of this idea that we have been able to find is PHLIQA's 'multi-level semantics', where the idea was applied to polysemy and homonymy of lexical items (Bronnenberg et al. 1979). Probably the first application of the idea to such linguistically interesting phenomena as quantifier scope ambiguity is as old as Schubert and Pelletier 1982, but this track of research did not gain great popularity until the late eighties, when researchers at SRI came up with their underspecified 'quasi-logical forms' (see e.g., Alshawi 1990). The ambiguous representations are typically not put to use until a separate module has disambiguated them into a non-ambiguous formula of a more traditional kind. In particular, the information in them is not used in logical inference, and they are not presented to the user of the system. Even so, the use of underspecified representations of meaning in NLP systems gives new urgency to the following questions:

- How can interpretations be identified and demarcated? The mere fact that a given sentence may be used for the truthful description of the models in two different classes, say C_{M_1} and C_{M_2}, is no sufficient ground for viewing the sentence as ambiguous, since there is always the possibility of viewing the sentence as a description of the one class of models that consists of the union $C_{M_1} \cup C_{M_2}$.

- What kinds of processing are possible on the basis of underspecified representations? In particular, how are different kinds of ambiguous information best represented and how can ambiguous information possibily enter logical inference?

- Ultimately, the use of underspecified semantic representations raises the question of under what conditions disambiguation is necessary. Even bolder, what is the significance of the notion of ambiguity? After all, if an ambiguous expression can be processed in much the same ways as a nonambiguous one (i.e., be used in the same mental activities), then what does the difference between them amount to?

Although the papers in this volume vary widely in terms of the specific problems they address, as well as in the particulars of the solutions they propose, they all deal with the subject matter just outlined, while also sharing a remarkable openness towards unconventional solutions. In this introductory chapter, we will refrain from giving a full summary of each individual paper. Instead, we will briefly indicate how each of them relates to the problem area of ambiguity and underspecification, and then draw some tentative conclusions.

The first paper in this collection, by **Georgia Green**, shows the huge difficulties involved in disambiguation. Green offers, among other things, a host of sentences that would normally be termed semantically ambiguous and argues convincingly, amplifying previous work by Nunberg (e.g., Nunberg 1987) and others, that many of them can only be resolved by pragmatic reasoning of a kind that can get arbitrarily complex. Consequently, the paper may serve as food for thought to those who view disambiguation as the only way to deal with ambiguous input, and this makes it an excellent start of the present book.

The two subsequent papers by Van der Does and Verkuyl, and by Hobbs are directly relevant to the question of what identifies an interpretation: Both papers happen to be direct follow-ups to earlier papers by the same authors (Verkuyl and Van der Does 1991 and Hobbs 1983) and both contradict received wisdom about what identifies a semantic interpretation. Even those who fail to be convinced by the details of their proposals will agree that they show that little about traditional views on the identification issue is obvious. One area in which the demarcation between interpretations is still hotly debated is that of distributive/collective quantification. **Jaap van der Does and Henk Verkuyl** contribute a new version of their earlier proposals in this difficult area, proposing that no more than two interpretations (or, in their terminology, one meaning, which can be specified according to two different 'modes' of interpretation) are needed to represent the semantics of a transitive sentence such as *Three girls mailed four letters*. The authors claim that their representation also covers the hitherto-problematic 'cumulative' interpretation of such sentences in a satisfactory fashion. Another area in which the question of what constitutes an interpretation has been discussed is that of quantifier scope. **Jerry Hobbs** returns to earlier work (Hobbs 1983) in which he proposed 'flat' representations, which are underspecified as to the scope of quantifiers, this time focusing on the treatment of monotone decreasing quantifiers (e.g., *few*), which was unsatisfying in his earlier proposal. The result is a highly unconventional account, in which the *semantics* of the sentence

Few men work simply says that there exists a set containing few men, all of which work. This is obviously not all that the sentence conveys, but the additional information that this set equals the set of all men who work, is provided by a *pragmatic*, abduction-driven component of interpretation.

The *representation* of ambiguous information and the subsequent *disambiguation* of ambiguous representations is discussed in each of the ten papers of this volume. (See, e.g., the remarkable unanimity in the rejection of 'disjunctive' representations of ambiguous information in the papers contributed by Buvač, by Poesio, and by van Deemter). But representation and disambiguation are probably discussed in most detail in the papers by Buvač, by Nakashima and Harada, and by Mineur and Buitelaar. **Hideyuki Nakashima and Yasunari Harada** observe that a sentence like *It is four o'clock*, when uttered in Japan, is equivalent to the sentence *It is four o'clock in Japan*, uttered anywhere. Reflecting this observation, they sketch a new variety of Situation Semantics which allows that semantic representations omit information that is present in the utterance situation. The omitted information may concern the time and place, as well as other properties of the utterance. The authors of the paper claim that this underspecification mechanism could have certain advantages in the representation of deixis as well as VP ellipsis. Other conceivable applications include the treatment of contextually restricted quantification of the kind described in Westerståhl 1985. **Saša Buvač** builds on his joint work with Ian Mason (Buvač et al. 1995), which was aimed at the formalization of the notion of context, as it is used in declarative AI. In the present paper, Buvač uses this highly general theory to deal with the representation and disambiguation of lexical ambiguities. In particular, Buvač formalizes the notion of a 'discourse context' as one which, among other things, constrains the interpretation of predicates. Crucially, information can be moved around between contexts by means of so-called lifting rules. (Compare e.g., McCarthy 1993.) A prime example of lifting occurs when the information in a special common-sense knowledge base is lifted into the knowledge base that is used for interpretation, thus allowing common-sense knowledge to assist in disambiguation. **Anne-Marie Mineur and Paul Buitelaar** focus on the representation and disambiguation of polysemous lexical items. (For example, the word *grammar* may either denote a system of linguistic rules, or the book in which such a system is described.) They explore an approach that is rather different from Buvač's context-based approach, using *type coercion*, a disambiguating device that is adopted from computer science, in combination with Pustejovsky's *qualia structures* (see e.g., Pustejovsky 1995), which can be viewed as underspecified representations of lexical meaning. The resulting proposal appears to be limited to the use of information in the immediate vicinity of the ambiguous item at hand, but has obvious advantages in the area of computational feasibility over more ambitious contenders.

Also dealing with the representation of ambiguity, but focusing on the issue of the *meaning* of an ambiguous expression are the papers by Alshawi and by Poesio. In his paper for the present volume, **Hiyan Alshawi**, one of the pioneers of ambiguous representation, explores the attribution of sets of truth values to underspecified logical forms. The logical forms contain not only quantifier-scope ambiguities, but also ambiguities of bracketing, as well as certain referentially ambiguous terms. Interestingly, Alshawi's formalism causes underspecification and uninterpretability to come out as opposite ends of the same scale, identifying the first with having more than one truth value, and the second with having no truth value at all. **Massimo Poesio**, in a paper that discusses much of the literature on ambiguity extant (see also Poesio 1994), defends a proposal in which ambiguous sentences are likewise represented by underspecified formulas characterized by having sets of truth values as their denotations, but he focuses on the interpretation process, which is modeled through a form of defeasible reasoning. Poesio argues that underspecified formulas can be perfectly valid as representations of meaning, but that the role they can play in an account of human language processing is constrained by various interpretive principles. For example, Poesio revives Pinkal's notion of 'H(omonym)-type' ambiguities (Pinkal 1995) and requires that all these ambiguities must be removed, or else the utterance is *perceived* as ambiguous, and consequently in need of further disambiguation.

The issue of *reasoning* with ambiguous premises and/or conclusions is touched upon in many of the papers of this volume, including those by Buvač and Hobbs. So far, there is no unanimity on the prospects for this kind of reasoning (cf., for example, the discussion by Poesio). Two papers in which the possibility of an 'ambiguous logic' is explicitly defended are the contributions by Van Deemter and by Reyle. **Kees van Deemter**, in a follow-up to van Deemter 1991, sets up a model theory for a many-sorted logic containing ambiguous constants, and explores the many different notions of logical consequence that can be defined using this model theory. He formulates a number of interpretive principles favouring interpretations that avoid 'inconsistency' as well as 'incoherence' of interpretation. For example, in the inference $F(a) \models F(a)$, coherence requires both occurrences of the predicate F to have the same interpretation even if F is ambiguous, and this is, arguably, what keeps the inference valid in an ambiguous setting. The paper by **Uwe Reyle**, which is the last one in this volume, explores one particular brand of ambiguous reasoning, in which the interpretations of the premises of an argument are quantified universally, while the interpretations of its conclusion are quantified existentially. Reyle investigates how this notion of inference can be applied to several ambiguities that involve plural noun phrases, and focuses on the issue of distributive/collective interpretations that is also the topic of Van der Does and Verkuyl's contribution. The framework used is an extension of Kamp's Discourse Representation Structures and constitutes a somewhat streamlined version of the author's earlier accounts of reasoning with underspecified DRS's (e.g., Reyle 1995).

We, as editors, feel that the papers of this volume go some way towards answering the three groups of questions that were formulated prior to our discussion of the individual papers. In particular, many of the papers contribute to our understanding of how ambiguous information may be represented, disambiguated, and otherwise processed. As a result, even the more difficult questions of what ambiguity is, and how the possible meanings of an ambiguous expression can be identified, may now be a little bit closer to being answered than before.

Given the scope of the topic, it is unavoidable that some questions in the area of ambiguity and underspecification are not discussed in as much detail as they deserve. This may be most obviously true for *psycholinguistic* aspects of ambiguity and underspecification, which always loom large in the background, but are seldom discussed in detail. The processing of ambiguous expressions has always been an extremely important topic in psycholinguistics. In particular, the question of whether different interpretations of an ambiguous expression tend to be available to an interpreter at the same time, has been investigated extensively. (See, for example, Seidenberg et al. 1982, for evidence suggesting a positive answer to this question.) Although the present volume does not contribute directly to the extensive work in this area of psycholinguistics, it does seem to raise some new questions in that area. For example, is there a psychological reality to (some) underspecified representations? Further, if and when humans draw conclusions from ambiguous input, which of all the *a priori* possible styles of reasoning do they employ? Likewise, if we agree that human interpreters do not always need full disambiguation, then *how much* disambiguation is required under what circumstances? We hope the present volume will encourage others to try to answer these and similar questions. The interested reader is referred to Hirst 1987 for an overview of older work on psycholinguistic aspects of ambiguity, and to Gorfein 1989 for an interesting collection of papers. A paper in which much of the recent literature is discussed and a new perspective on syntactic ambiguities is offered as well, is MacDonald et al. 1994.

Another area that is largely left out of consideration is the use of *statistical* techniques for disambiguation. Such methods have been used extensively for automatic part-of-speech tagging, but also for word-sense disambiguation in general (e.g. Brown et al. 1991, Gale et al. 1992). In this increasingly important area, on which much of the most recent work on ambiguity has focused, the current volume has little to offer, and the reader is referred to the above-mentioned papers (but see also Zernik 1991) for more information.

In what follows, we will briefly point out what we see as some of the main research challenges in the area of ambiguity and underspecification. Our perspective will be that of computational linguistics, and we will ask what research questions will have to be answered before meaning-oriented NLP systems (e.g., systems for question-answering or machine translation) can properly cope with ambiguous input.

We believe that the key to a better handling of ambiguity in NLP systems is a better understanding of what ambiguity is, and of how an interpretation of a given expression can be identified. To us at least, and judging from the contributions by Hobbs and by Van der Does and Verkuyl, it would come as no surprise if a proper understanding of this issue would allow semanticists to cut down on the number of interpretations that are now typically distinguished. Ideally, work in this area would also lead to better tests of ambiguity than are now available, which can then be used by the working (computational) linguist to determine whether an expression is ambiguous between two interpretations, or merely non-specific with respect to the distinction between them.

Further, NLP systems should ideally be capable of reliable disambiguation whenever the context allows it. It is in this area, of course, that traditional research into ambiguity has been most successful. New directions suggested by the papers in this volume include, among other things, the exploitation of information from the utterance situation, the use of type coercion, and the use of semantically-oriented principles of interpretation, including various principles of 'charitable' interpretation. Another idea that can be found in various papers of the present volume, and that we would like to emphasize here, is that of 'disambiguation by reasoning', according to which some kinds of disambiguation would become part of a genuine inference component that involves ambiguous propositions. Such an inference component could, among other things, use common-sense knowledge (perhaps of the kind described in Guha and Lenat 1990), if such information is available, as well as discourse information, to aid disambiguation.

It is important to note that if and when a reasoning component is in place that can deal with ambiguous premises, complete disambiguation is no longer always a necessity. For instance, suppose a user addresses a question-answering system asking an ambiguous yes-no question, and suppose the system is designed to answer questions by trying to prove their truth or falsity from premises that are stored in a database. Now if, for example, the negation of *each* interpretation of the question can be proven, then the reasoning component could infer that the answer to the question has to be negative. Consequently, disambiguation of the question is not necessary, and a negative answer can be given. (The case of an affirmative answer is, of course, completely analogous.) In those, more difficult, cases where disambiguation is necessary and yet cannot be performed with sufficient plausibility, 'querying the user' can be used as a last resort. Ideally, the results of this query would, again, enter the system as another bit of information which the system can then go on to use for disambiguation much like it can use common-sense information.

It must be added that reasoning with ambiguous sentences is still in its infancy. To become practical, ambiguous logics will have to move beyond semantic definitions of logical validity, towards the design of deductive systems to match the semantics, and towards computationally efficient implementations. We believe that this would be a very interesting way to go, and one that would accord nicely with the work reported in the present volume.

References

Alshawi, Hiyan. 1990. Resolving Quasi Logical Forms. *Computational Linguistics* 16: 133-144.

Bar Hillel, Yehoshua. 1960. The Present Status of automatic translation of languages. *Advances in Computers* 1, pp. 91-163.

Bronnenberg, W., H.C. Bunt, S.P.J. Landsbergen, R. Scha, W. Schoenmakers, and E. Van Utteren. 1979. The Question Answering System PHLIQA1. In *Natural Communication with Computers, Vol. II*, ed. L.Bolc. Carl Hanser Verlag, Muenchen & Wien.

Brown, Peter, Stephen Della Pietra, Vincent Della Pietra, and Robert Mercer. 1991. Word sense disambiguation using statistical methods. In *Proc. ACL 1991*, pp. 264-270.

Buvač, Sasa, Vanja Buvač, and Ian Mason. 1995. Metamathematics of Contexts. *Fundamenta Informaticae* 23(3). To appear.

Carbonel, Jaime. and Patrick Hayes. 1987. Natural Language Processing. In *Encyclopedia of Artificial Intelligence*, ed. S.Shapiro, D.Eckroth and G.Vallasi. Wiley & Sons, New York.

van Deemter, Kees. 1991. *On the composition of meaning; four variations on the theme of compositionality in natural language processing*. Ph.D. dissertation Amsterdam University, March 1991.

Gale, William, Kenneth W.,Church, and David Yarowsky. 1992. Estimating upper and lower bounds on the performance of word-sense disambiguation programs. In *Proc. of ACL 1992*.

Gorfein, D.S. ed. 1989. *Resolving Semantic Ambiguity*. Springer-Verlag, New York.

Guha, Ramanathan V. and Douglas B.Lenat. 1990. Cyc: A Midterm Report. *AI Magazine* 11(3):32-59.

Hirst, Graeme. 1987. *Semantic interpretation and the resolution of ambiguity*. Cambridge, UK. Cambridge University Press.

Hobbs, Jerry R. 1983. An improper treatment of quantification in ordinary English. In *Proc. of the 21st Annual Meeting, Association for Computational Linguistics*, pp. 57-63. Cambridge, Mass, June 1983.

McCarthy, John. 1993. Notes on Formalizing Context. In *Proceedings of the Thirteenth International Joint Conference on Artificial Intelligence*.

MacDonald, Maryellen C., Neal J. Pearlmutter, and Mark S. Seidenberg. 1994. The Lexical Nature of Syntactic Ambiguity Resolution. Psychological Review, vol. 101, No. 4.

Nunberg, Geoffrey. 1987. *The pragmatics of reference*. Ph.D. dissertation, CUNY. Bloomington, IN. Indiana Linguistics Club.

Pinkal, Manfred. 1995. *Logic and Lexicon*. Oxford.

Poesio, M. 1994. *Discourse interpretation and the scope of operators*. Ph.D. dissertation, University of Rochester, Dept. of Computer Science. Rochester, NY.

Pustejovsky, J. 1995. *The Generative Lexicon*. Cambridge. MIT Press.

Reyle, Uwe. 1995. On reasoning with ambiguities. In *Proc. EACL 1995*. Dublin.

Schubert,L.K. and F.J.Pelletier. 1982. From English to Logic: Context-Free Computation of 'Conventional' Logical Translations. *American Journal of Computational Linguistics* 10: 165-176.

Seidenberg, M.S., M.K.Tanenhaus, J.Leiman, and M.Bienkowski. 1982. Automatic access of the meanings of ambiguous words in context: some limitations of knowledge-based processing. *Cognitive Psychology* 14:489-537.

Verkuyl, Henk J. and Jaap M. van der Does. 1991. The Semantics of Plural Noun Phrases. In *Generalized Quantifier Theory and Applications*, Dutch Network for Language, Logic and Information, ed. Jaap M. van der Does and Jan van Eijck, pp. 403–441, Amsterdam. A revised version to appear in CSLI Publications.

Westerståhl, Dag. 1985. Determiners and context sets. In: J.van Benthem and A.ter Meulen (Eds.) *Generalized Quantifiers in Natural Language*. Dordrecht, The Netherlands: Foris, GRASS-4.

Zernik, Uri (ed.). 1991. *Lexical acquisition: Exploiting on-line resources to build a lexicon*. Lawrence Erlbaum Associates, Hillsdale, NJ.

1

Ambiguity Resolution and Discourse Interpretation

Georgia M. Green

1 Introduction

This paper compares the interpretive problem of resolving ambiguity [1] with the pragmatic problem of discourse interpretation generally. The conclusion is that the general character of the problem of resolving polysemies and attachment ambiguities is not significantly different from such problems of discourse interpretation as inferring the relevance of one utterance to another or inferring the referent of a pronoun or a definite description. Figuring out whether the pronoun *he* in a sentence like (1) refers to the individual described as the dean, the individual described as the student, or some individual not mentioned in the sentence depends on assumptions about what a speaker of (1) might reasonably assume the addressee of (1) knows about who might have done something incriminating, and who might have discovered it.

1. The dean expelled the student because he discovered something incriminating.

---

[1] I use GRAMMATICAL AMBIGUITY (which I occasionally specify further as either LEXICAL AMBIGUITY or SYNTACTIC AMBIGUITY) to refer strictly to instances where the grammar (syntax or lexicon) specifies two or more distinct interpretations for a linguistic expression. Grammatical ambiguity is thus distinct from the situation, termed by various writers vague, general, indeterminate, indefinite, neutral or unspecified (see Zwicky and Sadock (1975:2) for references and some discussion), in which the grammar provides a single representation that corresponds to a potentially infinite variety of states-of-affairs. It is not always clear which category an expression belongs to, but I try to stick to clear examples when I use the term *ambiguity*. Uncertainties of discourse interpretation are by definition not cases of grammatical ambiguity insofar as *grammar* refers to an account of the well-formed expressions in a particular language, and not an account of well-formed texts or discourses (cf. Morgan 1981, Morgan and Sellner 1980).

Semantic Ambiguity and Underspecification
Kees van Deemter and Stanley Peters, editors
Copyright © 1995, CSLI Publications

It cannot be resolved independently of a model of the context in which (1) might be used. The core of this paper is a demonstration that what is involved in the interpretation of an ambiguous word or phrase as in (2) or (3) is not significantly different from this.

   2. The count is 2 and 1.

   3a. Growers should plant disease-resistant hybrids and standard varieties.
   3b. I do not like green eggs and ham.

Whether (2) describes the status of an at-bat in a baseball game, or the win-loss record of some member of European royalty, whether (3a) advises growers to plant disease-resistant standard varieties, or standard varieties unrestrictedly, and whether (3b) describes dislike for green ham or only green eggs, can only be interpreted, like (1), in terms of a model of the context of use.

Consequently, insofar as systems for automatic natural language understanding have general techniques for discourse interpretation that model the behavior of natural language users, it should be possible to exploit those techniques for lexical and syntactic ambiguity resolution. To the extent that ambiguity resolution and discourse interpretation are interdependent, and the contexts essential to the resolution of both are not so much adjacent words and phrases as they are (abstractions from) secular situations of utterance, it is unreasonable to expect that ambiguity resolution independent of models of those situations can be satisfactory.

When the intended understanding of a sentence is unclear, for whatever reason, and a human interpreter recognizes a limited number of alternative interpretations, this recognition arises from the fact that it is not immediately evident which one it would have been most rational for the speaker to have intended in that context. When a human interpreter fails to recognize that more than one interpretation is possible, it is because it never enters his mind that the speaker might have intended anything other than what he takes her to have intended (cf. Hirst 1987:84). This works the same way whether it is lexicon, grammar, or discourse that makes more than one interpretation possible.

Thus, the view of disambiguation presented here provides a strict contrast to that of Hirst (1987), who considers (1987:4) semantic interpretation to be distinct from and computationally prior (and therefore, necessarily, logically prior) to discourse interpretation, including the resolution of deixis and anaphora, speech act identification, and non-literal usage (metaphor, sarcasm, etc.). Hirst (1987) discusses some of the psycholinguistic research on disambiguation (1987:84-95, 118-120), but its main concern is to describe and justify a computational implementation of a text-interpretation and disambiguation scheme that was submitted as a 1983 Brown University doctoral dissertation. In strict contrast to the view presented here, in which pragmatic information (in the form of the language user's system of beliefs about the content and context of the discourse) is argued to be central, Hirst relegates the role of inference to that of a last resort. Whether this is for computational convenience or is inspired by Hirst's interpretation of the psycholinguistic literature he reports is not clear. Hirst imagines (1987:85) three possible hypotheses about how language users interpret ambiguous words in context:

- mental representations (or neural structures) activated by linguistic processing of prior linguistic context determine a unique interpretation
- all interpretations are accessed before context influences the determination of the meaning in that context
- interpretations are accessed in order of their "frequency of usage"

The view presented here is distinct from all three of these. Framed in Hirst's terms, it would be something more consistent with the view of interpretation offered by Sperber and Wilson (1986), on the order of:

CONTEXT-ORDERED SEARCH: Interpretation of prior context biases the interpretive process before the ambiguity is encountered. The search for senses of an ambiguous word or phrase is determined by what the interpreter anticipates the speaker would have intended.

The parallels demonstrated here among semantic and structural disambiguation and discourse interpretation have their origin in the fact that language users interpret linguistic ACTS (utterances of linguistic forms by a speaker on an occasion for a reason), not linguistic objects abstracted away from contexts of use. For this reason, it would seem that both theoretical and practical models of this process ignore at their risk the fact that modelling the producer of a bit of language is an integral part of interpreting the product of her work.

The raison d'être of this paper is to provide additional arguments, and improvements on familiar arguments, for underappreciated ideas. No doubt the reason that some of the ideas are underappreciated and misunderstood is that the work in which they are articulated in greatest detail (Nunberg 1978) has not been widely accessible; it was never published by a commercial publisher, and was only circulated through the graces of the Indiana University Linguistics Club. Some of the conclusions are summarized in Nunberg (1979), but that work does not give an adequate representation of Nunberg's account of how the use of words by speakers in contexts facilitates reference.[2]

The basic claim is that that account of systematic polysemy is a striking subcase of a much more general account of language use which applies to all aspects of language behavior, including, for example, pronunciation, lexical choice, construction choice, content choice, and even code choice. When the generality of Nunberg's account is made clear, attempts to resolve lexical and structural ambiguity in natural language processing applications as isolated processes (useful as they might be for particular applications), independent of assumptions about beliefs held by members of the speech community about each other's beliefs, appears as a short-sighted quick fix which does not extend to other problems of interpretation, or to attempts to model speakers' ability to resolve lexical and structural ambiguities. Attempts (cf. Copestake and Briscoe 1994) to reduce systematic polysemy to systematic ambiguity by means of very specific lexical rules do not reduce the problem of interpretation insofar as interpretation depends on the same pragmatic principles in both cases. More recent work of Nunberg's (Nunberg 1995, Nunberg and Zaenen 1992) suggests that while for the most part, systematic polysemy arises from the exploitation of very general pragmatic principles, different cultures do conventionalize different isolated uses of them. Still, the strategies necessary to arrive at an interpretation remain the same whether the source of multiple possibilities is a pragmatic principle or a rule of grammar.

The argument proceeds by demonstrating that there are pervasive and systematic indeterminacies in interpretation at the discourse level. These cannot be a matter of structural or lexical ambiguity, but rather are a function of the possibility of reconstructing opposing plausible accounts of the speaker's goals in producing the discourse. These are compared to standard examples of lexical and structural ambiguity. The resolution of all three types of uncertainty depends on reconstructing rational goals and beliefs for the (assumed) speaker in the (assumed) context. In Section 3, I review Nunberg's (1978) argument that coping with systematic polysemy, whatever its source, requires the same kind of reconstruction of the speaker's goals and beliefs for its resolution. Despite being rule-governed (cf. Copestake and Briscoe 1994), an exhaustive account of systematic polysemy is not usefully treated as grammatical in character, insofar as the rules relate models of speech act participants. Treating systematic polysemy as essentially

---

[2]For example, Nunberg (1979) does not contain accounts of either the unextractability of interpretation from context (and the non-existence of null contexts), or the notion of a system of normal beliefs in a speech community. Yet both notions are central to understanding Nunberg's arguments for his conclusions about polysemy and interpretation.

pragmatic predicts that problematic indeterminacy can be resolved in a way parallel to resolution of other discourse uncertainties. Section 4 illustrates how the same general principles as are involved in discourse interpretation are invoked in disambiguation of a polysemous expression. The point being made here is not new. It is useful to discuss it at length, however, because it has been so widely misunderstood. Section 5 reviews the origin of much genuine lexical ambiguity in systematic polysemy, and shows a parallel in another kind of symbol use. Regardless of their diverse origins, however, all kinds of interpretive uncertainties require the same elements and principles for their resolution. The final section considers the implication of these observations for natural language understanding systems. The construction of truly robust and general natural language processing systems will have to reflect the fact that assessing speaker intentions is frequently required for disambiguation as well as for discourse understanding.

2 Some clearly pragmatic uncertainties of interpretation

It is clearly a matter of pragmatics, not a matter of grammar or lexicon, that in understanding an actual or putative utterance (e.g., a constructed example), we fix upon a particular interpretation out of several that might be plausible. In general, when someone says something to us, we do not know for certain exactly why the speaker said what she said, or said it the way she did, but as language users, and even as linguists going about our business, we are rarely cognizant of our ignorance, and are usually so confident of our interpretation that we do not recognize other possibilities. And yet, when we try to justify our interpretations, we typically discover much more often than we might have anticipated that we cannot know WHAT THE SPEAKER HAS SAID (at any level of analysis) without making assumptions about why she said it, or said it that way. This section describes several such examples, from the widest possible range of aspects of language use, and shows that they are indistinguishable from standard examples of syntactic and lexical ambiguity, in that in order to resolve them, the interpreter must attribute to the speaker beliefs that make the act of uttering that bit of language rational (Grice 1975, Green 1993a). Lexical ambiguity is treated in more detail in the following section.

One thing that it is essential to understand here is that what makes interpretation pragmatic is not just dependence on the language user's reasoning from "knowledge of the world," but its dependence on the language user's reasoning about her model of her interlocutor's beliefs and intentions (including her interlocutor's beliefs and intentions regarding her). Thus, any solutions or strategies that depend on treating the premises for such reasoning as being 1) absolute knowledge rather than defeasible belief, and/or 2) part of a fixed knowledge base are unlikely to extend to domains beyond the ones used to develop them.

When a sentence is grammatically ambiguous, it always has two (or more) distinct and (usually) incompatible interpretations, because there is either a single phonological form which conventionally refers to distinct and unrelated classes of referents, or a single constituent order which reflects distinct structural (and consequently, compositional-semantic) relations among the constituents of an expression. But grammatical ambiguity is not the only source for the possibility of two or more distinct and incompatible interpretations: any use of any linguistic form may have distinct interpretations because there are different plausible motivations (goals) for the act of uttering that form, just as there are an infinite number of potential motivations for any act.

2.1 Code choice

Perhaps the least likely, and thus the most striking, example of how interpreting a linguistic act depends on reconstructing the actor's intention in performing the act is provided by the case of choosing a language in which to conduct a particular interaction. When two bilingual speakers converse who have complementary competencies (that is, A speaks X natively and Y as a second language, and B speaks Y natively and X as a second language), and both share the feeling that in intercultural exchanges, all else being equal, converging to the language of the other person is an accommodating act,[3] either one may choose to speak in the native language of the other. A speaker might do this for self-centered reasons (to practice the second language, to show off, to build self-confidence etc, or the like) or for other-centered reasons (to be accommodating, maybe even deferential). Similarly, choosing to converse in one's native language might be an act of selfish convenience, or it might be intended as acknowledging the other's superior ability in using her second language. Burt (1994b) characterizes these reasons by the reactions they provoke:[4]

4a. How wonderful! An American who speaks German and is willing to do so.

4b. How arrogant! Does she think my English is not good enough for us to have a conversation in English?

5a. Typical American! Expects everybody to speak English!

---

[3]Burt 1994a uses these precise words to characterize Speech Accommodation Theory.

[4]Adapted from Burt 1994b.

5b. My English must be pretty good—a bilingual native speaker is speaking English to me!

The addressee does not know whether to feel generous (and gracious) when she maintains the conversation in her own language, or to feel patronized and insulted. Switching to the original speaker's native language in response could likewise have multiple interpretations. It might be understood as a retort to disabuse him of the mistaken idea that the non-native speaker was insufficiently competent in that language. Or it might be understood as a reciprocal courtesy, signalling only that he need not have gone to the trouble of speaking a foreign language. Or it might be taken insultingly, reflecting the judgement that the original speaker's use of his second language was inadequate to serve the presumed goals of the conversation. In any case, figuring out whether the choice of language reflects deference or disdain clearly requires being able to reconstruct likely beliefs of the speaker (e.g., about both interlocutors' ability in their second languages) in order to attribute particular social intentions to the speaker. Attribution of beliefs is even more clearly at issue in the next set of cases.

2.2 Discourse interpretation

The significance of what is communicated by choice of code may seem subtle, and peripheral to both practical and theoretical concerns. Determining the content of an utterance, however, generally seems less subtle, and is of both obvious practical and theoretical significance. When what is said is noncommittal on some point of intense interest to a hearer, the hearer may identify a small number of alternatives, but, unable to choose among them, feel that she does not even know what was said. Such cases of uncertainty about discourse involve vagueness rather than ambiguity, since further specification involves selection from an unconstrained domain rather than a few linguistically conventional alternatives. Some examples are given in (6-8).[5] Example (6) is the familiar example of the indeterminacy of pronominal reference.

6. The dean expelled Ignatius because he discovered something incriminating.

    Who discovered something incriminating? Ignatius? The dean? Someone else?

Examples (7-8) illustrate the familiar indeterminacy of implicature (Grice 1975:58). Example (7) involves inferring the source of an asserted impossibility, and example (8), the mechanism of an implicated causal relation.

7. Jack Sprat could eat no fat, his wife could eat no lean, and so betwixt the two of them, they licked the platter clean.

    Was Jack physically unable to eat fat, and therefore, thin?
    Or was Jack forbidden to eat fat because he was so overweight already?[6]
    Is there a lesson here? If so, what is it?

---

[5] It is self-evident that examples like (1) and (6) involve indefiniteness of reference rather than ambiguity. However, insofar as the opposed understandings in the other cases are privative opposites (one understanding including the other as a subcase), so-called "crossed readings" tests as in (i) cannot be used to demonstrate that the multiple understandings represent vagueness rather than ambiguity, because, as Zwicky and Sadock (1975:23-25) demonstrated, when one interpretation includes the other, or a more general interpretation includes both, nothing can force the more specific interpretation.

    i. John can play the tuba (but only after he does his chores), and so can Bill, now that he's grown.

While it appears to be possible to construct a "crossed readings" test case for (8), as in (ii), the available readings appear to be fewer than the claim of vagueness would predict: adding *who was frightened by the ranting rather than fascinated by it* reduces the plausibility of (ii) as a discourse.

    ii. Yesterday, Kim couldn't leave the car. Rush Limbaugh was on. Today, the same thing happened to Sandy.

However, this is exactly what is predicted by the use of a phrase like *the same thing*, since it is an identity-of-reference anaphor, like a personal pronoun, not an identity-of-sense anaphor of the sort that the crossed-readings tests depend on.

[6] I report, as evidence that these questions reflect a salient indeterminacy, the results of an informal experiment. Of eighteen adult volunteers who responded to a request to draw a picture of "the happy couple," fifteen drew a thin Jack and a fat Mrs. Sprat, while three drew a fat Jack and a thin missus. Many of the former volunteered that they may have been influenced by illustrations in books of nursery rhymes read to them decades ago. A smaller group responded to a similar request with respect to a prose rendition about Diana Herring and her husband; all three drew a thin male and a fat female. Possibly the numbers would have been different if respondents had been asked to draw a picture of "the unfortunate couple", but in any case, they testify to the fact that the discourse is silent on the issue in question. Interestingly, no one reported perceiving difficulty envisioning the situation. As mentioned above, and discussed again below, failure to recognize that an utterance admits of more than one interpretation is the norm for language understanding in

8. One afternoon last fall I found myself unable to leave my car when I arrived at the grocery store. On "All Things Considered" there was an excerpt from a series called "Breakdown and Back," the story of a mental breakdown as experienced by one woman, Annie. (*Patterns*, Feb. 1986, p. [4].)

   Was the story so frightening that the writer was afraid to leave the security of her car?
   Was it so compelling she had to hear all of it?
   Was it so emotionally involving that she feared losing control of her emotions if she listened to it on a personal stereo in a public place?

There are two points to note here. First, an interpreter may be aware of not finding in an utterance information that she considers essential to knowing what to make of that utterance—i.e., to knowing how to modify her knowledge base, since the brute facts themselves may be insufficiently informative (for example, if the interpreter cares whether Jack Sprat is fat or thin, knowing that he could not eat fat does not tell her enough). In that case, discourse understanding is as problematic as interpreting a sentence that is grammatically ambiguous in situations where both meanings are possible but relevantly different, so that it's crucial that there be further resolution. Interpreting motivations is an essential part of disambiguation when both interpretations are plausible, but relevantly different. This is true both with lexical ambiguity, as in (9a), and with structural ambiguity as in (9b), a standard example of an attachment ambiguity.

9a. Officials at International Seed Co. beefed up security at their South Carolina facility in the face of rumors that competitors would stop at nothing to get specimens of a newly-engineered variety, saying, "That plant is worth $5 million."

9b. (= (3b)) I do not like green eggs and ham.

Second, resolving both discourse vagueness and ambiguity (whether lexical or structural) involves making inferences about the speaker's intentions in making the utterance: was she explaining Jack's dietary preferences, or his doctor's orders? Does the speaker want us to believe that ISC officials were worried about biological material, or a building and the equipment in it? Is ham despised unconditionally, or only green ham?

In the following section, I review the arguments (originating in Nunberg 1978) that much of what is often considered polysemic lexical ambiguity is actually pragmatic underspecification, as a prelude to

---

context, regardless of whether the source of uncertainty is pragmatic, or originates in grammatical ambiguity.

showing that coping with systematic polysemy requires attributing to the speaker of a polysemous form beliefs and intentions that make one sense more rational for her to have intended in that context than others (Grice 1975, Green 1993a).

3 Polysemic lexical ambiguity

As has been often noted (cf. Ruhl 1989, Green 1993b), practically any word can be used to denote an almost limitless variety of kinds of objects or functions: *program* unremarkably refers to a goal, a schedule, a curriculum or course of study, a set of courses, a list of instructions for a computational device, a written representation of any of these, a show broadcast on radio or TV, and potentially to a person responsible (in any relevant sense) for any of these.

10a. The program of this group is to subvert the youth of America.
10b. Their program calls for 10 pushups three times a day.
10c. She entered the program in 1977.
10d. We're expanding our program with the addition of two new faculty members, and six new courses.
10e. The program would not execute.
10f. The programs are all smudged.
10g. If you have a VCR you can tape your programs while you're at work or asleep.
10h. The program just called and said she'd be late.

Likewise, in addition to referring to a fruit, or a defective automobile, *lemon* might refer to the wood of the lemon tree, as in (11a), to the flavor of the juice of the fruit (11b), to the oil from the peel of the fruit (11c), to an object which has the color of the fruit (11d), to something the size of the fruit (11e), and to a substance with the flavor of the fruit (11f). These are only the most obvious uses from an apparently limitless set.

11a. Lemon has an attractive grain, much finer than beech or cherry.
11b. I prefer the '74 because the '73 has a lemon aftertaste.
11c. Lemon will not penetrate as fast as linseed.
11d. The lemon is too stretchy, but the coral has a snag in it.
11e. Shape the dough into little lemons, and let rise.
11f. Two scoops of lemon, please, and one of Rocky Road.

The idea that what a word can be used to refer to might vary indefinitely is clearly unsettling. It makes the fact that we (seem to) understand each other most of the time something of a miracle, and it makes the familiar, comfortable Conduit Theory of Communication,[7] according to which speakers encode ideas in words and sentences and

---

[7]Critiqued in Reddy (1979).

send them to addressees to decode, quite irrational. But the conclusion that as language users, we are free to use any word to refer to anything at all, any time we want is unwarranted. Lexical choice is always subject to the pragmatic constraint that we have to consider how likely it is that our intended audience will be able to correctly identify our intended referent from our use of the expression we choose. What would really be irrational would be using a word to refer to anything except what we estimate our addressee is likely to take it to refer to, because it would be self-defeating. Thus, rationality severely limits what a speaker is likely to use a term to refer to in a given context. By this I mean only that since people assume that people's actions are goal-directed (so that any act will be assumed to have been performed for a reason), a speaker must believe that, all things considered, the word she chooses is the best word to further her goals in its context and with respect to her addressee.

We frequently exploit the freedom we have, within the bounds of this constraint, referring to movies as turkeys, cars as lemons, and individuals in terms of objects associated with them, as when we say that the flute had to leave to attend his son's soccer game, or that the corned beef spilled his beer. Perhaps this makes communication sound very difficult to effect, and very fragile. We are probably less successful at it than we think we are, but in general, we are just not conscious of the work that is required, and it is probably not all that fragile. Believing in the convenient fiction that words have fixed meanings is what makes using them to communicate appear to require no effort. If we were aware of how much interpretation we depended on each other to do to understand us, we might hesitate to speak.

The point is that we all ACT as if we believe, and believe that everyone else believes, that the denotation an individual word may have on an occasion of use is limited, somewhat arbitrarily, as a matter of linguistic convention. Let us follow Nunberg (1978) in calling this sort of belief a normal belief, and say that the relation *normally-believe* holds of a speech community and a proposition P when people in that community believe that it is normal (i.e., unremarkable, to be expected) in that community to believe P and to believe that everyone in that community believes that it is normal in that community to believe P. (*Speech community* as used here (again following Nunberg's (1978) usage) is not limited to geographical or political units, or even institutionalized social units, but encompasses any group of individuals with common interests. Thus, we all belong simultaneously to a number of speech communities, depending on our interests and backgrounds; we might be women and mothers and Lutherans and lawyers and football fans and racketball players, who knit and surf the Internet, and are members of countless speech communities besides these.[8]) Illustrating the relevance to parsing and disambiguation of the notion of normal belief, it is normal beliefs about cars and trucks, and about what properties of them good old boys might find relevant,[9] that would lead someone to parse the coordination in (12a) with narrow adjectival scope and that in (12b) with wider scope.

12a. The good ol' boys there drive fast cars and trucks.
12b. The good ol' boys there drive red cars and trucks.

This technical use of *normal belief* should not be confused with other notions that may have the same name. A normal belief in the sense intended is only remotely related to an individual's belief about how things normally are, and only remotely related (in a different direction) to a judgement that it is unremarkable to hold such a belief. The beliefs that are normal within a community are those that "constitute the background against which all utterances in that community are rationally made" (Nunberg (1978:94-95)). McCawley (1985), for another purpose, defines the notion of unmarked belief in much the same way (1985:24):

> For example, in most American communities, belief that there is a god (indeed, belief that there is a god of the sort that listens to prayers, judges the souls of dead persons, etc.) is unmarked. This does not mean that members of that society all believe in a god or are kept from expressing beliefs to the contrary, but it does mean that members of that society treat one another as believing in a god except when there is reason to impute a contrary belief to someone, and expressions of nonbelief in a god are expected to be accompanied by apologies and/or justifications.

When it comes to using words to refer to things, properties, and events, what it is considered normal to use *tack* or *host* or *rock* or *metal* to refer to varies with the community. These are social facts, facts about societies, and only incidentally and contingently and secondarily facts

---

[8]McCawley gives, in a somewhat different context, an example that is a little closer to home (1985:34):

Just as persons in general normally belong to several overlapping communities, (e.g. a neighborhood, one's workmates, a church congregation, the clientele of a particular pub), so too those engaged in research normally belong to several overlapping scientific communities. Being a member of, say, the Montague grammar community, in which relating syntactic structure to model-theoretic semantic interpretation is a prime goal, does not prevent one from also being a member of a larger community of syntacticians in which such a goal either is not recognized at all or is accepted in a weakened form and assigned low priority.

[9]E.g., that because of the aerodynamic properties of trucks relative to cars, *fast truck* is almost an oxymoron.

about words. More precisely, they are facts about what speakers believe other speakers believe about conventions for using words.

Thus, it is normal among field archaeologists to use mesh bound in frames to sift through excavated matter for remnants of material culture, and it is normally believed among them that this is normal, and that it is normal to refer to the sieves as *screens*. Likewise, among users of personal computers, it is normally believed that the contents of a data file may be inspected by projecting representations of portions of it on an electronic display tube, and it is normally believed that this belief is normally held, and that it is normal to refer to the display tube as a *screen*. Whether *screen* is (intended to be) understood as (normally) referring to a sort of sieve or to a video display depends on assumptions made by speaker and hearer about the assumptions each makes about the other's beliefs, including beliefs about what is normal in a situation of the sort being described, and about what sort of situation (each believes the other believes) is being discussed at the moment of utterance.[10] This is what is irreducibly pragmatic about word meaning.

Importantly, this sense of *normal use* has nothing to do with verifiable frequency of use,[11] and is only indirectly related to perceived frequency of use. Normal use is defined in terms of normal belief, and normal belief is an intensional concept. If everybody believes that everybody believes that it is normal to believe P, then belief in P is a normal belief, EVEN IF NOBODY ACTUALLY BELIEVES P.

In light of all this, we are led to a view of word usage in which, when a speaker rationally uses a word w to refer to some intended referent a, she must assume that the addressee will consider it rational to use w to refer to a in that context. She must assume that if she and her addressee do not in fact have the same assumptions about what beliefs are normal in the community-at-large, and in every relevant subgroup, at least the addressee will be able to infer what relevant beliefs the speaker imputes to the addressee, or expects the addressee to impute to the speaker, and so on, in order to infer the intended referent.

If we define an additional, recursive relation *mutually-believe* as holding among two sentient beings A and B and a proposition P when A believes the proposition, believes that B believes the proposition, believes that B believes that A believes the proposition, and so on (cf. Cohen and Levesque 1990),[12] then we can articulate the notion 'normal

---

[10]Nunberg (1978) gives numerous examples of this.

[11]If there is such a thing, which there probably is not, since no sample would accurately reflect any individual's experience, and all individuals have different histories of exposure to language use, from which any perception of frequency of use would have to arise.

[12]Thus, mutual belief does not involve perfect mutual knowledge.

meaning': some set (or property) m is a normal meaning (or denotation) of a referential expression w insofar as it is normally believed that w is used to refer to m. A meaning m for an expression w is normal in a context insofar as speaker and addressee mutually believe that it is normally believed that w is used to refer to m in that context. We can then say that 'member of the species *canis familiaris*' is a normal meaning for the word *dog* insofar as speaker and addressee mutually believe that it is normally believed in their community that such entities are called *dogs*.

The notion of *normal meaning* provided here must not be confused with notions like 'normal reference out of context.' Researchers who perceive the dependence of the referential use of expressions on users' beliefs about each other's beliefs as inconvenient sometimes try to circumnavigate it by articulating a theory of meaning that is independent of particular contexts in that it depends instead on a so-called null context, where speaker and hearer make no assumptions about each other. This is a dead end, however, because (as discussed by Nunberg (1978)) there are no such null contexts in which utterances could be interpreted. As Crain and Steedman put it (1985:338), the so-called null context is no more than an unknown and uncontrolled context. When we are asked to act as informants, and make judgements about expressions or their meanings "out of context" or "in a null context," we cannot help but imagine SOME context consisting of a speaker directing that expression as an utterance to some audience. We differ, as individuals, and on occasions, in how much context we import into the judgement task, and in what we are willing to imagine when we try to construe the expression as a sensible thing to utter on an occasion of the sort we assume.[13] Consequently, if we abstract away from systems of normal beliefs that inhere in all the various possible groups of users of a language (say, English), we do not arrive at anything that looks much like what we imagine for a notion of either "normal English user" or "normal English." The usage of such a "normal user", depending on whether we abstract by intersecting or by unioning memberships, would either be that of a person who belonged to no subgroups within the English-speaking world (imagine it—a person with no family, no country, no religion, no occupation, no avocations, no ethnic background–it would be the epitome of a social misfit, and we would be saying it represented a normal user), or it would be a person who was a member of every subgroup (a Welsh Kikuyu Catholic Jewish evangelical Christian Muslim Hindu (etc.) needleworker professor literary critic computer hacker

---

[13]cf. Schmerling 1978, Green 1993b.

multi-sport athlete insurance salesman) and his[14] usage would reflect the sum of all possible usages, and the problem of unlimited polysemy would be staring us in the face again.

Some uses of referential expressions like those exemplified in (10) and (11) are not so much abnormal or less normal than others as they are normal in a more narrowly defined community. In cases of systematic polysemy, all the use-types (or senses), whether normal in broadly defined or very narrowly exclusive communities, are relatable[15] to one another in terms of functions like 'source of', 'product of', 'part of', 'mass of',[16] which Nunberg (1978) characterized as REFERRING FUNCTIONS.[17] For example, using the word *milkshake* as in (13) to refer to someone who orders a milkshake exploits the referring function 'purchaser of', and presumes a mutual belief that it is normal for restaurant personnel to use the name of a menu item to refer to a purchaser of that item, or more generally, for sales agents to use a description of a purchase to refer to the purchaser.

13. The milkshake claims you kicked her purse.

This is in addition, of course, to the mutual belief it presumes about what the larger class of English speakers normally use *milkshake* to refer to, and the mutual belief that the person identified as the claimant ordered a milkshake.

In general, we are able to understand each other because we all use language in accordance with Grice's Cooperative Principle, which entails (cf. Grice 1957) that a speaker will only use a referential term x when the speaker believes that the addressee will be able to identify the intended referent FROM the reference to it by that term and will believe that the speaker intended him to do so.

The assumption that people's actions are purposeful, so that any act will be assumed to have been performed for a reason, is a universal normal belief—everyone believes it and believes that everyone believes it (cf. Green 1993a). The consequence of this for communicative acts is that people intend and expect that interpreters will attribute particular intentions to them, so consideration of just what intention will be attributed to speech actions must enter into rational utterance planning (cf. Green 1993a, also Sperber and Wilson 1986). This is the Gricean foundation of this theory (cf. also Neale 1992).

---

[14]Or her, if you like; the mind boggles at imagining the sex and gender of such an individual.

[15]For example, in lexical or (more likely—cf. Nunberg 1978, Green 1989, 1993a, Helmreich 1994) semantic or pragmatic rules.

[16]Portioning and Grinding (Pelletier and Schubert 1986, Nunberg and Zaenen 1992, Copestake and Briscoe 1994) are thus two functions out of a much larger, indeed, potentially infinite class (Nunberg 1978:30).

[17]cf. also Helmreich 1994.

The arguments against trying to represent in a finite lexicon all the possible meanings any term might have in some context are obvious. If the number of such meanings is truly indefinitely extendable (as it appears to be), or even merely very large, it is impractical in the extreme to try to list them. But the usual solution to the problem of representing an infinite class in a finite (logical) space is as available here as anywhere else, at least to the extent that some potential denotations can be described in terms of composable functions on other denotations, and typically, this is the case (Nunberg 1978:29-62). It is enough to know, Nunberg argues, that if a term can be used to refer to some class X, then it can be used, given appropriate context, to refer to objects describable by a (recognizable) function on X. This principle can be invoked recursively, and applies to functions composed of other functions, and to expressions composed of other expressions, enabling diverse uses like those for *program* and *lemon* to be predicted in a principled manner.

Because the intended sense (and thence the intended referent) of an utterance of any referential term ultimately reflects what the speaker intends the hearer to understand from what the speaker says by recognizing that the speaker intends him to understand that, interpreting an utterance containing a polysemic ambiguity (or indeed, any sort of ambiguity) involves doping out the speaker's intent, just as understanding a speaker's discourse goals does. The next section discusses this sort of ambiguity resolution in detail.

4 Ambiguity resolution

When a reader or hearer recognizes that an utterance is ambiguous, resolving that ambiguity amounts to determining which interpretation was intended. When recognizing an ambiguity affects parsing, resolving it may involve grammar and lexicon, as for example, when it involves a form which could be construed as belonging to different syntactic categories (e.g., *The subdivision* **houses** *most of the officers* vs. *The subdivision* **houses** *are very similar*, or **Visiting relatives** *is a lot of fun* vs. **Visiting relatives** *are a lot of fun*). But grammar and lexicon may not be enough to resolve such ambiguities, as in the case of familiar examples like (14).

14a. I saw her duck.
14b. Visiting relatives can be a lot of fun.

They will rarely suffice to resolve polysemies or attachment ambiguities (like *I returned the key to the library*). In all of these cases, it is necessary to reconstruct what it would be reasonable for the speaker to have intended, given what is known or believed about the beliefs and goals of the speaker, exactly as when seeking to understand the relevance of an unambiguous utterance in a conversation—that is, to understand why the speaker bothered to utter it, or to say it the way she said it.[18] The literature on natural language understanding contains numerous demonstrations that the determination of how an ambiguous or vague term is intended to be understood depends on identifying the most likely model of the speaker's beliefs and intentions about the interaction. To mention just two demonstrations of how this is determined, Nunberg (1978:84-87) discusses the beliefs and goals that have to be attributed to him in order for his uncle to understand what he means by *jazz* when he asks him if he likes jazz. Green (1989:115-117) describes what is involved in identifying what is meant by *IBM, at,* and *seventy-one* in *Sandy bought IBM at 71.* At the other end of the continuum of grammatical and pragmatic uncertainty is Sperber and Wilson's (1986:239-241) discussion of the process of understanding irony and sarcasm, as when one says *I love people who don't signal,* intending to convey 'I hate people who don't signal.'[19] Nonetheless, it may be instructive to examine here how a salient lexical ambiguity can be resolved.

For example, understanding the officials' statement in example (9a) (repeated here) involves comparing how different assumptions about mutual beliefs about the situation are compatible with different interpretations, in order to determine whether *plant* refers to a vegetable organism or to the production facility of a business (or perhaps just to the apparatus for controlling the climate within it, or maybe to the associated grounds, offices and equipment generally), or even to some sort of a decoy.

9a. Officials at International Seed Co. beefed up security at their South Carolina facility in the face of rumors that competitors would stop at nothing to get specimens of a newly-engineered variety, saying, "That plant is worth $5 million."

If the interpreter supposes that what the company fears is simply theft of samples of the organism, she will take the official as intending *plant* to refer to the (type of the) variety: being able to market tokens of

---

[18]Crain and Steedman 1985, and Altmann and Steedman 1988 offer evidence that experimentally controllable aspects of context that reflect speakers' beliefs about situations affect processing in more predictable ways than such mechanistic strategies as Minimal Attachment.

[19]A further step in the process is required to interpret *I love people who signal!* as intended to convey the same thing; the difference is subtle, because the contextual conditions likely to provoke the two utterances are in a subset relation. One might say *I love people who don't signal* to inform an interlocutor of one's annoyance at someone who the speaker noticed did not signal, but *I love people who signal* is likely to be used sarcastically only when the speaker believes that it is obvious to the addressee that someone should have signalled and did not.

that type represents a potential income of $5 million. On the other hand, if the interpreter supposes that the company fears destruction of (part of) their production facility or the property surrounding it—say, because she knows that samples of the organism are not even located at the production facility any more, and/or that extortionists have threatened to destroy that company property if samples of the organism are not handed over, she is likely to take *plant* as intended to refer to buildings and grounds or equipment. Believing that the company believes that potential income from marketing the variety is much greater than $5 million would have the same effect. If the interpreter believes that the statement was made in the course of an interview where a company spokesperson discussed the cost of efforts to protect against industrial espionage, and mentioned how an elaborate decoy system had alerted them to a threat to steal plant specimens, she might even take *plant* as intended to refer to a decoy. The belief that officials believe that everyone relevant believes that both the earnings potential of the organism, and the value of relevant structures and infrastructure are way more or way less than $5 million would contribute to this conclusion, and might even suffice to induce it on its own.

Two points are relevant here. First, depending on how much of the relevant information is salient in the context in which the utterance is being interpreted, the sentence might not even be recognized as ambiguous. This is equally true in the case of determining discourse intents. For example, identifying sarcastic intent is similar to understanding the reference of an expression in that it depends on attributing to the speaker intent to be sarcastic. (Such an inference is supported by finding a literal meaning to be in conflict with propositions assumed to be mutually believed, but this is neither necessary nor sufficient for interpreting an utterance as sarcastic.) Being misled in the attribution of intent is a common sort of misunderstanding (in fact, it is a sort that is likely to go undetected).

Second, there is nothing linguistic about the resolution of the lexical ambiguity in (9a). All of the knowledge that contributes to the identification of a likely intended referent is (encyclopedic or contextual) knowledge of (or beliefs about) the relevant aspects of the world, including the beliefs of relevant individuals in it (e.g., the speaker, the (presumed) addressees of the quoted speech, the reporter of the quoted speech, and the (presumed) addressees of the report). That disambiguation of an utterance in its context may require encyclopedic knowledge of a presumed universe of discourse is not a new observation. Indeed, it has been a commonplace in the linguistics and AI literature for decades. Nonetheless, its pervasiveness and its significance seem to have been underappreciated.

A similar demonstration could be made for many structural ambiguities, including some of the ones mentioned at the beginning of this section. Insofar as language users resolve ambiguities that they recognize by choosing the interpretation most consistent with their model of the speaker and of the speaker's model of the world, modelling this ability of theirs by means of probability-based grammars and lexicons (e.g., Copestake and Briscoe 1994) is likely to provide an arbitrarily limited solution.[20] When language users fail to recognize ambiguities in the first place, it is surely because beliefs about the speaker's beliefs and intentions in the context at hand which would support alternative interpretations are not salient.

Building on analyses of speech acts as the execution of plans (Cohen and Perrault 1979, Cohen and Levesque 1980) and of language users as rational agents (Cohen and Levesque 1985, 1990),[21] Cohen and Levesque (1991) outline a set of axioms defining cooperative behavior. When these are applied to the task of communicating, they provide a vehicle for modelling a proper understanding (cf. Neale 1992, Green 1993a) of Grice's account of communicative behavior as a subcase of intentional action which includes interpretation and disambiguation. Indeed, Cohen and Levesque suggest that their analysis of joint intention enables one to understand "the *social contract* implicit in engaging in a dialogue in terms of the conversants' jointly intending to make themselves understood, and to understand the other" (1991:509). In their analysis, a team of agents jointly intends to do an action p (relative to some condition q, under which the action ceases to be desired), just in case the members have a joint persistent goal (relative to q) of their having done the action, and of having done it mutually believing throughout that they were doing it (1991:501). The fact that doing p is a joint persistent goal means that the members of the team mutually believe p is currently false, that they mutually know that they all want p to eventually be true, and that until it is mutually believed that it is either achieved or abandoned, they will all strive to achieve it, and that any member who discovers that it is achieved or unachievable or q is false will adopt the goal of making that fact mutually believed by all team members (1991:498, 499). In other words, communication is viewed as being undertaken under a set of assumptions about other participants' assumptions which have to be constantly monitored. This

---

[20]Parsers and text-interpreters that are probability-driven can only reflect the source of the statistics on which they are based, and there is never a guarantee that the source will reliably represent relevant properties of the next bit of input text. It is no doubt a truism that if you make predictions probabilistically, you will probably be wrong some of the time.

[21]These analyses are readily seen as themselves inspired by Grice's (1957, 1975) account of natural language.

view treats disambiguation, at all levels, as indistinct from interpretation, insofar as both involve comparing an interpretation of a speaker's utterance with goals and beliefs attributed to that speaker, and rejecting interpretations which in the context are not plausibly relevant to the assumed joint goal for the discourse.

5 Grammatical ambiguity; Plus ça change, plus c'est la même chose

I have argued that although uncertainties of discourse interpretation may differ from grammatical ambiguities in character, the constructs required to resolve the former are very often required to resolve the latter as well. Thus, discourse indeterminacies (anaphora (1), polysemy (10-11), relations among parts of discourses (8)) are unlimited (because the constellation of beliefs that underlie them are unlimited) and predictable (insofar as they depend on the assumption that all parties to a discourse are behaving rationally (i.e., with a goal and in the belief that their discourse action will contribute to achieving that goal (Grice 1975, Green 1993a)), while lexical ambiguity[22] (homonymy (9a)) and structural ambiguity (9b) are limited to a finite set of alternatives, and lexical ambiguity is unpredictable. However, these differences are insignificant in the face of the fact that settling on one interpretation for a parsed sentence out of however many there might be regularly requires determining what it would have been most rational for the speaker to have meant in the context in which the sentence was uttered. This does not mean that grammatical ambiguity is a subcase of discourse indeterminacy. They are distinct phenomena, albeit as a result of natural accidents, rather than as an unanalyzable universal of language.

As linguists know, grammatical ambiguities often reflect the fossilized results of natural phonological and pragmatic processes.[23] Neutralization of a phonological difference that was once distinctive is responsible for a good part of the homonymy that is characteristic of English (e.g., *pair* and *pear*, *ear* of corn and *ear* 'hearing organ', *pain* and *pane*, *plait* and *plate*). But another source of lexical ambiguity is fossilization of what was once part of a systematic polysemy: a meaning that is available as a normal meaning in a restricted context gets conventionalized and detached from the more general meaning it is functionally related to, through natural pragmatic processes (cf. Bréal (1900), Horn (1984)). Insofar as these processes are pragmatic, and depend on individuals' beliefs about normal beliefs, differences that result

---

[22]Excluding the boundary case of systematic polysemy.

[23]This is probably true much more often of lexical ambiguity than of structural ambiguity (on which, more below). However, it is not unknown in the development of structural ambiguity—cf. Horn 1989.

from them can be expected to vary from speaker to speaker. This is how *vest* comes to refer to either a short, tight-fitting, sleeveless garment or a sleeveless undergarment, and how *watch* can refer either to a period of time (part of a night or day), or a portable device for keeping time, and so on. As conventionalization supplants functional relations, fewer speakers are aware of any rationale for calling the distinct categories of experience by the same name, and more speakers are surprised to learn that the two terms have a common etymology. As more meanings that are normal only in specialized contexts become contextualized as normal names for a subcategory of experience, the meaning that was originally the normal meaning in widest use may come to seem very narrowly specialized itself. No one now uses *vest* to refer to just any garment, or *watch* to just the fact or act of staying awake and alert.

The fossilization of uses (as conventionalization, and eventually as grammaticalization) is quite transparently observable in other domains of language use as well. The often deplored extensions of the use of quotation marks provide a conspicuous example. Presumably the original use of quotation marks is to demarcate words explicitly attributed to someone other than the speaker. With this kind of basic function, it is a short step to using them as so-called "scare" quotes to demarcate expressions which are not being used literally, and are implicitly attributed to someone else.[24] Both literal and scare quotes are realized phonologically with a pause that precedes the quoted material. The quoted material has an independent intonation, and some speakers apparently take this phonological realization to be a (potential) primary function of quotation marks, leading to their use as an emphatic device, as in the signs that say *"No" dogs allowed.*[25] Here the pause and independent intonation of the quoted material seems to be intended to convey that that material is especially important. The obviously related, but presumably secondary, use of (single or double) quotation marks to indicate mention (as opposed to use) of an expression, especially in order to denote a meaning of some other expression, may also contribute to the exploitation of quotation marks for emphasis.

One might, as a simplifying assumption, dismiss the processes of language change that are constantly at work on the evolving competences of individual speakers. Even then, the fact that senses that

---

[24]Insofar as the use of scare quotes is a convention of written language (itself an artifact), their representation as double quotes ("scare" quotes) or single quotes ('scare' quotes) varies among academic disciplines, and probably even among the style sheets of journals within the same discipline.

[25]The use of quotation marks for emphasis has been commonplace in public notices (e.g., signs), especially in smaller commercial establishments such as stores and restaurants throughout the U.S. for at least the last forty years, and recurs as an object of vilification by self-appointed prescriptivists.

may once have been transparent polysemes now seem so unrelated that grammar writers and dictionary makers treat them as representing a grammaticalized ambiguity has no consequences for processes of natural language understanding. Language users typically do not know, and do not care, whether an uncertainty of interpretation arises from a grammatically conventionalized ambiguity or from the fact that distinct goals might have motivated the speaker to say what she said (the way she said it), because they must deal with it the same way: if they consider the difference among possible intended meanings important, they must figure out which one the speaker most likely intended, and if they can't resolve it, ask for clarification. If the difference is not important, it can be left unresolved. Speakers, of course, have to calculate whether their addressees are likely to understand them as they intend, and choose their words accordingly.

Resolving syntactic ambiguities that persist through parsing involves the same procedures. The most salient structural ambiguities (attachment ambiguities like those in (9b) and (15), and coordination ambiguities as in (16)) directly reflect semantic intentions.

15a. Fifty-two others were reported as injured, either by ambulance surgeons who attended them at the scene of the accident, or by physicians to whom they went for treatment later in the day.
15b. The conviction carries a penalty of one to ten years in California.

16a. At the pancake supper there will be men flipping the flapjacks and costumed waitresses.
16b. Stir in nutmeg and parsley or chervil and thyme.

Determining whether some modifier attaches high or low amounts to (and one might say, ultimately is incidental to) divining which of the corresponding intentions to attribute to the speaker—did she mean that the doctors reported the injuries, or caused them?

Other cases of structural homonymy are language-specific, arbitrary, and (like most lexical ambiguities) accidents of the history and structure of the language. An example is the structural syncretism of infinitive adjuncts as in (17).[26]

17. We bought a book to read on the train.

Another is the ambiguity of noun-noun compounds with participial

---

[26]The purpose, rationale, and relative infinitive interpretations of this structure are evident in (i-iii) respectively. cf. Green (1992).

   i. We bought it$_i$ to show t$_i$ to the children.
   ii. We shopped to pass the time.
   iii. They lost the books$_i$/*them$_i$ to read t$_i$ to the children.

modifiers and nouns with markerless relative clause modifiers as in (18).

18. An incipient forest fire drew workmen, today, from the task of mastering a burning gusher which had killed nine men and destroyed oil statisticians estimated in value up to $200,000.

The cross-categorial sense extensions (noun/verb ambiguities) that make so many English verbs homophonous with nouns (*flower, flour, drive, heat, race, trumpet*, etc.) reflect morphological facts that are specific to the English language. That is, they reflect the fact that English is unusual in having category-changing rules of derivational morphology that do not mark the derived category with a phonologically substantial affix. This typically does not make sentences containing such words ambiguous. Syntactic co-occurrence properties are usually enough for disambiguation as in (19), but when they are not, as in syntactically impoverished utterances like newspaper headlines ((20)), or even the occasional well-formed sentence as in (21), interpreters have to rely on the familiar strategy of attributing likely intentions to the speaker in order to understand what was said.

19a. Bunkersfield houses | the smallest public library in the state.
19b. Bunkersfield houses | have withstood floods, tornadoes, and an invasion of California crickets.

20a. Lodgepole, Potter men to soil offices (Omaha *World Herald*)
20b. Dealers will hear car talk Friday noon (Newark (NJ) *News*)
20c. Governor hopeful Netsch to stop in area (Champaign-Urbana (IL) *News-Gazette*)
20d. French army cooks women (San Antonio *News*)
20e. Trade shows increase

21a. Never break your bread or roll in your soup. (Nashville *Tennesseean*)
21b. Owners cannot be required to stop barking. (El Dorado (AR) *Evening Times*)

6 Conclusion

I have argued, and I hope, demonstrated, that resolving ambiguities that arise from the fact that grammars provide more than one interpretation for certain words, or more than one structure for sequences of certain constituent types, frequently boils down to the familiar pragmatic problem of determining what motivates any linguistic act in the first place. Lexical and structural ambiguities that persist through parsing are resolved exactly as are such uncertainties of discourse intention as code choice, pronominal reference, and relevance of one utterance to another—by attributing likely locutionary and perlocutionary intentions to the speaker. Insofar as resolving lexical and structural ambiguity and understanding discourse require the same sort of information to proceed, it is unreasonable to suppose that automated ambiguity resolution can succeed without reference to models of speakers and addressees (as well as of the substantive domain of the discourse) any more than natural language understanding in general can do this.

Much progress has been made in the last ten years on the problem of parsing unrestricted text. To take only the example that I am most familiar with, Russell (1993) describes a system which unifies syntactic and semantic information from partial parses to postulate (partial) syntactic and semantic information for unfamiliar words. This progress suggests that a promising approach to the problem of understanding unrestricted texts would be to expand the technique to systematically include information about contexts of utterance, especially since it can be taken for granted that words will be encountered which are being used in unfamiliar ways.[27] The chief requirement for such an enterprise is to reject (following Reddy 1979) the simplistic view of linguistic expressions as simple conduits for thoughts, and model natural language use as action of rational agents who treat the exchange of ideas as a joint goal, as Grice, Cohen, Perrault, and Levesque have been suggesting over the last three decades. This is a nontrivial task, and if it does not offer an immediate payoff in computational efficiency, ultimately it will surely pay off in increased accuracy, not to mention in understanding the subtlety of communicative and interpretive techniques.

References

Altmann, Gerry, and Mark Steedman. 1988. Interaction with context during sentence processing. Cognition 30:191–238.

Bréal, Michel. 1900. Semantics: studies in the science of meaning. London: William Heinemann.

Burt, Susan M. 1994a. Code choice in intercultural conversation: speech accommodation theory and pragmatics. Ms.

Burt, Susan M. 1994b. Where does sociopragmatic ambiguity come from? Paper presented at the 8th International Conference on Pragmatics and Language Learning. Urbana, Illinois.

Cohen, Philip R., and Hector J. Levesque. 1980. Speech acts and the recognition of shared plans. Proceedings of the 3rd biennial conference, Canadian Society for Computational Studies of Intelligence, Victoria, B.C.

Cohen, Philip R., and Hector J. Levesque. 1985. Speech acts and rationality. Proceedings of the 23rd annual meeting, Association for Computational

---

[27]I have estimated the percent of unfamiliar noun, verb, and adjective senses in descriptive English prose at between 10% and 20% of noun, verb, and adjective uses (Green 1989:56. For more discussion see Green and Morgan (to appear)).

Linguistics. Chicago, Illinois: ACM.

Cohen, Philip R., and Hector J. Levesque. 1990. Rational interaction as the basis for communication. Intentions in communication, ed. by Philip R. Cohen, Jerry Morgan, and Martha E. Pollack, 221–256. Cambridge, Mass.: MIT Press.

Cohen, Philip R., and Hector J. Levesque. 1991. Teamwork. Nous 25:487–512.

Cohen, Philip R., and Raymond Perrault. 1979. Elements of a plan-based theory of speech acts. Cognitive Science 3:177–212.

Copestake, Ann, and Ted Briscoe. 1994. Semi-productive polysemy and sense extension. Journal of Semantics, in press.

Crain, Stephen, and Mark Steedman. 1985. On not being led up the garden path; the use of context by the psychological parser. Natural language parsing, ed. by David R. Dowty, Lauri Karttunen, and Arnold M. Zwicky, 320–358. Cambridge, England: Cambridge University Press.

Green, Georgia M. 1989. Pragmatics and natural language understanding. Hillsdale, NJ: Lawrence Erlbaum Associates.

Green, Georgia M. 1992. Purpose infinitives and their relatives. The Joy of grammar, ed. by Diane Brentari, Gary N. Larson, and Lynn A. MacLeod, 95–128. Amsterdam: John Benjamins.

Green, Georgia M. 1993a. Rationality and Gricean inference. Cognitive Science Technical Report UIUC-BI-CS-93-09. Urbana, IL: University of Illinois at Urbana-Champaign.

Green, Georgia M. 1993b. Nondescriptional accounts of word meaning and reference. Cognitive Science Technical Report UIUC-BI-CS-93-12. Urbana, IL: University of Illinois at Urbana-Champaign.

Green, Georgia M., and Jerry L. Morgan. In prep. A note on using larger lexicons to expand application domains.

Grice, H. Paul. 1957. Meaning. Philosophical Review 66:377–388.

Grice, H. Paul. 1975. Logic and conversation. Syntax and semantics, vol. 3: Speech acts, ed. by Peter Cole and Jerry L. Morgan, 41–58. NY: Academic Press.

Helmreich, Stephen. 1994. Pragmatic referring functions in Montague grammar. Ph.D. dissertation. University of Illinois at Urbana-Champaign.

Hirst, Graeme. 1987. Semantic interpretation and the resolution of ambiguity. Cambridge, England: Cambridge University Press.

Horn, Laurence R. 1984. Toward a new taxonomy for pragmatic inference: Q-based and R-based implicature. Georgetown University Round Table on Language and Linguistics 1984: Meaning, form and use in context: Linguistic applications, ed. by Deborah Schiffrin, 11–42. Washington, DC: Georgetown University Press.

Horn, Laurence R. 1989. The natural history of negation. Chicago: University of Chicago Press.

McCawley, James D. 1985. Kuhnian paradigms as systems of markedness conventions. Linguistics and philosophy; essays in honor of Rulon S. Wells, edited by Adam Makkai and Alan K. Melby, 23–43. Amsterdam: John Benjamins Publishing Co.

Morgan, Jerry L. 1981. Discourse theory and the independence of sentence grammar. Georgetown University Round Table on Language and Linguistics 1981: Analyzing discourse: text and talk, ed. by Deborah Tannen, 176–204. Washington, DC: Georgetown University Press.

Morgan, Jerry L., and Manfred Sellner. 1980. Discourse and linguistic theory. Theoretical issues in reading comprehension, ed. by Rand J. Spiro, Bertram C. Bruce, and William F. Brewer, 165–200. Hillsdale, NJ: Lawrence Erlbaum Associates.

Neale, Stephen. 1992. Paul Grice and the philosophy of language. Linguistics and philosophy 15:509–559.

Nunberg, Geoffrey. 1978. The pragmatics of reference. Ph.D. dissertation, CUNY. Bloomington, IN: Indiana University Linguistics Club.

Nunberg, Geoffrey. 1979. The non-uniqueness of semantic solutions: polysemy. Linguistics and philosophy 3:145–185.

Nunberg, Geoffrey. 1995. Transfers of meaning. To appear in Semantics.

Nunberg, Geoffrey and Annie Zaenen. 1992. Systematic polysemy in lexicology and lexicography. Proceedings of Euralex92. Tampere, Finland.

Pelletier, F. J., and L. K. Schubert. 1986. Mass expressions. Handbook of philosophical logic, vol. 4, ed. by D. Gabbay and F. Guenthner. Dordrecht: Reidel.

Reddy, Michael. 1979. The conduit metaphor–a case of frame conflict in our language about language. Metaphor and thought, ed. by Andrew Ortony, 284–324. Cambridge, England: Cambridge University Press.

Ruhl, Charles. 1989. On monosemy; a study in linguistic semantics. Albany: State University of New York Press.

Russell, Dale W. 1993. Language acquisition in a unification-based grammar processing system using a real-world knowledge base. Report No. UIUCDCS-R-93-1822, UILU-ENG-93-1737. Urbana, Illinois: Department of Computer Science, University of Illinois.

Schmerling, Susan F. 1978. Synonymy judgements as syntactic evidence. Syntax and semantics, vol. 9: Pragmatics, ed. by Peter Cole, 299–314. NY: Academic Press.

Sperber, Dan, and Deirdre Wilson. 1986. Relevance; communication and cognition. Cambridge, MA: Harvard University Press.

Zwicky, Arnold, and Jerrold M. Sadock. 1975. Ambiguity tests and how to fail them. Syntax and semantics, vol. 4, ed. by John Kimball, 1–36. New York: Academic Press.

2

Quantification and Predication

JAAP VAN DER DOES AND HENK VERKUYL

1 Introduction

In this paper, we will consider sentences like (1) and (2) from the point of view of quantification and predication.

(1)   Three girls mailed a letter

(2)   Three girls mailed four letters

As to the issue of quantification, Verkuyl & Van der Does 1991 tried to reduce the large numbers of readings often assigned to these sentences to just one by adopting a so-called scalar approach. This approach is based on the following observation.

Scha 1981 stipulated that NPs are ambiguous between a distributive (D) reading and two collective readings (C_1 and C_2). In sentences with two NPs, combinations of these three readings lead to at least nine readings for (2): DD, DC$_1$, ..., C_2C_2. For example, on the DD-reading of (2), each of the girls mailed four letters, each letter on a different occasion. On the C_1C_1- reading, the girls mailed the four letters together on one occasion. The C_1C_2-reading would say that the three girls as a group mailed four letters, say on one occasion one letter, and one day later the three other letters. Observe that C_2 allows both 1+3- and 2+2-configurations of the set of four letters. In fact, it also comprises D and C_1. On the C_1C_2- reading just mentioned, C_2 allows also the 4- and the 1+1+1+1-configuration. Here the idea of a scale comes up quite naturally, but this idea was not taken up by Scha himself, nor did Link 1984 pay attention to it.

Verkuyl & Van der Does 1991 decided to take a strengthening of the C_2-reading as basic, in fact as the only reading that can be attached

Semantic Ambiguity and Underspecification
Kees van Deemter and Stanley Peters, editors
Copyright © 1995, CSLI Publications

to (1) and (2). They chose (3) as the format for the analysis of the denotation of NPs like *three girls* in sentences such as (1) and (2):

(3) $\quad \lambda \mathbf{P}.\exists X[X \subseteq [\![\text{girl}]\!] \wedge |X| = 3 \wedge \exists \mathbf{Q}[\bigcup \mathbf{Q} = X \ \& \ \mathbf{Q} = \mathbf{P}|_{[\![\text{girl}]\!]}]]$

It says that there is a set X of three girls that can be covered by a collection $\mathbf{Q}$ which is the predicate $\mathbf{P}$ restricted to the set of girls.[1] In this way, we obtain Scha's D just in case $\mathbf{Q}$ is partitioned into three singletons whereas (an instance of) Scha's C_1 is obtained when $\mathbf{Q} = \mathbf{P}|_{[\![\text{girl}]\!]} = \{X\}$.

The leading idea of the scalar approach is the empirical fact that sentences like (1) and (2) do not give away which configuration is actualized, and that the variant of C_2 in (3) seems the right way of expressing this. It includes the whole range between and including the extremes D and C_1. However, although (3) has the virtue of scalarity and thus captures the underdeterminedness of information inherent in (1) and (2), it still has some shortcomings. For one, it does not capture the so-called cumulative reading of these sentences. In case of (2) this reading would say that the total number of girls mailing letters is three and that the total number of letters being mailed is four. This cannot be obtained by (3) because the predicate $\mathbf{P}|_{[\![\text{girl}]\!]}$ will always contain information about the second argument NP, whereas the cumulative reading requires the scope of the two NPs to be independent.

At this point, the second conjunct of the title of the present paper comes in: one cannot have a theory of (collective) quantification without a theory of (collective) predication which tells us how exactly the argument denotations and their members are involved in the predication itself; i.e., we want to account for the possible ways in which the members of the argument NP satisfy the predicate. The problem is—informally speaking—that in (1) we use the predicate *mail a letter* whereas in fact we might speak about mailing three letters. Sentences like (4) show the problem even more clearly.

(4)   Four men lifted three tables

They allow us to speak about between three and twelve tables which were lifted, whereas the predicate is 'lift three tables'. This means that in order to maintain our scalarity thesis we need the formal means to provide underdeterminedness as to how the different tables in (4) have been involved in the predication, and to establish how this affects the quantification expressed by the NP.

---

[1]Below we shall strengthen coverings to partitions, which require the sets in the cover to be disjoint. For a discussion on other forms of covering see Verkuyl & Van der Does 1991, Van der Does 1993.

It is this perspective which will be worked out in detail here. We will formalize such notions as VP-predication, Path, and 'mode' within the framework of generalized quantification, but with the explicit purpose of integrating in it some points of view from the linguistic tradition called *localism*. Sentences like (1) express a change of state which in a localistic approach is analyzed in terms of an abstract "movement" from a point of origin to a point at which the predicate is satisfied. In

(5)   Mary mailed a letter

one may say that Mary is "going through" a Path as a way of saying that she underwent the predication. Similar things can be said of the set of three girls, in the sense that we need to pay attention to the way in which each of the girls undergoes the predication, i.e., has an individual Path. In particular we are interested in the way the individual Paths of the girls may interfere. In Verkuyl 1988 it was argued that only two modes are available in this respect: either the Paths are totally disjoint or they are essentially one. It is obvious that the metaphoric way of introducing the intuitive notion of localism—change in time expressed by a verb like *mail* can be dealt with in terms of a cumulative structure built up from an origin to an end—is to be replaced by a precise formalism. This has been done in Verkuyl 1993 and a simplified version will be used in section 3.1. We shall show that the incorporation of localistic insights into the model-theoretic approach of generalized quantification makes it possible to reduce ambiguities.

This paper has the following structure. In section 2 we give an overview of our earlier attempt to reduce the ambiguity of plural sentences, and also of the problems this gave rise to. Next, section 3 introduces the linguistic tradition of localism and its core concept of a Path. After formalizing this notion, we focus on two 'modes' namely the one in which the relevant members of the external object have distinct verbal Paths, and the one in which they share the same verbal Path. These extremes are called the π-injective and the π-constant modes. In section 4, we prove that the π-constant mode, which captures a special kind of collectivity, gives an impressive collapse of plural as well as of polyadic readings. We therefore suggest to capture the readings by means of the two π modes combined with iterated neutral plural quantification, but to use no further representation within the semantics.

2   The Scalar Approach

In this section we formally characterize our earlier attempts to reduce the ambiguity of sentences like (1) and (2). To this end, section 2.1 first discusses the quantifier liftings in Van der Does 1993, which generalize the treatment of numerals in Scha 1981. In section 2.2 we give a short overview of the considerations which led to the attempt in Verkuyl and Van der Does 1991 to reduce ambiguities, and of the subsequent discussion it gave rise to. Finally, in section 2.3 we discuss some problems we and others have with that proposal. So, the present section paves the way for a further development of our theory in section 3 and section 4.

2.1   Quantifier liftings

Determiners as they are studied in the theory of generalized quantification live in type $(et)(ett)$; they are relations among sets. These relations have to satisfy some constraints. In particular, most natural language determiners are conservative, and have extension and isomorphy.

Definition 1 A determiner $\mathbf{D}$ is a functor which assigns to each non-empty domain E an element from $\wp(\wp(E) \times \wp(E))$. $\mathbf{D}$ is *conservative* (CONS) iff for each E and all $A, B \subseteq E$: $\mathbf{D}_E AB \Leftrightarrow \mathbf{D}_E AA \cap B$. $\mathbf{D}$ has *extension* (EXT) iff for all $E, E' \supseteq A, B$: $\mathbf{D}_E AB \Leftrightarrow \mathbf{D}_{E'} AB$. $\mathbf{D}$ has *isomorphy* (ISOM) iff for all bijections $f : E \longrightarrow E'$: $\mathbf{D}_E AB \Leftrightarrow \mathbf{D}_{E'} f[A] f[B]$, where $f[X] := \{f(x) : x \in X\}$. $\mathbf{D}$ is a *quantifier* iff $\mathbf{D}$ has CONS, EXT, and ISOM.

Due to EXT we may forget about E and stipulate that $\mathbf{D} AB$ iff for some E: $\mathbf{D}_E AB$. Also, for a quantifier $\mathbf{D}$ the truth of $\mathbf{D} AB$ only depends on the two cardinals: $|\{a \in A : a \notin B\}|$ and $|\{a \in A : a \in B\}|$. In this article, we shall often use *positive* determiners which require their arguments to be non-empty: $\mathbf{D} AB$ implies $A \neq \emptyset \neq B$.

The above treatment of determiners does not cover the phenomena typical of plural noun phrases. Following up on a suggestion in Van Benthem 1991, Van der Does 1992,1993,1994 studies different approaches to plural quantification by means of liftings from type $(et)((et)t)$ to type $(et)(((et)t)t)$. In the latter type the verbal part of a quantifier can be taken to hold of sets instead of just atoms, which makes quantification over these sets possible. The relevant liftings, given in (6), turn out to be generalizations of the numeral denotations in Scha 1981.[2]

(6)   D $\mathbf{D(D)}XY \Leftrightarrow \mathbf{D}X\{d \mid \{d\} \in \mathbf{Y}\}$
       C $\mathbf{C(D)}XY \Leftrightarrow \exists Z[\mathbf{D}XZ \wedge X \cap Z \in \mathbf{Y}]$
       N $\mathbf{N(D)}XY \Leftrightarrow \mathbf{D}X\bigcup(\mathbf{Y} \cap \wp(X))$

The names of the liftings are mnemonic for 'distributive', 'collective', and 'neutral', respectively. On the conceptual side they are based on the three perspectives we seem to employ in describing collections. We either quantify over 'atomic' partless individuals (D), or over genuine collections (C, Scha's C_1), or over the atoms which take part in certain

---

[2]Scha (1981) discerns two forms of collective quantification instead of collective and neutral quantification.

collections (N, Scha's C_2)). In the latter situation we remain neutral as to the precise structure and size of these collections.[3]

Disregarding scopal ambiguities and non-iterative forms of quantification, the determiner readings in (6) make (4) *Four men lifted three tables* nine times ambiguous. The readings are summarized in (7).

Nine readings is a bit much for the simple (4), and it is tempting to try to do with less. In the next subsection, we give an overview of our earlier proposal in that direction.[4]

(7)

NP_1/NP_2	D	N	C
D	DD	DN	DC
N	ND	NN	NC
C	CD	CN	CC

2.2 The One-Reading Hypothesis

The proposal in Verkuyl and Van der Does 1991 grew out of Verkuyl's idea to reduce the number of readings of (4) to one by taking the neutral reading of numerals as their plural denotation. The distributive and the collective readings could then be seen as depending on the nature of its verbal argument in a particular context. The verbal argument takes its value on a scale ranging from sets of singletons at the one end via several intermediate cases to singletons of sets at the other. The endpoints yield the distributive and collective 'reading', which, however, need not be represented at logical form.[5] As proposition 1 shows, the liftings in (6) can be used to formalize and generalize these intuitions.

---

[3]It is perhaps misleading to talk about distributive quantification as pointed out in Verkuyl 1994. The quantification is over atoms (i.e., the elements of type e or, equivalently, the singletons in type (et)), so 'atomic quantification' seems more accurate (Van der Does 1992, 1993). A *predicate* of sets can be distributive in that it is closed under non-empty subsets. Atomic predicates, which only contain singletons, are trivially distributive in this sense. Yet, the two notions should not be confused. E.g., a predicate can also be distributive up to a certain size, if it is closed under subsets of this size and larger. Still the concepts are intimately related: each atomic predicate gives rise to a unique predicate which is closed under non-empty subsets and arbitrary unions. Van der Does calls such sets of sets strictly distributive as opposed to the partly distributive ones, which are closed under subsets of size greater than one. A quantifier $D(\mathbf{D})$ is equivalent to a relation between sets and (strictly) distributive sets of sets, and it derives its name from the latter (cf., Van der Does *ibidem*).

[4]We do not discuss Link's proposal not to discern between C and N 'for methodological reasons' (Link 1991). The logical differences between the denotations do not sustain this strategy (cf., Van der Does 1993 for details).

[5]Of course the proposal is limited to the NPs which allow the readings. Inherently distributive (i.e., atomic) NPs, such as *every man*, are obtained via the D-denotation of its determiner.

Proposition 1 (FIN) *Call* **Y** *positive iff* $\emptyset \notin$ **Y**. *For all positive* **Y** $\cap$ $\wp(A)$ *it holds that* $\forall X \in$ **Y** $\cap \wp(A)[|X| = 1]$ *iff for all* **D**, X: N(**D**)XY *and* D(**D**)XY *are equivalent. For all* **Y** *it holds that* $|\textbf{Y} \cap \wp(A)| = 1$ *iff for all conservative* **D** *and all* X: N(**D**)XY *and* C(**D**)XY *are equivalent.*

PROOF. It is plain that for the appropriate **Y** N(**D**) is either equivalent to D(**D**) or to C(**D**). For the other directions we need FIN.[6] By way of example we show the distributive case. Assume that **Y**$\cap \wp(A)$ contains a Z which is not a singleton. Since **Y** $\cap \wp(A)$ is positive $|Z| > 1$. By FIN $|\{d \in A : \{d\} \in \textbf{Y}\}| < |\bigcup(\textbf{Y} \cap \wp(A))|$. Set $n = |\bigcup(\textbf{Y} \cap \wp(A))|$, and let **n** be the corresponding determiner. Then N(**n**)AY but not D(**n**)AY. □

Given proposition 1 it seems natural to give (2) only its NN reading and leave the other interpretations to context. However, there are some problems with this strategy.

2.3 Problems

The problems concern neutral readings of the external argument NP in a sentence with a complex VP. They are followed by suggested solutions.

Problem I In his reaction to an earlier version of Van der Does 1993, Lønning 1991 pointed out that the neutral reading allows a splitting of the collections quantified over. For example, on the neutral reading of *four men* in (4) the sentence may be true if there is a single man who lifted three tables besides a set of three men who also lifted three tables. That this is so, is best seen by means of (8), which is equivalent to N(**D**)XY for conservative **D**:

(8) $\exists Y \subseteq X[\textbf{D}XY \wedge \exists \textbf{Z} \text{ cv } Y : \textbf{Z} = \textbf{Y} \cap \wp(X)]$

Here the relation **Z** cv Y—**Z** *covers* Y,—is defined by $\bigcup \textbf{Z} = Y$. For (4), **Y** is the set of Z such that 'Z lifted three tables'. On the subject neutral reading (8) says: there is a set Y of four men and a cover **Z** of Y which is identical to the set of 'men-parts' of the collections Z which lifted three tables. But such a cover could be of the form $\{\{m_1\}, \{m_2, m_3, m_4\}\}$. The judgements whether or not these truth-conditions are correct differ widely.

Problem II Van der Does 1993 observes that the application of neutral quantifiers is also limited for another reason. Call a quantifier *bounded* iff there is an n such that for all A, B: if **D**AB then $|A \cap B| \leq n$ (cf., Westerståhl 1989). Numerals are prime examples of bounded quantifiers. In sentence (4), which iterates two numerals n and m, one expects under the normal scoping that the number of tables described lies between m and $n * m$. But neutral plural quantification allows an

---

[6]'FIN' indicates that we assume the models to have a finite domain.

upper bound of $2^n * m$. In the truth-conditions of (4) as given by (8) $\mathbf{Z}$ may vary over the poorest cover $\{Y\}$ of Y via intermediate alternatives to its richest cover $\wp(Y)$. Thus, a neutral reading of the subject in (4) allows the number of tables to range from three to $2^4 * 3$.

2.4 Suggested Solutions

Problem II can be solved by strengthening the notion of cover in (8) to that of partition, mimimal cover, or pseudo-partition (cf., Verkuyl and Van der Does 1991, Van der Does 1993, for details). On the localistic analysis advocated in Verkuyl 1993, and introduced in section 3, partitions are a natural choice. As we shall point out in sections 3.1 and 4.1 the subject NP should then vary over the partition which arises from the equivalence relation 'to share the same Path'. However, this strategy offers no solution to Problem I.

As an alternative solution to Problem II, one could use a referential rather than a quantificational treatment of the NP, as suggested by Van der Does 1993,1994. To be precise, (8) could be replaced by (9).[7]

(9) $\mathbf{D} X \bigcup \mathbf{P} \wedge \mathbf{P} \; partitions \bigcup \mathbf{P} \wedge \mathbf{P} = \mathbf{Y} \cap \wp(X)$

Here $\mathbf{P}$ is a contextually given set of sets. On this view the meaning of a determiner is a Kaplanian character; it needs contextual information to yield a denotation. In uttering (4) $\mathbf{P}$ remains underspecified, but (4) will be false with respect to any situation that does not comply with its structure. Note that this solution, too, leaves Problem I unsolved. The partitional reading still allows the spliced subject NP noted by Lønning. Verkuyl (1992, 1994) has some examples where such a split is not unlikely, and there may be pragmatical principles which rule out the remaining odd cases.

Van der Does 1993 feels uncomfortable with the spliced subjects. He seeks a semantical solution by holding that they only occur in case of non-iterative forms of quantification, such as the cumulative reading. On this reading arbitrary covers are allowed, for it leaves the quantificational elements of the internal argument NPs outside the scope of the external one. In the case of iterations there is an asymmetry between the external and the internal argument NP (cf., section 3.1). The internal argument NP favours a neutral reading—again allowing for covers,—while the external argument may be either distributive or

---

[7]Recall that a set of sets $\mathbf{Y}$ *partitions* a set X iff (i.e., if and only if) the following three requirements are met: (i) $\bigcup \mathbf{Y} = X$, (ii) $\forall X, Y \in \mathbf{Y}[X \neq Y \Rightarrow X \cap Y = \emptyset]$, (iii) $\emptyset \notin \mathbf{Y}$.

collective. On this view a simple transitive sentence can have one of the following three readings:

(10) DN $D(\mathbf{D}_1)AN(\mathbf{D}_2)B\mathbf{R}$
  CN $C(\mathbf{D}_1)AN(\mathbf{D}_2)B\mathbf{R}$
  NN $N(\mathbf{D}_1)A\,\mathrm{DOM}(\mathbf{R}\cap\wp(A)\times\wp(B))$
  $\wedge\;N(\mathbf{D}_2)B\,\mathrm{RNG}(\mathbf{R}\cap\wp(A)\times\wp(B))$

Van der Does does not explain why these readings are realized and no others. Below we point out that the first two readings are strict analogues of Verkuyl's π_{inj} and π_{con} modes (cf., section 3.2 and 4.2). Here π is the localistic Path- function accounting for the participancy of the members of the NP-denotation. The next section gives a detailed exposition of a formalization of this localistic notion. This prepares the ground for clearing up how Verkuyl's localistic approach figures within the wider landscape of plural and polyadic quantification.

3 Two modes of Predication

3.1 The π-function

Linguists have a long tradition of analyzing sentences like (1) and (11) into a NP VP structure, as in figure 1. In generative grammar, there are two independent lines of thought which lead to the idea of a certain asymmetry between the two NPs in figure 1.

(11) John loves Mary

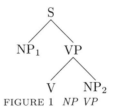

FIGURE 1 *NP VP*

The first line is syntactic and it shows up in the issue about whether or not languages are configurational, the leading hypothesis being that this is universally the case. Around 1980 it became standard to distinguish in sentences like (11) between the external NP_1-argument *John* and an internal NP_2-argument *Mary*. This means that the basic format of the sentences of natural language is the one in figure 1. The second line is the localistic one as it has developed in the generative framework. In Jackendoff (1978;1983;1990) and in Verkuyl (1978;1987;1993), the internal argument has closer ties with the verb than the external argument, at least when temporal structure is taken into account. Jackendoff (1972) still analyzed change expressed in sentences like

(12)   a.   John went to New York
        b.   John became angry

in terms of the 3-place format GO(X,Y,Z), where in (12a) X = John, Y = some point of departure and Z = New York, whereas in (12b) X = John, Y = some peace of mind, and Z = the state of being angry, but in his later work he comprised the last two arguments of the GO-predicate into a Path obtaining asymmetry. Verkuyl (1972:106) accepted the NP VP asymmetry in view of the composition of aspectuality and has maintained it.

For the purpose of this paper, the notion of compositionally formed aspectuality is best discussed in terms of features assigned to the verb and its arguments. These features have a precise model-theoretic interpretation which is given in Verkuyl 1993. It would carry too far to discuss the formal machinery dealing with aspectuality here. It suffices to observe that sentences like (5) are called terminative, i.e., have terminative aspectuality: they pertain to a bounded event as opposed to sentences like *Mary mailed letters*, *Mary mailed no letter* and *Nobody mailed a letter*. These are called durative: they pertain to events that can be prolonged indefinitely or to non-events. One of the standard litmus tests is given in (13):

(13)   a.   #For hours Mary mailed a letter
        b.   For hours Mary mailed letters
        c.   For hours nobody mailed a letter

Sentence (13a) is odd: it enforces a queer sort of repetition. In any case, it blocks the one-event reading of (5). The other two sentences in (13) have a normal interpretation: they pertain to the same sort of event or non-event as the sentences without the durational adverbial. In Verkuyl's compositional theory (simplified here to an algebra of features) the terminative aspectuality in (13), in (12) and in (1) and (2) are due to the fact that these sentences all satisfy two conditions: (a) their verb is a [+ADD TO]-verb, i.e., a nonstative verb, which builds up a cumulative index structure;[8] (b) the arguments of the verb are [+SQA]-NPs. The abbreviatory label SQA stands for Specified Quantity of A, where A is the head noun denotation. The idea behind the

---

[8]Nonstative verbs, i.e., verbs expressing change, like *walk*, *talk*, *eat*, etc. are distinguished from stative verbs like *hate*, *love*, by their being able to invoke an interpretation in which their arguments participate in a temporal structure. One may call the nonstative verbs [+ADD TO] and the stative verbs [−ADD TO] to distinguish them lexically. To say that a verb compositionally contributes to the formation of the VP is taken to say that it contributes semantic information to the VP by interacting with the NP_2-information.

model-theoretic definition is that in a type-logical analysis of the NP as a semantic object of type ($ettt$) the basic format of the representation is ...$\exists X[X \subseteq A \wedge |X| = k...]$. In *four letters* $k = 4$, in *a letter* $k = 1$, in *some letters*, $k \geq 1$, etc. Compositionally, for the verb the aspectually relevant information of NPs (with Count Nouns) is the cardinality information, either explicitly expressed (numerals, *both*) or implicitly given (*some, many, few*), in order to establish terminative aspectuality.

In the theory of aspectuality of Verkuyl 1993 VP-aspectuality is essentially different from sentential aspectuality. Intuitively, the terminativity in sentences like (1) and (2) must be dealt with exactly in the way we deal with the quantificational structure of these sentences: if the girls each mailed a letter, then aspectually we must end up with three terminative events, whereas if they mailed just one letter we should end up with one terminative event. Localistically, this is just another way of saying that the Path of each of the girls is assigned at the VP-level. Note that the Path in (1) is bounded, whereas in *Three girls mailed letters*, which is durative, the Path is unbounded.

The above informal introduction of the aspectual asymmetry is our point of departure for explicating the functions associated with the information expressed by figure 1, which are depicted in figure 2. Intuitively, two functions, π and ℓ, are involved in the interaction be-

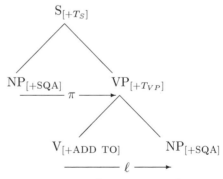

FIGURE 2 *Basic structure of aspect construal.*

tween the temporal ([+ADD TO]) information expressed by verbs like *mail, lift, eat,* (but not *love* and *believe*), and the atemporal ([+SQA]) information expressed by their arguments. In terms of the informal notions used above: ℓ is the function defining a Path, whereas π determines how the members of the external argument NP$_1$ are mapped onto the Path assigned to them by the predication.

This intuition can be formalized as follows. For the sake of the present exposition, let verbs take their denotation in type $e(i(et))$, with i the type of indices. Then π is the function from $\text{DOM}(\llbracket V \rrbracket \cap \llbracket N_1 \rrbracket \times \llbracket N_2 \rrbracket)$ to the function space

$$\mathbf{D}_i \longrightarrow \wp(\text{RNG}(\llbracket V \rrbracket \cap \llbracket N_1 \rrbracket \times \llbracket N_2 \rrbracket))$$

where the ℓ's take values. To be precise, for each $a \in \text{DOM}(\llbracket V \rrbracket \cap \llbracket N_1 \rrbracket \times \llbracket N_2 \rrbracket)$ $\pi(a)$ is the ℓ_a defined by: $\lambda i \lambda d' \in \llbracket N_2 \rrbracket . \llbracket V \rrbracket aid'$. So, $\ell_a(i)$ is the set of $\llbracket N_2 \rrbracket$'s a is $\llbracket V \rrbracket$-related to at i. For (4), *Four men lifted three tables*, this says that the function π assigns to each of the relevant men m a function ℓ_m, which is a map from indices to subsets of the tables. E.g., the function π could be spelled out as in (14) with the situation sketched in (15) as a possible outcome of its application (only non-zero values of ℓ_n are depicted).

(14)　　$m_1 \mapsto \ell_1$　　$m_2 \mapsto \ell_2$
　　　　$m_3 \mapsto \ell_3$　　$m_4 \mapsto \ell_4$

(15)　　$m_1 \mapsto \{\langle i, \{t_1, t_2\}\rangle, \langle j, \{t_3\}\rangle\}$　　$m_2 \mapsto \{\langle j, \{t_4, t_5, t_6\}\rangle\}$
　　　　$m_3 \mapsto \{\langle j, \{t_1\}\rangle, \langle m, \{t_7, t_8\}\rangle\}$　　$m_4 \mapsto \{\langle i, \{t_1\}\rangle, \langle k, \{t_9, t_{10}\}\rangle\}$

In fact, the notion of Path in Verkuyl 1993 is much richer, as it involves the use of structured indices in an essential way. In particular, a [+ADD TO] -verb V is interpreted over intervals of natural numbers, which model progress in time among other things. Moving from the beginpoint of an interval, an object a makes successive steps to go through its V-Path. Each possible step from the beginpoint to the endpoint of an interval contributes a cell of a partition of the set $\ell_n(a)$. The partition is warranted on the basis of the equivalence relation 'being lifted at the same index as'.[9] In this way, ℓ as part of the definition of π ensures that in a sentence like (4) the number of tables may vary from 3 to 12, and that a large number of different situations are captured, among which (15).

One of the purposes of the present paper is to investigate how far we can get without using indices. Our wish to abstract away from indices is to provide for a common ground for the treatment of [+ADD TO]-verbs like *lift* and [−ADD TO]- verbs like *love*, for which the π-function has not been defined. After this, it may be easier to account for the difference between these verbs in domains with temporal structure.

There are two ways of disregarding indices, which become plain by considering an intermediate step of abstraction where they are structureless. At this level, a transitive verb can be of type $e(i(ett))$ or of

---

[9]Recall that partitions are closely related to equivalence relations (i.e., two-place relations which are reflexive, symmetrical, and transitive). For if $\mathbf{Y}$ partitions X, then Rxy iff $\exists Y \in \mathbf{Y}[x, y \in Y]$ is an equivalence relation. In section 4.1 we give the canonical way to turn an equivalence relation into a partition.

type $e(i(et))$. In the first case, the way in which the set of objects comes about while going through an index, is represented within the second argument as a set of sets. In the second case only the set itself is given. To start with, we concentrate on the first option. Without indices, it leads us to consider a transitive verb R as of type $e(ett)$, so that $\pi_R(a)$ is a set of sets for each $a \in \text{DOM}(R)$. It should be kept in mind, however, that intuitively such an a is R-related to $\bigcup \pi_R(a)$; i.e., the set obtained after 'processing' the entire interval.

3.2 Two Modes

Verkuyl (1988) proposed to put an empirically motivated restriction on π by assuming that it should either be an injection or a constant function. This amounts to holding that the elements in the domain of π_V either have their own Path (injective) or all share the same Path (constant).[10] In (15) π_{lift} is an injection, due to the fact that none of the men has the same Path, even when sometimes the same tables have been lifted at different indices. In particular, $\langle i, \{t_1\}\rangle \neq \langle i, \{t_1, t_2\}\rangle \neq \langle j, \{t_1\}\rangle$ because t_1 occurs in different index-set pairs. But π_{lift} can also map all the originals to one and the same image, as in (16):

(16) $m_1 \mapsto \{\langle i, \{t_1, t_2, t_3\}\rangle\}$
         $m_2 \mapsto \{\langle i, \{t_1, t_2, t_3\}\rangle\}$
         $m_3 \mapsto \{\langle i, \{t_1, t_2, t_3\}\rangle\}$
         $m_4 \mapsto \{\langle i, \{t_1, t_2, t_3\}\rangle\}$

The function π_{lift} is now constant. At this point the notion of kolkhoz-collectivity comes in. At the index i, the men are not just related to the same collection of three tables but this collection is required to be unique.[11] None of the men can be said to have his own Path, so it is impossible for the relevant members of the N_1- denotation to be 'held responsible' for the satisfaction of the predicate 'lift three tables'. The

---

[10]A function $f : A \longrightarrow B$ is an injection iff for all $a, a' \in A$: if $f(a) = f(a')$, then $a = a'$. The function is constant iff for all $a, a' \in A$: $f(a) = f(a')$. In section 4 it will appear that Verkuyl's intuition should be formalized by: *relative to an index i* the function π_R^i, defined by $\lambda d \lambda d' . \pi_R did'$, should be either constant or injective.

[11]We use the term 'collection' to remain neutral with respect to their precise nature (sets, sums, groups). In this article, we use sets. Also, Verkuyl (1994) took kolkhoz-collectivity to be about collections which are minimal within the VP. But now we hold that this notion should be strengthened to uniqueness (cf., Van der Does' (1994) discussion of kolkhoz-collectivity in terms of maximized, minimized, and referential collective readings). The use of maximized, not necessarily unique sets in collective readings is also an important theme in Van den Berg 1995 (and earlier).

following sentences show that this is in fact a frequently used mode of predication:

(17)   a.   The twelve passengers killed that horrible man
          b.   Hans and Uwe wrote a book about DRT
          c.   500 Dutch firms own 6000 American computers

In (17a) none of the passengers may claim that he or she killed that horrible man. The purpose of the sentence seems to be to evade such a claim. In (17b) neither of the two men may claim 'I have written a book about DRT'. The essence of the information is that they did it together, blurring the individual contribution to the satisfaction of the VP- predicate. In a sense, Scha's famous (17c) appears to fall under the notion of kolkhoz- collectivity as well. It can be seen as a claim about a unique set of Dutch firms and a unique set of American computers which somehow stand in the own-relation to each other (cf., section 4.3).

In section 4, we will argue that the distinction between the constancy and injectivity of π underlies two basic modes of predication. Moreover, these modes should provide for a considerable reduction of ambiguity of sentences like (1) and (2). Rather than specifying many different readings in terms of NP denotations or quantificational structures, we aim to show that to a large extent these 'readings' are encompassed by the modes of π. In particular we want to argue that the difference between the distributive and the totalizing collective use of a sentence is a matter of mode rather than of representation.

In the above, the two modes of handling verbal information are made dependent on indices. The function ℓ has indices in its domain, and the distinction between the two forms of π is based on indices as well. In section 4 we show that the two modes are available without any appeal to indices. This does not imply that indices are not necessary. Rather it implies that the intuition on which the modes are based are independent of them.

Now, we want to clarify how the modes of π are related to the readings in terms of plural NP denotations. As a first step in that direction we give an explicit account of the intuitions concerning Kolkhoz-collectivity. We do so by means of liftings and lowerings of the basic relations, and characterize the higher level relations which arise in this manner (section 4.1). It is shown what reduction in readings is effected if attention is restricted to these relations (section 4.2), and how they can be used to give a connection between plural and polyadic quantification (section 4.4).[12] In this way we make precise how these readings relate to the modes of predication.

4 The Present Framework

Localistically, a standard model can be seen to give what is the case at a certain index (interval, event, ...). In the previous section we noted that on this view it is natural to take a two-place relation as carrying information concerning maximal, even unique sets. On the one hand there is for each $a \in A$ in the domain of the relation the unique set of B's standing in the R-relation to it (i.e., the set of Bs on a's R-path). On the other hand, there are the unique sets of A's which stand in the R-relation to the same B's (i.e., the set of A's which share the same R-path as restricted to B).[13] As soon as the totalizing nature of this is made explicit at the level of relations among sets, it suggests that at the higher level not all relations are admissible. We now characterize the relations which are obtained in this manner. Intuitively, only those transitive verb denotations are allowed which relate two unique sets per index. In fact, we prove a slightly more general result to enable a discussion of the options concerning transitive verbs in type $e(et)$ and in type $e(ett)$ discerned above.

4.1 Lifting Relations

Let R be a two-place relation of type $\alpha(\beta t)$. Define

$$\pi_R : \text{DOM}(R) \longrightarrow \wp(\text{RNG}(R))$$

by: $\pi_R(a) \mapsto R_a$ with $R_a := \{b : Rab\}$, and define $\langle \text{DOM}(R), \sim_R \rangle$ by:

$$a \sim_R a' \text{ iff } \pi_R(a) = \pi_R(a')$$

Clearly $\sim_R$ is an equivalence relation, which induces a partition of $\text{DOM}(R)$. The cells of this partition are:

$$[a]_R := \{a' \in \text{DOM}(R) \mid a' \sim_R a\}$$

Using these notions, we define a lifting $\uparrow$ from type $\alpha(\beta t)$ to type $(\alpha t)(\beta tt)$ as follows:

(18) $\uparrow_\pi (R) XY$ iff $\exists a \in \text{DOM}(R)[X = [a]_R \text{ and } Y = \pi_R(a)]$

The subscript π is dropped if no confusion is likely. Notice that we have R_a as the value of $\uparrow(R)$ on $[a]_R$: $\uparrow(R)([a]_R) = R_a$. In fact, the relations within the image of $\uparrow$ can be characterized as the partitional injections

---

[12]Such a connection is first noted in the appendix of Hoeksema 1983. The question is often raised by Van Benthem (cf., the issues for further study in Westerståhl 1994).

[13]Another view on models takes each tuple in a relation as a unique 'atomic' event. With explicit indices, this would satisfy: $Rx_1 \ldots x_n i$ and $Rx_1 \ldots x_n i'$ implies $i = i'$.

in type $(\alpha t)(\beta tt)$; i.e., the injections $\mathbf{R} : \text{DOM}(\mathbf{R}) \longrightarrow \text{RNG}(\mathbf{R})$ with $\text{DOM}(\mathbf{R})$ partitions $\bigcup \text{DOM}(\mathbf{R})$.

Proposition 2 *The partitional injections $\mathbf{R}$ in type $(\alpha t)(\beta tt)$ are precisely those of the form $\mathbf{R} = \uparrow(R)$ for an R of type $\alpha(\beta t)$.*

PROOF. It is clear from its definition that $\uparrow(R)$ is a function with a partitioned domain. To see that it is even an injection, assume for X, $X' \in \text{DOM}(\uparrow R)$ that $X \neq X'$. There are a, $a' \in \text{DOM}(R)$ such that $X = [a]_R$ and $X' = [a']_R$. Since $[a]_R \neq [a']_R$, also $\pi_R(a) \neq \pi_R(a')$. That is, $\uparrow R(X) \neq \uparrow R(X')$.

In order to show that any partitional injection $\mathbf{R}$ is of the form $\uparrow(R)$, we introduce the lowering $\downarrow$ defined by:

(19) $\downarrow(\mathbf{R})xy$ iff $\exists XY[\mathbf{R}XY$ and $x \in X$ and $y \in Y]$

That is, $\downarrow\mathbf{R} := \bigcup\{X \times Y \mid \mathbf{R}XY\}$. Our proof is complete if we can show that for all the $\mathbf{R}$'s under consideration $\uparrow(\downarrow\mathbf{R}) = \mathbf{R}$. So, let $\mathbf{R}$ be an partitional injection. Then, $\downarrow(\mathbf{R}) = \bigcup\{X \times \mathbf{R}(X) \mid X \in \text{DOM}(\mathbf{R})\}$. Here the X's are pairwise disjoint and $\mathbf{R}(X)$ is only assigned to X. Consequently, for all $a \in \text{DOM}(\downarrow(\mathbf{R}))$: $\pi_{\downarrow\mathbf{R}}(a) = \mathbf{R}(X)$, where X is the unique $X \in \text{DOM}(\mathbf{R})$ with $a \in X$. But then for all $a \in \text{DOM}(\downarrow(\mathbf{R}))$: $[a]_{\downarrow\mathbf{R}}$ is that X as well. Thus, $\mathbf{R}XY$ iff $\exists a \in \text{DOM}(\downarrow\mathbf{R})[X = [a]_{\downarrow\mathbf{R}} \ \& \ Y = \pi_{\downarrow\mathbf{R}}(a)]$ iff $\uparrow(\downarrow\mathbf{R})$; as required. □

Proposition 2 highlights once more the notion of kolkhoz-collectivity. First, the sets of objects which share the same Path occur uniquely within the domain of $\mathbf{R}$. Second, these unique sets are $\mathbf{R}$-related to a unique set in the range of $\mathbf{R}$.

A next step is to determine the specific form of $\uparrow(R)$ in case π_R has special properties. It is at this point that clear connections with collective quantification emerge. The properties of π we are interested in are given in the formulation of proposition 3, which can be proved along the same lines as proposition 2.

Proposition 3 *The atomic injections $\mathbf{R}$ in type $(\alpha t)(\beta tt)$ – i.e., the injections with a domain which consists of singletons – are precisely those of the form $\mathbf{R} = \uparrow_\pi(R)$ for an R of type $\alpha(\beta t)$ and π an injection. The singletons $\mathbf{R}$ in type $(\alpha t)(\beta tt)$ are precisely those of the form $\mathbf{R} = \uparrow_\pi(R)$ for an R of type $\alpha(\beta t)$ and π constant.* □

The above observations are preliminary to showing how iterative quantification at the lower level is related to a form of iterative quantification at the level of sets. It is this relation which allows us to establish in what way the readings at the higher level vary with the nature of a Path function π.

4.2 Plural Quantification

In this section we take transitive verbs to be of type $e(ett)$ (cf., section 3.1). These denotations are obtained from their denotation in type $e(i(ett))$ by fixing a certain index i. In Verkuyl 1993 the indices are totally ordered. The Path-function π_R of a verb R of type $e(ett)$ assigns to each individual in its domain a set of sets, which intuitively comes about by going through the ordered index i. For example, one could have the injective (20) or the constant (21):

(20) $m_1 \mapsto \{\{t_1, t_2\}\}$, $m_2 \mapsto \{\{t_3\}, \{t_4\}\}$, $m_3 \mapsto \{\{t_3\}, \{t_5\}\}$

(21) $m_1, m_2, m_3 \mapsto \{\{t_1, t_2\}\}$

To be able to adapt to this diversity, the internal argument NP should receive a neutral plural interpretation. As to the plural interpretation of the external argument NP, the lifting used in section 4.1 may yield an arbitrary partition as the domain of the shifted verbal denotation. Therefore, the plural form of this NP should be neutral as well. The basic connection between the atomic and the plural version of the external argument is given by proposition 4.

Proposition 4 *Let A and B be sets of type (et), and R a relation of type $e(ett)$. One has for all $\mathbf{D}_1$ and all positive $\mathbf{D}_2$:*

$$N(\mathbf{D}_1)A\{X \mid N(\mathbf{D}_2)B{\uparrow}(R)(X)\} \Leftrightarrow \mathbf{D}_1 A N(\mathbf{D}_2)BR$$

N.B. We write $\uparrow(R)(X)$ rather than $\uparrow(R)_X := \{\mathbf{Y} : \uparrow(R)X\mathbf{Y}\}$ (with $\uparrow$ as in (18)). The latter is a set of sets of sets, which is one level too high.

PROOF. It follows from the positivity of $\mathbf{D}_2$ that a–c are true:

    a. $\{X : N(\mathbf{D}_2)B{\uparrow}(R)(X)\}$
        $= \{X \in \text{DOM}(\uparrow(R)) \mid N(\mathbf{D}_2)B{\uparrow}(R)(X)\}$
    b. $\bigcup\{X \in \text{DOM}(\uparrow(R)) \mid N(\mathbf{D}_2)B{\uparrow}(R)(X)\}$
        $= \{a \in \text{DOM}(R) \mid N(\mathbf{D}_2)BR_a\}$
    c. $\{a \in \text{DOM}(R) \mid N(\mathbf{D}_2)BR_a\}$
        $= \{a \mid N(\mathbf{D}_2)BR_a\}$

Given these identities, the required equivalence is almost immediate.

□

Observe that the plural forms of the NPs show the NN configuration. This was also our point of departure in section 2.2, but it was found problematic in section 2.3 since not all neutral NPs can take scope over each other. In the present situation the NN configuration is unproblematic, because $\uparrow(R)$ is not just any relation between sets and sets of sets. In particular, proposition 2 shows its domain to be a partition. As we have seen in section 2.4, moves like this eliminate the unwanted effects of a wide-scope N reading.

Proposition 5 determines the effects of the π-modes in terms of plural NP denotations.

Proposition 5 (FIN) *Let A, B be of type (et), and R of type $e(ett)$. We write $R\lceil_{A,B}$ for $R \cap A \times \wp(B)$.*

i) $\pi_{R\lceil_{A,B}}$ *is an injection iff for all positive $\mathbf{D}_1$ and $\mathbf{D}_2$ $\mathbf{D}_1 AN(\mathbf{D}_2)BR$ is equivalent to $D(\mathbf{D}_1)A\{X : N(\mathbf{D}_2)B{\uparrow}(R)(X)\}$.*

ii) $\pi_{R\lceil_{A,B}}$ *is constant iff for all positive $\mathbf{D}_1$ and $\mathbf{D}_2$ $\mathbf{D}_1 AN(\mathbf{D}_2)BR$ is equivalent to $C(\mathbf{D}_1)A\{X : N(\mathbf{D}_2)B{\uparrow}(R)(X)\}$.*

PROOF. We prove the characterization of $\pi_{R\lceil_{A,B}}$ injective. Since $\mathbf{D}_1$ and $\mathbf{D}_2$ are conservative, $\mathbf{D}_1 AN(\mathbf{D}_2)BR$ is equivalent to $\mathbf{D}_1 AN(\mathbf{D}_2)BR\lceil_{A,B}$. By proposition 4 this, in turn, is equivalent to

a) $N(\mathbf{D}_1)A\{X : N(\mathbf{D}_2)B{\uparrow}(R\lceil_{A,B})(X)\}$

Further, $\mathbf{D}_2$ is positive, so (a) is equivalent to:

$N(\mathbf{D}_1)A\{X \in \text{DOM}(R\lceil_{A,B}) : N(\mathbf{D}_2)B{\uparrow}(R\lceil_{A,B})(X)\}$

Since $\mathbf{D}_1$ is positive too, the set

$\{X \in \text{DOM}({\uparrow}(R\lceil_{A,B})) \mid N(\mathbf{D}_2)B{\uparrow}(R\lceil_{A,B})(X)\}$

is non-empty. In case $\pi_{R\lceil_{A,B}}$ is an injection, proposition 3 with $\alpha = e$ and $\beta = (et)$ says that the domain of ${\uparrow}(R\lceil_{A,B})$ is atomic. So proposition 1 in combination with the above observations shows that $\mathbf{D}_1 AN(\mathbf{D}_2)BR$ and $D(\mathbf{D}_1)A\{X : N(\mathbf{D}_2)B{\uparrow}(R)(X)\}$ are equivalent.

As to the converse direction of (i), assume that $\pi_{R\lceil_{A,B}}$ is not an injection. Then there are $a, a' \in \text{DOM}(R\lceil_{A,B})$ with $\pi_{R\lceil_{A,B}}(a) \neq \pi_{R\lceil_{A,B}}(a')$. Set $n = |\pi_{R\lceil_{A,B}}(a)|$. Since $a \in \text{DOM}(R\lceil_{A,B})$, $\mathbf{n}$ is positive. Next, set $m = |\bigcup\{X \in \text{DOM}({\uparrow}R\lceil_{A,B}) : N(\mathbf{n})B{\uparrow}(R\lceil_{A,B})(X)\}|$. Since

$N(\mathbf{n})B{\uparrow}(R\lceil_{A,B})([a]_{R\lceil_{A,B}})$

$\mathbf{m}$ is positive, too. Also, $N(\mathbf{m})A\{X : N(\mathbf{n})B{\uparrow}(R\lceil_{A,B})(X)\}$, and so with proposition 4 and the conservativity of the numerals: $\mathbf{m}AN(\mathbf{n})BR$. But by FIN *not* $D(\mathbf{m})A\{X : N(\mathbf{n})B{\uparrow}(R\lceil_{A,B})(X)\}$, for the set of singletons in $\{X \in \text{DOM}({\uparrow}R\lceil_{A,B}) : N(\mathbf{n})B{\uparrow}(R\lceil_{A,B})(X)\}$ is strictly smaller than the number of elements in the union of this set. For one, the cel $[a]_{R\lceil_{A,B}}$ is in this set but is not a singleton. The characterization of $\pi_{R\lceil_{A,B}}$ constant is proved along similar lines. □

Proposition 5 proves the external argument to be distributive iff the relevant A's have their own Path. They share the same Path iff the argument is collective. As to the internal argument, recall that the sets of sets within the image of π represents how the set of elements to which an element j is V-related comes about while going through a well-ordered index. Therefore, this set has information on the nature of the internal argument NP at a particular index. If the set is given one atom after the other, the internal argument is used distributively; if the set is given in one go, its use is collective; etc.

According to proposition 5 there is a strict analogue between the readings (10DN) and (10CN) proposed by Van der Does (1993), and the present formalization of the injective and constant mode of π in Verkuyl 1988. These treatments are essentially the same but for their treatments of transitive verbs. In Van der Does (1993) these verbs are relations among sets, whereas on the present interpretation Verkuyl (1988) uses relations among individuals and sets of sets. This difference is eliminated by means of the lift operation.

The status of the cumulative reading (10NN) remains. Here we do not find such characterizations as the above. But we shall show that the π-constant mode is a strong assumption, which makes several readings collapse. To this end, we concentrate on polyadic quantification in section 4.3, and then on a connection between polyadic and collective quantification in section 4.4.

4.3 Polyadic Quantification

In this section we give examples of cases where the readings of sentences 'collapse' given specific information concerning the lowest level of predication. In particular we show that the iterative, the cumulative, and a branching reading of a transitive quantificational sentence are equivalent as soon as π is a constant function for the transitive verbs of type $e(et)$.

For the next two sections we first concentrate on the relation between iterative and cumulative quantification, and then on the relation between cumulative quantification and some simple versions of branching quantification. We observe that they are all equivalent iff $\pi_{R\lceil_{A,B}}$ is constant.

4.3.1 Iterative and Cumulative Quantification

The most familiar notion of quantification is iterative. It corresponds to subsequently combining the internal argument NP with the transitive verb and then combining the result of this with the external argument NP to yield a sentence. Formally:

(22) $\text{IT}(\mathbf{D}_1, \mathbf{D}_2)ABR \equiv \mathbf{D}_1 A\{a : \mathbf{D}_2 BR_a\}$

Cumulative quantification is due to Scha (1981), and is defined by:

(23) $\text{CM}(\mathbf{D}_1, \mathbf{D}_2)ABR \equiv \mathbf{D}_1\text{ADOM}(R \cap A \times B) \wedge \mathbf{D}_2\text{BRNG}(R \cap A \times B)$

In case of (4) it says that the total number of men who lifted tables is 4 and that the total number of tables lifted by men is 3. $\mathbf{D}_1$ and $\mathbf{D}_2$ are used to determine the size of two unique sets: the domain and range of $R \cap A \times B$. Lemma 6 describes the logical relation between $\text{IT}(\mathbf{D}_1, \mathbf{D}_2)ABR$ and $\text{CM}(\mathbf{D}_1, \mathbf{D}_2)ABR$. Its proof is close to that of the product decomposition lemma's of Keenan (1992) and Westerståhl (1993).

Lemma 6 (FIN) *For all A, B, R: $R \cap A \times B$ is a non-empty product iff for all positive $\mathbf{D}_1$, $\mathbf{D}_2$: $\mathrm{IT}(\mathbf{D}_1, \mathbf{D}_2)ABR$ and $\mathrm{CM}(\mathbf{D}_1, \mathbf{D}_2)ABR$ are equivalent.*

PROOF. [$\Rightarrow$:] First note that if $R \cap A \times B$ is the non-empty product $X \times Y$, one has:

  i) $\forall a \in X : (R \cap A \times B)_a = Y$
  ii) $\{a \mid \mathbf{D}_2 B (R \cap A \times B)_a\} = X$, if $\neg \mathbf{D}_2 B \emptyset$ and $\mathbf{D}_2 BY$.

Assume $\mathrm{CM}(\mathbf{D}_1, \mathbf{D}_2)ABR$, i.e.: $\mathbf{D}_1 \mathrm{ADOM}(R \cap A \times B)$ and $\mathbf{D}_2 \mathrm{BRNG}(R \cap A \times B)$. Since $R \cap A \times B = X \times Y$, also $\mathbf{D}_1 AX$ and $\mathbf{D}_2 BY$. Given (i) and (ii), it follows that $\mathrm{IT}(\mathbf{D}_1, \mathbf{D}_2)ABR \cap A \times B$. But $\mathbf{D}_1$ and $\mathbf{D}_2$ are conservative, so this is equivalent to $\mathrm{IT}(\mathbf{D}_1, \mathbf{D}_2)ABR$.

Conversely, assume $\mathrm{IT}(\mathbf{D}_1, \mathbf{D}_2)ABR$ and that $R \cap A \times B = X \times Y \neq \emptyset$. Conservativity gives $\mathrm{IT}(\mathbf{D}_1, \mathbf{D}_2)ABR \cap A \times B$, i.e., $\mathbf{D}_1 A \{a \mid \mathbf{D}_2 B (R \cap A \times B)_a\}$. $\mathbf{D}_1$ is positive, so there is a $a \in \mathrm{DOM}(R \cap A \times B)$ with $\mathbf{D}_2 B (R \cap A \times B)_a$. But $(R \cap A \times B)_a = Y$ for all $a \in \mathrm{DOM}(R \cap A \times B)$, so $\mathbf{D}_2 BY$. Since $\mathbf{D}_2$ is positive as well, it follows from (ii) that:

$$\{a \mid \mathbf{D}_2 B (R \cap A \times B)_a\} = X$$

so $\mathbf{D}_2 AX$. All in all, we see that $\mathbf{D}_1 \mathrm{ADOM}(R \cap A \times B)$ and $\mathbf{D}_2 \mathrm{BRNG}(R \cap A \times B)$. That is, $\mathrm{CM}(\mathbf{D}_1, \mathbf{D}_2)ABR$.

[$\Leftarrow$:] Let $R \cap A \times B$ fail to be a product, and let $n = |\mathrm{DOM}(R \cap A \times B)|$ and $m = |\mathrm{RNG}(R \cap A \times B)|$. Since $n, m > 0$, the quantifiers (exactly) $\mathbf{n}$ and $\mathbf{m}$ are positive, and clearly $\mathrm{CM}(\mathbf{n}, \mathbf{m})ABR$. But not $\mathrm{IT}(\mathbf{n}, \mathbf{m})ABR$. For this would imply that $|R \cap A \times B| \geq n * m$, which in a finite model only holds if the relation is a product. $\square$

It is an almost immediate consequence of this lemma that iteration and cumulation are indistinguishable as soon as π is constant for the given relation and sets. Indeed, the remaining step consists in observing the simple truth of lemma 7.

Lemma 7 *For all A, B, and R: π_R is constant iff $R \cap A \times B$ is a product.*

PROOF. Plainly, if $R \cap A \times B = X \times Y$ $\pi_R(a)$ is constant. Assume for a contradiction that $R \cap A \times B$ is no product. Then there is a $\langle d, d' \rangle \in (\mathrm{DOM}(R \cap A \times B) \times \mathrm{RNG}(R \cap A \times B)) \setminus R \cap A \times B$. This implies that $d' \notin \pi_R(d)$. But also that there is a d'' with $d' \in \pi_R(d'')$. So, $\pi_R(d) \neq \pi_R(d'')$, i.e., π_R is not constant. $\square$

Combining the lemma's 6 and 7 we get a proof of the following proposition:

Proposition 8 (FIN) *For all A, B, and R: the function*

$$\pi_R : \text{DOM}(R \cap A \times B) \longrightarrow \wp(\text{RNG}(R \cap A \times B))$$

is constant iff: $\text{IT}(\mathbf{D}_1, \mathbf{D}_2)ABR$, *and* $\text{CM}(\mathbf{D}_1, \mathbf{D}_2)ABR$ *are equivalent, for all positive* $\mathbf{D}_1, \mathbf{D}_2$. □

Along these lines we obtain a logical reconstruction of the claim in Verkuyl 1994 that the cumulative reading is brought about by π constant. Proposition 8 says that in this case iteration and cumulation collapse. As a corollary we see that under these circumstances the issue of scope ambiguity does not arise:

Corollary 9 (FIN) *For all A, B, and R: if* π_R *is constant then for all positive* $\mathbf{D}_1, \mathbf{D}_2$ *(i) and (ii) are equivalent.*

   i) $\text{IT}(\mathbf{D}_1, \mathbf{D}_2)ABR$

   ii) $\text{IT}(\mathbf{D}_2, \mathbf{D}_1)BAR^{-1}$

PROOF. Since $\text{CM}(\mathbf{D}_1, \mathbf{D}_2)ABR$ is equivalent to $\text{CM}(\mathbf{D}_2, \mathbf{D}_1)BAR^{-1}$, the corollary is immediate from proposition 8. □

Of course we should not conclude from proposition 8 that in general iterations and cumulations are identical. As is well-known, their logical behaviour differs widely. Verkuyl's claim is rather an empirical one: cumulation is only used when π is constant. This is an issue which is open for further discussion. As an argument in favour of it, Verkuyl (1994) highlights the notion of totalization, which also plays a crucial role in the way we lifted relations. In section 4.2, on plural quantification, we have already seen that the constancy of π is closely tied up with this notion.

This ends our discussion of the relationship between iterative and cumulative quantification. We now turn to similar observations concerning cumulative and branching quantification.

4.3.2   Branching quantification

Hintikka (1973) claimed that natural language quantification is sometimes branching. Barwise (1979) found convincing arguments to support this claim by considering generalized quantifiers (rather than just first-order ones). He considered the most prominent readings of (24).

(24)
$$\begin{bmatrix} \text{Few} \\ \text{Two} \\ \text{Most} \end{bmatrix} \text{ of these girls and } \begin{bmatrix} \text{at most four} \\ \text{three} \\ \text{quite a few} \end{bmatrix} \text{ of those boys}$$
all dated each other

E.g., for the monotone increasing *most* and *quite a few*, (24) comes to mean: there are sets X and Y containing most girls and quite a few boys such that the product $X \times Y$ is part of the relation denoted by *to date*. Similarly for the other cases. Formally, we have the schemes:

Definition 2 [branching quantification]

i) Monotone decreasing: $\mathrm{BR}^{\mathrm{md}}(\mathbf{D}_1, \mathbf{D}_2)ABR \equiv$
$\exists XY[\mathbf{D}_1 AX \wedge \mathbf{D}_2 BY \wedge R \cap A \times B \subseteq X \times Y \cap A \times B]$

ii) Non-monotone: $\mathrm{BR}(\mathbf{D}_1, \mathbf{D}_2)ABR \equiv$
$\exists XY[\mathbf{D}_1 AX \wedge \mathbf{D}_2 BY \wedge X \times Y \cap A \times B = R \cap A \times B]$

iii) Monotone increasing: $\mathrm{BR}^{\mathrm{mi}}(\mathbf{D}_1, \mathbf{D}_2)ABR \equiv$
$\exists XY[\mathbf{D}_1 AX \wedge \mathbf{D}_2 BY \wedge X \times Y \cap A \times B \subseteq R \cap A \times B]$

These schemes are partial, in that they apply depending on the monotonicity behaviour of the determiners.[14] The schemes for monotone quantifiers are due to Barwise (1979), and the one for non- monotone quantifiers to Van Benthem (cf., Westerståhl 1987, 274).[15] A more general definition for continuous determiners is in Westerståhl 1987.[16] Recently there is a renewed attention for the phenomena. For instance, Sher (1990) and Spaan (1993) argue that branching quantification involves a notion of maximality which is lacking in the earlier proposals. Here we concentrate on the simpler notions of branching given above.

We want to know how the schemes relate to other forms of quantification, and in particular to cumulative quantification. In case of $\mathrm{BR}^{\mathrm{md}}$ we can be quick, since Westerståhl (1987, 285) observes that for monotone decreasing determiners $\mathrm{BR}^{\mathrm{md}}$ and CM are equivalent. The scheme for non-monotone quantifiers is more interesting. Although the observation below holds for the intended class, we shall in fact treat it as a general scheme. Lemma 10 describes the logical relationship between BR and cumulative quantification for arbitrary quantifiers.

Lemma 10 *For all A, B, R: $R \cap A \times B$ is a product iff for all quantifiers $\mathbf{D}_1$, $\mathbf{D}_2$ $\mathrm{CM}(\mathbf{D}_1, \mathbf{D}_2)ABR$ is equivalent to $\mathrm{BR}(\mathbf{D}_1, \mathbf{D}_2)ABR$.*

PROOF. [$\Rightarrow$:] First note that branching quantification is stronger than cumulative quantification. Conversely, if we know $\mathrm{CM}(\mathbf{D}_1, \mathbf{D}_2)ABR$ and in addition that $R \cap A \times B$ is a product, then $\mathrm{BR}(\mathbf{D}_1, \mathbf{D}_2)ABR$. For in this case, $R \cap A \times B = \mathrm{DOM}(R \cap A \times B) \times \mathrm{RNG}(R \cap A \times B)$.

---

[14] A determiner $\mathbf{D}$ is (right) monotone decreasing iff for all A, B, C: if $\mathbf{D}AC$ and $B \subseteq C$ then $\mathbf{D}AB$. $\mathbf{D}$ is (right) monotone increasing iff for all A, B, C: if $\mathbf{D}AB$ and $B \subseteq C$ then $\mathbf{D}AC$.

[15] In fact, we use slight variations in order to get a better fit with the notion of collective quantification in (6).

[16] A determiner $\mathbf{D}$ is *continuous* iff for all A, B, C, D: if $\mathbf{D}AB$, $B \subseteq C \subseteq D$, and $\mathbf{D}AD$, then $\mathbf{D}AC$.

[⇐:] It is sufficient to observe that if $R \cap A \times B$ is not a product, $(\text{DOM}(R \cap A \times B) \times \text{RNG}(R \cap A \times B)) \setminus R \cap A \times B \neq \emptyset$. So, CM(**some**, **some**)ABR, but not BR(**some**, **some**)ABR. □

Branching for monotone increasing quantifiers remains. As it happens, we can use the previous proof to give the same kind of characterization here.[17]

Lemma 11 (FIN) *For all* A, B, R: $R \cap A \times B$ *is a product iff for all monotone increasing* $\mathbf{D}_1$, $\mathbf{D}_2$ CM($\mathbf{D}_1, \mathbf{D}_2$)$ABR$ *and* $\text{BR}^{\text{mi}}(\mathbf{D}_1, \mathbf{D}_2)ABR$ *are equivalent.*

PROOF. For monotone increasing $\mathbf{D}_1$ and $\mathbf{D}_2$, BR^{mi} implies CM. On the other hand, if $R \cap A \times B$ is a product, it follows from lemma 10 that CM is equivalent to BR for all quantifiers. But BR implies BR^{mi}, and this holds in particular for monotone increasing quantifiers. Finally, whenever $R \cap A \times B$ is not a product, we can adapt the proof of lemma 6 to show that

CM(**at least n**, **at least m**)ABR

while not BR^{mi}(**at least n**, **at least m**)ABR for certain n and m. □

Let us take stock. We have shown that as soon as $R \cap A \times B$ is a product, branching is indistinguishable from cumulation. As a consequence we have:

Corollary 12 (FIN) *For all* A, B, R: $R \cap A \times B$ *is a non-empty product (that is:* $\pi_{R \lceil A, B}$ *is constant) iff for all positive* $\mathbf{D}_1$, $\mathbf{D}_2$: IT($\mathbf{D}_1, \mathbf{D}_2$)$ABR$, CM($\mathbf{D}_1, \mathbf{D}_2$)$ABR$, *and* BR($\mathbf{D}_1, \mathbf{D}_2$)$ABR$ *are equivalent.* □

With a view to the reduction of ambiguity, corollary 12 suggests to consider to treat (2ii) as a general scheme. This would have the drawback that $R \cap A \times B$ is required to be a product, which seems too strict, even in case of non-monotonic quantifiers. However, in order to enforce a branching reading one often has to resort to such linguistic means as reciprocals. And it might well be possible to interpret the reciprocal used so as to turn a transitive verb into a product; e.g., by selecting a contextually salient or maximal product part of its denotation. Cf. Schwarzchild 1992. For the present case one might have:

(25) $[\![EO]\!](R, A, B) \in \{X \times Y : X \times Y \subseteq R \cap A \times B\}$

---

[17]Checking the proof one notes that lemma 11 also holds in case BR^{mi} quantifies over products which are maximal with respect to the inclusion relation, as in Sher 1990.

Consequently, the meaning of (24) can either be written as (26a) or as (26b).

(26)   a. $CM(\mathbf{D}_1, \mathbf{D}_2)AB[\![EO]\!](R, A, B)$
       b. $BR(\mathbf{D}_1, \mathbf{D}_2)AB[\![EO]\!](R, A, B)$

If so, the linguistic use of branching could be dispensed with in favour of cumulative quantification. And if the quantifiers are positive, even to 'standard' iterative quantification (cf., lemma 6). Needless to say that this observation disregards the many subtleties concerning the other meanings of reciprocals. Cf. Dalrymple et al. 1994.

This finishes our discussion of polyadic quantification. In the next section we shall use the present observations to give a connection between polyadic and collective quantification.

4.4   Polyadic vs. Collective Quantification

It remains to clarify the status of the cumulative and other non-iterative forms of quantification in case π_R is constant, for R a plural verb. To this end, recall that on the localistic view we took such verbs to be of type $e(ett)$ in order to represent the main effect of 'passing through' a structured index. Now, if π_R is constant, this set of sets is the same for all $a \in \text{DOM}(R)$. This correctly predicts that a collective use of (4), which more or less corresponds to a use of (27), allows for some variation with respect to the internal argument NP.

(27)   Three men lifted two tables together

The men may have jointly lifted two different tables, or they may have lifted two tables in one go. That is, in case of (27) the constancy of π_R is compatible with such configurations as in (28).

(28) $m_1, m_2, m_3 \mapsto \{\{t_1, t_2\}\}$
       $m_1, m_2, m_3 \mapsto \{\{t_1\}, \{t_2\}\}$

It should be observed, however, that the underlying set of tables the men turn out to be related to is the same.

Formally, one may abstract from the process of generation by means of the type-shift ABS:

$$\text{ABS} := \lambda R_{e(ett)} \lambda x_e \lambda y_e . \exists Z_{(et)} (RxZ \wedge y \in Z)$$

Then the above observation becomes: for all $R_{e(ett)}$, if π_R is constant, so is $\pi_{\text{abs}(R)}$. The converse need not be true: at an index i one can ultimately be R-related to the same set ($\pi_{\text{abs}(R)}$ is constant), even though this set is arrived at in different ways within i (π_R is not).

It might be clear now how the constancy of π_R within type $e(ett)$ connects collective with polyadic quantification. In that circumstance two unique sets are related to each other. The collective use takes these sets as they come, while the polyadic forms of quantification uses their product. Proposition 15 has the details, but first some lemma's.

Lemma 13 *Let* $\mathbf{R}$ *be a relation between sets, and* $\mathbf{D}_1$ *and* $\mathbf{D}_2$ *positive determiners. If* $|\mathbf{R}| = 1$ *then* (i) *and* (ii) *are equivalent.*

  i) $N(\mathbf{D}_1)AN(\mathbf{D}_2)B\mathbf{R}$
  ii) $C(\mathbf{D}_1)AC(\mathbf{D}_2)B\mathbf{R}$

PROOF. In case $\mathbf{R}$ is a singleton, it follows from the positivity of $\mathbf{D}_2$ and proposition 1 that:

$$\{X \mid N(\mathbf{D}_2)B\mathbf{R}_X\} = \{X \mid C(\mathbf{D}_2)B\mathbf{R}_X\}$$

Since $\mathbf{D}_1$ is positive: $|\{X \mid C(\mathbf{D}_2)B\mathbf{R}_X\}| = 1$. So the equivalence follows by applying proposition 1 once more. □

The converse of this lemma is false. For take $\mathbf{R} \subseteq \wp(A) \times \wp(B)$ to be: $\{\langle\{a\}, \{b\}\rangle, \langle\{a\}, \{c\}\rangle, \langle\{d\}, \{c\}\rangle\}$. Then, $C(1)AC(1)B\mathbf{R}$ is equivalent to $N(1)AN(1)B\mathbf{R}$, but $\mathbf{R}$ is no singleton. Lemma 14 proves a similar equivalence between the doubly collective and the branching reading.

Lemma 14 *Let* $\mathbf{R}$ *be a relation between sets. If* $|\mathbf{R}| = 1$ *then* (i) *and* (ii) *are equivalent.*

  i) $C(\mathbf{D}_1)AC(\mathbf{D}_2)B\mathbf{R}$
  ii) $BR(\mathbf{D}_1, \mathbf{D}_2)AB{\downarrow}(\mathbf{R})$

PROOF. First define $\mathbf{R}{\lceil}_{A,B} := \mathbf{R} \cap \wp(A) \times \wp(B)$. If $|\mathbf{R}| = 1$, ${\downarrow}(\mathbf{R}{\lceil}_{A,B}) = {\downarrow}(\mathbf{R}) \cap A \times B$. Using this, we reason as follows:

$$C(\mathbf{D}_1)AC(\mathbf{D}_2)B\mathbf{R}$$
$$\Leftrightarrow \quad \exists XY[\mathbf{D}_1 AX \wedge \mathbf{D}_2 BY \wedge \mathbf{R}X \cap AY \cap B]$$
$$\Leftrightarrow \quad \exists XY[\mathbf{D}_1 AX \wedge \mathbf{D}_2 BY \wedge X \times Y \cap A \times B = {\downarrow}(\mathbf{R}{\lceil}_{A,B})]$$
$$\Leftrightarrow \quad \exists XY[\mathbf{D}_1 AX \wedge \mathbf{D}_2 BY \wedge X \times Y \cap A \times B = {\downarrow}(\mathbf{R}) \cap A \times B]$$
$$\Leftrightarrow \quad BR(\mathbf{D}_1, \mathbf{D}_2)AB{\downarrow}(\mathbf{R})$$

□

Again the converse of lemma 14 is false. The constancy of π_R with R of type $e(ett)$ can now be shown to have the following effect.

Proposition 15 *Let A and B be sets, R a relation of type $e(ett)$, and* $\mathbf{D}_1$ *and* $\mathbf{D}_2$ *positive determiners. If π_R is constant, $(i - iv)$ are equivalent.*

  i) $N(\mathbf{D}_1)A\{X : N(\mathbf{D}_2)B{\uparrow}(R)(X)\}$
  ii) $N(\mathbf{D}_1)A\{X : N(\mathbf{D}_2)B{\uparrow}(\text{ABS}(R))\}$
  iii) $C(\mathbf{D}_1)A\{X : C(\mathbf{D}_2)B{\uparrow}(\text{ABS}(R))\}$
  iv) $BR(\mathbf{D}_1, \mathbf{D}_2)AB\,\text{ABS}(R)$

According to theorem 8 similar equivalences hold with respect to the iterative and cumulative reading.

PROOF. Observe that for all $X \in \text{DOM}(R)$: $\bigcup(\uparrow R(X)) = (\uparrow \text{ABS}(R))_X$. The equivalence of (i) and (ii) now follows from the positivity of $\mathbf{D}_2$. Moreover, if π_R is constant so is $\pi_{\text{abs}(R)}$. Proposition 3 with $\alpha = \beta = e$ gives that $\pi_{\text{abs}(R)}$ is a singleton. Therefore, lemma 13 and 14 can be used to obtain the remaining equivalences. $\square$

On this view, the differences in readings merely result from a shift in perspective on the underlying collections. The crudest view pertains in case of the kolkhoz-collective use, which states that at an index two unique collections are related to each other. The doubly neutral use, on the other hand, relates the same two collections, but employs the way the second collection is generated within the index. Finally, branching takes the members of the two collections to be all related to each other, which yields perhaps the finest perspective possible. For the present investigations it is important to note that these uses cannot be distinguished in terms of truth-conditions. We therefore suggest to capture them by means of the π_{inj}- and the π_{con}-mode of the verbal components combined with iterated neutral quantification, but to use no further representation within the semantics.

5 Conclusions

In 1991 the present authors agreed upon the need to reduce the ambiguity of sentences like (1) and (2) and decided to embark on an enterprise to end up with just one reading to these sentences rather than the usual six, eight, nine or more.

Verkuyl 1988 offered the intuition to bring back the number of readings to just two by means of the two modes of the π-function. This reduction was possible due to the integration of an important linguistic tradition called *localism* with the theory of generalized quantification. At the time of our common enterprise the constant and the injective functions appeared to be two sides of a coin, so our optimism seemed to be justified, as we suggested in Verkuyl and Van der Does 1991.

In separate studies—Van der Does 1993,1994 and Verkuyl 1993, 1994—it became clear that there were some problems. Even if it were possible to reduce Scha's nine readings to one on the basis of the scale approach, the cumulative reading required a special treatment. Van der Does 1993 ended up with the three readings in (10) as the minimal number of readings to be assigned to sentences like (1) and (2), and Verkuyl 1994 ended up with one reading for the combinations predicted by a scalar approach and one reading which was called kolkhoz-collectivity.

In the present paper, the number of readings is reduced to two by analyzing the relation between kolkhoz-collectivity and Scha's cumulativity. Whenever π is constant, a transitive doubly collective sentence is equivalent to a cumulative one. To show this, among other things, we introduced an abstract notion of Path. The main insight is that the notion of kolkhoz-collectivity, i.e., the π constant mode, can be used to connect the different forms of quantification.

Kolkhoz-collectivity arises naturally within the localist framework, but it is also of independent interest. Plainly, this notion requires a strong appeal to context, and we suggest to use indices for this purpose. It is shown that the two modes of predication, which correspond to natural restrictions on the Paths provided by a verb, covers the 'readings' discerned in the literature. We would wish to maintain that it is less natural to speak about two readings rather than modes; the difference between the reading corresponding to the $\pi_{injective}$-function and the kolkhoz-collective $\pi_{constant}$-function is not visible in the logical form. Of course, the restriction on the denotation of the verb can be seen in terms of a representational clue, but linguistically it makes more sense to continue to think about this matter in terms of modes.

References

Barwise, Jon. 1979. On Branching Quantification in English. *Journal of Philosophical Logic* 8:47–80.

Benthem, Johan F. A.K. van. 1991. *Language in Action*. Amsterdam: North-Holland.

Berg, Martin van den. 1995. *The Internal Structure of Discourse*. Doctoral dissertation, University of Amsterdam, Amsterdam. To appear.

Does, Jaap M. van der. 1994. On Complex Plural Noun Phrases. In *Dynamics, Polarity, and Quantification*, ed. Makoto Kanazawa and Chris Piñon. 81–115. Stanford, California: CSLI Publications.

Does, Jaap van der. 1992. *Applied Quantifier Logics. Collectives, Naked Infinitives*. Doctoral dissertation, University of Amsterdam, Amsterdam.

Does, Jaap van der. 1993. Sums and Quantifiers. *Linguistics and Philosophy* 16:509–550.

Hintikka, J. 1973. Quantifiers vs. Quantification Theory. *Dialectica* 27:329–358.

Hoeksema, Jack. 1983. Plurality and Conjunction. In *Studies in Modeltheoretic Semantics*, ed. Alice G.B ter Meulen. 63–83. Dordrecht: Foris Publications.

Jackendoff, Ray S. 1990. *Semantic Structures*. Current Studies in Linguistics, Vol. 18. Cambridge (Mass.): The M.I.T. Press.

Keenan, Edward L. 1992. Beyond the Fregean Boundary. *Linguistics and Philosophy* 15:199–221.

Landman, Fred. 1989. Groups I & II. *Linguistics and Philosophy* 12:559–605 and 723–744.

Link, Godehard. 1984. Hydras. In *Varieties of Formal Semantics*, ed. Fred Landman and Frank Veltman. Groningen-Amsterdam Studies in Semantics, Vol. 3, 245–257. Dordrecht: Foris Publications.

Link, Godehard. 1991. Plural. In *Semantics. An International Handbook of Contemporary Research*, ed. Dieter Wunderlich and Arnim von Stechow. Berlin and New York: De Gruyter.

Lønning, Jan Tore. 1987. Collective Readings of Definite and Indefinite Noun Phrases. In *Generalized Quantifiers*, ed. Peter Gärdenfors. 203–235. Dordrecht: Reidel.

Lønning, Jan Tore. 1991. Among Readings. In *Quantification and Anaphora*, ed. Jaap van der Does. 37–52. Edinburgh: DYANA deliverable R2.2.b.

Scha, Remko. 1981. Distributive, Collective and Cumulative Quantification. In *Formal Methods in the Study of Language*, ed. Jeroen Groenendijk, Theo Janssen, and Martin Stokhof. 483–512. Amsterdam: Mathematical Tracts.

Schein, Barry. 1993. *Plurals and Events*. Cambridge (Mass.): The M.I.T. Press.

Schwarzschild, Roger. 1992. Types of Plural Individuals. *Linguistics and Philosophy* 15:641–675.

Sher, G. 1990. Ways of Branching Quantification. *Linguistics and Philosophy* 13:393–422.

Spaan, Martijn. 1995. Parallel Quantification. In *Generalized Quantifier Theory and Applications*, ed. Jaap van der Does and Jan van Eijck. Amsterdam: CSLI Publications. to appear.

Verkuyl, Henk J. 1972. *On the Compositional Nature of the Aspects*. Foundation of Language Supplementary Series, Vol. 15. Dordrecht: Reidel.

Verkuyl, Henk J. 1988. Aspectual Asymmetry and Quantification. In *Temporalsemantik. Beiträge zur Linguistik der Zeitreferenz*, ed. Veronika Ehrich and Heinz Vater. 220–259. Tübingen: Niemeyer Verlag.

Verkuyl, Henk J. 1992. Some Issues in the Semantics of Plural NPs. In *Plural Quantification*, ed. F. Hamm and E. Hinrichs. Dordrecht: Kluwer. to appear.

Verkuyl, Henk J. 1993. *A Theory of Aspectuality. The Interaction between Temporal and Atemporal Structure*. Cambridge Studies in Linguistics, Vol. 64. Cambridge: cup.

Verkuyl, Henk J. 1994. Distributivity and Collectivity: a Couple at Odds. In *Dynamics, Polarity, and Quantification*, ed. Makoto Kanazawa and Chris Pi non. 49–80. Stanford, California: CSLI Publications.

Verkuyl, Henk J., and Jaap M. van der Does. 1991. The Semantics of Plural Noun Phrases. In *Generalized Quantifier Theory and Applications*, ed. Jaap M. van der Does and Jan van Eijck. 403–441. Amsterdam: Dutch Network for Language, Logic and Information. A revised version to appear in CSLI Publications.

Westerståhl, D. 1989. Quantifiers in Formal and Natural Languages. In *Handbook of Philosophical Logic. Part IV: Topics in the Philosophy of Language*, ed. Dov Gabbay and Frans Guenthner. 1–131. Dordrecht: Reidel.

Westerståhl, Dag. 1987. Branching Generalized Quantification and Natural Language. In *Generalized Quantifiers*, ed. P. Gärdenfors. 269–298. Dordrecht: Reidel.

Westerståhl, Dag. 1994. Iterated Quantifiers. In *Dynamics, Polarity, and Quantification*, ed. Makoto Kanazawa and Chris Piñon. 173–209. Stanford, California: CSLI Publications.

3

Monotone Decreasing Quantifiers in a Scope-Free Logical Form

JERRY R. HOBBS

1 Introduction

In Hobbs (1983) (henceforth, ITQ) and Hobbs (1985) (OP) I developed the outlines of an approach to semantic representation in which the logical form of an English sentence is a flat (i.e., scope-free) conjunction of existentially quantified, positive literals, with roughly one literal per morpheme. In this representation scheme the logical form of a sentence is vague with respect to quantifier-scoping decisions, and further information about scoping relations is encoded in the form of further existentially quantified postitive literals. In the DIALOGIC system for syntactic analysis, developed in the early and middle 1980s, translations into such a logical form were implemented for a great majority of English syntactic constructions, and this system was used successfully in a number of applications. In Hobbs et al. (1993) (IA) my colleagues and I developed an approach to the interpretation of discourse in which to interpret a text is to find the least-cost abductive proof of the logical forms of the sentences of the text, essentially by back-chaining on mostly Horn-clause axioms in the knowledge base and making assumptions when necessary.

One shortcoming of the proposal advanced in ITQ was in the treatment of monotone decreasing quantifiers, such as "few" and "no" (cf. Barwise and Cooper, 1981). A monotone increasing quantifier, like

I have profited from discussions about this work with Mark Gawron, David Israel, Bob Moore, Kees van Deemter, Ed Zalta, and especially Massimo Poesio. They of course do not necessarily endorse nor even condone the proposals made here. This material is based on work supported by the National Science Foundation and Advanced Research Projects Agency under Grant IRI-9304961 (Integrated Techniques for Generation and Interpretation).

Semantic Ambiguity and Underspecification
Kees van Deemter and Stanley Peters, editors
Copyright © 1995, CSLI Publications

"most", is "monotone increasing" because when the predicate in the body of the quantified expression is made less restrictive, the truth value is preserved. Thus,

Most men work hard.

entails

(1) Most men work.

By contrast, for monotone decreasing quantifiers, when the predicate in the body of the quantified expression is made less restrictive, the truth value is not necessarily preserved. Quite the opposite. It is preserved when the body is made *more* restrictive.

(2) Few men work.

entails

Few men work hard.

Since "x works hard" entails "x works", a flat, scope-free representation for "few men work hard" runs into problems, because it would seem to allow the incorrect inference "few men work".

In ITQ, I suggested very briefly a logical form for such sentences in which the quantifier "few" is translated into a predicate that means "all but a few", and the predication of the body of the quantified expression is negated. Thus, sentence (2) would be interpreted as if it were

All but a few men don't work.

This solves the entailment problem. "x doesn't work" entails "x doesn't work hard." Thus, "Few men work" would be equivalent to "all but a few men don't work", which entails "all but a few men don't work hard," which would be equivalent to "few men work hard." This approach is similar to that of van Eijck (1983).

However, this is not a felicitous solution, since the negation of the main verb makes the compositional semantics of the quantifier nonlocal, in that information from the noun phrase other than its referent is required in the interpretation of the rest of the sentence.

In this paper, I use the insights afforded by IA to propose a different analysis of monotone decreasing quantifiers, one in which the right interpretation arises from a combination of a single rule for interpreting quantifiers, both monotone increasing and monotone decreasing, and the pragmatic process of specializing or strengthening interpretations that is the basis of the abduction approach. Along the way I redo or repair several other features of the ITQ approach that were infelicitous or incorrect in the original, and I mention in passing the scope-neutral representation of functional dependencies among quantified variables that this approach makes possible. The result is a picture wherein syntactic analysis and semantic translation yields a representation that makes fewer distinctions than we might wish, but is strictly locally compositional, and strengthening to the desired representation is done by pragmatic processes that already have such strengthening as their task.

2 Background

The IA approach may be thought of as dividing the interpretation of a sentence into a "compositional semantic" phase, in which the explicit content of the sentence is represented in a logical notation (referred to here as the logical form), and a "pragmatic" phase that inferentially determines the contextually appropriate specific information that the speaker intended to convey (although, in fact, both phases use the same abductive inferential mechanism and can intermix freely). The compositional semantic phase is strictly local, in the sense that the interpretation of noun phrases does not require information from elsewhere in the sentence, and the only information about a noun phrase that is used in the semantic interpretation of the rest of the sentence is a variable indicating its referent.

Using as the logical form of a sentence a flat conjunction of existentially quantified positive literals becomes possible through an approach to representation called "ontological promiscuity", in which there is extensive reification of such things as eventualities, possible and even impossible individuals, sets, typical elements of sets, and so on. The introduction of eventualities is a key move. In addition to having predications of the form

$$work(J)$$

saying that John works, we also have predications of the form

$$work'(E, J)$$

saying that E is the eventuality of John's working. This eventuality may or may not obtain in the real world. If it does, this is just another one of its properties, expressed by

$$Rexists(E)$$

Existential quantification in this approach is over a Platonic universe of possible (or impossible) individuals, that may or may not exist in the real world.

The relationship between primed and unprimed predicates is captured by the following axiom schema:

(3) $(\forall x)[p(x) \equiv (\exists e)[p'(e,x) \wedge \text{Rexists}(e)]]$

That is, p is true of x if and only if there is an eventuality e that is the eventuality of p being true of x and e exists in the real world. In fact, whenever in this paper the notation $p(x)$ is used, it should be viewed as an abbreviation for the right side of the biconditional.

Those desiring to use model theory to strengthen their intuitions about eventualities can think of the denotation of E in $p'(E, X)$ as the ordered triple of the intension of p, the denotation of X, and an integer serving as an index. The function of the index is to allow multiple events with the same predicates and arguments. There will normally be many events of John's working.

The approach to quantifiers taken in ITQ and the present paper is motivated by two considerations. The first is the desire to treat quantifiers in the same way that every other morpheme in the language is treated, in accordance with a principle that might be stated

All morphemes are created equal.

Every morpheme in English conveys information, and this information can be encoded in the form of a proposition consisting of a predicate applied to one or more arguments. One aim of ITQ and the present paper is to show this is as possible for quantifiers as it is for every other morpheme.

Another consequence of this principle, by the way, is that in the OP approach virtually every morpheme has a corresponding eventuality, even conjunctions. Thus,

John works and George sleeps.

has the logical form

$(\exists e, e_1, e_2)[\text{Rexists}(e) \wedge \text{and}'(e, e_1, e_2) \wedge \text{work}'(e_1, J)$
$\wedge \text{sleep}'(e_2, G)]$

That is, the eventuality e that both e_1 and e_2 hold holds, where e_1 is John's working and e_2 is George's sleeping. It will be convenient in this paper to use the abbreviation $e_1 \& e_2$ to stand for the eventuality e such that $\text{and}'(e, e_1, e_2)$.

The second consideration motivating the approach to quantifiers is the need for scope-neutral representation of quantifiers. The sentence

In most democratic countries most politicians can fool most of the people on almost every issue most of the time.

has 120 readings. Moreover, they are distinct, in that for any two readings one can find a model under which one is true and the other isn't. Yet when people hear this sentence, they have the impression they understand it. They do not compute the 120 possible readings and then choose the best among them. Rather, they use world knowledge to constrain some of the dependencies among quantified expressions and leave other dependencies unresolved. For example, for me, the sets of politicians and the sets of people depend on the country, but I have no view on whether or not the politicians outscope the people. A representation is needed that allows this underspecification of meaning.

In brief, the approach to quantifiers advocated in ITQ consisted of four principles:

1. Sets are individuals. Quantifiers are relations between sets.
2. Sets have typical elements. Ordinary elements inherit the properties of typical elements.
3. Functional dependencies are expressed as relations between typical elements.
4. Disambiguating scope is done by learning functional dependencies.

The first two elements of this approach are discussed in some detail here. The last two are orthogonal to our present purposes and are discussed only briefly below, but they are one of the foci of ITQ.

To begin with, if we accept sets as first-class objects, then a determiner like "most" can be viewed as expressing a relation between sets. The expression $most(s_2, s_1)$ says that set s_2 is a subset of s_1 consisting of more than half the elements of s_1. Then sentence (1) can be represented as follows:

(4) $(\exists s)[most(s, \{x \mid man(x)\}) \wedge (\forall y)[y \in s \supset work(y)]]$

That is, there is a set s that is most of the set of all men (i.e., it is a subset with more than half the elements), and for every entity y in s, y works.

We can unwind this into a flat notation by introducing two new predicates. The first is *typelt*, and it takes two arguments—a typical element of a set and the set itself. The expression

   $typelt(y, s)$

says that y is the typical element of the set s. The precise nature of typical elements is discussed in Section 3, but for now they can be viewed as a kind of reified, universally quantified variable. (McCarthy (1977) suggests a similar approach.) I will write about typical elements as though each set had a unique typical element, although this property will not be required (except once) in this paper. The principal property that typical elements should have is that their properties should be inherited by the ordinary elements of the set. A first cut at expressing this property is the following axiom schema:

(5)　$(\forall x, s)[typelt(x, s)$
$\qquad \supset [p(x) \equiv (\forall y)[y \in s \supset p(y)]]]$

That is, if x is the typical element of set s, then p is true of x if and only if p is true of every ordinary element y of s.

Two obvious problems with this rule are as follows:

1. Because of the Law of the Excluded Middle, it would seem that for any predicate p, either $p(x)$ or $\neg p(x)$ would be true of the typical element x. Then by (5), the elements of s could not differ on any properties. They all would inherit either p or $\neg p$ from x.

2. There is a question as to whether the typical element of a set is itself an element of the set. Both choices seem to lead to difficulties.

The solution to these problems is described briefly in Section 3 and at length in ITQ.

There is another problem that was not dealt with in ITQ. The statement of this rule is not quite right because of the flat notation we are using, and it must be complicated somewhat, as described in Section 4 below.

The fact that sets have typical elements is captured by the axiom

$\qquad (\forall s)[set(s) \supset (\exists x)typelt(x, s)]$

The second new predicate, *dset*, is more specific than *typelt* in that it relates not only a set and its typical element, but also its defining condition. It takes three arguments—a set, its typical element, and the defining condition of the set. The expression

$\qquad dset(s, x, e)$

says that s is a defined set whose typical element is x and whose defining condition is the eventuality e. If e is, for example, the eventuality of x's being a man

$\qquad man'(e, x)$

then s is a defined set whose typical element is x and whose defining condition is the eventuality e of x's being a man, or the set of men. Thus, the expression

(6)　$(\exists s, x, e)dset(s, x, e) \wedge man'(e, x)$

is equivalent to the more conventional expression

(7)　$(\exists s)\, s = \{x \mid man(x)\}$

The principal property we need for the predicate *dset* is expressed, at a first cut, in the following axiom schema:

(8) $(\forall s)[[(\exists x, e)dset(s, x, e) \wedge p'(e, x)]$
$\equiv (\forall y)[y \in s \equiv p(y)]]$

That is, s is the defined set whose typical element is x, and whose defining condition is the eventuality e of p being true of x if and only if for all y, y is in the set if and only if p is true of y. Again, this encoding will have to be revised in Sections 3 and 4, but modulo this revision, Axiom Schema (8) implies the equivalence of (6) and (7), since the left side of the outer biconditional in (8) is equivalent to (7).

The relation between the predicates *dset* and *typelt* is expressed in the following axiom:

(9) $(\forall s, x, e)[dset(s, x, e) \supset typelt(x, s)]$

If s is the defined set whose typical element is x and whose defining condition is the eventuality e, then x is the typical element of s. The predicate *dset* is thus a specialization of the predicate *typelt*, a fact that will play an important role in the treatment of monotone decreasing quantifiers.

There should probably not be a rule of the form

$(\forall x, s)[typelt(x, s) \supset (\exists e)dset(s, x, e)]$

since this would entail that every set is definable by some eventuality. This strikes me as an undesirable property. Some linguistically described sets, such as the set referred to by "all men", have natural defining properties. Others, such as the set referred to by "many men", do not, but they are sets nevertheless. In any case, we will not need this property.

The predicates corresponding to quantifiers, such as *most* and *few*, will be viewed as expressing relations, (e.g., comparing cardinalities) between two sets. The principal properties of specific quantifiers can be stated as axioms. For example, one property of "few" and "most" is that they pick out subsets:

(10) $(\forall s_1, s_2)[most(s_2, s_1) \supset subset(s_2, s_1)]$
(11) $(\forall s_1, s_2)[few(s_2, s_1) \supset subset(s_2, s_1)]$

The monotone increasing and monotone decreasing properties can also be expressed as axioms:

(12) $(\forall s_1, s_2) most(s_2, s_1) \wedge subset(s_2, s) \wedge subset(s, s_1)$
      $\supset most(s, s_1)$
(13) $(\forall s_1, s_2) few(s_2, s_1) \wedge subset(s, s_2) \wedge \neg null(s)$
      $\supset few(s, s_1)$

That is, if s_2 is most of s_1 and s_2 is a subset of s which in turn is a subset of s_1, then s is also most of s_1. This is the monotone increasing property. If s_2 constitutes few members of s_1, then so does a non-null subset s of s_2. This is the monotone decreasing property.

Further axioms specify that the arguments of *subset* are both sets.

$(\forall s_1, s_2) subset(s_2, s_1) \supset set(s_1)$
$(\forall s_1, s_2) subset(s_2, s_1) \supset set(s_2)$

With this machinery, we can now rewrite logical form (4) as follows:

(14) $(\exists s_2, s_1, x, e, y)[most(s_2, s_1) \wedge dset(s_1, x, e)$
      $\wedge man'(e, x) \wedge typelt(y, s_2) \wedge work(y)]$

That is, there is a set s_1 defined by the property e of its typical element x being a man, there is a set s_2 which is most of s_1 and has y as its typical element, and y works. Accepting Axiom Schemas (5) and (8) as written, it is straightforward to show that (14) is equivalent to (4).

Although this property will not be required in this paper, it is easy to see that distinct sets must have distinct typical elements.

It is easy to see how a logical form like (14) could be generated compositionally in a strictly local fashion. The common noun "men" introduces a set, its typical element, and its defining property, generating the conjuncts $dset(s_1, x, e) \wedge man'(e, x)$. The determiner "most" introduces another set and its typical element, along with the conjuncts $most(s_2, s_1) \wedge typelt(y, s_2)$. The latter typical element becomes the logical subject of the predication of the main verb, which generates the conjunct $work(y)$.

The logical form for

Most men like several women.

is

$(\exists s_2, s_1, e, x, y, z, s_3)[most(s_2, s_1) \wedge dset(s_1, x, e)$
$\wedge man'(e, x) \wedge typelt(y, s_2) \wedge like(y, z) \wedge several(s_3)$
$\wedge typelt(z, s_3) \wedge woman(z)]$

That is, there is a set s_1 defined by the property e of its typical element x being a man, there is a set s_2 which is most of s_1 and has y as its typical element, and y likes z, where z is the typical element of a set s_3, z is a woman, and s_3 has several members.

This is a scope-neutral representation. In the course of further processing, we may discover that s_3 is an *actual* set of several women, corresponding to wide scope for "several", or we may discover that s_3 is functionally dependent upon s_2, in which case s_3 is the typical element of a set of sets of women, one for each man in s_2, corresponding to the narrow scope.

This treatment of functional dependencies is elaborated on in ITQ, and is similar to the ordering constraints of Allen (1987) and Poesio (1991).

Section 3, sketchily, and Section 4, more thoroughly, discuss two complications that arise in this approach. The aim of the complications, however, is to bring us back to the original simplicity of notation.

3 The Nature of Typical Elements

There are three ways one might try to view typical elements:

1. The typical element of a set is one of the ordinary elements, but we will never know which one, so that anything we learn about it will be true of all.

2. The typical element is not an element of the set, and only special kinds of predicates are true of typical elements.

3. The typical element is not an element of the set, and ordinary predicates are true of them, except in set-theoretic axioms, which must be formulated carefully.

The first alternative is similar to the stance one takes toward instantiations of universally quantified variables in proofs. In proving $(\forall x \in s)p'(x)$, one might consider an element a of s and show $p(a)$ while relying only on properties of a that are true for all elements of s. This alternative seems dangerous, however. The set consisting of John and George would have as its typical element either John or George, so by the desired properties (5) and (8), any property one has the other has too. The variable a in the proof is used only in a very limited context and in a very constrained way, whereas we want typical elements to exist in a persistent fashion in the Platonic universe and sometimes in the real world as well.

The second approach was taken in ITQ. The problem that arises when the typical element is assumed to be something other than an element of a set is that if the property p in Axiom Schema (5) is taken to be $\lambda x[x \notin s]$, then we can conclude that none of the members of the set are members of the set. I worked around this difficulty in ITQ by introducing a complex scheme of indexing predicates according to the kinds of arguments they would take. Essentially, for every predicate p, there was a basic level predicate p_0 that applied to ordinary individuals that are not typical elements, and a number of other predicates p_s that applied to the typical element of set s. More precisely, if x is the typical element of s, then $p_s(x)$ was defined to be true if and only if $p(y)$ was true for every y in s, and otherwise p_s was equivalent to p_0.

Axiom (5) can then be stated

$$(\forall x, s)[typelt(x, s)$$
$$\supset [p_s(x) \equiv (\forall y)[y \in_0 s \supset p_0(y)]]]$$

This solves the first difficulty with formulation (5). It is true that either $p_s(x)$ or $\neg(p_s)(x)$ holds, but this does not imply that all elements of s have all the same properties. That would hold only if either $p_s(x)$ or $(\neg p)_s(x)$ were true, but this is not what the Law of the Excluded Middle entails. The difference is the same as the difference between having negation outscope universal quantification and having universal quantification outscope negation.

The second difficulty with formulation (5) is solved as well. Suppose x is the typical element of s. We can simply stipulate that $x \notin_0 s$, and since this is a basic level rather than an indexed predicate, no consequences follow for real elements. To determine whether $x \in_s s$ is true, by the indexed version of Axiom (5), we have to ask whether

$$(\forall y)[y \in_0 s \supset y \in_0 s]$$

and this of course is trivially true. So $x \in_s s$ is true.

This solution is inconvenient, however, because it forces us to carry around complex indices in many contexts where they are irrelevant to the content being expressed. For example, the axiom

$$(\forall x)[man(x) \supset person(x)]$$

is true regardless of whether x is an ordinary individual or a typical element of a set. If all the members of a set are men, they are all persons. We would not like to have to specify indices in such axioms, and most axioms are exactly of this nature.

The primary place where the indices must be attended to is in set theoretic axioms. If x is the typical element of s, then $x \notin_0 s$ but $x \in_s s$. Thus, axioms that depend crucially on whether an entity is or is not in a set must be stated in terms of indexed predicates.

This leads to the third alternative, which we will adopt. We can avoid the complexity of indices by considering a bit how they are actually used in discourse processing. One must reintroduce the unindexed predicate p to use in the logical form of sentences, before interpretation, that is, before quantifier scope ambiguities are resolved. The relation between the indexed and unindexed predicates can be expressed, *inter alia*, by the following axiom schemas:

$$(\forall x)[p_0(x) \supset p(x)]$$
$$(\forall s, x)[p_s(x) \supset p(x)]$$

That is, the indexed predicates are specializations or strengthenings of the unindexed predicates, and in the course of discourse interpretation by abduction, one of the things that happens is that, as the existentially quantified variables are resolved to ordinary entities or to typical elements, the predicates that apply to them are specialized to the corresponding indexed predicate.

In this context of use, the indexing of the predicate is uniquely determined by the nature of its arguments. This would hold if constraints such as the following were stipulated:

$$(\forall x, s)[p(x) \land typelt(x, s)$$
$$\supset [p_s(x) \land \neg p_0(x) \land (\forall s_1)[s_1 \neq s \supset \neg p_{s_1}(x)]]]$$

That is, if p is true of the typical element x of a set s, then the specialization p_s of p is true of x, and no other indexing of p is true of x.

A more thorough development of this idea depends on a treatment of functional dependencies, and therefore is beyond the scope of this paper.

It is worth noting that the consistency of the formulation I have given of typical elements can be demonstrated by taking as a model one in which the denotation of the typical element of a set is the set itself. In this case, $typelt$ is simply identity. However, I wish to admit as well interpretations in which the set and its typical element are distinct, since there are a number of contexts in which this distinction is a useful one to make, including representing the difference between collective and distributive readings.

For the remainder of this paper, only the unindexed predicates are used.

4 Substitution

As noted above, there is a problem with the statement of Axiom Schemas (5) and (8) that arises because what in more conventional logical notations is represented via embedding gets strung out in the OP notation. Consider

> John believes men work.

The logical form of this sentence is

(15) $(\exists e_1, m, s, e_2)believe(J, e_1) \land work'(e_1, m)$
$\land dset(s, m, e_2) \land man'(e_2, m)$

That is, John believes the eventuality e_1 to obtain where e_1 is the eventuality of m working, where m is the typical element of a set s whose defining property is the eventuality e_2 of m's being a man.

Suppose John believes George is a man, and thus in the set s. We would like to conclude that John believes George works. But this does not follow from axiom schemas (5) and (8). The entity m is the typical element of s, John believes m works, and so John should believe that George works. The predication $p(x)$ in axiom (5) would have to be "John believes m works". If p is restricted to be an atomic predicate, this won't do, because "John believes m works" is not represented by an atomic predicate. Suppose p can be an arbitrary lambda expression. Then given that m is the typical element of s, Axiom (5) implies that any property of m must also hold of G, specifically, for the property

$$\lambda m[believe(J, e_1) \wedge work'(e_1, m)]$$

Thus it would follow from (15) that

$$believe(J, e_1) \wedge work'(e_1, G)$$

But this is the wrong result. The problem is that e_1 is the eventuality of men working, not the distinct eventuality of George's working. If Sam is also a man, then this approach leads to e_1's also being the eventuality of Sam's working.

To get around this difficulty, we can introduce a predicate *Subst* that expresses substitution relations among expressions directly. In a way, it mimics in the flat notation what substitution does in conventional notations, and one may thus suspect it is just a formal trick. However, I think that substitution itself is one particular formalization of an intuitive, commonsense concept—that of "playing the same role". $Subst(a, e_1, b, e_2)$ can be read as saying that a plays the same role in e_1 that b plays in e_2. (*Subst* differs from "playing the same role" in one aspect noted below.) Viewing it in this way, one need feel no compunction about applying the predicate to entities other than reified, universally quantified variables or typical elements. For example, if

$$work'(e_2, G) \wedge work'(e_3, S)$$

then

$$Subst(G, e_2, S, e_3)$$

since George plays the same role in George's working that Sam plays in Sam's working.

Subst turns out to be a useful concept in discourse interpretation wherever the similarity of two entities must be established.

In conventional notations, the first important property of substitution is the following:

$$p(t_1, \ldots, t_n)|_b^a = p(t_1|_b^a, \ldots, t_n|_b^a)$$

That is, the substitution of a predicate applied to a number of terms is the predicate applied to the substitution of the terms.

We can remain maximally noncommittal about the identity conditions among eventualities if we translate this schema into the following four axiom schemas, where p is now restricted to atomic predicates.

(16) $(\forall a, b, e_1, e_2, \ldots, u_i, \ldots)[Subst(a, e_1, b, e_2)$
$\qquad \wedge p'(e_1, \ldots, u_i, \ldots)$
$\qquad \supset (\exists \ldots, v_i, \ldots)[p'(e_2, \ldots, v_i, \ldots)$
$\qquad\qquad \wedge \ldots \wedge Subst(a, u_i, b, v_i) \wedge \ldots]]$

This says that if a plays the same role in e_1 that b plays in e_2, p is the predicate of e_1, and the arguments of e_1 are u_i, then e_2 also is an eventuality with predicate p and arguments v_i where a plays the same role in each u_i that b plays in the corresponding v_i. This allows us to proceed in substitution from predications to their arguments.

(17) $(\forall a, b, e_1, \ldots, u_i, v_i, \ldots)[\ldots \wedge Subst(a, u_i, b, v_i) \wedge \ldots$
$\qquad \wedge p'(e_1, \ldots, u_i, \ldots)$
$\qquad \supset (\exists e_2)[p'(e_2, \ldots, v_i, \ldots) \wedge Subst(a, e_1, b, e_2)]]$

This says that if e_1 is an eventuality with predicate p and arguments u_i, where a plays the same role in each u_i that b plays in a corresponding v_i, then there is an eventuality e_2 whose predicate is p and whose arguments are v_i and a plays the same role in e_1 that b plays in e_2. This allows us to proceed from arguments to predications involving the arguments.

Two more axiom schemas are required because of the fact that eventualities are not necessarily uniquely determined by their predicates and arguments. $p'(E_1, X)$ and $p'(E_2, X)$ can both be true without E_1 being identical to E_2. The above two axiom schemas guarantee a "substitution" eventuality of the right structure. The next two axiom schemas say that an eventuality is of the right structure if and only if it is a substitution eventuality.

(18) $(\forall a, b, e_1, e_2, \ldots, u_i, v_i, \ldots)[Subst(a, e_1, b, e_2)$
$\qquad \wedge p'(e_1, \ldots, u_i, \ldots)$
$\qquad \supset [p'(e_2, \ldots, v_i, \ldots)$
$\qquad\qquad \equiv \ldots \wedge Subst(a, u_i, b, v_i) \wedge \ldots]]$

This says that if a plays the same role in e_1 that b plays in e_2, p is the predicate of e_1, and the arguments of e_1 are u_i, then e_2 also is an eventuality with predicate p and arguments v_i if and only if a plays the same role in each u_i that b plays in the corresponding v_i.

(19) $(\forall\, a, b, e_1, e_2, \ldots, u_i, v_i, \ldots)[\ldots \wedge Subst(a, u_i, b, v_i) \wedge \ldots$
$\wedge\, p'(e_1, \ldots, u_i, \ldots)$
$\supset [p'(e_2, \ldots, v_i, \ldots) \equiv Subst(a, e_1, b, e_2)]]$

This says that if e_1 is an eventuality with predicate p and arguments u_i, where a plays the same role in each u_i that b plays in a corresponding v_i, then the eventuality e_2 has predicate p and arguments v_i if and only if a plays the same role in e_1 that b plays in e_2.

The next two axioms enable substitution to bottom out.

(20) $(\forall\, a, b) Subst(a, a, b, b)$

That is, a plays the same role in a that b plays in b.

(21) $(\forall\, a, b, c) \neg eventuality(c) \wedge c \neq a \supset Subst(a, c, b, c)$

That is, if c is not an eventuality and not equal to a, then a plays the same role in c that b plays in c.

Notice that Axiom (21) allows c to be b. Substituting b for a in b results in b. This is the one asymmetry in the *Subst* predicate, and the reason it is really more like substitution than like playing the same role. This asymmetry will allow us to draw from the fact that everyone in a set including John likes John the conclusion that John likes himself. That is, from $typelt(x, s)$, $p(x, y)$, and $y \in s$, we can conclude $p(y, y)$. The one constraint on *Subst* is that the first and fourth arguments cannot be the same. Substitution for the first argument would have eliminated such occurrences.

(22) $(\forall\, a, b, t_1, t_2)[a \neq b \wedge Subst(a, t_1, b, t_2) \supset a \neq t_2]$

That is, substituting b for a will never result in a.

The axiom schemas (5) and (8) can now be recast as Axioms (23) and (24), respectively.

(23) $(\forall\, x, s, e)[typelt(x, s)$
$\supset [(\exists\, e_1)[Subst(x, e, x, e_1) \wedge Rexists(e_1)]$
$\equiv (\forall\, y)[y \in s \supset (\exists\, e_2)[Subst(x, e, y, e_2)$
$\wedge\, Rexists(e_2)]]]]$

This property is now expressed as an axiom rather than an axiom schema. The explicit specification of the structure $p'(e, x)$ has been eliminated here. Instead the eventuality e represents that pattern and the predicate $Subst$ is used to stipulate that other eventualities exhibit the same pattern. This axiom says that if e is such a pattern and x is the typical element of s, then there is a really existing eventuality e_1 exhibiting that pattern if and only if for every ordinary element of s, there is a corresponding eventuality e_2 exhibiting the same pattern that really exists.

Suppose, in (23), that x is the typical element of s. If e is not an eventuality, then it is either x or something else. If it is x, then $e = e_1 = x$ and $e_2 = y$, so the axiom is valid. If it is something else, then $e = e_1 = e_2$, and the axiom is valid. Suppose e is an eventuality and $p'(e, x)$ holds. Then $p(x)$ is equivalent to $(\exists e_1)p'(e_1, x) \wedge Rexists(e_1)$, which is equivalent to $(\exists e_1)Subst(x, e, x, e_1) \wedge Rexists(e_1)$. Similarly, $p(y)$ is equivalent to $(\exists e_2)Subst(x, e, y, e_2) \wedge Rexists(e_2)$. Thus, Axiom (23) captures the intent of Axiom (5).

Replacing Axiom (8) is Axiom (24):

(24) $\quad (\forall s, x, e)[eventuality(e)$
$\qquad \supset [(\exists e_1)[dset(s, x, e_1) \wedge Subst(x, e, x, e_1)]$
$\qquad \equiv (\forall y)[y \in s \equiv (\exists e_2)[Subst(x, e, y, e_2)$
$\qquad \wedge Rexists(e_2)]]]]$

That is, if e is an eventuality (representing a pattern expressed in terms of the typical element x of a set s), then there is an eventuality e_1 of the same pattern that is the defining eventuality for s if and only if for every ordinary element y of s there is a corresponding eventuality e_2 of the same pattern that really exists. Here it is necessary to express the constraint that e be an eventuality, because the third argument of $dset$ must be an eventuality.

Let us return to (15). If $dset(s, m, e_2)$ and $man'(e_2, m)$ hold and George is a man, then we have

$$man(G) \equiv man'(e_3, G) \wedge Rexists(e_3) \qquad \text{(by 3)}$$
$$\equiv Subst(m, e_2, G, e_3) \wedge Rexists(e_3) \qquad \text{(by 19)}$$
$$\equiv G \in s \qquad \text{(by 24)}$$

Suppose $Rexists(e_0)$, $believe'(e_0, J, e_1)$, and $work'(e_1, m)$ all hold. Since $typelt(m, s)$ holds, and letting e and e_1 in (23) both be e_0, there is, by (23), an e_4 such that

$\qquad Subst(m, e_0, G, e_4) \wedge Rexists(e_4)$

By (16) there is an e_5 such that

$\qquad believe'(e_4, J, e_5) \wedge Subst(m, e_1, G, e_4) \wedge Rexists(e_4)$

By (19),

$\qquad believe'(e_4, J, e_5) \wedge work'(e_5, G) \wedge Rexists(e_4)$

By (3),

$$believe(J, e_5) \wedge work'(e_5, G)$$

That is, John believes George works. (I ignore here the problem of what inferences it is legitimate to draw inside belief contexts. Think of this expression as saying that, merely by virtue of the fact that George is a man, John believes George, whoever he may be, works.)

5 Monotone Decreasing Quantifiers

Virtually every utterance describes a situation in a more general fashion than the speaker actually means to convey. If I say, "I went to Tokyo," you are likely to interpret this as saying that I *flew* to Tokyo, even though I did not specify the means of transportation, and I would expect you to interpret it in this way. Indexicality is one example of this phenomenon. If I say "He went to Tokyo," I am saying that a male person went to Tokyo, but my listener will generally use contextual information to arrive at a more specific interpretation. This observation is at the core of the IA framework. To interpret a sentence is to find the "best" proof of its logical form, together with the selectional constraints that predicates impose on their arguments, allowing for coercions to handle metonymy, making assumptions where necessary. In brief, we must find the best set of specific facts and assumptions that imply the generalities conveyed explicitly by the utterance.

The parts of the logical form that we are able to prove is the *given* information that provides the referential anchor for the sentence. The assumptions that we must make in order to interpret a sentence constitute the *new* information; this is what the sentence is asserting. Typically, information in the main verb is what is asserted, and information that is grammatically subordinated is given, or presupposed. But this is not necessarily the case. In

An innocent man was convicted today.

the listener may already know that someone was convicted, and the new, asserted information is that the man was innocent. Similarly, in

I have a sore throat.

you know I have a throat. The new information is that it is sore. Reinterpreting what is asserted by the sentence will be a key move in dealing with monotone decreasing quantifiers.

The solution to the problem of monotone decreasing quantifiers that I propose consists of three steps.

1. We first generate the logical form of the sentence exactly as we would for other quantifiers. For sentence (2), the logical form would be analogous to (14), namely,

(25) $(\exists s_1, s_2, x, y, e_1, e_2) few(s_2, s_1) \land dset(s_1, x, e_1)$
$\land man'(e_1, x) \land typelt(y, s_2) \land work'(e_2, y)$
$\land Rexist(e_2)$

That is, there is a set s_1 defined by the property e_1 of its typical element x being a man, there is a set s_2 which is few of s_1 and has y as its typical element, and the eventuality e_2 of y's working exists in the real world. Note that all of this is true, as far as it goes; there is a set consisting of few men, and the members of this set work. It just doesn't go far enough, because it does not rule out a much larger set.

2. The next step is to specialize or strengthen the predication $typelt(y, s_2)$ to the more specific $dset(s_2, y, e_2 \& e_3)$, by back-chaining on axiom (9), and instantiating the defining eventuality to the conjunction of the two eventualities we see in the sentence, or rather, in place of the eventuality e_1 the "substitution" eventuality e_3 such that

$Subst(x, e_1, y, e_3)$

That is, we have further specified the set s_2 to be not just some subset of s_1 that has few elements, but the subset defined by the conjunction of conditions e_3 and e_2, where

$man'(e_3, y) \land work'(e_2, y)$

which, by (24), is the set of men who work.

It is axiom (9) that places this interpretation in the space of possible interpretations, but nothing so far guarantees that this is the interpretation that will be selected. I would like to suggest one way this could happen, without, however, denying other possible accounts.

To promote this particular strengthening, we can associate as a selectional constraint on the arguments of few the requirement that its first argument be a set with a defining property.

(26) $few(s_2, s_1)$: $(\exists y, e) dset(s_2, y, e)$

This requirement then becomes something that has to be proven in addition to the logical form to arrive at an interpretation. It forces us to look for an eventuality e that defines the set s_2. The three most readily available eventualities are those explicit in the sentence itself— e_1 (or rather, e_3), e_2 and the conjunction of the two. e_3 (being a man) is impossible as a defining condition for s_2 since it is the defining condition for s_1, of which s_2 is a proper subset. e_2 (working) is also impossible as a defining condition, since the members of s_2 are men, and more than just men work. That leaves the conjunction $e_2 \& e_3$. The set s_2 is the set of men who work.

3. The proposition $few(s_2, s_1)$ is taken to be the assertion of the sentence, rather than $work(y)$. That is, the sentence would be interpreted as saying

The men who work are few.

Increasing the plausibility of this part of the analysis is the fact that it is hard to unstress the word "few" when it is functioning as a monotone decreasing quantifier, and high stress is an indication that the information conveyed by the morpheme is new.

In order to demonstrate that this approach goes through, under this formulation, I need to show that from "Few men work" we can indeed conclude "Few men work hard," (assuming anyone works hard) once these two sentences have been interpreted as in Steps 1-3, and assuming, for the sake of this paper, that we have an axiom

(27) $(\forall x)work\text{-}hard(x) \supset work(x)$

The logical form of "Few men work", generated in Step 1, is given in (25). By Step 2, $typelt(y, s_2)$ is strengthened to $dset(s_2, y, e_3 \& e_2)$. Since this sentence is the premise, we assume the strengthened logical form is all true.

The logical form of the sentence "Few men work hard" is

$$(\exists s_1, s_4, x, z, e_1, e_4)few(s_4, s_1) \wedge dset(s_1, x, e_1)$$
$$\wedge man'(e_1, x) \wedge typelt(z, s_4) \wedge work\text{-}hard'(e_4, z)$$
$$\wedge Rexist(e_4)$$

By Step 2, we strengthen $typelt(z, s_4)$ to $dset(s_4, z, e_5 \& e_4)$, where

$Subst(x, e_1, z, e_5)$.

Step 3 tells us that what is asserted is $few(s_4, s_1)$, while the rest is presupposed. Thus, we assume the rest is true, and we must demonstrate $few(s_4, s_1)$.

The conclusion $few(s_4, s_1)$ will follow from Axiom (13) if we can demonstrate $few(s_2, s_1)$ and $subset(s_4, s_2)$. But $few(s_2, s_1)$ is part of the premise assumed above. To demonstrate that $subset(s_4, s_2)$ holds, we need to show that any member v of s_4 is also a member of s_2. We do this in three steps. First we show, using the premises $dset(s_4, z, e_5 \& e_4)$, $man'(e_5, z)$ and $work\text{-}hard'(e_4, z)$, together with a rightward use of the inner biconditional in Axiom (24), that any member v of s_4 is a man and works hard. We then use Axiom (27) to conclude that v works. We then use Axiom (24) in a leftward direction to show that v is in the set s_2. This establishes that the monotone decreasing property of the word "few" is preserved in this formulation.

It would be good if the predicate few used in "Few men work" captured the same notion of few-ness that is expressed in "A few men work." I will only sketch a possible account in which this would be the case. Consider

A few men work.

The word "a" expresses a relationship between the entity referred to by the noun phrase and the description it provides; it says roughly that the entity is not uniquely identifiable in context solely on the basis of that description. The logical form of this sentence would be almost the same as (25). But we need first to introduce the eventuality e_0 corresponding to the few-ness relation between s_2 and s_1—$few'(e_0, s_2, s_1)$. Then to express the relation conveyed by the determiner "a" we add the predication $a(y, e_0 \& e_3)$, saying that y is not uniquely identifiable in context on the basis of the properties e_0 and e_3. If we were to proceed in Step 2 as before and specialize $typelt(y, s_2)$ to $dset(s_2, y, e_2 \& e_3)$, then we would have a contradiction, for the properties e_2 and e_3 would uniquely identify y as the typical element of the set defined by these properties (assuming sets have a unique typical element). The word "a" thus blocks this strengthening of "few", the eventuality e in (26) remains unresolved, and we are left with only the few relation between the sets s_2 and s_1.

It is often argued that one way of drawing the line between compositional semantics (Step 1) and pragmatics (Step 2) is to say that the results of compositional semantics are not defeasible whereas the results of pragmatics are. This would appear to be an argument against the approach suggested here, since the interpretation of "Few men work" as "The men who work are few" does not seem to be defeasible. But another force that strongly constrains likely interpretations is conventionalization. The IA account of discourse comprehension traces out a space of possible interpretations and provides a graded mechanism for choosing among them, given a context. But conventionalization picks out among the possible interpretations a particular interpretation of a given word, phrase, or grammatical structure. It collapses the space of possible interpretations to only the conventional interpretation. It thus eliminates the defeasibility one ordinarily associates with pragmatic processing.

An example of this, unrelated to quantifiers, involves "let's". This is a contraction of "let us". But the sentence "Let us go" could be said by two victims to a kidnapper, whereas the sentence "Let's go" would not be. The general meaning of "Let us go"—

Don't cause us not to go.

is, for the contraction, conventionally specialized to

Don't cause us (inclusive) not to go by not going yourself.

The favored interpretations of "few men" and "a few men" are no doubt conventionalized, even though they can be derived *de novo* according to the accounts given above.

"Only" could be viewed as a determiner, and as such it would be monotone decreasing. Its interpretation would be derived very much as that of "few", but differing in one crucial respect.

"Only" is indeed monotone decreasing, since "Only men work" entails "Only men work hard." But unlike "few" it is not conservative. The conservativity property can be illustrated as follows: The sentence "Few men are men who work" entails "Few men work," and "few" is hence conservative. By contrast, "Only men are men who work" does not entail "Only men work." In fact, the first is tautologically true, and the second is false. "Only" is hence nonconservative (cf. van Benthem, 1983). This means the process of interpreting "only" must differ at some point from the process of interpreting "few". In fact, it differs in Step 2.

The logical form of "Only men work" would parallel (25).

$$(\exists s_1, s_2, x, y, e_1, e_2) only(s_2, s_1) \wedge dset(s_1, x, e_1)$$
$$\wedge man'(e_1, x) \wedge typelt(y, s_2) \wedge work'(e_2, y)$$
$$\wedge Rexist(e_2)$$

Under this analysis, as before, "only" will be taken to express a relation between a set s_2 and the set s_1 of all men, and the noun phrase "only men" will be taken to refer to the set s_2 in the sense that it is the members of s_2 who work. Thus, Step 1 in the analysis of "only" does not differ from Step 1 in the analysis of "few".

In Step 2, however, the set s_2 is not specialized to the set of men who work. Rather it is specialized to the set of workers. That is, $typelt(y, s_2)$ is strengthened to $dset(s_2, y, e_2)$. The relation that *only* expresses between s_2 and s_1 is then simply the subset relation. The set of workers is a subset of the set of men. That is, only men work.

Step 3 is the same as for "few". The predication $only(s_2, s_1)$ is picked as the assertion of the sentence. That is, "Only men work" is interpreted as though it were "The set of workers is a subset of the set of men," or "All workers are men."

This is a limited account of the interpretation of "only" as a determiner. In fact, a proper account would encompass adverbial uses as well. My real view is that *only* is a predicate of three arguments—an entity or eventuality x, a scale s that has x as its lowest element, and a property that is true of x but not of the other, higher elements of s. In "John only walked", x is John's walking, s is a scale of actions ordered, say, by energy requirements, and the property is the property of having John as an agent. When used as a determiner, x is the entity or set referred to by the NP, s is the set of subsets containing x and ordered by inclusion, and the property is the main predication of the sentence. In "Only men work", x is a set of men, s is the set of subsets of the relevant entities containing x, and the property is working. The sentence says that the members of x work, but the members of no larger set in s works. This implies that the workers are a subset of all men, the meaning of "only" assumed in the account above.

6 Conclusion

The interpretation of quantifiers is a complex area of semantics, and one's simple, elegant notions of how the information in sentences can be represented run up against difficulties as soon as quantifiers are considered. Everyone who examines quantifiers is obliged to introduce substantial complexities into their logical notation to accommodate them. My approach has been no exception. The appeal to eventualities in Section 2, the indexing of Section 3, and the treatment of substitution of Section 4 are all examples of these complexities. But whereas in most approaches to semantics, the logical notation *remains* complex, the whole aim of my detour into the complexities was to regain the original simplicity and elegance, and I believe this has been achieved. The logical form of a sentence is still an existentially quantified conjunction of atomic predications, roughly one for each morpheme in the sentence. Once such a logical form has been generated for the sentence, only one interpretation process is needed, namely, the abductive process of determining the facts and assumptions that will provide the most economic proof of that logical form.

References

Allen, James, 1987. *Natural Language Understanding*, Benjamin Cummings, Menlo Park, California.

Barwise, Jon, and Robin Cooper, 1981. "Generalized Quantifiers and Natural Language", *Linguistics and Philosophy*, Vol. 4, No. 2, pp. 159-219.

Hobbs, Jerry R., 1983. "An Improper Treatment of Quantification in Ordinary English", *Proceedings of the 21st Annual Meeting, Association for Computational Linguistics*, pp. 57-63. Cambridge, Massachusetts, June 1983.

Hobbs, Jerry R. 1985. "Ontological Promiscuity." *Proceedings, 23rd Annual Meeting of the Association for Computational Linguistics*, pp. 61-69. Chicago, Illinois, July 1985.

Hobbs, Jerry R., Mark Stickel, Douglas Appelt, and Paul Martin, 1993. "Interpretation as Abduction", *Artificial Intelligence*, Vol. 63, Nos. 1-2, pp. 69-142.

McCarthy, John, 1977. "Epistemological Problems of Artificial Intellegence", *Proceedings, International Joint Conference on Artificial Intelligence*, pp. 1038-1044, Cambridge, Massachusetts, August 1977.

Poesio, Massimo, 1991. "Scope Ambiguity and Inference", Technical Report 389, Computer Science Department, The University of Rochester, Rochester, New York, July 1991.

van Benthem, Johan, 1983. "Determiners and Logic", *Linguistics and Philosophy*, vol. 6, pp. 447-478.

van Eijck, Jan, 1983. "Discourse Representation Theory and Plurality", in A.G.B. ter Meulen, ed., *Studies in Modeltheoretic Semantics*, Foris Publications, Dordrecht, Netherlands, pp. 85-106.

4

Situated Disambiguation with Properly Specified Representation

HIDEYUKI NAKASHIMA AND YASUNARI HARADA

1 Introduction

When we communicate through (natural) languages, we do not explicitly say everything. Rather, both the speaker and the hearer utilize information supported by the utterance situation. For example, if we say in Japan "it is four o'clock," it means "it is four o'clock in Japan". The "in Japan" part is not made explicit in the utterance because it is obvious from the situation. However, existing semantic representation frameworks either do not reflect the difference, or cannot properly handle the relation between sentences (a) "it is four o'clock" uttered in Japan and (b) "it is four o'clock in Japan" uttered somewhere else.

In this paper, we will discuss relationships between the representation of the semantic (or truth conditional) contents of linguistic expressions on the one hand, and how they are manipulated by the inference process that has close connections with the interpretation of linguistic expressions on the other, and go on to present a model of the internal mechanisms of communicating agents, including the human being, computer programs, or mechanical automata such as intelligent robots. This model is meant to be an idealization of the actual mechanisms (for example, programs) used by humans or intelligent robots.

Situation Theory formalizes the relation between situations and information from the theorist's point of view (cf. Barwise and Perry 1983, p. 59). As a particular application, it formalizes informational state of

Part of the research presented here was conducted while both authors were visiting CSLI, Stanford. The authors thank CSLI for giving us the opportunity. Discussions with Kees van Deemter, Yasuhiko Den, Stanley Peters, Ichiro Ohsawa and Yoshiki Kinoshita were useful. Koiti Hasida as well as editors of the book gave us useful comments on the earlier version of the paper.

Semantic Ambiguity and Underspecification
Kees van Deemter and Stanley Peters, editors
Copyright © 1995, CSLI Publications

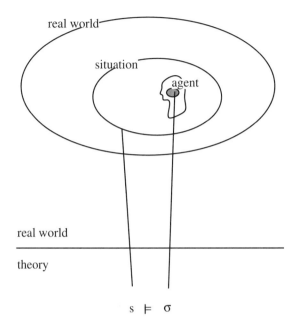

$$s \models \sigma$$

FIGURE 3 Situation Theory

a reasoning agent and the environment it is situated in as depicted in figure 3. In this view, when an agent has some information (σ) about a situation (s), it is formalized as $s \models \sigma$. When the agent reasons about the world using the information it has, the validity of the reasoning is supported by the situation out there in the world. Taking advantage of this, the agent can perform efficient reasoning with situated rules, i.e., the agent can forget about background conditions and still do valid reasoning.

Now, let us imagine a situation where a second agent in the world takes the position of the theorist and models the original agent's reasoning. The observing agent will have some information *about* the situation s in which the reasoning agent resides, as well as some information about the reasoning agent's information σ about the situation. The observing agent can talk about whether the information of the reasoning agent is correct or not. However, the knowledge of the observer cannot affect the behavior of the reasoner, *i.e.*, it is just a description and cannot be used by the reasoner to plan the future behavior of the reasoner.

On the other hand, when the reasoner is observing its own reasoning process, it can make plans or actions in accordance with its own observation. This self-observing agent is depicted in figure 4. It

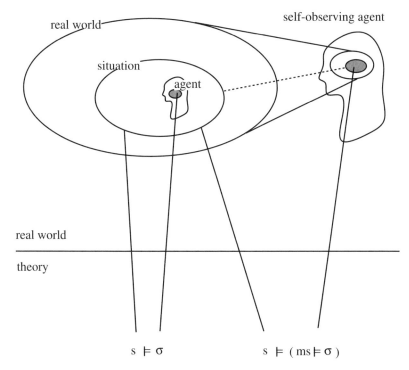

FIGURE 4 Our extension

has an ability to reflect upon its own situation: it can manipulate the information it has about itself and about the situations it is in (cf. Nakashima and Tutiya 1991). Of course this judgment may be wrong because the agent is not an omniscient theorist. Nevertheless, the agent can only rely on its own observation.

To distinguish such self-observation from the theorist's formalization, we will use the term "mental" in our theorist's formalization of the self-observing agent. In figure 4, a mental representation of the situation s is shown as ms, and a mental infon is shown as $m\sigma$.

An infon is about the world, from the theorist's point of view. A mental infon, on the other hand, is something an agent has about the world, from the agent's point of view. Therefore in a situation s supporting σ, it is possible that the agent has a different representation $m\sigma$. Thus we need both $s \models \sigma$ and $ms \models m\sigma$ about the same situation.

Devlin 1991 (page 164) describes a mental version of, say,

$$e \models \langle\!\langle \text{raining,t;1} \rangle\!\rangle$$

as

$\langle\langle$Bel, $e^\sharp$,raining$^\sharp$,now$^\sharp$;1$\rangle\rangle$.

But we do not want to use Bel operators because that is *not* a part of agent's representation. We use $ms \models m\sigma$ which expresses that $m\sigma$ is supported by ms.

The embedding $s \models (ms \models m\sigma)$ says that this is true according to s. In other words, the reasoner has the information that $m\sigma$ is supported by his mental representation. As formalized later, a mental situation may correspond to not only one of the real situations but also to one of the situation types.

When the self-observing agent believes that it has the correct information, it can disregard its mental representation of the situation and perform situated reasoning. It can leave its knowledge about the situation in, so to speak, its long term memory and load only related rules into its working memory. On the other hand, when the agent believes that the situation has changed or finds out that it is in a different situation than it thought, it can switch back to a non-situated mode and explicitly reason about its situation. In this case, efficiency of reasoning is sacrificed to flexibility and robustness of reasoning.

Similarly in dialog, when an agent uses less-than-fully specified representations, (variously referred to as "underspecified representations", "situated representations" or "ambiguous representations") as discussed in this paper, switching from situated mode to non-situated mode is sometimes required. As long as the underspecified representation works well because it matches the situation, there is no need for either the speaker or the hearer to reflect upon their situations. However, cases arise in which the situation must be explicitly mentioned to shift the topics or to correct misunderstandings.

Let us focus on situated cases for a while. We do not explicitly say everything. Rather, both the speaker and the hearer make maximal use of information readily available from the situation of the utterance. For example, if we say in Japan, either in English or in Japanese, that "it is four o'clock," what we usually mean is that "it is four o'clock in Japan at this particular moment". The "in Japan" part is not made explicit in the utterance because it is obvious from the situation.

Barwise calls these elements *unarticulated constituents* and points out that they play, together with *background conditions*, an important role in situated inference [Barwise 1989, page 152]:

> Natural languages have an important feature that suggests another strategy for embodying situated inference, namely the ability to leave parameters implicit in some circumstances, yet make them explicit in others. Compare "It is raining" with "It is raining here" or "It is raining there", or compare "I am flying" with "I am flying to Canberra, from Sydney, on Sunday, July 1". Natural language

allows us great flexibility in making reference to whatever parameters are relevant for the task at hand, but leaving them implicit when they are irrelevant.

Our motivation in proposing the framework of situated representation of natural language semantics is to develop a formal language of reasoning that reflects the kind of characteristics we find in natural languages as mentioned above.

In contrast to natural languages, an expression in most formal languages, a logical formula, for example, must literally contain all the bits and pieces of information to express the relevant truth value, according to the traditional view. Therefore, if we use logical formulae to represent the semantic contents of natural language sentences, the translation mechanism must supply all the missing information. This, however, is computationally implausible.

On the other hand, formal languages such as programming languages or command languages make full use of flexibility and efficiency that are usually considered distinguishing characteristics of natural languages. For instance, when you are navigating through a file system of say, UNIX or MS-DOS, most of the time you specify the relative file path rather than the absolute. Also, when you are copying files from one directory to another, you are often not required to spell out the target file name, as long as the new file name is identical to the old. Without such efficient use of the relative path specification and the default mechanism, command languages would be too bothersome to handle for human users.

In our view, it is not correct to say that the information that is not made explicit is *omitted* because it is obvious. In many cases, we are not even aware that those pieces of information are an important part of our communication. The time zone we are in or the current directory in a file system are simple examples of such cases. Our thought/inference itself is situated and thus makes certain aspects of information concealed from outside manipulation and this fact is reflected in our use of language, natural or formal.

Situation Semantics [Barwise and Perry 1983] formalizes the relation between the situation (called discourse situation) and the meaning of the utterance. However, its main purpose is to describe mappings from elements in the sentences (like "here" and "now") to their "meanings" (like loc-1 and time-1). Treatment of unarticulated elements (for example, the location and the time of a sentence like "It is raining."), namely, whether they should be included in the semantic representation of the utterance is not discussed.

We argue that those elements *should not* be included in the semantic representation. There are two reasons:

1. By eliminating elements which are decidedly guaranteed to be fixed, an agent can keep the representations and their manipulation to the minimum, making inference that much more efficient.
2. Moreover, it is practically impossible to supply all those missing elements. This task requires complete representation of the utterance situation but this is in principle and in practice an impossible task.

However, as the context shifts, pieces of information previously considered fixed may have to be viewed as variable. For instance, if you are making a phone call to someone outside your time zone, mentioning time or date simply would not do. In such a case, the system must "re-present" the information explicitly. What we need is a representational framework in which information can be passed from situation to representation. The system can forget about the surrounding situation to efficiently reason within the situation, or it can objectivize the situation to reason about the complex structure of the situations.

2 Proper Specification

What we will discuss in this paper crucially concerns the relationships among representations of semantic contents of linguistic expressions and the way these representations are utilized in the inferencing and reasoning mechanisms of intelligent agents. In this section, we will informally sketch general ideas behind our approach toward the problem of situated disambiguation. In section 3, we formalize the notion of situated representation and in the first part of section 4, we come back to the example cited below and show how our formalism is utilized in the proper treatment of disambiguation.

Let us take an example of an ambiguous sentence in (1) [Dalrymple *et. al.* 1991].

(1)   John adores his wife and Bill does so too.

According to the traditional linguistic wisdom, (1) has at least two possible interpretations, one in which Bill adores John's wife and one in which Bill adores his own wife.[1] Traditionally, this has been described by positing two different semantic representations such as (2) and (3) for the first conjunct of the sentence in (1) and then interpreting the pro-verb phrase *do so* on the basis of the predicate of the first conjunct.

(2) λx adore(x, wife(x)) John

(3) λx adore(x, wife(John)) John

This analysis amounts to the claim that the first conjunct in (1) is ambiguous between the meaning expressed in (2) and that in (3).

---

[1]In both cases that we are considering here, 'his' in the first conjunct is to be interpreted as anaphorically related to 'John'.

On the other hand, Dalrymple et al. 1991 argue that the kind of varied interpretation as seen in (4) cannot be attributed to ambiguity of the first conjunct and propose a higher-order unification approach to the interpretation of this kind of elliptical expressions.

(4)   John realizes that he is a fool, but Bill does not, even though his wife does.

In the representation schema that we discuss later in this paper, the situation expressed in the first conjunct of (1) can be represented as shown in (5), disregarding various details that do not concern us here.

(5) $S_{\text{JOHN}} \models \langle\!\langle \text{adore, x} \rangle\!\rangle, \langle\!\langle \text{his wife, x} \rangle\!\rangle$

This is to be understood to mean that in the mental model of John that the speaker or the hearer of the sentence in (1) has, it holds that there is some entity x which he adores and which is his wife. (How this works in detail will be discussed in section 4.3). One possible reading of the second conjunct of the sentence in (1) can be obtained by copying into the situation $S_{\text{BILL}}\text{m}$, i.e., the mental model of Bill, whatever content of the semantic representation we find in the situation S_{JOHN} in (5), thus we get something like (6).

(6) $S_{\text{BILL}} \models \langle\!\langle \text{adore, x} \rangle\!\rangle, \langle\!\langle \text{his wife, x} \rangle\!\rangle$

This is to be understood to mean that in our mental model or representation of Bill, it holds that there is some entity x which he adores and which is his wife.

A second possible reading of the second conjunct of the sentence in (1) can be obtained by copying into the situation S_{BILL}, whatever content of the semantic representation we find in the situation S_{JOHN} in (5), but replacing the second expression ($\langle\!\langle \text{his wife, x} \rangle\!\rangle$) by a slightly different formula ($\langle\!\langle \text{his wife, John, x} \rangle\!\rangle$, meaning that x is John's wife) [2] (How this is done and the reasons behind this kind of treatment are discussed in section 4.3):

(7) $S_{\text{BILL}} \models \langle\!\langle \text{adore, x} \rangle\!\rangle, \langle\!\langle \text{his wife, John, x} \rangle\!\rangle$

Note that $\langle\!\langle \text{his wife, x} \rangle\!\rangle$ and $\langle\!\langle \text{his wife, John, x} \rangle\!\rangle$ had the same meaning in the situation S_{JOHN}, but not in S_{BILL}. The above is somewhat reminiscent of the difference between call-by-name and call-by-value in programming languages. The same piece of program may work differently depending on the larger context in which that particular subroutine is placed, just as the same expression in a natural language may mean different things depending on the context. What we are trying to address

---

[2]In our view, a shift of attentional states requires different representation of the same situation. We believe that there are various constraints on when one piece of a situation can be copied to another and in the discussions to follow, we will give proposals as to when one form of representations can be converted to another, or which ones can be manipulated by the inferencing or reasoning process.

in this paper is this fundamental problem of situatedness of linguistic expressions, be it a natural language, a programming language, or a logical system.

3 Situated Representation for Inference and Communication

In this section, we describe the framework of situated representation to properly reflect the level of underspecification of sentences. It is then applied to the model of communication. Our basic idea is that both the speaker and the hearer are situated. Not only their representation and inference mechanisms are situated, but also the language used in the communication reflects its situatedness. In this sense, our approach can be viewed as an attempt to formalize Barwise's "unarticulated constituent" [Barwise 1989].

Situated inference can be defined as inference in which an agent takes advantage of being in a situation. The agent need not consider or represent all the conditions (potentially) relevant for valid inference, if the conditions are guaranteed to be true in the situation. We call such inference "inference **in** a situation". Situation theory has supplied conceptual equipment to analyze how this kind of inference works making use of information made relevant by contexts and goals. Note that the situation mentioned here includes mental states of the agent. In the case of dialog, those mental situations may not be shared between the speaker and the hearer. Therefore we need another type of inference called "inference **about** situations" [Nakashima and Tutiya 1991]. This involves explicit mention of situations as well as meta-level inference of "changing" the situation that the agent believes it is in.

Changing a situation may sound strange when the situation is taken to be the real one out there in the world. We instead talk about mental representation of situations as stated earlier.

3.1 Situated Representation

As an example, let us consider the problem of representing locations of objects for robot planning. When we consider a situation in which a robot is scanning its visual image and making an internal map of the outside objects, it is natural to represent them as something like the following:

at(object1, location(3.5, 4.8)).[3]

Here we assume that the robot is using an x-y coordinate system to represent the location of objects. When the robot moves object1, it

---

[3]Details of the syntax for the representation language are not at issue here. Only the informational content counts.

can easily update its location by changing the x-y coordinates of the representation. However, when the robot wants to remember all the history of the locations of objects or wants to plan future positions of them, it becomes necessary to represent both time and location:

at(object1, location(3.5, 4.8), time(1994-01-01, 17:33:05)).

The "time" information was not newly introduced. It is always there. It was the robot that did not require the information. The representation of the robot (without time) was correct because it matched the actual situation at that moment although "that moment" was not explicitly represented. In other words, the representation "at(object1, location(3.5, 4.8))" at 17:33:05, January 6th, 1995, is equivalent to the representation "at(object1, location(3.5, 4.8), time(1995-01-06, 17:33:05))" at any time. We say that the former representation is *attuned to* the situation. Therefore, we will borrow the notation of situation theory and write this as

{a situation whose time is "time(1994-01-01, 17:33:05)"}
$\models$ at(object1, location(3.5, 4.8))

or else as,

s $\models$ time(1994-01-01, 17:33:05) $\rightarrow$
s $\models$ at(object1, location(3.5, 4.8))

However, the latter representation does not reflect the asymmetry between explicitly represented information and implicit information in the situation. For our purpose, we will use a variant of the former. We will describe how to represent implicit information a bit later.

Now, let us go a bit further. A robot may want to plan its path through a room. In the planning, the robot must represent its own location, for instance, as

at(Robby, in-front-of(table1)).

However, a program usually uses internal representation such as:

at(in-front-of(table1)).

The reason is that in planning of this kind, the agent of various actions is always the robot itself. Thus we can say that a representation "at(in-front-of(table1))" is equivalent to a representation "at(Robby, in-front-of(table1))" for Robby planning its own movement. Furthermore, the representation without the agent is portable to other robots without modification.

Therefore, when a planner focuses on the action sequence of a particular agent, there is no need to represent the agent. In the same sense, when a planner is focusing on moving a particular object, there is no need to represent the object in the plan. Thus a two-place relation "on(a, b)" may be represented as a one place relation "on(b)".

There are two computational advantages obtained by not explicitly representing the object that is the focus of attention:

1. Efficiency: When the object is represented, the planner or the executor must verify that the object in focus is actually the object represented. A more trivial drawback is that the parameter specifying the object must be passed to sub-routines.

2. Portability:

   a. The acquired plan can be applied to other objects. Suppose that Robby made a plan to move from room A to room B. This plan may be shared by other robots. But when the plan contains the explicit mention of Robby, it cannot be used by other robots without further modification.

   b. A housekeeping robot having a plan to prepare breakfast at 7:00 am can function properly regardless of the time zone. But if the robot has the representation of the time as "7:00 am JST," it must be re-programmed to be used in the U.S.

As the representational framework, we need a situated mechanism to freely move some of the arguments into the background situation. We assume that the information is represented as a set of infons [Devlin 1991] about the situation. Infons are used to represent some properties of the situation. We write an infon as:

$$\langle\!\langle R, {}^{r_1}a_1, \ldots, {}^{r_n}a_n \rangle\!\rangle$$

where R is an n-ary relation and r_i and a_i are its argument roles and arguments respectively. We write

$$s \models \sigma$$

to mean that s makes an infon σ true, or the infon is *supported* by the situation s. The situation part is *not* used by the reasoner unless the inference process needs to reflect on its own context.

Since we are interested in the internal mechanisms of reasoners, we use s as the representation of the actual situation by the reasoner. A reasoner may have multiple representations of the same situation.

Any argument role of a relation may be turned into background information. The information is then considered as a part of the situation, and the reasoner can forget about it while it is in the situation. If we call such a new situation s' that has additional information to the original one s, then as far as information is concerned, $s' = s + {}^{r_i}a_i$. To reflect this, we will write s' as $s/{}^{r_i}a_i$. The formal definition is given later (definition 11).

Now the following transformation is allowed:

$$s \models \langle\!\langle R, {}^{r_1}a_1, ..., {}^{r_{i-1}}a_{i-1}, {}^{r_i}a_i, {}^{r_{i+1}}a_{i+1}, ..., {}^{r_n}a_n \rangle\!\rangle$$
$$\rightarrow$$
$$s' \models \langle\!\langle R, {}^{r_1}a_1, ..., {}^{r_{i-1}}a_{i-1}, {}^{r_{i+1}}a_{i+1}, ..., {}^{r_n}a_n \rangle\!\rangle$$

Note that the symbol s refers to the situation of which the agent is making a representation. The set of infons used to describe the situation by no means represents the total information about the situation. It is impossible to fully describe an actual situation by a finite number of infons. A situation is rather characterized by the infons which the situation supports.

Note also that the argument roles cannot be identified by the position anymore. We must explicitly name each argument role. The formal treatment is given in the next section.

3.2 Situated Representation

Here, we formally describe our representation language which is an extension of situation theory. Details not described here are the same as in situation theory. The basic idea of the extension is how *not* to represent information that is obvious in the situation.

We will use the term "mental" to denote that "situations" and "infons" we are talking about are not out there in the world, but rather they should be considered as mental representations. The following description is based on Nakashima et al. 1991.

3.2.1 Mental Infon

Since we must explicitly name each argument role, we first introduce *argument roles* to distinguish different arguments of relations.

Definition 1 AR : a set of argument roles.

Here we are not committed to whether argument roles are specific to each relation or universal to all relations. If they are specific, then the effect of specialization (definition 11) is limited to several infons that share the relation. If not, all infons may be affected.

Definition 2 ME : a set of mental entities. They are given as primitives.

Mental entities here correspond to "parameters" in situation theory. They are used to point to the entities in the world. In our formalism, mental situations are also mental entities.

A mental infon consists of a triplet of a relation, a set of role-value pairs and a polarity.

Definition 3 A mental infon is a triple $\langle r, f, p \rangle$ where

1. $r \in ME$: a relation name,

2. $f : AR \xrightarrow{f} ME$ is a finite mapping from AR to ME, and

3. $p \in \{0,1\}$: the polarity.

Notation 3.1 A mental infon $\langle r, f, p \rangle$ is written as

$$\langle\!\langle r, {}^{role_1} a_1, \ldots, {}^{role_n} a_n; p \rangle\!\rangle$$

where $role_i \in \text{domain}(f)$ and $a_i \in \text{range}(f)$. p may be omitted when it is 1 (meaning positive).

For example, an infon with relation = kill, killer = Brutus and killee = Caesar is written as

$$\langle\!\langle \text{kill}, {}^{killer}\text{Brutus}, {}^{killee}\text{Caesar} \rangle\!\rangle,$$

or

$$\langle\!\langle \text{kill}, {}^{killee}\text{Caesar}, {}^{killer}\text{Brutus} \rangle\!\rangle.$$

Note that Brutus and Caesar are mental entities. Mental entities form their own mental situations around them as described in the next section.

Note also that the arguments are order-free. [4]

Definition 4 MI: the set of all mental infons.

Definition 5 The negation of an infon σ is written as $\overline{\sigma}$.

3.2.2 Primitive Mental Situation

Definition 6 A primitive mental situation is a pair $\langle n, i \rangle$ where

1. $n \in ME$: the unique identifier of the primitive mental situation, and

2. $i \subseteq MI$: the set of mental infons which the primitive mental situation supports.

The name corresponds to the agent's conception of the mental situation and can be any element of ME, including relations.

There can be two mental situations with exactly the same set of mental infons but with different names. In this case, they correspond to two distinct concepts which accidentally have the same characteristics.

Definition 7 PMS : the set of all primitive mental situations ($ME \times 2^{MI}$)

Notation 7.1 For all $s \in PMS$, $s.ME$ denotes ME associated with s, and $s.MI$ denotes the set of MI (2^{MI}) associated with s.

Definition 8 $\forall \sigma \in MI$, $\forall s \in PMS$, $s.ME \models \sigma \overset{def}{=} \sigma \in s.MI$

Thus, a mental infon σ is supported by a primitive mental situation s just in case s contains σ as an element of its set of mental infons.

---

[4]This feature of situated representation is best suited for syntactic and semantic analysis of Japanese, in which complement phrases can appear almost in any order.

A typical primitive mental situation we are considering corresponds to our conceptualization of a certain entity. For example, a primitive mental situation for Caesar[5] is a pair of a mental entity *Caesar* and a set of infons about Caesar. We can write this as follows using definition 8:

Caesar $\models$ $\langle\!\langle$name, ^{family}Caesar, ^{given}Julius$\rangle\!\rangle$
Caesar $\models$ $\langle\!\langle$position, ^{rank}general, ^{city}Rome$\rangle\!\rangle$
Caesar $\models$ $\langle\!\langle$kill, ^{killee}Caesar, ^{killer}Brutus$\rangle\!\rangle$
Caesar $\models$ ...

Note that we use a mental entity to denote the mental situation associated with it.

For readers familiar with knowledge representation frameworks in AI, we point out that our formalism of *primitive* mental situations has a simple mapping (table 1) to the frame system [Minsky 1975].

our framework	the frame system
mental situation	frame
relation	slot
role	facet
value	value

TABLE 1 Correspondence to the frame system

However, the frame system presupposes fixed cluster of frames, and do not support operations like specialization or globalization described below. Another shortcoming of the frame system is that it has no formal framework for reasoning other than inheritance. The user must provide procedural knowledge for reasoning.

3.2.3 Mental Situation

Starting from a primitive mental situation, and applying a sequence of either specializations or globalizations, definitions of which are given later in this section, the inferencer can reach any form of (non-primitive) mental situations. The detailed mechanism to allow this operation is not important in this paper, and makes the definition more complex. Therefore, we will just consider specialization in the following definitions of mental situations.

Definition 9 A mental situation is a triplet $\langle s, i, an \rangle$ where

1. $s \in ME$ is the name,
2. $i \subseteq MI$ is the set of mental infons it supports, and
3. $an \in 2^{AR \times ME}$ is information about some of the missing argument roles.

---

[5]This idea is parallel to Devlin's "oracle" [Devlin 1991].

Definition 10 MS: the set of all mental situations ($PMS \times 2^{AR \times ME}$).

A primitive mental situation is a mental situation with $an = \phi$. A primitive mental situation is specialized by fixing one of its argument roles with a particular value. For example, a primitive mental situation s supporting an infon $\langle\!\langle \text{kill}, \, ^{killer}\text{Brutus}, \, ^{killee}\text{Caesar} \rangle\!\rangle$ is specialized by fixing the value of ^{killer} to Brutus. Once it is fixed, we do not have to mention it explicitly. Thus we can write the infon as $\langle\!\langle \text{kill}, \, ^{killee}\text{Caesar} \rangle\!\rangle$. We attach the fixed part to s.

Definition 11 Let $\langle s_1, i_1, an_1 \rangle$ and $\langle s_0, i_0, an_0 \rangle$ be mental situations, a be a role and n be a mental entity. Then $\langle s_1, i_1, an_1 \rangle$ is defined to be a specialization of $\langle s_0, i_0, an_0 \rangle$ with a and n, if and only if the following conditions are satisfied:

1. $\forall \langle r_1, f_1, p_1 \rangle \in MI,$

$$s_1 \models \langle r_1, f_1, p_1 \rangle \iff \begin{array}{l} (\exists f_0, \ s_0 \models \langle r_1, f_0, p_1 \rangle \ \wedge \quad f_0(a) = n \\ \wedge \ \text{domain}(f_1) = \text{domain}(f_0) \setminus \{a\} \\ \wedge \ \forall x \in \text{domain}(f_1), f_1(x) = f_0(x)) \ \vee \\ (s_0 \models \langle r_1, f_1, p_1 \rangle \ \wedge a \notin \text{domain}(f_1)) \end{array}$$

2. $an_1 = an_0 \cup \{\langle a, n \rangle\}$

The above definition claims that a specialized mental situation s_1 supports a mental infon only when one of the following conditions holds:

1. When the original mental situation s_0 supports a mental infon with the designated role a and value n, then s_1 supports an infon without a and n, with all values of other roles remaining unchanged.

   Example 11.1
   $s_0 \models \langle\!\langle \text{time}, ^{clock}\text{4:00}, ^{period}\text{pm}, ^{zone}\text{JST} \rangle\!\rangle$
   $\qquad\qquad \Downarrow$ specialization with ^{zone}JST
   $s_1 \models \langle\!\langle \text{time}, ^{clock}\text{4:00}, ^{period}\text{pm} \rangle\!\rangle$

2. When s_0 supports a mental infon which does not contain a, then s_1 supports the same mental infon.

   Example 11.2
   $s_0 \models \langle\!\langle \text{time}, ^{clock}\text{4:00}, ^{period}\text{pm}, ^{zone}\text{JST} \rangle\!\rangle$
   $\qquad\qquad \Downarrow$ specialization with ^{actor}John
   $s_1 \models \langle\!\langle \text{time}, ^{clock}\text{4:00}, ^{period}\text{pm}, ^{zone}\text{JST} \rangle\!\rangle$

Note that the following proposition follows from the definition: when s_0 supports a mental infon with the designated role a but with a different value, then s_1 does not support it, unless s_0 accidentally supports an infon without a and n, but with all the values of other roles being the same.

Example 11.3

$$s_0 \models \langle\langle \text{time},^{clock}4{:}00,^{period}\text{pm},^{zone}\text{JST}\rangle\rangle$$
$$\Downarrow \text{ specialization with } ^{zone}\text{GMT}$$
$$s_1 \not\models \langle\langle \text{time},^{clock}4{:}00,^{period}\text{pm},^{zone}\text{JST}\rangle\rangle$$

Example 11.4

$$s_0 \models \langle\langle \text{time},^{clock}4{:}00,^{period}\text{pm},^{zone}\text{JST}\rangle\rangle$$
$$s_0 \models \langle\langle \text{time},^{clock}11{:}00,^{period}\text{pm},^{zone}\text{PST}\rangle\rangle$$
$$s_0 \models \langle\langle \text{in},^{loc}\text{solar-system}\rangle\rangle$$
$$\Downarrow \text{ specialization with } ^{zone}\text{JST}$$
$$s_1 \models \langle\langle \text{time},^{clock}4{:}00,^{period}\text{pm}\rangle\rangle$$
$$s_1 \models \langle\langle \text{in},^{loc}\text{solar-system}\rangle\rangle$$

Notation 11.1 $s/^r n$ denotes a specialization of s with a role r and a value n.

When the specialization is applied to a situation, the information used for specialization is said to be moved from infons to the situation. Therefore, the following two sentences express exactly the same information.

$$s \models \langle\langle \text{time},^{clock}4{:}00,^{zone}\text{JST}\rangle\rangle$$
$$\Updownarrow$$
$$s/^{zone}JST \models \langle\langle \text{time},^{clock}4{:}00\rangle\rangle$$

The constituent "JST" is implicit in the $s/^{zone}JST$ (corresponding to Japan) situation while it is explicit in the s (corresponding to the world) situation. When an intelligent agent makes an inference, it uses $s/^{zone}JST$ rather than just the situation s.

The result of a sequence of specializations on different argument roles does not depend on the order in which they are applied:

$$\forall s \in MS, a_1, a_2 \in AR, n, m \in ME \quad s/^{a_1}n/^{a_2}m \equiv s/^{a_2}m/^{a_1}n$$

3.2.4 Globalization

Globalization is the inverse operation of specialization to be used to make mental infons less situation dependent. It has also been called context lifting (for example, McCarthy 1985).

When the mental situation at hand is a specialized one, then the inverse operation is trivial.

There are cases, however, when one must globalize a primitive mental situation. For example, a child in Japan may begin by representing time as

$$\langle\langle \text{time},^{clock}4{:}00\rangle\rangle$$

without knowing the existence of other roles. And later when (s)he grows up to know that there are other countries, (s)he needs a more global representation such as

$$\langle\!\langle \text{time},^{clock}4{:}00,^{zone}\text{JST}\rangle\!\rangle.$$

4 Application to NL Semantics

4.1 Communication as Passing Infons

In the remainder of this paper we will make use of a highly simplified model of communication.

Now that we observed that language and situated representation share the same characteristics, we can formalize communication through (natural) languages using infons. When we say "hungry", the information

$$\langle\!\langle \text{hungry}\rangle\!\rangle$$

is passed from the speaker to the hearer (figure 5).

FIGURE 5 Communication as passing infons

In this process, an infon (representing the semantics of the utterance) is first detached from the speaker's mental situation and then stored in the hearer's mental situation. If the hearer can choose a proper mental situation to store the infon, the communication is successful. If not, it may cause some misunderstandings. For example, $\langle\!\langle \text{hungry}\rangle\!\rangle$ may be stored in the situation of the speaker (in which case it conveys the information that the speaker is hungry), or it may be stored in the situation of the hearer (in which case it conveys the information that the hearer is hungry).

Now, let us describe how a hearer might identify the situation. The hearer maintains the following lists of situations: [6]

- The current (mental) situation, called C(urrent)-sit, on which attention is focused.
- An ordered list of situations, called D(efault)-sits.

The attention is focused on a particular situation either through (a)

---

[6]This is a rather naive approximation of what humans might do.

inference, or (b) linguistic guidance. One example of such guidance in Japanese is the use of the particle "wa". "NP wa" is a signal to the hearer that indicates that the speaker is going to focus on (the referent of) NP.

The primary candidate situation where infon must be interpreted is C-sit. However, when such interpretation leads to an immediate contradiction (for example, when C-sit contains the negation of the infon), other alternatives must be searched. D-sits gives a list of such candidates.

The procedure can be formalized as follows:

1. Linguistically obtained information is stored in C-sit.
2. Conflict checking is achieved locally on C-sit.
3. If there is no conflict detected, then end.
4. If there is a conflict, determine which information to remove.
5. The removed information is put into the first situation of D-sits. (If D-sits is empty, then the procedure terminates with failure.) That situation becomes C-sit. Then, steps from 2 to 5 are repeated.

Note incidentally, that the notions of C-sit and D-sits have close analogues in traditional linguistic concepts. C-sit designates what the focus of attention is and D-sits helps determine interpretation of various zero elements in a sentence, and thus is related to the notion of center [Kameyama 1988].

4.2   Placing Information

Our next example treats the problem of placing information into a proper situation. Since the missing elements of an infon are supplied by the situation, placing the same infon into different situations alters the meaning of the infon. We will show how infons can be placed properly in the case of dialogs in Japanese.

Since Japanese is a pro-drop language, we encounter numerous cases of subject-less sentences in naturally occurring conversations. However, speakers of Japanese usually find little difficulty in interpreting those utterances appropriately, although in certain circumstances, misunderstandings do occur. Identification of intended subject, however, is not a simple matter.

For instance, if you utter the one-word assertion "hungry," you would very likely be understood as saying that you are hungry. On the other hand, a one word question such as "hungry?" would be interpreted as asking if the hearer is hungry. Where does the different supply for the missing argument come from? The following simplistic hypothesis fails.

Information in a declarative sentence should be attributed to the speaker, while information in an interrogative sentence should be on the hearer.

An obvious counterexample is "pale", meaning "*You* look pale".

Let us consider some combinations of typical situations and typical utterances. More detailed analyses on various cases are given in Nakashima and Harada 1994.

Situations:

A: Speaker and Hearer looking at each other.

B: Speaker and Hearer monitoring the blood sugar rate of the hearer.

Utterances (here, we assume that all the utterances are in the form of assertion):

1. Hara-ga hette iru. (HUNGRY)
2. Kaoiro-ga warui. (PALE)
3. Tukarete iru. (TIRED)

In the following table, "S" means the subject is the speaker, "H" the hearer and "T" a third person (or object).

	A	B
hungry	S	H/S
pale	H	T
tired	S/H	H/S/T

TABLE 2 Combination of utterances and situations

See how each case differs in interpretation. We will examine each case and give proper explanations.

HUNGRY

Situations:

A: Speaker and Hearer looking at each other.
The hearer knows whether he/she is hungry or not. And the appropriateness of the interpretation of the infon when it is placed in C-sit depends on the hearer's situation. If the hearer knows that he/she is *not* hungry, even when C-sit indicates to attribute the infon to the hearer, the conflict resolution mechanism may reject the interpretation (in that case, D-sit is searched).
As a result, it is most likely that the information is attributed to the SPEAKER. We want to put emphasis on the fact that the attribution of the information to the speaker is reached "as a result" of reasoning. There is no predefined rules to determine the missing information.

B: Speaker and Hearer monitoring the blood sugar rate.

C-sit is most likely the blood sugar rate. A similar inference as used in expert systems takes place, and the information is attributed to the owner of the blood.

PALE

Situations:

A: Speaker and Hearer looking at each other.

Suppose visual information is dominant. Then if the speaker is pale, "pale" is attributed to the speaker. If not, the conflict resolution process searches through D-sits for another situation to store the information.

Assuming usual situations, where only the hearer is pale, then it will be attributed to the hearer since the hearer is most likely to be high in D-sits when they are talking about themselves.

As a result, it is most likely that the information is attributed to the HEARER.

B: Speaker and Hearer monitoring the blood sugar rate.

The blood sugar rate carries no information on whether the subject is pale or not. The information is most likely about another thing (such as the color of the blood) in C-sit.

TIRED

Situations:

A: Speaker and Hearer looking at each other.

C-sit is used to determine the referent. Both visual and internal cues are possibly available. Therefore both of the SPEAKER (with visual cue) and the HEARER (with internal cue) are likely.

B: Speaker and Hearer monitoring the blood sugar rate.

Closer to HUNGRY than PALE since blood sugar rate carries partial information on the subject's level of exhaustion. C-sit is used to determine the referent.

4.3 Copying Information

Now let us go back to sentence (1):

(1) John adores his wife, and Bill does so too.

The first conjunct of the sentence may be represented as

John $\models \langle\!\langle$adore, ^{obj}X$\rangle\!\rangle, \langle\!\langle$his-wife, ^{wife}X$\rangle\!\rangle$

Here we use "John" to denote a mental situation corresponding to the mental model of John, following the definition 8. Note that infon $\langle\!\langle$his-wife, ^{wife}X$\rangle\!\rangle$ itself is underspecified unless its situation is given. Suppose John's wife is Mary and Bill's wife is Susan, then the following holds:

John $\models \langle\langle$his-wife, ^{wife}Mary$\rangle\rangle$
Bill $\models \langle\langle$his-wife, ^{wife}Susan$\rangle\rangle$

Now "Bill does so too" can be represented by copying the infons, $\langle\langle$adore, ^{obj}X$\rangle\rangle$ and $\langle\langle$his-wife, ^{wife}X$\rangle\rangle$, into S_{BILL}. There are two ways of doing this.

1. Just copy the infons as they are (figure 6).
2. Globalize the infons, and make specializations of them into S_{BILL} (figure 7).

We would like to stress that the representations for the first conjunct of the sentence, i.e., those in John and in S_{hearer}[7] situations, are truth-conditionally one and the same thing in both cases. However, it is interesting to note that the literal difference among various representations results in the subtle difference in the interpretation of the second conjunct of the sentence.

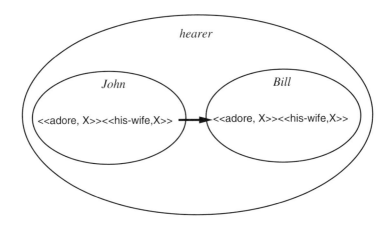

FIGURE 6 Direct copy of an infon

In the latter case (copying through globalization), by "Bill does so", we know that the actor must be changed to Bill. This can be realized by turning John into a variable when the infon is moved outside the situation S_{JOHN}.[8]

---

[7]The situation representing the mental state of the hearer is written as S_{hearer}. However, in normal cases, the hearer certainly knows the identity of the hearer. Therefore, this can be replaced by the mental situation for the hearer, say Tom, or *me* using the essential indexical [Perry 1979].

[8]This treatment (variablization) is the same as *abstraction of primary occurrences* in higher order unification used in their analysis of VP ellipsis [Dalrymple et al. 1991].

1. The original representation:

   John $\models \langle\!\langle$adore,^{obj}X$\rangle\!\rangle$,$\langle\!\langle$his-wife, ^{wife}X$\rangle\!\rangle$

2. Copy the infons into S_{hearer} by globalizing them:

   $S_{hearer} \models \langle\!\langle$adore,^{actor}John,^{obj}X$\rangle\!\rangle$, $\langle\!\langle$his-wife,^{husband}John,^{wife}X$\rangle\!\rangle$

3. Turn the actor into a variable:

   $S_{hearer} \models \langle\!\langle$adore,^{actor}A,^{obj}X$\rangle\!\rangle$, $\langle\!\langle$his-wife,^{husband}John,^{wife}X$\rangle\!\rangle$

4. Specialize the situation with actor=Bill:

   $S_{hearer}/^{actor}$Bill $\models \langle\!\langle$adore, ^{obj}X$\rangle\!\rangle$, $\langle\!\langle$his-wife,^{husband}John,^{wife}X$\rangle\!\rangle$

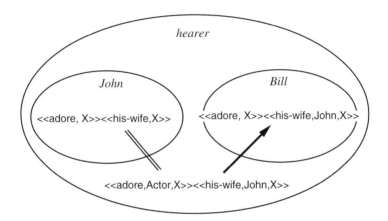

FIGURE 7 Copying through globalization

We propose that the following conditions separate the above two cases:

1. When C-sit is S_{hearer}, for example when they have been talking about the hearer, then it is more likely that the infons are copied directly as in figure 6.

2. When C-sit is John, then the hearer must once globalize the situation to shift into a new situation that is currently outside of C-sit (figure 7).

We must conduct an experiment to verify the above proposal. Instead, let us just suggest another support by examining the corresponding case in Japanese, about which the authors have better intuition. In the following two sentences, both of which are translations of our same English example, (8) more likely matches the "copy" case, and (9) the "globalize" case respectively. This observation is consistent with our hypothesis that the particle "wa" is used to force the hearer to go into the situation denoted by its antecedent, while "ga" does not have that function.

(8)   John   ga   tsuma   wo   shitatteiru.
       (John   SBJ   wife   OBJ   adores.)
       Bill   mo   shitatteiru.
       (Bill   too   adores.)

(9)   John   wa   tsuma   wo   shitatteiru.
       (John   Shift-Situation   wife   OBJ   adores.)
       Bill   mo   shitatteiru.
       (Bill   too   adores.)

5 Conclusion

We presented a formalism of situated representation suitable for situated inference with the following characteristics:

- Representation of situation and representation of properties holding in the situation are distinguished.
- Part of the information can be turned into the background, or pulled to the foreground.

We then applied the formalism to representation of natural language semantics.

Our motivation in proposing the framework of situated representation of natural language semantics was to develop a formal language that reflects the kind of characteristics we find in natural languages. In this sense, our objective was to implement the ideas informally suggested by Barwise, and can be construed as partial attainment of the research goals that originated from him and that were briefly discussed in the Introduction of this paper.

The question of giving the right interpretation to unexpressed elements in a sentence against the background of the situation of the utterance has far-reaching consequences for linguistic studies. Work on implicit arguments, VP ellipsis, and reduced coordination in English and studies of zero-pronominals in Japanese come to mind immediately. Here, we discussed just a few simple examples of related problems, but the authors believe that the representation language proposed in this paper has a much wider range of possible applications in related studies in linguistic semantics.

References

Barwise, Jon. 1989. *The Situation in Logic.* CSLI Lecture Notes, No. 17, CSLI Publications.

Barwise, Jon, and John Perry. 1983. *Situations and Attitudes.* MIT Press.

Dalrymple, Mary, Stuart M. Shieber, and Fernando C. N. Pereira. 1991. Ellipsis and Higher-Order Unification. *Linguistics and Philosophy* 14(4):399–452.

Devlin, Keith. 1991. *Logic and Information I: Infons and Situations.* Cambridge Univ. Press.

Kameyama, Megumi. 1988. Japanese zero pronominal binding: where syntax and discourse meet. In *Papers from the Second International Workshop on Japanese Syntax. Stanford, CA*, ed. William Poser. 47–74.

McCarthy, John. 1985. Notes on Formalizing Context. In *Proc. of IJCAI 93*, 555–560.

Minsky, Marvin. 1975. A Framework for Representing Knowledge. In *The Psychology of Computer Vision*, ed. Patric Winston. McGraw Hill.

Nakashima, Hideyuki, and Yasunari Harada. 1994. Situated dialog model for software agents. *Speech Communication* 15:275–281.

Nakashima, Hideyuki, Ichiro Ohsawa, and Yoshiki Kinoshita. 1991. Inference with Mental Situations. TR-91-7. ETL.

Nakashima, Hideyuki, and Syun Tutiya. 1991. Inference *in* a Situation *about* Situations. In *Situation Theory and its Applications, 2.* 215–227. CSLI Lecture Notes no. 26, CSLI Publications.

Perry, John. 1979. The Essential Indexical. *Noûs* 13:3–21.

5

Resolving Lexical Ambiguity using a Formal Theory of Context

Saša Buvač

1 Introduction

Many words and phrases used in natural language discourse are ambiguous. Their interpretation (and/or meaning) depends on which context they are uttered in. The English word "bank" is one such example. It is ambiguous because it can be interpreted either as a financial institution or a river shore. The choice of interpretation depends on the context in which the word bank is used.[1] This type of ambiguity in natural language is called *lexical ambiguity*; for example, see Hirst 1987 for a discussion of ambiguity in natural language processing.

Our goal is to be able to write computer programs which will be able to deal with ambiguous expressions. They should be able to disambiguate most ambiguous terms which come up in discourse. The first step in this direction is to provide computers with a language enabling them to declaratively represent that a predicate symbol is ambiguous. Intuitively, this representation will correspond to lexical ambiguity in natural language. The goal of this paper is to provide such a language

The author thanks Vanja Buvač, Tom Costello, Ian A. Mason, John McCarthy, Johan van Benthem, Kees van Deemter, and the three anonymous reviewers for their valuable comments. This research is supported in part by the Advanced Research Projects Agency, ARPA Order 8607, monitored by NASA Ames Research Center under grant NAG 2-581, by NASA Ames Research Center under grant NCC 2-537, NSF grants CCR-8915663, and IRI-8904611 and Darpa contract NAG2-703. Other papers on context are available to WWW browsers at `http://sail.stanford.edu/buvac` and are also available by anonymous FTP from `sail.stanford.edu`.

[1] Note however, that the context is not always sufficient to disambiguate an ambiguous utterance, but is something that needs to be considered in the interpretation of natural language.

Semantic Ambiguity and Underspecification
Kees van Deemter and Stanley Peters, editors
Copyright © 1995, CSLI Publications

and show how it can be used in conjunction with a data base of general common sense knowledge to resolve ambiguity.

We will use the logic of context, as developed in declarative AI, to represent and reason about ambiguity. The logic of context provides a language in which contexts are treated as formal objects. The logic extends classical first-order logic by introducing a modality, $\text{ist}(c, \phi)$, used to express that the formula, ϕ, holds in the context c. Using contexts and the ist modality we can state that an expression is interpreted differently in different discourse contexts; this serves as the basis for our definition of ambiguous expression. Disambiguating an ambiguous expression involves finding its interpretation in the particular discourse context in which it is used. The above is also expressible in our logic; this enables us to define disambiguation.

The remainder of this paper is organized as follows. In the next section we briefly sketch the logic of context. We then introduce the two types of contexts needed to define ambiguity, knowledge base contexts and discourse contexts, in sections §3. In section §4 we show how ambiguity can be represented in the logic of context. In section §5 a data base of general common sense knowledge is used to reason about and resolve ambiguity. We put together all the concepts developed in the paper to show in section §6 how context change occurring in simple discourse segments is represented and reasoned about. Section §7 contains conclusions and plans for future work.

2 Formal Theory of Context

The logic of context extends classical 2-sorted predicate calculus with identity to enable representing facts about contexts and reasoning with contexts. Our logic has the following four basic features. Firstly, contexts are treated as formal objects, that is, objects in the semantics which can be denoted by terms in the language and which we can quantify over. Consequently, we can state properties of contexts in the same way we state properties of any other objects. Secondly, rather than being given in isolation, all formulas are stated in some context. We write $\kappa : \phi$ when formula ϕ is given in context κ. Thirdly, the language is extended with a new modality, $\text{ist}(\kappa, \phi)$, (ist is pronounced "is true"). It is used to express that the formula, ϕ, is true in the context κ. Fourthly, the formal system contains rules for entering and exiting a context; the proofs which use these rules mirror the intuitive patterns of contextual reasoning. In §4.2 we discuss why these non-classical features of the context logic are useful for capturing ambiguity. In this section we will briefly sketch a basic logic of context which is a trivial generalization of the propositional logic presented in Buvač et al. 1995. Detailed treatment of the subject including soundness, completeness, decidability, and correspondence theorems, as well as a formal comparison of our logic to other modal logics can be found in the latter paper.

2.1 Syntax

A first-order language, $\mathcal{L}$, will be used to express the state of affairs which holds in a particular context as well as the state of a discourse. It is defined in the usual way. If $\mathbb{A}$ is a set of constant symbols, and for each $i \geq 0$ $\mathbb{P}^i$ is a countable set of predicate symbols which take i arguments, then the language $\mathcal{L}$ is a collection of these sets of symbols.

Definition ($\mathcal{L}$): $\mathcal{L} = \mathbb{A} \cup \bigcup_{0 \leq i} \mathbb{P}^i$.

Let $\mathbb{V}$ be the set of variable symbols. We define the set of terms, $\mathbb{T}$, in the usual way to be the union of constant symbols $\mathbb{A}$ and the variable symbols $\mathbb{V}$.

Let $\mathbb{K}$ be the set of all contexts.[2] The set, $\mathbb{W}$, of well-formed formulas (wffs) is the set of classical first-order formulas closed under `ist` modality.

Definition ($\mathbb{W}$): The set $\mathbb{W}$ is the least set satisfying

$$\mathbb{W} = \mathbb{P}^i(\mathbb{T}_1, \ldots, \mathbb{T}_i) \cup (\neg \mathbb{W}) \cup (\mathbb{W} \to \mathbb{W}) \cup (\forall \mathbb{V})(\mathbb{W}) \cup \mathtt{ist}(\mathbb{K}, \mathbb{W})$$

The operations $\exists$, $\wedge$, $\vee$ and $\leftrightarrow$ are defined as abbreviations in the usual way. We adopt the following notational conventions: κ and c will range over $\mathbb{K}$; p will range over $\mathbb{P}$; t will range over $\mathbb{T}$; v will range over $\mathbb{V}$; and lower case Greek letters will range over $\mathbb{W}$.

2.2 Model Theory

Intuitively, a context is modelled by a set of first-order structures that describe what is true in that context. As we will argue later, this will reflect either the possible states of affairs of a knowledge base context or the epistemic state of a discourse context. Thus a model will associate a set of first-order structures with every context. These first-order structures reflect the states of affairs which are possible in a knowledge base context or the epistemic state (i.e., what is known) in a discourse context. For a formula to be true in a context it has to be satisfied by all the first-order structures associated with that context. Therefore the `ist` modality is interpreted as validity: $\mathtt{ist}(\kappa, \rho)$ is true iff the atomic formula ρ is true in all the first-order structures associated with context κ. A system which models a context by a single truth assignment, thus interprets `ist` as truth, can be obtained by placing simple restrictions on the definition of a model, and enriching the set

---

[2]Note that contexts are thus primitive objects of the theory.

of axioms. Treatment of `ist` as validity also corresponds to Guha's proposal for context semantics, Guha 1991, which was motivated by the Cyc knowledge base.

Definition (STR($\mathcal{L}$)):   We let STR($\mathcal{L}$) be the set of first-order structures of the language $\mathcal{L}$.

By convention, gothic letters will range over elements of STR($\mathcal{L}$). We use $\mathcal{I}(\mathfrak{A})$ to refer to the interpretation function of the first-order structure $\mathfrak{A}$, and $|\mathfrak{A}|$ to refer to the domain of the structure $\mathfrak{A}$. If X is a set, then $\mathbf{P}(X)$ is the set of subsets of X.

Definition ($\mathfrak{M}$):   A *model*, $\mathfrak{M}$, is a function from contexts to sets of first-order structures of some language $\mathcal{L}$,

$$\mathfrak{M} : \ \mathbb{K} \to \mathbf{P}(\mathrm{STR}(\mathcal{L})),$$

provided (1) all the contexts have the same domains, i.e., $(\forall \mathfrak{A} \in \mathfrak{M}(\kappa))(\forall \mathfrak{B} \in \mathfrak{M}(\kappa'))|\mathfrak{A}| = |\mathfrak{B}|$; (2) all the domain objects are distinct from the contexts, i.e., the sets $\mathbb{K}$ and $\cup_{\kappa \in \mathbb{K}} \cup_{\mathfrak{A} \in \mathfrak{M}(\kappa)} |\mathfrak{A}|$ are disjoint; and (3) all constants are *rigid designators*, i.e., for any $\mathfrak{A} \in \mathfrak{M}(\kappa_1)$ and $\mathfrak{B} \in \mathfrak{M}(\kappa_2)$, and for any constant a we have $\mathcal{I}(\mathfrak{A})(a) = \mathcal{I}(\mathfrak{B})(a)$.

Definition (variable assignment):   A variable assignment is a function from the set of variables, $\mathbb{V}$, to the set of all objects, $|\mathfrak{A}|$ (where $\mathfrak{A} \in \mathfrak{M}(\kappa)$ for any κ). We extend the variable assignment to constants; this is trivial since all the constants are rigid designators.

By convention, the Greek letter σ will range over variable assignments. Instead of writing $\sigma(v)$, we will use the common notation and write $v[\sigma]$.

We introduce $\models$ which is a relation on a model, a first-order structure, a context, a formula, and a variable assignment. It is written

$$\mathfrak{M}, \mathfrak{A} \models \kappa : \phi \, [\sigma],$$

and should be interpreted as a *satisfaction relation*: we say that the model $\mathfrak{M}$, the first-order structure $\mathfrak{A}$, and the variable assignment σ satisfy the formula ϕ in context κ. Note that since every formula is given in a context, the satisfaction relation will also need a context argument.

Definition ($\models$):   If $\mathfrak{A} \in \mathfrak{M}(\kappa)$ then $\mathfrak{M}, \mathfrak{A} \models \kappa : \chi \, [\sigma]$ is defined by induction on the structure on χ, as follows:

$\mathfrak{M}, \mathfrak{A} \models \kappa : p_j^i(t_1, \ldots, t_i) \, [\sigma]$ iff $< \mathcal{I}(\mathfrak{A})(t_1[\sigma]), \ \ldots \ , \ \mathcal{I}(\mathfrak{A})(t_i[\sigma]) > \in \mathcal{I}(\mathfrak{A})(p_j^i)$

$\mathfrak{M}, \mathfrak{A} \models \kappa : \neg\phi \, [\sigma]$ iff   not $\mathfrak{M}, \mathfrak{A} \models \kappa : \phi \, [\sigma]$

$\mathfrak{M}, \mathfrak{A} \models \kappa : \phi \to \psi \, [\sigma]$ iff $\mathfrak{M}, \mathfrak{A} \models \kappa : \phi \, [\sigma] \ \Rightarrow \ \mathfrak{M}, \mathfrak{A} \models \kappa : \psi \, [\sigma]$

$$\mathfrak{M}, \mathfrak{A} \models \kappa : (\forall v)\phi\,[\sigma] \quad \text{iff} \quad \text{for all } d \in |\mathfrak{A}| \quad \mathfrak{M}, \mathfrak{A} \models \kappa : \phi\,[\sigma(v := d)]$$

$$\mathfrak{M}, \mathfrak{A} \models \kappa : \mathtt{ist}(\kappa_1, \phi)\,[\sigma] \quad \text{iff} \quad \text{for all } \mathfrak{B} \in \mathfrak{M}(\kappa_1) \quad \mathfrak{M}, \mathfrak{B} \models \kappa_1 : \phi\,[\sigma]$$

We write $\mathfrak{M}, \mathfrak{A} \models \kappa : \phi$ iff for all $\sigma \quad \mathfrak{M}, \mathfrak{A} \models \kappa : \phi\,[\sigma]$; and $\mathfrak{M} \models \kappa : \phi$ iff $(\forall \mathfrak{A} \in \mathfrak{M}(\kappa)) \quad \mathfrak{M}, \mathfrak{A} \models \kappa : \phi$. Finally, we write $\models \kappa : \phi$ iff $(\forall \mathfrak{M})$ $\mathfrak{M} \models \kappa : \phi$, which corresponds to the provability relation we will define in the formal system.

We conclude the presentation of the model theory with some intuitive clarifications of the satisfaction relation. Firstly, the satisfaction of an atomic formula only depends on the first-order structure, $\mathfrak{A}$, and the variable assignment, σ, in which it is evaluated, and not on the model, $\mathfrak{M}$, and the context, κ. Note, however, that this first-order structure $\mathfrak{A}$ has to be in $\mathfrak{M}(\kappa)$ in order for the satisfaction relation to be defined. Secondly, the set of first-order structures $\mathfrak{M}(\kappa_1)$ reflects the possible states of affairs in context κ_1. Since the $\mathtt{ist}(\kappa_1, \phi)$ is to be interpreted as ϕ being valid in context κ_1, the $\mathtt{ist}$ clause of the satisfaction relation quantifies over all the first-order structures in $\mathfrak{M}(\kappa_1)$. Thirdly, note that the context κ does not appear in the right hand side of the $\mathtt{ist}$ clause. Consequently, a context will appear the same regardless which context it is being viewed from. We call this property *flatness*; although it is not desirable in the most general case (see Buvač et al. 1995), flatness is a convenient simplification which we are willing to accept for the purposes of this paper.

2.3 Proof Theory

The formal system contains rules for entering and exiting a context; the proofs which use these rules mirror the intuitive patterns of contextual reasoning. Intuitively, we derive a formula in some context by first entering that context, performing some inferences with the formulas true in that context in order to derive our goal formula, and finally exiting the context. To capture this style of reasoning we define derivability as a relation on a formula ϕ given in a context κ. We also introduce the inference rules (**Enter**) and (**Exit**) which enable the reasoning system to enter and exit a context.

This style of reasoning also has the advantage that at any given point in time the reasoner will only consider the facts which are true in the current context, rather than all the facts given in the knowledge base. The relevance of entering and exiting contexts will become evident in later sections when we give examples of derivations in our logic.

We now present the formal system. Since every formula is given in a context, the provability relation will also need a context argument. Provability is a relation on a context and a wff, which is written

$$\vdash \kappa : \phi$$

and we say that formula ϕ is provable in context κ.

Definition ($\vdash\kappa : \phi$):   A formula ϕ *is provable in the context κ* (formally $\vdash\kappa : \phi$) iff $\vdash\kappa : \phi$ is an instance of an axiom schema or follows from provable formulas by one of the inference rules. Formally, iff there is a sequence $[\vdash\kappa_1 : \phi_1, \ldots, \vdash\kappa_n : \phi_n]$ such that $\kappa_n = \kappa$, and $\phi_n = \phi$ and for each $i \leq n$ either $\vdash\kappa_i : \phi_i$ is an axiom, or is derivable from the earlier elements of the sequence via one of the inference rules. In the case of assumptions, formula ϕ is provable from assumptions T in context κ (formally $T\vdash\kappa : \phi$) iff there are formulas $\phi_1,\ldots,\phi_n \in$ T, such that $\vdash\kappa : (\phi_1 \wedge \cdots \wedge \phi_n) \to \phi$.
The axiom schemas and inference rules naturally divide into three groups.

1.   Classical Predicate Calculus.

(PL) $\vdash\kappa : \phi$ provided ϕ is an instance of a propositional tautology

(UI) $\vdash\kappa : (\forall v)\phi(v) \to \phi(t)$

(MP) $\dfrac{\vdash\kappa : \phi \quad \vdash\kappa : \phi \to \psi}{\vdash\kappa : \psi}$

(UG) $\dfrac{\vdash\kappa : \phi \to \psi(v)}{\vdash\kappa : \phi \to (\forall v')\psi(v')}$ provided v is not free in ϕ

2.   Propositional Properties of Contexts.

(K) $\vdash\kappa : \mathtt{ist}(\kappa', \phi \to \psi) \to (\mathtt{ist}(\kappa', \phi) \to \mathtt{ist}(\kappa', \psi))$

($\triangle$) $\vdash\kappa : \mathtt{ist}(\kappa_1, \mathtt{ist}(\kappa_2, \phi)\vee\psi) \to \mathtt{ist}(\kappa_1, \mathtt{ist}(\kappa_2, \phi))\vee\mathtt{ist}(\kappa_1, \psi)$

(Flat) $\vdash\kappa : \mathtt{ist}(\kappa_2, \mathtt{ist}(\kappa_1, \phi)) \to \mathtt{ist}(\kappa_1, \phi)$

(Enter) $\dfrac{\vdash\kappa' : \mathtt{ist}(\kappa, \phi)}{\vdash\kappa : \phi}$ (Exit) $\dfrac{\vdash\kappa : \phi}{\vdash\kappa' : \mathtt{ist}(\kappa, \phi)}$

3.   Quantificational Properties of Contexts.

(BF) $\vdash\kappa : (\forall v)\mathtt{ist}(\kappa', \phi) \to \mathtt{ist}(\kappa', (\forall v)\phi)$

We briefly comment on the axioms and inference rules. The first set of axioms and rules guarantees that all valid formulas of classical predicate calculus hold in every context, and every context is closed with respect to the classical rules of inference. The second set of axioms and rules captures the propositional modal properties of contextual reasoning. The axiom schema (**K**) guarantees that every context is closed with respect to logical consequence. A property we call *contextual omniscience* is captured by the ($\triangle$) axiom. Intuitively, every context "knows" what is true in every other context. Thus, although a context need not have complete information about what is true in the world, it will have complete information about other context's view of the world. If we interpret contexts as knowledge bases, then contextual omniscience states that every knowledge base "can see" into any other knowledge base. The axiom schema (**Flat**) tells us that every context looks the same regardless of which context it is being viewed from. Although in natural language it is not always the case that only the most deeply embedded context is needed for interpretation, in this paper we restrict our attention to such simpler examples. In Buvač et al. 1995 we present a more general logic which does not make this assumption. Rules (**Enter**) and (**Exit**) allow the formal system to respectively enter and exit a context. Note that the (**Enter**) rule is the converse of the (**Exit**) rule. The third set of axioms and rules captures the quantificational properties of contexts. The Barcan formula (**BF**) states that the domains of all the first-order structures in all of the contexts are the same. Although it will not be desirable in the general case, we assume it for simplicity of presentation.

There are clear parallels between our formal system and the normal systems of modal logic. For example, the rule (**Exit**) is similar to the rule of necessitation in normal systems of modal logic. However, our derivability relation, $\vdash \kappa : \phi$, differs from the usual modal logic derivability relation, $\vdash \phi$. This choice was influenced by the intuition that every formula is given in some context and that the reasoning system can enter and exit a context. Thus when proving that some formula is true in a context, rather than doing all the reasoning in the outermost context (as is done in modal logic), we can enter the indicated context, prove the formula in that context, and exit the context. If we were willing to give up these features we could define derivability in the style standard to modal logics.

Notational Convention: when a formula is given without specifying a context, we are implicitly assuming that it is stated in some outer context $c0$. Formally, when we write ϕ without giving a context, we mean $c0 : \phi$. See McCarthy 1993 for a discussion on the outer context $c0$.

2.4 A Brief Discussion

There is a clear parallel between our logic of context and standard multi-modal logics. In Buvač et al. 1995 we show that the propositional logic of context exactly corresponds to a multi-modal logic in which all modalities satisfy axiom schemas ($\triangle$) and (**Flat**). These results extend trivially to the logic presented in this section. Furthermore, it is straightforward to show that the logic we use in this paper can be reduced to classical first-order logic. Finally, in terms of expressive power, typed lambda calculus, Barendregt 1992, is also at least as powerful as context logic. Although originally typed lambda calculus was not designed for explicitly using multiple contexts, De Bruijn 1991 gives a reduction, referred to as *telescoping*, which enables explicitly representing properties and relations of multiple contexts.

However, apart from being interesting theoretical results, such reductions tell us very little about how to use the formalism, what kind of information should be represented, and for the purposes of this paper: how ambiguity should be represented and resolved. For example, we can take this line of reasoning a step further and reduce all of the above mentioned formalisms to Turing machines. But this does not make Turing machines the only interesting formalism. Instead, it demonstrates that a particular formalism is useful if and only if its semantics are appealing, that is, if it allows us to represent facts about the world and the domain of study in a simple, concise and intuitive fashion.

3 Two Types of Contexts

In this section we identify two types of contexts: knowledge base contexts and discourse contexts. The former have been widely used in AI. The latter need to be introduced in order to represent and reason about ambiguity and context change.

3.1 Knowledge Base Contexts

Knowledge base (kb) contexts reflect some possible states of affairs. By "possible" we mean that a knowledge base context need not completely specify what holds in the world. In other words, it might "not be committed" about some propositions. For example, the context of a common sense knowledge base of Stanford University might contain the proposition "kids drive BMW's" reflecting on the states of affairs at Stanford in which kids drive BMW's. The set of first-order structures which a model associates with a kb context reflect this possible states of affairs of that context. The modality $\text{ist}(\kappa, \phi)$ expresses that the formula ϕ holds in all the possible states of affairs described by the kb context κ. In the above example, we would say $\text{ist}(\text{Stanford}, \text{kids drive BMW's})$. This clarifies the need for the universal quantification in the ist clause in the satisfaction relation. A model, $\mathfrak{M}$, satisfies the formula $\text{ist}(\text{Stanford}, \text{kids drive BMW's})$ iff the proposition "kids drive BMW's" holds in all the possible states of affairs that $\mathfrak{M}$ associates with the context of Stanford. In other words, if all the first-order structures $\mathfrak{A} \in \mathfrak{M}(\text{Stanford})$ satisfy the proposition "kids drive BMW's". Formally, we can write

$$\mathfrak{M} \models \text{Stanford} : \text{kids drive BMW's}$$

which by the `ist` clause of the satisfaction relation can be written as

$$(\forall \mathfrak{A} \in \mathfrak{M}(\text{Stanford})) \quad \mathfrak{M}, \mathfrak{A} \models \text{Stanford} : \text{kids drive BMW's}$$

and naively translating the English sentence "kids drive BMW's" into logic enables us to apply the atomic clause of the satisfaction relation to obtain

$$(\forall \mathfrak{A} \in \mathfrak{M}(\text{Stanford})) \quad <\text{kids}, \text{BMW's}> \in \mathcal{I}(\mathfrak{A})(\text{drive}).$$

In the above derivation we have disregarded variable assignments since only constants appeared as terms in our formula. Finally, note that in this paper we are assuming that all the contexts have the same domains. Thus, contrary to one's intuitions, the context of Stanford does not determine the domain of discourse to contain all the objects in Stanford as elements. All the objects are present in all contexts and the context only determines what relations hold between these objects. By convention, c_{kb} will be used to refer to knowledge base contexts.

The problem of generality was the primary motivation for the use of contexts in AI. KB contexts are central for dealing with this problem. A simple manifestation of the problem of generality is that AI systems cannot coherently use knowledge bases which were not originally intended to be used together, which in fact might, on the surface, seem inconsistent. For example, assume a common sense knowledge base of Stanford University contains the proposition "kids drive BMW's". A common sense knowledge base of Berkeley, which was not originally intended to be used with the above mentioned Stanford knowledge base, will probably contain the negation of this proposition.[3] A logic dealing with kb contexts enables a reasoning system to use such seemingly inconsistent knowledge bases without deriving a contradiction. Every knowledge base will be given in a separate context and *lifting axioms* will be used to relate the two contexts. For a detailed exposition of this style of reasoning see McCarthy 1993, McCarthy and Buvač 1994.

3.2 Discourse Contexts

To represent and reason about ambiguity in the framework of the formal theory of context, we identify a new class of contexts, the *discourse contexts*. Previously studied *knowledge base* contexts are characterized only by the sentences which are true in them. Discourse contexts, however, are not only characterized by the sentences which are true in

---

[3]A note for non-US audience: this example makes use of University pop culture according to which Stanford students, unlike Berkeley students, are often stereotyped to be spoiled children who drive expensive cars.

them but also by the interpretation of their predicate symbols, which might vary from one discourse context to the next.

Discourse contexts are used to represent a particular state in a discourse. In our simple model, the discourse state consists of the

epistemic state consisting of the facts established in a discourse or facts which are known based on the discourse, and the

semantic state describing the interpretation of predicate symbols in the discourse context by relating them to predicate symbols in some kb context.

By convention, c_d will refer to a discourse context.

To illustrate the notion of the discourse state, we examine a simple discourse context c_d, resulting in me uttering a single propositional sentence "Vanja is running" to my mother. The epistemic state of c_d will contain (only) the fact that Vanja is running. The semantic state of c_d describes the meaning of predicate symbols "being named Vanja" and "running". Since I was talking to my mother the intended interpretation of "Vanja" is my brother Vanja, and since Vanja is an exercise freak, the intended interpretation of running is the standard athletic one. Formally, the semantic state of c_d will be a relation between the predicate symbol "Vanja" (or "being named Vanja") in c_d and a predicate symbol "is-Saša-Buvač's-only-brother" in some knowledge base context containing facts about my family. It will also include the relation between the predicate symbol "running" in the discourse context c_d and the predicate symbol "running" in some knowledge base context containing descriptions of exercising. Later we will give more elaborate examples of how our formalism can be used to represent discourse states.

The epistemic state of a discourse context is similar to the state of affairs which is captured by kb contexts. In the model theory, the first-order structures which a model associates to a discourse context capture the epistemic state of the discourse context, that is, what is known to be said in the discourse. In the logic, we talk about the epistemic state of a discourse context using the ist modality. In the above example, we would express the epistemic state of c_d by saying $\mathtt{ist}(c_d, \text{Vanja is running})$.

The semantic state of a discourse context captures the interpretation of predicate symbols used to express the epistemic state of the discourse context, that is, the *interpretation of discourse predicate symbols*. This is done by relating the truth of predicate symbols in the discourse context to the truth of formulas in some kb context. This can also be represented in the basic context language using the ist modality.

Definition (interpreting discourse predicate symbols): Predicate symbol p in the discourse context c_d is interpreted as ϕ in the kb context c_{kb} if

$$\text{ist}(c_d, p(\vec{x})) \leftrightarrow \text{ist}(c_{kb}, \phi(\vec{x}))$$

As is common in logic, we assume that free variables are implicitly universally quantified. Note that the semantic state is an intuitive notion which is not captured directly by the formalization. Unlike the epistemic state of a context which is captured by the set of first-order structures associated with that context, we can not point to a formal construct and say "look, this is the semantic state." The above formula expresses a relation between a discourse context and a kb context. In other words, the formula describes the semantic state only given a context of a knowledge base.

Although the above formula defines a very simple, extensional relation between p and ϕ, it is sufficiently expressive to capture all the notions we are currently working on. Returning to the above example, to give the interpretation of the discourse predicate symbol "Vanja" we would say

$$\text{ist}(c_d, \text{Vanja}(x)) \leftrightarrow \text{ist}(c_{kb}, \text{is-Saša-Buvač's-only-brother}(x))$$

and the interpretation of the discourse predicate symbol "run" would be given by

$$\text{ist}(c_d, \text{run}(x)) \leftrightarrow \text{ist}(c_{kb}, \text{run}(x))$$

where c_{kb} is the context of some knowledge base containing facts both about athletics and about my family.

Since we are not concerned with solving the syntactic and semantic problems addressed by the natural language community, we are assuming the system is given the discourse utterances in the form of logical formulas. This assumption is in line with McCarthy 1990a; in McCarthy's terminology we would say that the discourse has been processed by both the parser and the understander to produce a logical theory. Note that the process of producing this theory is not precisely defined, and it is not completely clear how much common sense information is needed to generate it. It might turn out that producing such a theory requires the solution of the problem we had set out to solve. But for the time being let us take a positive perspective and assume the discourse theory is given.

To this point, discourse contexts have not been studied in formal theories of context because they are not as central to the problem of generality as the kb contexts. However, they seem relevant to AI as tools for analyzing discourse as well as a canonical example of contexts associated with particular circumstances. Although in later sections we will only deal with question-answer discourses (i.e., discourses consisting of a sequence of questions and answers), at this point we consider discourse in the general sense.

Note that our simple model does not claim to capture all aspects of discourse interpretation. We have refrained from modeling some phenomena that have been studied by semanticists and computational linguists. In particular, Discourse Representation Theory, Kamp 1981, includes a third aspect of discourse interpretation, namely discourse entities known as *reference markers*. Reference markers, each of which can be accessible at a given point in a discourse, are now viewed as an essential element of most theories of context that deal with anaphoric reference. Furthermore, we have ignored pragmatic aspects relevant to discourse analysis; see Grosz and Sidner 1986. These include resolving references by keeping track of which objects are salient in a discourse, and inferring the intentions of agents based on their speech acts. Extending the notion of a discourse state to deal with these and other linguistic phenomena is part of our plans for future research.

4 Representing Ambiguity

The same predicate symbol will often be interpreted differently in different discourse contexts. For example, in some discourse contexts the predicate symbol *bank* will be interpreted as a shore of a river and in other discourse contexts it will be interpreted as a financial institution. We say that such predicate symbols are ambiguous.

Ambiguity is a property of the semantic states of discourse contexts. First, we introduce the notion of unambiguous interpretation.

Definition (unambiguous interpretation):   Predicate symbol p is interpreted unambiguously as ϕ in the kb context c_{kb}, if p in every discourse context c_{d} is interpreted as ϕ in c_{kb}.

Now we define ambiguous interpretation.

Definition (ambiguous interpretation):   Predicate symbol p is interpreted ambiguously as ϕ or as ϕ' in the kb context c_{kb}, if p in every discourse context c_{d} is interpreted as ϕ in c_{kb} or is interpreted as ϕ' in c_{kb}; formally

$$(\forall \vec{x})(\texttt{ist}(c_{\text{d}}, p(\vec{x})) \leftrightarrow \texttt{ist}(c_{\text{kb}}, \phi(\vec{x})))\vee$$
$$\vee(\forall \vec{x})(\texttt{ist}(c_{\text{d}}, p(\vec{x})) \leftrightarrow \texttt{ist}(c_{\text{kb}}, \phi'(\vec{x})))$$

where ϕ and ϕ' are not logically equivalent. Note that in the above definition an ambiguous interpretation can be ambiguous in only two different ways. The definition generalizes in a natural way for allowing an arbitrary number of ambiguities, although as long as only lexical ambiguities are concerned the number is likely to be small for the cases that actually come up in natural language.

Finally, we introduce the notion of disambiguating.

Definition (disambiguating): Disambiguating is determining the interpretation of an ambiguous predicate symbol p in a particular discourse context c_d.

Our notion of ambiguous interpretation is defined in terms of predicate symbols in a logical language. However, when one thinks of ambiguous interpretation one is usually concerned with natural language utterances. If we assume some *prima facia* translation of natural language into logic, ambiguous interpretation as defined above will correspond closely to *lexical ambiguity*. This will be illustrated with a concrete example in section §4.1.

Our formalism treats ambiguity as a disjunction of the ist modalities. This should be distinguished from the treatment of ambiguity as disjunction in classical logic. We discuss this issue further after giving an example.

4.1 The Bank Example

The predicate symbol *bank* is ambiguous. It can be used to either refer to a financial institution or to a river shore. The choice of interpretation depends on the discourse context in which the word bank is used. This ambiguity is an example of homonymy; in section §6.3.3, we give an example of ambiguity which is based on polysemy.

Assume a knowledge base is given in a context c_kb. Also assume the predicate symbol *at* is unambiguous

$$(\forall x, y)\mathtt{ist}(c_\mathrm{kb}, at(x, y)) \leftrightarrow \mathtt{ist}(c_\mathrm{d}, at(x, y)). \tag{1}$$

Since the predicate symbol *bank* is ambiguous, we have the axiom

$$(\forall x)(\mathtt{ist}(c_\mathrm{kb}, river\text{-}bank(x)) \leftrightarrow \mathtt{ist}(c_\mathrm{d}, bank(x)))\vee \tag{2}$$
$$(\forall x)(\mathtt{ist}(c_\mathrm{kb}, financial\text{-}bank(x)) \leftrightarrow \mathtt{ist}(c_\mathrm{d}, bank(x)))$$

The utterance "Vanja is at a bank" might result in a particular discourse context c_d containing the sentence

$$c_\mathrm{d}: \quad (\exists x)bank(x) \wedge at(Vanja, x). \tag{3}$$

Therefore, by exiting context c_d, the following is true in the knowledge base:

$$\mathtt{ist}(c_\mathrm{d}, (\exists x)bank(x) \wedge at(Vanja, x)). \tag{4}$$

Note that this defines the epistemic state of the context c_d. Since the domains of all contexts are the same, which is given by the (**BF**) axiom, we get

$$(\exists x)\texttt{ist}(c_{\text{d}}, bank(x) \wedge at(Vanja, x)). \tag{5}$$

Using the fact that ist distributes through a conjunction, which follows trivially from the axiom schema (**K**), we have

$$(\exists x)\texttt{ist}(c_{\text{d}}, bank(x)) \wedge \texttt{ist}(c_{\text{d}}, at(Vanja, x)). \tag{6}$$

Since the *at* predicate symbol is unambiguous, using axiom 1 we get

$$(\exists x)\texttt{ist}(c_{\text{d}}, bank(x)) \wedge \texttt{ist}(c_{\text{kb}}, at(Vanja, x)). \tag{7}$$

Using the ambiguity of the *bank* predicate symbol given in axiom 2 we get

$$(\exists x)(\texttt{ist}(c_{\text{kb}}, river\text{-}bank(x)) \vee \texttt{ist}(c_{\text{kb}}, financial\text{-}bank(x))) \wedge \tag{8}$$
$$\wedge \texttt{ist}(c_{\text{kb}}, at(Vanja, x)).$$

Thus we have shown that the unambiguous interpretation of the predicate symbol *at* and the ambiguous interpretation of the predicate symbol *bank* allows us to conclude in the kb context that Vanja is either at a river bank or at a financial bank, but we do not know which.

4.2 Treating Ambiguity as Disjunction

Naïvely, ambiguity could be treated as a classical disjunction. In this light, the fact that the predicate symbol *bank* is ambiguous would be given by

$$(\forall x)\texttt{ist}(c_{\text{kb}}, river\text{-}bank(x) \vee financial\text{-}bank(x)) \leftrightarrow \texttt{ist}(c_{\text{d}}, bank(x)) \tag{9}$$

and the utterance "Vanja is at a bank", given in formula 3, would allow us to derive

$$(\exists x)(\texttt{ist}(c_{\text{kb}}, (river\text{-}bank(x) \vee financial\text{-}bank(x)) \wedge at(Vanja, x))). \tag{10}$$

We feel that the treatment of ambiguity using classical disjunction is inadequate. Intuitively, in the above example, it is not the case that we are communicating that Vanja is either at the river bank or at the money bank. Instead, it is the case that we are either communicating that Vanja is at the river bank, or we are communicating that Vanja is at the money bank. Therefore, associated to the knowledge base context in which the utterance "Vanja is at a bank" is interpreted should not be two first-order structures, one where Vanja is at the river bank and another where Vanja is at the money bank. Instead, there should be a single first-order structure, either the one in which Vanja is at the river bank or the one in which Vanja is at the money bank. Thus we advocate formula 8 over formula 10 as the correct reading of "Vanja is at a bank." Formally, formula 8 is logically stronger than 10 because 8 requires that all the first order structures interpret bank as river bank or all the first order structures interpret bank as financial bank, whereas 10 does not require this unanimity. Since this reading which we are trying to capture is not expressible in classical first-order logic (in a straightforward fashion) we are proposing the use of context logic to represent ambiguity.

5 Disambiguating via Common Sense Knowledge

In this section we illustrate how the context formalism makes it simple, in principle, to use general common sense knowledge to resolve ambiguity. The utility of this approach will be amplified

The necessity to use common sense knowledge in natural language processing is now widely acknowledged, and has recently been argued for in detail in Kameyama 1994. Contrasting Kameyama's examples with the example that follows should convince the reader of advantages the context formalism has (at least in terms of elegance).

The use of common sense knowledge is one of many possible ways of resolving ambiguity. In section §6.3.3 disambiguation is performed by directly asking the speaker which particular meaning of the word was desired. This, "direct asking", approach to disambiguation is significantly simpler since no common sense knowledge is needed, but it requires more logical machinery (to represent the sequence of utterances which make up a discourse). What we will probably want in the long run is a combination of the two approaches. The "obvious" ambiguities will be resolved using common sense knowledge, and where that fails the computer program will go back to the user and ask him or her to clarify what they said.

Now we use an example to show how common sense knowledge can be used to resolve ambiguity. We will conclude this section by explicating some assumptions underlying our approach and comparing our form of disambiguation to existing linguistic theories.

5.1 Disambiguating the Bank Example

The utterance which we examined previously, "Vanja is at a bank", can not be disambiguated without additional information. Thus we now turn our attention to the utterance "Vanja is getting money at a bank", in which "bank" should intuitively refer to a financial bank. Assume it is uttered in some discourse context c_d. We thus have

$$c_{\mathrm{d}} : \quad (\exists x) bank(x) \wedge get(money, Vanja, x). \qquad (11)$$

A derivation similar to the one in section §4.1 will give us

$$(\exists x)(\mathtt{ist}(c_{\mathrm{kb}}, river\text{-}bank(x)) \vee \mathtt{ist}(c_{\mathrm{kb}}, financial\text{-}bank(x))) \wedge \qquad (12)$$
$$\wedge \mathtt{ist}(c_{\mathrm{kb}}, get(money, Vanja, x)).$$

Assume a common sense knowledge base, $C_{\mathrm{common\text{-}sense}}$, contains general common sense facts, including:

$$C_{\mathrm{common\text{-}sense}} : \quad get(money, x, y) \rightarrow financial\text{-}institution(y) \quad (13)$$

$$C_{\mathrm{common\text{-}sense}} : \quad river\text{-}bank(x) \rightarrow \neg financial\text{-}institution(x). \quad (14)$$

In order to use this information, we will need to *lift* it into our knowledge base:

$$\mathtt{ist}(C_{\mathrm{common\text{-}sense}}, \phi) \rightarrow \mathtt{ist}(c_{\mathrm{kb}}, \phi) \qquad (15)$$

For more examples and discussion on lifting see McCarthy and Buvač 1994. The above formulas 12–15 allow us to disambiguate formula 11 and infer

$$(\exists x)\mathtt{ist}(c_{\mathrm{kb}}, financial\text{-}bank(x) \wedge get(money, Vanja, x)) \qquad (16)$$

telling us that Vanja is getting money at a financial bank. The derivation is straightforward.

5.2 Some Underlying Assumptions

We point to two assumptions which need to be made in order for our approach to be useful in practice.

Once we are given a particular instance of an ambiguous expression it is easy to write a few common sense axioms which will be used to disambiguate it. However, the reader might be skeptical about the existence of a large common sense knowledge base which contains enough information to disambiguate most expressions that come up in natural language discourse and were not anticipated in advance. This is in fact a valid concern, and the practical utility of our approach to disambiguation is contingent on the existence of such a knowledge base. In our defense we point to (1) active research in logical AI, the goal of which is creating such knowledge bases of common sense facts; and (2) the Cyc system, Guha and Lenat 1990, which is an existing large common sense knowledge base of facts usable in various arbitrary circumstances.

Our solution also hinges on the assumption that all common sense knowledge is shared by all speakers, and thus can be lifted not only into the kb context, but also into the context of what we know about the knowledge of the speaker. When I say "Vanja goes to the bank because he needs money," my information about Vanja's knowledge is what counts. We consider this assumption to be reasonable because all participants in natural language discourse ought to have common sense (which is why it is called "common" sense). If the reader is not comfortable with this assumption then our approach can be viewed as a useful approximation.

5.3 Comparison to Existing Approaches

Many linguistic theories are concerned with resolving ambiguity. Probably the two best known formal frameworks are *discourse representation theory*, Kamp 1981, and *typed lambda calculus*, Barendregt 1992. Since the latter is more general than the former, in the sense that the structures of discourse representation theory are embeddable in expressions of typed lambda calculus (see Ahn and Kolb 1990), we will compare our disambiguation approach to the one commonly used in typed lambda calculus.

A naïve system that uses types for lexical disambiguation might handle the disambiguation problem presented in section §5.1 in the following fashion. We would have types *location* and *financial-institution* for objects that are locations or financial institutions, respectively. We assume that river banks are of type *location* but not of type *financial-institution*. The phrase "getting money" would take an object of type *financial-institution*. Consequently, "Vanja is getting money at a bank" could not mean that Vanja is getting money at a river shore but only that Vanja is getting money at a financial bank.

Using the formal theory of context has the advantage over type-based disambiguation strategies like the one described above. It makes it simple to use general common sense knowledge which is stated in full first-order logic rather than having to be encoded consequences of common sense facts in terms of types of arguments. To illustrate this point we will introduce some pragmatic issues thus making the above example slightly more complicated. Assume that the ambiguous sentence was "Vanja is going to the bank because he needs money." Common sense knowledge could be used to disambiguate "bank" in the following fashion. We are told that Vanja needs money. It follows that he has the goal of getting money. Therefore he is performing actions to achieve the goal of getting money. Going to a financial bank is a way of achieving the goal, where as going to a river bank is not. Thus "bank" will refer to a financial bank. Formalization of goals and actions needed to achieve them is the kind of information that should be found in common sense knowledge bases. Encoding facts about goals and actions in form of types does not seem natural.

6 Context Change in a Discourse Segment

In previous sections we have examined discourse contexts in isolation. We have assumed that a particular discourse context was given, and we focused on characterizing it and relating it to some kb context. Now we focus on context change: we will use discourse contexts to represent and reason about the change that takes place in simple sequences of questions and answers.

We examine question/answer discourse segments which are simply sequences of questions and answers. In this simple model we allow two types of questions:

propositional questions are used to inquire whether a proposition is true or false; they require a yes or no answer. In the language we introduce a special proposition *yes* which is used to answer these questions. In linguistics these are commonly referred to as YN questions.

qualitative questions are used to find the objects of which a formula holds; in the language we introduce a unary predicate symbol *answer* which holds of these objects. In linguistics these are commonly referred to as WH questions.

In order to know what is being communicated in a discourse, as well as reason about a discourse in general, we need a way of representing the discourse. We represent a discourse segment with a sequence of discourse contexts, each of which in turn represents the discourse state after an utterance in the discourse. Our attention is focused only on discourse segments which are sequences of questions and replies: $[q^1, r^1, q^2, r^2, \ldots, q^n, r^n]$. Thus, we can represent such a discourse segment with a sequence of discourse contexts:

$$[c_d, \texttt{query}(c_d, q^1), \texttt{reply}(\texttt{query}(c_d, q^1), r^1), \ldots$$

$$\ldots, \texttt{reply}(\texttt{query}(\texttt{reply}(\cdots \texttt{reply}(\texttt{query}(c_d, q^1), r^1) \cdots, r^{n-1}), q^n), r^n)]$$

such that (i) c_d is some discourse context in which the initial question (q^1) was asked; (ii) the function $\texttt{query}$ takes a question ϕ and some discourse context c_d (representing the discourse state before the question ϕ) and returns the discourse context representing the discourse state after asking the question ϕ in c_d; (iii) the function $\texttt{reply}$ takes a reply ϕ and some discourse context c_d (representing the discourse state before replying ϕ) and returns the discourse context representing the discourse state after replying ϕ in c_d. In order to reason about the discourse segment we now only need the properties of the functions $\texttt{query}$ and $\texttt{reply}$.

6.1 The Logic of query and reply

In this section we give the properties of the functions query and reply, which are central for representing question/answer discourse segments.

For simplicity of presentation we will not change our basic logic. Thus the query and reply functions will not be in the language of the logic, but at the meta-level. Consequently the axioms that the two functions admit, which are given below, are meant as meta-syntaxis and could be referred to as *meaning postulates* in the style of meaning postulates of Montague Grammar. Extending the basic logic of context to incorporate query and reply as logical functions is straightforward.

We begin with some intuitions. Intuitively, the query function will set up a context in which the reply to the question will be interpreted. For example, the context resulting in asking some proposition p will have the property that *yes* in that context will be interpreted as p. Thus query only changes the semantic state of the discourse context. The reply function will do a simple update of information: the formulas true in the context resulting in replying p in c_d will be exactly those formulas which are conditionally true on p in c_d. Thus the reply function only changes the epistemic state of the discourse context. We now make these notions more precise.

The following axioms characterize the functions query and reply.

interpretation axiom (propositional) if ϕ is a closed formula, then

$$\texttt{ist}(\texttt{query}(\kappa, \phi), \phi \leftrightarrow \textit{yes})$$

frame axiom (propositional) if ϕ is a closed formula, and *yes* does not occur in ψ, then

$$\texttt{ist}(\kappa, \psi) \rightarrow \texttt{ist}(\texttt{query}(\kappa, \phi), \psi)$$

interpretation axiom (qualitative) if x is the only variable occurring free in ϕ, then

$$\texttt{ist}(\texttt{query}(\kappa, \phi(x)), \phi(x) \leftrightarrow \textit{answer}(x))$$

frame axiom (qualitative) if x is the only variable occurring free in ϕ, and *answer* does not occur in ψ, then

$$\texttt{ist}(\kappa, \psi) \rightarrow \texttt{ist}(\texttt{query}(\kappa, \phi(x)), \psi)$$

reply axiom

$$\texttt{ist}(\texttt{reply}(\kappa, \phi), \psi) \leftrightarrow \texttt{ist}(\kappa, \phi \rightarrow \psi)$$

Assume that *no* is defined as an abbreviation for $\neg yes$. We proceed to illustrate the axioms and their use with an example.

6.2 Example: Air Force–GE Discourse

We examine the following hypothetical discourse taking place between the Air Force and General Electric:

1. AF: Will you bid on the engine for the FX22?
2. GE: Yes.
3. AF: What is your bid?
4. GE: $2M.
5. AF: Does that include spares?
6. GE: Yes.

We transcribe the above discourse segment in our logic as a sequence of discourse contexts, s.t.

$c1 = \texttt{query}(c, \textit{will-bid-on}(\text{FX22-engine}))$
$c2 = \texttt{reply}(c1, \textit{yes})$
$c3 = \texttt{query}(c2, \textit{price}(\text{FX22-engine}, x))$
$c4 = \texttt{reply}(c3, \textit{answer}(\$2M))$
$c5 = \texttt{query}(c4, \textit{price}(x) \leftrightarrow \texttt{ist}(c_{\text{kb}}, \textit{price-including-spares}(x)))$
$c6 = \texttt{reply}(c5, \textit{yes})$

where c is the initial discourse context.

6.3 Deriving Properties of the Air Force–GE Discourse

We now show some properties of the discourse segment which can be derived with our logic.

6.3.1 First Question: Propositional Case

The discourse segment begins with a propositional question. We show how the first two utterances modify the discourse state.

Proposition ($c2$): $\texttt{ist}(c2, \textit{will-bid-on}(\text{FX22-engine}))$

Proof ($c2$): Instantiating the first axiom for the propositional questions, we get

$$\texttt{ist}(\texttt{query}(c, \textit{will-bid-on}(\text{FX22-engine})), \textit{will-bid-on}(\text{FX22-engine}) \leftrightarrow \textit{yes}) \tag{17}$$

which, by definition of $c1$, can be written as

$$\texttt{ist}(c1, \textit{will-bid-on}(\text{FX22-engine}) \leftrightarrow \textit{yes}) \tag{18}$$

Instantiating the axiom for reply we have

$$\texttt{ist}(\texttt{reply}(c1, \textit{yes}), \textit{will-bid-on}(\text{FX22-engine})) \leftrightarrow \tag{19}$$
$$\leftrightarrow \texttt{ist}(c1, \textit{yes} \rightarrow \textit{will-bid-on}(\text{FX22-engine}))$$

and it follows from the two lines above that

$$\texttt{ist}(\texttt{reply}(c1, \textit{yes}), \textit{will-bid-on}(\text{FX22-engine})) \qquad (20)$$

which by definition of $c2$ we can write as

$$\texttt{ist}(c2, \textit{will-bid-on}(\text{FX22-engine})) \qquad (21)$$

$\square_{\mathbf{c2}}$

6.3.2 Second Question: Qualitative Case

The reasoning for this qualitative question is similar to the propositional question.

Proposition ($c4$): $\texttt{ist}(c4, \textit{price}(\text{FX22-engine}, \$2M))$

Proof ($c4$): We begin with an instance of the first axiom for qualitative questions

$$\texttt{ist}(\texttt{query}(c2, \textit{price}(\text{FX22-engine}, x)), \qquad (22)$$
$$\textit{price}(\text{FX22-engine}, x) \leftrightarrow \textit{answer}(x))$$

which, by definition of $c3$, can be written as

$$\texttt{ist}(c3, \textit{price}(\text{FX22-engine}, x) \leftrightarrow \textit{answer}(x)) \qquad (23)$$

Instantiating the axiom for reply we have

$$\texttt{ist}(\texttt{reply}(c3, \textit{answer}(\$2M)), \textit{price}(\text{FX22-engine}, \$2M)) \leftrightarrow \qquad (24)$$
$$\leftrightarrow \texttt{ist}(c3, \textit{answer}(\$2M) \rightarrow \textit{price}(\text{FX22-engine}, \$2M))$$

and it follows from the two lines above that

$$\texttt{ist}(\texttt{reply}(c3, \textit{answer}(\$2M)), \textit{price}(\text{FX22-engine}, \$2M)) \qquad (25)$$

which by definition of $c4$ we can write as

$$\texttt{ist}(c4, \textit{price}(\text{FX22-engine}, \$2M)) \qquad (26)$$

$\square_{\mathbf{c4}}$

Due to the frame axioms, the conclusion established in the first question, which is given in formula 21, also holds in context $c4$.

Proposition (frame): $\texttt{ist}(c2, \textit{will-bid-on}(\text{FX22-engine}))$

Proof (frame): We first instantiate the second axiom for qualitative questions to get

$$\texttt{ist}(c2, \textit{will-bid-on}(\text{FX22-engine})) \rightarrow \qquad (27)$$

$\rightarrow$ ist(query($c2$, $price$(FX22-engine, x)), $will$-bid-on(FX22-engine))

The two lines above imply

$$\text{ist(query}(c2, price(\text{FX22-engine}, x)), will\text{-}bid\text{-}on(\text{FX22-engine})) \quad (28)$$

which, by definition of $c3$, can be written as

$$\text{ist}(c3, will\text{-}bid\text{-}on(\text{FX22-engine})) \quad (29)$$

Now we apply the following instance of the reply axiom

$$\text{ist(reply}(c3, answer(\$2M)), will\text{-}bid\text{-}on(\text{FX22-engine})) \leftrightarrow \quad (30)$$

$$\leftrightarrow \text{ist}(c3, answer(\$2M) \rightarrow will\text{-}bid\text{-}on(\text{FX22-engine}))$$

to get

$$\text{ist(reply}(c3, answer(\$2M)), will\text{-}bid\text{-}on(\text{FX22-engine})) \quad (31)$$

which, by definition of $c4$, can be written as

$$\text{ist}(c4, will\text{-}bid\text{-}on(\text{FX22-engine})) \quad (32)$$

$\square$**frame**

6.3.3 Third Question: Dealing with Ambiguity

We are assuming that the predicate symbol *price* is ambiguous in the discourse contexts since it can be interpreted as either *price-including-spares* or as *price-not-including-spares* in some knowledge base. Note that although this is still a lexical ambiguity, it is an example of polysemy, rather than of homonymy as was the case with "bank". In the third question the predicate symbol is disambiguated for context $c6$. Since in the setting of this discourse it was unclear what common sense knowledge could be utilized to resolve ambiguity, the disambiguation is not based on general common sense knowledge (as was the case in section §5.1) but instead on asking the participant in the discourse about the meaning of the ambiguous word. Note that although this "asking the participant" discourse strategy is simpler, it relies on a stronger logical machinery which has the ability to represent a sequence of utterances as a discourse. By asking the speaker to clarify themselves we can prove that the GE bid on the FX22 engine is $2M including spare parts. Note that we will have to state the above in the kb context because the discourse contexts are not expressive enough to distinguish between the price including spares and the price excluding spares (which in fact was the source of ambiguity).

Proposition (kb):

ist(c_{kb},*price-including-spares*(FX22-engine,\$2M))

Proof (kb):   By reasoning similar to the first question, we can conclude

$$\text{ist}(c6, price(x,y)) \leftrightarrow \text{ist}(c_{kb}, price\text{-}including\text{-}spares(x,y)) \qquad (33)$$

From the frame axioms we get

$$\text{ist}(c6, price(\text{FX22-engine}, \$2M)) \qquad (34)$$

similarly to the frame derivation in the second question. Now the proposition follows from the above formulas. $\square_{\textbf{kb}}$

7   Conclusions and Future Work

Our original motivation for developing the formal theory of context was to address the problem of generality in AI, as introduced in McCarthy 1987. McCarthy's concern with the existing AI systems has been that they can reason only about some particular, predetermined task. When faced with slightly different circumstances than the ones intended, they need to be completely rewritten to incorporate a new description of the world. In other words, AI systems lack generality. As was argued in McCarthy 1993 and Guha 1991, a logic of context enables a reasoning system to coherently use theories which were not originally intended to be used together.

In this paper, by identifying and focusing on the contexts associated with a particular state of discourse, we have shown how the formal theory of context can be used to represent lexical ambiguity, represent context change in simple discourse segments, and how a general common sense knowledge base can be used to resolve ambiguity. We are currently investigating whether and how other types of ambiguity (see, for example, Hirst 1987) can be handled using the formal theory of context.

Linguists, philosophical logicians, and natural language researchers have already studied similar notions of context. However, in their work context is often represented implicitly, and not treated as a formal object. Treating context as a formal object enables us to represent and reason about contextual phenomena in the framework of logic. In most cases where linguists and philosophers do have explicit theories of context (like DRT and typed lambda calculus, which we discussed in §5.3), these theories lie embedded in the analysis of specific linguistic constructions, so that identifying the relations to our formal theory of context is itself a research challenge. We are currently investigating these relations.

References

Ahn, R., and H. Kolb. 1990. Discourse representation meets constructive mathematics. In *Papers from the second symposium on logic and language*, ed. L. Kálmán and L. Pólós. Akadémia Kiadó, Budapest.

Barendregt, Henk. 1992. Lambda Calculi with Types. In *Handbook of Logic in Computer Science*, ed. Abramsky, Gabbay, and Maibaum. Oxford University Press.

Buvač, Saša, Vanja Buvač, and Ian A. Mason. 1995. Metamathematics of Contexts. *Fundamenta Informaticae* 23(3). To appear.

De Bruijn, N.G. 1991. Telescopic mappings in typed lambda calculus. *Information and Computation* 91:189–204.

Grosz, Barbara J., and Candace L. Sidner. 1986. Attention, Intention, and the Structure of Discourse. *Computational Linguistics* 12:175–204.

Guha, R. V. 1991. *Contexts: A Formalization and Some Applications*. Doctoral dissertation, Stanford University. Also published as technical report STAN-CS-91-1399-Thesis, and MCC Technical Report Number ACT-CYC-423-91.

Guha, Ramanathan V., and Douglas B. Lenat. 1990. Cyc: A Midterm Report. *AI Magazine* 11(3):32–59.

Hirst, Graeme. 1987. *Semantic Interpretation and the Resolution of Ambiguity*. Cambridge University Press.

Kameyama, Megumi. 1994. Indefeasible semantics and defeasible pragmatics. In *Quantifiers, Deduction, and Context*, ed. Makoto Kanazawa, Christopher Pinon, and Henriette de Swart. CSLI, Stanford, CA. Also SRI International Technical Note 544 and CWI Report CS-R9441,1994.

Kamp, Hans. 1981. A Theory of Truth and Discourse Representation. In *Formal Methods in the Study of Language*, ed. J. Groenendijk, T. Janssen, and M. Stokhof. Amsterdam: Mathematical Centre Tracts 135.

McCarthy, John. 1987. Generality in Artificial Intelligence. *Comm. of ACM* 30(12):1030–1035. Also in *ACM Turing Award Lectures, The First Twenty Years*, ACM Press, 1987; and reprinted in McCarthy 1990b.

McCarthy, John. 1990a. An Example for Natural Language Understanding and the AI Problems it Raises. In *Formalizing Common Sense: Papers by John McCarthy*. 355 Chestnut Street, Norwood, NJ 07648: Ablex Publishing Corporation.

McCarthy, John. 1990b. *Formalizing Common Sense: Papers by John McCarthy*. 355 Chestnut Street, Norwood, NJ 07648: Ablex Publishing Corporation.

McCarthy, John. 1993. Notes on Formalizing Context. In *Proceedings of the Thirteenth International Joint Conference on Artificial Intelligence*.

McCarthy, John, and Saša Buvač. 1994. Formalizing Context (Expanded Notes). Technical Note STAN-CS-TN-94-13. Stanford University.

6

A compositional treatment of polysemous arguments in Categorial Grammar

ANNE-MARIE MINEUR AND PAUL BUITELAAR

1 Introduction

Categorial Grammar is a compositional theory. The representation of the meaning of a whole is a function of the representation of the meaning of its parts. Since Categorial Grammar has only been interested in modelling predicate-argument structure, scope and the like, a simple representation of the nominal lexical semantics was sufficient in most cases[1]. As observed by several researchers however, such a basic Fregean concern with composition is not enough for a cognitive or computational system (Pustejovsky 1995; Sowa 1992). Frequently, there is additional information in between the composing parts, which is inferred by heuristic reasoning, e.g., by *metonymy* as in (1), which has to be interpreted as 'John beginning to do something with/to a novel', probably 'reading' or 'writing' it (Pustejovsky 1995).

(1)   John began a novel.

To account for this kind of inferences in Categorial Grammar some additions have to be made to its present way of representing word meaning. We borrow from Generative Lexicon theory (Pustejovsky 1995) in

This paper has benefitted from discussions with Hiyan Alshawi, Johan Bos, Bob Carpenter, Ann Copestake, Kees van Deemter, David Milward, Michael Moortgat, Gerald Penn, James Pustejovsky, Hans Uszkoreit, Marc Verhagen, Kees Vermeulen, Leon Verschuur, our colleagues at Brandeis, Saarbrücken and Utrecht and from suggestions by an anonymous reviewer. As always, we are solely responsible for any remaining errors. We would like to thank Kees van Deemter also for inviting us to write this paper.

[1] Although some of the work on *meaning postulates* developed a more elaborate lexical semantics (Dowty 1979).

Semantic Ambiguity and Underspecification
Kees van Deemter and Stanley Peters, editors
Copyright © 1995, CSLI Publications

defining the multiple meanings of a word by the use of a polymorphic representation. Instead of giving a traditional enumeration of word senses, we now relate them to one another into one coherent structure (*qualia structure*). This also allows for a generation of senses in context, that is in a dynamic fashion by means of *coercion*. We see this in an object-oriented way, where objects derive their meaning from the procedures that operate on them. Each procedure addresses a different aspect or quality (*'qual'*) of an object.

We want to stress that we are not talking about syntactic polymorphism, like a noun that is ambiguous between nominative and accusative (Pullum and Zwicky 1986; Ingria 1990; Bayer 1994). In this paper, we are interested in how the meaning of one word influences that of another and thus how semantics is built up by association while still maintaining compositionality. In fact, what we are saying is that there are no such things as uninterpretable, syntactically well-formed sentences. To our minds the sentence 'Colourless green ideas sleep furiously', that Chomsky (1957) claimed proved the autonomy of syntax, only proves that people assign an interpretation to almost any syntactically well-formed sentence—and that they have a very flexible imagination.

In short, form (morphology) and structure (syntax) serve meaning, in the sense that they indicate to the hearer how to interpret the concepts that are communicated, and in what way those are related. The less well-formed a sentence, the less clear it is which relation exists between which objects, and the more complicated to fit subcategorization and argument. Once it is clear which argument belongs to which subcategorization, the limits to coercion seem very flexible.

From a computational angle however, certain limits have to be dealt with. Currently, it does not seem feasible to compute whatever interpretation for any given syntactically well-formed sentence. This is why computational linguistic theories like Categorial Grammar seem rather to ignore semantic anomalies as they occur in sentences like (1). In this paper however we try to deal with them in some computationally acceptable way, while at the same time acknowledging the fact that not every possible interpretation can or even should be computed. If one assumes a semantic network for a given language in which words are ultimately (through recursive links) related to every other word in the language, it must be obvious that not every interpretation to be obtained from this network should be computed. Therefore, we take the simple but effective heuristic of computing only one level deep. Only the semantic elements to be found in the immediate qualia structure of a word are to be considered for interpretation, which takes the form of a selection of the right interpretation(s) from this lexical semantic

structure. The compositional process selects the appropriate semantic element(s) (*sorts*) out of the qualia structure, which is represented
as a *set*. Such an approach reinterprets Pustejovsky's *coercion* as a
form of type *selection* rather than type *shifting*, which makes it also a
monotonic operation[2].

The reason for choosing Categorial Grammar as the grammar formalism is rather arbitrary, although not entirely. Both Categorial
Grammar and Generative Lexicon theory are descendants from Montague Grammar, and share a number of assumptions (lexicalism, compositionality). The multi-level approach that is pursued nowadays in
sign-based Categorial Grammar facilitates adding an extra autonomous
level, and constitutes an interesting extension to Categorial Grammar.

2   Compositionality

2.1   Functors and Arguments

In Categorial Grammar one defines a category in terms of its domain
and its yield. An intransitive verb requires a noun phrase to yield a
sentence; a transitive verb requires a noun phrase to yield an intransitive verb; an article requires a noun to yield a noun phrase. Even
complex arguments are possible—take for instance a modifier to a VP
(i.e., an NP\S): it requires an NP\S to yield an NP\S.

(2)   Intransitive verb: NP\S
         Article: NP/N
         Transitive verb: (NP\S)/NP
         VPmodifier: (NP\S)/(NP\S)

Directionality is indicated by the direction of the slash; an X/Y ('X
over Y') seeks a Y to its right to yield an X, whereas a Y\X ('Y *under*
X') seeks a Y to its left to yield an X.

The basic categories we use are N (for noun), NP (for noun phrase)
and S (for sentence). All basic categories are categories. Complex
categories are of the form X/Y or X\Y, where X and Y must also be
categories.

This categorial approach has two immediate effects, first that all the
combinatorial information is transferred to the lexicon, so that every
entry has all the information it needs (*lexicalization*), secondly that the
set of rules is reduced to two rules, that do nothing more than describe
the behavior of the connectives / ('slash') and \ ('backslash'):

(3)   X/Y, Y → X
         Y, Y\X → X

---

[2]The observation that in such an approach coercion becomes a monotonic operation is due to Hans Uszkoreit (personal communication).

2.2   Logical Representation

It follows naturally to extend this compositional approach of constituent structure with a logical representation. Since in Categorial Grammar the choice to call something a functor is usually based both on content and on form, we find the same division as is found in the categories to be reflected in the logical representation. The result of applying a functor to an argument in terms of a logical form is the *logical representation* of the functor applied to the *logical representation* of the argument.

(4)

$$\langle\, (X/Y) : functor\, \rangle, \langle\, Y : argument\rangle \rightarrow \langle\, X : functor(argument)\rangle$$
$$\langle\, Y : argument\, \rangle, \langle\, (Y\backslash X) : functor\, \rangle \rightarrow \langle\, X : functor(argument)\rangle$$

As we use these rules recursively, and as each of the lexical entries carries its own bit of information, the logical representation of the whole is composed *exclusively* of the logical representation of the subparts. If we follow the traditional Montagovian way of representing meaning, then the lexical entries for 'explained, 'a speaker' and 'an example' would be:

(5)

explained	$\rightsquigarrow$	$(NP\backslash S)/NP$	$: \lambda qp.explain(p, q)$
an example	$\rightsquigarrow$	NP	$: \lambda R.\exists y.example(y) \wedge R(y)$
a speaker	$\rightsquigarrow$	$S/(NP\backslash S)$	$: \lambda P.\exists x.speaker(x) \wedge P(x)$

Then the representation of (6a) would be derived straightforwardly as (6b). (Albeit with the intervention of some simple meaning postulates to account for the equivalence of a term and its η-normal form, see (Montague 1974):

(6)   a. A speaker explained an example.

   b. $\exists x.speaker(x) \wedge \exists y.example(y) \wedge explain(x, y)$

This lambda-term can on the one hand be seen as the output of the derivation procedure (which functors applied to which arguments) and on the other hand as the input for the interpretation function (the interpretation in the model).

However, there are some shortcomings to this approach. First, (6b) can hardly be considered an exhaustive representation of (6a). It does not show that a 'speaker' is a person; nor does it represent the information that 'to explain' means that you exemplify something to an audience; nor that an 'example' is something that is chosen because of its typical properties or behaviour. Secondly, nothing prevents sentences like (7a) through (7c):

(7)   a. An example explained an example

   b. A speaker explained a speaker

   c. An example explained a speaker

These sentences have some semantic mismatch in them, but—and this is an important observation—we still can construct some meaning, albeit with increasing difficulty. That is, if we use all the knowledge that we have available on each of these words. As was mentioned before, meaning is more than an addition of the single atomic senses.

The idea of a semantic mismatch is mirrored quite well in the way some semanticists (e.g., Pollard and Sag 1987) formulate it: 'explain' has not just syntactic expectations considering its arguments, but also expects their meaning to meet certain *selection restrictions*, see (8). The first SUBCAT NP has to fulfill the role of the explainer, the second that of the explained.

(8)   explain → [SUBCAT : $\langle$ NP$_{\boxed{1}\ explainer}$, NP$_{\boxed{2}\ explained}\rangle$]

If we look at the representation in (6b) none of this shows. All (6b) does is indicate what the predicate is and what the arguments, and what relations there are between them.

3   Lexical Semantics

3.1   Towards a Lexical Semantics

If we want to talk about natural language not only in terms of predicate-argument schemata, but also in terms of associations and the bridging of semantic gaps, then we have to consider *all* the semantic relations that exist between the words in the lexicon. We have to take into account not only verbs and their arguments, but also the lexical semantics of other categories, more in particular of nouns.

We claim that it is virtually impossible for any word to have only one strict interpretation. By their very nature words adapt to their context. The hearer as well as the speaker use their imagination and select the one aspect of the concept (relating to a particular word) that fits best to the requirements of the situation (see also (Bartsch 1987)). In short: polysemy is everywhere.

In the following sections, we will discuss the systematic nature of this semantic polymorphism, as well as the way in which it interacts with context.

3.2   Polysemy and Complementary Versus Contrastive Senses

As observed by Weinreich (1964), distinctive interpretations or *senses* of words are either of a *contrastive* or a *complementary* nature. Contrastive senses (or *homonyms*) are unrelated to each other, see, for instance, the different meanings of the word 'bank' in (9a) and (9b):

(9)   a. We walked along the bank of the Charles river
       b. Did he have an account at the HBU bank?

Complementary senses on the other hand do not contrast each other, but seem to be related in a systematic way. For instance, a *brand name* like 'BMW' has at least the following complementary senses[3]:

(10) a. *the company*:
       BMW stocks gained two points yesterday.

      b. *the company building*:
       BMW takes up half this block.

      c. *a spokesperson with the company*:
       BMW announced a new model last week.

      d. *the product*:
       This year around 10,000 BMWs will be sold.

      e. *the design or production process*:
       They started a new BMW last year.

The systematic relation between complementary senses has to some extent been investigated in the literature (Weinreich 1964, Apresjan 1973, Nunberg 1979, Bierwisch 1982); most recently by Pustejovsky (1995) who termed it *logical polysemy*. Some other examples are:

INSTITUTIONS In the case of *institutions* we quote the well known 'school' example (Bierwisch 1982):

(11) a. *as a group of people*:
       The school went for an outing

      b. *as a learning process*:
       School starts at 8.30

      c. *as an institution*:
       The school was founded in 1910

      d. *as a building*:
       The school has a new roof

ARTIFACT-EVENT In the following sentences we see a *metonymic* relation between an *artifact* ('novel') and an *event* ('reading') that typically involves that *artifact*.

(12) a. John began the novel
      b. John began reading the novel

This is a general pattern, which is productive for all *artifact* denoting words. Another example is a 'model' and the *event* of 'producing' it.

(13) a. The president of BMW announced a new model
      b. The president of BMW announced that they will produce a new model

---

[3]Note that (10a) through (10c) refer to the company, hence 'BMW' is used as a proper name, where (10d) and (10e) refer to the car BMW, and hence 'BMW' is used as a common noun.

FIGURE-GROUND Pustejovsky and Anick (1988) give several examples of so-called *figure-ground* nominals that are either to be interpreted as the physical object themselves (figure) or the open space they leave behind upon removal (ground).

(14) a. *figure*:
        John painted the door blue

   b. *ground*:
        John walked through the door quickly

Interestingly, we can also construct the following perfectly acceptable example where *figure* and *ground* interpretations occur at the same time:

(14) c. Go through the red door on your right.

That this can not always be done is shown by the following two examples with *book*, which is both of sort *information* and *physical object*— apparently *to buy* doesn't trigger the *physical object*-aspect of *book*, or not as much as *to throw* does.

(15) a.   I love the book you bought me.
      b. ?? I love the book you threw at me.

ANIMAL-FOOD *Grinding* (see e.g., (Copestake and Briscoe 1992)) is the systematic relation between an *animal* and the *food* those animals produce after being killed.

(16) a. *the animal*:
        You won't find *badgers* living around here.

   b. *the food it produces*:
        Badger is a delicacy in China.

3.3 Lexical Semantics and Context

Natural language is at the same time the most powerful and the most limited knowledge representation language. Most powerful, because in no artificial language can we express what we mean so vividly and full of interpretations. Most limited, because the number of possible interpretations that are somehow conveyed in natural language is just too big to yield any precision. This would mean that one is never able to point out what exactly the meaning of an expression is. However, humans are able to communicate in a sensible way most of the time. This leads us to believe that in fact there are two levels of semantic reasoning, one operating on information that can be obtained from the lexicon, and one that involves real-world knowledge. We illustrate this distinction with the following example:

(17) The newspaper that fell off the table, fired its chief editor.

Technically speaking sentence (17) could have a meaning: one might imagine a talking, acting, living newspaper that can both fall off the table and fire people[4], but given our knowledge about the physical world, it is not a very likely one. In other words: in our theory *newspaper* will be coerced to *human* and then some interpretation can be assigned to the sentence, but unless we use it in an Alice-in-Wonderland setting, real-world knowledge will rule it out.

In this paper we will only deal with the compositionally construable aspects of systematic polysemy without looking at any specific context dependent interpretation.

4 Lexical Semantic Structure

4.1 Four Levels of Interpretation

We adopt Pustejovsky's (1995) model of lexical semantic structure, which introduces four interrelated levels of interpretation:

Argument Structure Specification of number and type of logical arguments, and how they are realized syntactically[5].

Event Structure Definition of what sort of event a lexical item represents. Sorts include STATE, PROCESS and TRANSITION. Events may have sub-eventual structure.

Qualia Structure Modes of explanation, composed of FORMAL, CONSTITUTIVE, TELIC and AGENTIVE roles. In more common AI terms these roles correspond to the IS-A, PART-OF/HAS-A, PURPOSE and CAUSE relations respectively.

Lexical Inheritance Structure Identification of how a lexical object is hierarchically related to other objects in a lattice that constitutes the global organization of the lexicon.

4.2 Qualia Structure

In Pustejovsky 1995 qualia structure is seen as a polymorphic representation with the different qualia roles expressing different aspects of the lexical semantic object that it represents. An example is a qualia structure for 'BMW' given in figure (18). The values of the qualia roles are meant to be defaults (the "..." are to be filled in depending on context). They reflect typical knowledge related to the concept 'BMW'.

---

[4]The proposition that we do not allow any word to have an ambiguous meaning, or, in our case, to use multiple aspects of its meaning at a time, is motivated extensively by Bayer (1994). There is reason to believe that this proposition does not hold for all situations, take for instance example (15), as well as the following sentence: "The school that starts at 9 am, burnt down this morning", which uses two aspects of the word's meaning that apparently do unify.

[5]Notice that there is a difference between Pustejovsky's (1995) notion of Argument Structure, where three types of arguments are distinguished (logical, default and shadow arguments) and the CG notion of predicate-argument structure, which only accounts for those arguments that are actually realized—logical arguments, in Pustejovsky's terms.

(18)

$$
\begin{bmatrix}
\text{FORMAL} & : company(bmw) \\
\text{CONSTITUTIVE} & : \exists y.spokesperson\_of(y, bmw), \ldots \\
\text{AGENTIVE} & : \exists e.\exists x.human(x) \wedge establish(e, x, bmw), \ldots \\
\text{TELIC} & : \exists e.\exists z.produce(e, bmw, z), \ldots
\end{bmatrix}
$$

This structure reads as follows: If we take BMW as a company (FORMAL), then depending on what qualia role is highlighted, it can also be seen as the group of people who constitute it, one of whom is the spokesperson (CONSTITUTIVE); it entails the process of being established (AGENTIVE); and it entails its default purpose, which is the production of cars (TELIC). In other words, in this case 'BMW' is polymorphic between the predicates 'company', 'spokesperson_of', 'establish' and 'produce'.

4.3 Coercion

If qualia structure is to be seen as a polymorphic representation, then *coercion* is the generation process that produces each individual sense that is represented in the qualia structure. This notion of *coercion* is similar to the original notion of the same name in the context of object-oriented and functional programming languages (Cardelli and Wegner 1985).

Essentially, the original notion of coercion is restricted to changing the type of an object if a particular function that takes the object as input requires it. From the standpoint of natural language semantics this can be seen as some form of interpretation. The context of the object forces, *coerces* it to be interpreted differently, to take on another denotation.

In natural language interpretation this happens all the time, but unlike Pustejovsky 1995, we prefer to see this as a selection out of a set of possible interpretations rather than as some form of meaning shift. In the sentences on BMW above we saw an example of such a set of interpretations to choose from: a company, a car, a building, a collection of people and a process.

In the following section we will try to formalize this in a Categorial Grammar framework.

5 A Categorial Treatment of Polysemous Arguments

5.1 Motivation

The rules for functional application in *traditional* Categorial Grammar (Bar-Hillel 1953), when labeled with a logical representation, as given in (4) are repeated here:

(19) $\langle X/Y : f \rangle, \langle Y : a \rangle \to \langle X : f(a) \rangle$
      $\langle Y : a \rangle, \langle Y\backslash X : f \rangle \to \langle X : f(a) \rangle$

That is, a type X can be derived from the concatenation of a functor
X/Y with an argument Y on its right, or a functor Y\X with an argument Y on its left. In terms of its logical representation the functor is
applied to the argument.

But now we are proposing to insert lexical semantic information
(qualia structure) into these combinatorial rules. We want to do it in
such a way that it does not influence the derivability of a sentence, nor
the compositionality of the logical representation. Whether we want the
lexical semantic information to be reflected in the logical representation
is another matter. We insist on maintaining compositionality. However,
since our representation of the composing parts (i.e., the lexical objects)
will be more elaborate, this may effect the representation of the whole
(i.e., the sentence), and it may in fact influence its denotation.

5.2 The Categorial Sign

The nucleus of the categorial sign is the category, which describes the
combinatorial behaviour. A number of labels may be attached to it,
each of which represents a different dimension (e.g., denotational semantics, prosody) (Gabbay 1991). The rules that describe the behaviour of the categories will also specify the combinatorial behaviour
of the representation of the other dimensions. Properties that apply
to the category need not apply to the labels: the way a sequence is
proven to be derivable does not matter for the prosodics of the utterance, and for the representation of the denotation of an utterance it
does not matter in which order the arguments were found. In other
words: bracketing can be omitted in the prosodics dimension, order is
irrelevant for predicate-argument structure.

In sign-based Categorial Grammar (Moortgat 1992, Morrill 1994),
every lexical entry is represented by a sign that contains two dimensions: prosody and denotational semantics. The sign, the basic element
of the framework, looks as follows:

(20) $\langle C : (\lambda, P) \rangle$

> where C = combinatorics;
> λ = denotational semantics;
>   P = prosody

The combinatorics is the category as it is inductively built up from the
basic categories NP, N and S. The basic categories will carry with them
those features that can influence the combinatorial properties of the
word, whether they are semantically relevant or not. Number, person,
gender and case are typically combinatorially relevant properties. The
denotational semantics is in fact the predicate-argument structure of

the sentence; the constants that are used are only mnemonic identifiers, as we know them from the Montague-literature (Montague 1974). The prosodic dimension represents word order, and could be extended to represent constituent structure and intonation.

Denotational semantics is a standard label in the existing work on sign-based Categorial Grammar. For the sake of simplicity we will omit prosody. The categorial sign as we use it then becomes:

(21) $\langle$ C : (λ, Q) $\rangle$

   where C = combinatorics;
   $\quad \lambda$ = denotational semantics;
   $\quad$ Q = qualia structure

The introduction of a qualia structure is new. The qualia structure of a phrase will consist of the information of its composing parts; it grows as more lexical objects are added. The interpretation of the lexical objects, however, gets more precise: context disambiguates.

5.3   The Representation of Qualia Structure

In (Buitelaar and Mineur 1994) we explored the consequences of including the qualia structure in the *combinatorics*, together with all the other features that described the category's lexical properties. In this way, we gave the qualia structure combinatorial power, and made it possible for an application to fail because of conflicting qualia structures. However, this is not consistent with what we stated above, namely that people will assign an interpretation to any syntactically well-formed sentence[6]. Chomsky's example shows that its lexical semantics will not make a sentence ungrammatical, the arguments will always adapt to their selectional restrictions—this clearly illustrates the appropriateness of the term *coercion*.

In our current proposal qualia structure is an extra semantic dimension, next to the logical form. It serves to license coercions, where otherwise a semantic mismatch would have occurred between the argument and the selection restriction of the functor for that argument.

Qualia structures are represented as sets of *sorts*[7] and are indexed by the *entity* they correspond to in the model. For instance:

(22) QS_{bmw}: {**company**, **spokesperson_of**, **establish**, **produce**}

Note that with this representation of qualia structure we are abstracting away from the use of qualia role names like FORMAL, etc. (see

---

[6]In this respect it is interesting to compare (Verschuur 1994), who explores metonymy in a many-sorted version of Categorial Grammar—using sorts instead of types as basic categories. Like in our current approach this system ties syntactically well-formedness to a flexible form of semantic interpretation.

[7]Specifications on a basic type that correspond to subsets of the set of entities that correspond to the basic type in the model.

figure (18)). We acknowledge that subdividing the qualia set by role names adds additional structure to the lexical semantic representation, but we refrain from exploiting this for now, in order to keep the representation legible. Not adding role names, we think, does not damage the fundamental ideas behind a polymorphic lexical semantic representation.

Sorts are hierarchically organized in a lattice, where sub-sorts are subsumed by their super-sorts. In the case where a sub-sort is unified with its super-sort, the result will be the sub-sort. For instance, the subsorts **read** and **write** share the same super-sort **event**, and unification with **event** would result in **read** and **write**, respectively. In general,

(23) $\mathbf{x} \leq \mathbf{y} \Longrightarrow \mathbf{x} \sqcup \mathbf{y} = \mathbf{x}.$

Basic categories carry one qualia structure, while complex categories have lists of qualia structures (one for the functor and one for the argument[8]):

(25)

basic $\langle\, X : (\lambda,\, QS_a : \{q_1 \ldots q_n\})\,\rangle$

complex $\langle\, X/Y : (\lambda,\, [QS_f : \{q_1 \ldots q_m\}, QS_a : \{q_1 \ldots q_p\}])\,\rangle$ or
$\langle\, Y\backslash X : (\lambda,\, [QS_f : \{q_1 \ldots q_m\}, QS_a : \{q_1 \ldots q_p\}])\,\rangle$

We chose to represent qualia structure as a set and not as a conjunction or disjunction. The use of conjunction would imply incorrectly that all values need to be present all the time. The use of disjunction would imply that values can be maintained, as long as one of the other values is applicable, even if they are not wanted. Clearly, this is not correct either. We want to be able to make a selection, and only use those values that apply in a given context.

5.4 The Calculus

We will not go into detail about all the varieties of functional application that occur in the literature. For that we refer the reader to (Moortgat 1992) and (Morrill 1994) on Lambek-style Categorial Grammar. What we claim with respect to functional application of a functor to an adjacent argument, may be generalized to any form of adjacent or non-adjacent argument resolution.

In order to have a complete calculus, we not only need to have rules for functional application, but abstraction (or conditionalization) as

---

[8] With the embedding of the categories, the qualia structures of complex categories will also be embedded—a transitive verb ((NP\S)/NP) will typically have a qualia structure of the form

(24) $\begin{bmatrix} QS_f : \begin{bmatrix} QS_{f'} : \{x_1 \ldots x_n\}, \\ QS_{a'} : \{x_1 \ldots x_m\} \end{bmatrix}, \\ QS_a : \{x_1 \ldots x_p\} \end{bmatrix}$

well. The use of abstraction can best be demonstrated by an example: the derivation of a VP. A sequence of types that reduces to form a VP will in categorial terms be said to reduce to a sentence that lacks a noun phrase on its left (NP\S). This sequence can be reformulated in the following way. We can assume that the missing noun phrase is present as the leftmost type in the sequence and try to prove that this sequence combines to form a (complete) sentence. Like in any other equation, we can simply add a category on both sides. This category is hypothetical, and so are all the labels that are attached to it. In the denotational semantics dimension this materializes by the introduction of a lambda operator.

To represent the relation between the original sequence and the reformulated one in a rule, we need a notation that can show the derivability between two sequences. We also need such a notation to generalize the simple rule for application—we want to be able to capture any sequence of categories that resolves to the argument. Only in the final stage, when the categories are reduced to basic categories, will there be a check for identity between the given category and the required one—the axiom. The set of rules for the basic fragment are based on Moortgat (1988) and are shown in the following section.

5.5 The Original Rules

Application is given in (26), where a functor X/Y (or Y\X, respectively), preceded by left context U and followed by right context V, takes some sequence of categories T on its right (or on its left, respectively) as its argument if T reduces to Y, and the resulting category X with U and V reduces to the same Z.

(26)

$$[\text{L}/] \quad U, \langle \ X/Y{:}f \ \rangle, T, V \to Z \text{ if} \quad [\text{L}\backslash] \quad U, T, \langle \ Y\backslash X{:}f \ \rangle, V \to Z \text{ if}$$
$$T \to \langle Y{:}a \ \rangle \text{ and} \qquad\qquad\qquad T \to \langle \ Y{:}a \ \rangle \text{ and}$$
$$U, \langle \ X{:}f(a) \ \rangle, V \to Z \qquad\qquad U, \langle \ X{:}f(a) \ \rangle, V \to Z$$

Abstraction is given in (27), where a sequence of categories T reduces to some functor X/Y (or Y\X, respectively) if T followed by Y (or preceded by it, respectively) reduces to X.

(27)

$$[\text{R}/] \quad T \to \langle \ X/Y{:}f \ \rangle \text{ if} \qquad\qquad [\text{R}\backslash] \quad T \to \langle \ Y\backslash X{:}f \ \rangle \text{ if}$$
$$T, \langle \ Y{:}a \ \rangle \to \langle \ X{:}\lambda a.f \ \rangle \qquad\qquad \langle \ Y{:}a \ \rangle, T \to \langle \ X{:}\lambda a.f \ \rangle$$

The axiom rule (28) shows that any basic category reduces to itself (identity).

(28) $[\text{Ax}] \quad \langle X{:}t \ \rangle \to \langle X{:}t \ \rangle$

5.6 Qualia Structure in Categorial Grammar

Application In (29) and (30) we present a revised version of the rules for functional application. Note that the difference between the rule for left application (X/Y) and right application (Y\X) is only in where the argument is found. Neither the predicate-argument structure nor the qualia structure are order-sensitive (see subsection (5.2) at page 134).

(29)

$$[L/] \quad U, \langle\, X/Y : (f, [QS_f, QS_{a'}])\,\rangle, T, V \to Z \text{ if}$$

$$T \to \langle\, Y : (a, QS_a)\,\rangle \text{ and}$$

$$U, \langle\, X : (f(a), [QS_f, QS])\,\rangle, V \to Z$$

if Y is basic then $QS = \{\, q \sqcup q' \mid q \epsilon QS_a \ \& \ q' \epsilon QS_{a'} \ \& \ q \sqcup q' \neq \emptyset \,\}$; QS_a otherwise

(30)

$$[L\backslash] \quad U, T, \langle\, Y\backslash X : (f, [QS_f, QS_{a'}])\,\rangle, V \to Z \text{ if}$$

$$T \to \langle\, Y : (a, QS_a)\,\rangle \text{ and}$$

$$U, \langle\, X : (f(a), [QS_f, QS])\,\rangle, V \to Z$$

if Y is basic then $QS = \{\, q \sqcup q' \mid q \epsilon QS_a \ \& \ q' \epsilon QS_{a'} \ \& \ q \sqcup q' \neq \emptyset \,\}$; QS_a otherwise

The functor usually has limited selection restrictions ($QS_{a'}$) on its argument, whereas the argument itself tends to have a more elaborate qualia structure (QS_a). A functor may for instance require its argument to be of sort **human**, whereas the argument may have **boy** as one value of its qualia structure, next to a few other ones.

We take the qualia structure of the resulting type (the result of applying the functor to the argument) to be the set of qualia roles of the argument that unify with requirements of the functor. In other words: that subset of the qualia structure of the argument that meets some requirements of the functor. From the set of qualia roles of the argument it takes only those that unify with any of the requirements of the functor.

The case where the unification of $QS_{a'}$ and QS_a is empty—there is no value that unifies some qualia role from the argument and some qualia role from the functor—indicates that no interpretation can be found on the basis of the present information. Such a restriction of the interpretation process to coercion from the initial qualia structure, working only with stipulated values, implies accepting that the process may fail at some point.

A sentence like (31), where an address should be coerced to the function of the person who works there, the prime minister, and from there to his or her spokesperson, will fail.

(31)   Downing Street denied all knowledge today.

The fact that our theory does not capture all possible readings a sentence may have, constitutes a departure from what was stated earlier. But to capture all possible readings, we would need a recursive application of coercion to avoid failing, and derive values also from the embedded qualia structures. Such an approach may be computationally uncontrollable and we therefore pursue it no further here[9].

Abstraction The rules for abstraction are given in (32) and (33). Since the resulting category X/Y (Y\X, respectively) is hypothetical, the requirements $(QS_{a'})$ for the embedded argument can not be lexically given, but will result from the derivation. Similarly, the introduced category Y has only a hypothetical qualia structure QS_a, that must be instantiated *on the fly*, i.e., through argument cancelation elsewhere in the derivation.

(32)

$$[R/] \quad T \to \langle\ X/Y : (f, [QS_f, QS_{a'}])\ \rangle \text{ if}$$
$$T, \langle\ Y : (a, QS_a)\ \rangle \to \langle\ X : (\lambda a.f, [QS_f, QS_{a'}])\ \rangle$$

(33)

$$[R\backslash] \quad T \to \langle\ Y\backslash X : (f, [QS_f, QS_{a'}])\ \rangle \text{ if}$$
$$\langle\ Y : (a, QS_a)\ \rangle, T \to \langle\ X : (\lambda a.f, [QS_f, QS_{a'}])\ \rangle$$

Axiom The identity case, the axiom, is given in (34). This now is the place where the final type-check occurs. Note that this is *not* where coercion takes place, coercion is typically a process between functor and argument.

(34)

$$[Ax] \quad \langle\ X : (t, QS_t)\ \rangle \to \langle\ X : (t, QS_t)\ \rangle$$

5.7   Examples

5.7.1   'begin a novel'

In the following example we demonstrate how the transitive verb *begin* combines with the noun phrase *a novel* to constitute the verb phrase *begin a novel*.

---

[9]In (31) one might think of looking into the qualia structure of *Downing Street*, finding the address of the Prime Minister; then looking into the qualia structure of *Prime Minister* and finding an entry for *spokesperson* there.

(35)

$$begin : \langle\ (NP\backslash S)/\ S/(NP\backslash S) : (\lambda R\lambda x.R(\lambda y\exists e.begin(e,x,y)),$$

$$\begin{bmatrix} QS_f: & \begin{bmatrix} QS_{f'}:\{x_1\ldots x_n\}, \\ QS_{a'}:\{\textbf{human}\} \end{bmatrix}, \\ QS_a: & \begin{bmatrix} QS_{f''}:\{y_1\ldots y_n\}, \\ QS_{a''}: & \begin{bmatrix} QS_{f'''}:\{z_1\ldots z_n\}, \\ QS_{a'''}:\{\textbf{event}\} \end{bmatrix} \end{bmatrix} \end{bmatrix})\rangle,$$

$$a\ novel : \langle\ S/(NP\backslash S) : (\lambda P.\exists z.novel(z) \wedge P(z),$$

$$\begin{bmatrix} QS_f:\{x_1\ldots x_n\}, \\ QS_a: & \begin{bmatrix} QS_{f'}:\{y_1\ldots y_n\}, \\ QS_{a'}:\{\textbf{artifact, read, write}\} \end{bmatrix} \end{bmatrix})\rangle \to$$

$$begin\ a\ novel : \langle\ NP\backslash S : (\lambda x.(\exists z.novel(z) \wedge (\exists e.begin(e,x,z))),$$

$$\begin{bmatrix} QS_f: & \begin{bmatrix} QS_{f'}:\{x_1\ldots x_n\}, \\ QS_{a'}:\{\textbf{human}\} \end{bmatrix}, \\ QS_a: & \begin{bmatrix} QS_{f''}:\{y_1\ldots y_n\}, \\ QS_{a''}: & \begin{bmatrix} QS_{f'''}:\{z_1\ldots z_n\}, \\ QS_{a'''}:\{\textbf{read, write}\} \end{bmatrix} \end{bmatrix} \end{bmatrix})\rangle$$

where: **read, write** $\leq$ **event**.

The functor with category $(NP\backslash S)/NP$ applies to the argument with category NP, to yield an $NP\backslash S$. The semantics of the functor (f) applies to the semantics of the argument (a) and results in $f(a)$. The qualia structure of the functor QS_e remains unaffected, as well as the selection restrictions of the subject argument ({**human**}). The selection restrictions of the object argument ({**event**}) are intersected with the qualia structure of the NP ({**artifact, read, write**}) which results in {**read, write**}, following **read, write** $\leq$ **event**.

5.7.2 'BMW announced ...'

This example demonstrates how a predicate combines with its subject argument. The transitive verb 'announced' combines with the noun phrase 'BMW' to constitute the incomplete sentence 'BMW announced ...'[10]

(36) $BMW : \langle\ NP : (bmw, QS_a:\{\textbf{company, spokesperson,...}\ \}) \rangle,$

    $announced : \langle\ (NP\backslash S)/NP : (\exists e.\lambda yx.announce(e,x,y),$

---

[10]Another way to look at it would be to assume a VP, and not a transitive verb, if one wishes to introduce bracketing. In that case the qualia structure of the object argument would have been specified. For our present purposes this is of no relevance.

$$\left[QS_f: \begin{array}{l} \left[\begin{array}{l} QS_{f'}:\{y_1 \ldots y_n\}, \\ QS_{a'}:\{\mathbf{human}\} \end{array} \right], \\ QS_a:\{\mathbf{event}\} \end{array} \right]$$

$BMW\ announced : \langle$ S/NP $: (\exists e.\lambda y.announce(e, bmw, y)$,

$$\left[QS_f: \begin{array}{l} \left[\begin{array}{l} QS_{f'}:\{y_1 \ldots y_n\}, \\ QS_{a'}:\{\mathbf{spokesperson}\} \end{array} \right], \\ QS_a:\{\mathbf{event}\} \end{array} \right] \rangle$$

where: $\mathbf{spokesperson} \leq \mathbf{human}$.

The functor with category (NP\S)/NP applies to the argument with category NP, to yield an S/NP. The semantics of the functor (f) applies to the semantics of the argument (a) and results in $f(a)$. Again, the qualia structure of the functor (QS_e) and the selection restrictions of the object argument ($\{\mathbf{event}\}$) remain unaffected. The selection restrictions of the subject argument ($\{\mathbf{human}\}$) are intersected with the qualia structure of the NP ($\{\mathbf{company, spokesperson}, \ldots\}$), which results in $\{\mathbf{spokesperson}\}$, following $\mathbf{spokesperson} \leq \mathbf{human}$.

6 Conclusion

The main criticism one may have against our work, is that it introduces a new combinatorial explosion in Categorial Grammar, that already suffers from the problem of spurious ambiguity (Hendriks 1993). A noun may have any finite number of values in its qualia roles, and this may cause computational problems. This is a valid objection. However, our objective is to derive all the possible readings a sentence could have. In other words, we show how compositionality might work with functions that operate on polysemous arguments. However, any research into the modelling of constraints on interpretation that are set by our knowledge of the (im)possibilities of the physical world is beyond the scope of this paper.

In addition, and related to the previous problem, the semantics / pragmatics interface remains problematic. It is not yet clear to what extent pragmatic inference is compositional, and in this paper we have restricted ourselves to aspects that can be dealt with compositionally[11].

However, we believe we did succeed in increasing the semantic potential of Categorial Grammar, while maintaining compositionality. We

---

[11]Some constraints on the interface of semantics and pragmatics may come from presuppositions. Bos, Buitelaar and Mineur (1995) study the parallel between qualia roles and presuppositions and takes coercion to operate on the presuppositions that lexical entries trigger. This does not effect the truth values for the entities that are denoted by these lexical items.

have dealt with polymorphism in lexical semantics. Instead of stipulating some n monomorphic types for one word, we adopted Pustejovsky's approach to stipulate one polymorphic type which through coercion will generate all n monomorphic types. Such an approach explains in part the creative use of language, which we find, for instance, in the use of metonymy. On the other hand, we acknowledged that Pustejovsky's approach will not be helpful in cases of strict homonymy (bank/bank).

References

Apresjan, J. 1973. Regular Polysemy. *Linguistics* (142).

Bar-Hillel, Y. 1953. A quasi-arithmetical notation for syntactic description. *Language* 29:47–58.

Bartsch, R. 1987. The construction of Properties under Perspectives. *The Journal of Semantics*, 5:293–320.

Bayer, S. 1994. The Coordination of unlike Categories. Paper of a conference presentation at the 1993 LSA meeting in Los Angeles, May.

Bierwisch, M. 1982. Semantische und konzeptuelle Repräsentation lexikalischer Einheiten. In *Untersuchungen zur Semantik*, ed. R. Ružička and W. Motsch, 61–99. Berlin: Akademie-Verlag.

Bos, J., P. P. Buitelaar and A.-M. Mineur. 1995. Bridging as Coercive Accommodation. In *Computational Logic for Natural Language Processing—Workshop Proceedings*, ed. Suresh Manandhar et.al. South Queensferry, Scotland, 3rd - 5th April, 1995

Buitelaar, P. P., and A. M. Mineur. 1994. Coercion and Compositionality in Categorial Grammar. In *Proceedings of the 9th Amsterdam Colloquium*, ed. P. Dekker and M. Stokhof, 175–188. Amsterdam. ILLC.

Cardelli, L., and P. Wegner. 1985. On Understanding Types, Data Abstraction, and Polymorphism. *Computing Surveys* 17(4):22–29.

Chomsky, Noam. 1957. *Syntactic Structures*. Janua linguarum, Ser. minor, Vol. 4. 's Gravenhage: Mouton.

Copestake, A., and E. Briscoe. 1992. Lexical Operations in a Unification-Based Framework. In *Lexical Semantics and Knowledge Representation. Lecture Notes in Artificial Intelligence 627*, ed. J. Pustejovsky and S. Bergler, 22–29. Berlin. Springer Verlag.

Dowty, David R. 1979. *Word Meaning and Montague Grammar*. Dordrecht, Holland: Reidel.

Gabbay, D. 1991. *Labelled Deductive Systems*. Oxford University Press. (to appear).

Hendriks, Herman. 1993. *Studied Flexibility*. Doctoral dissertation, Institute for Logic, Language and Information, Amsterdam, December.

Ingria, R. J. 1990. The Limits of Unification. In *Proceedings of the 28th Annual Meeting of the ACL*, 194–204.

Moortgat, M. 1992. Labelled Deductive Systems for categorial theorem proving. Technical Report OTS-WP-CL-92-003, Onderzoeksinstituut voor Taal en Spraak, Utrecht.

Moortgat, M. J. 1988. *Categorial Investigations. Logical and Linguistic Aspects of the Lambek Calculus*. Vol. 9 of Groningen-Amsterdam Studies in Semantics. Dordrecht, Holland: Foris.

Montague, Richard. 1974. In Richard Thomason, editor, *Formal Philosophy. Selected papers of Richard Montague*. New Haven: Yale University Press.

Morrill, Glyn V. 1994. *Type-logical Grammar*. Dordrecht: Kluwer Academic Publishers.

Nunberg, G. D. 1979. The nonuniqueness of semantic solutions: Polysemy. *Linguistics and Philosophy* 3.

Pollard, C., and I. A. Sag. 1987. *Information-based Syntax and Semantics*. Vol. 1, Fundamentals of CSLI Lecture Notes, Number 13. CSLI.

Pullum, G. K., and A. M. Zwicky. 1986. Phonological Resolution of Syntactic Feature Conflict. *Language* 62:751–773.

Pustejovsky, J. 1995. *The Generative Lexicon*. Cambridge: MIT Press.

Pustejovsky, J., and P. Anick. 1988. On the Semantic Interpretation of Nominals. In *Proceedings Coling88*. Boedapest.

Sowa, J. 1992. Logical structures in the lexicon. In *Lexical Semantics and Knowledge Representation. Lecture Notes in Artificial Intelligence*, ed. J. Pustejovsky and S. Bergler, Vol. 627, 577–613. Berlin: Springer Verlag.

Verschuur, L. 1994. Flexibly Disambiguating Metonymy. Technical Report 52, ITK, Tilburg, June. MMC Research Report.

Weinreich, U. 1964. Webster's third: A critique of its semantics. *International Journal of American Linguistics* 30:405–409.

7

Underspecified First Order Logics

HIYAN ALSHAWI

1 Logics of Underspecification

Traditional theories of natural language semantics involve mapping natural language sentences into expressions of an unambiguous artificial language. An alternative is to express the semantics of sentences via expressions of a representation which is still ambiguous but for which the underspecification of meaning can be formalized precisely. In this paper, we present two closely related examples of such a formal language. These are both first order languages with non-deterministic truth valuation. We will give model-theoretic definitions of the semantics of these languages and discuss their relevance to natural language interpretation.

1.1 Partiality and Underspecification

The logics we introduce are intended to capture one of two types of partiality that seem necessary if models of language and reasoning are to reflect incomplete knowledge and vagueness of expression. Much of the work addressing partiality has concentrated on partiality of the information under which expressions (of logic or natural language) are interpreted. This has often taken the form of partial models and the resulting partial logics (Blamey 1986, Langholm 1988). The development of Situation Semantics (Barwise and Perry 1983) and the use of 'infons' to express no more and no less information than is necessary can also be seen in terms of partiality of models.

Another type of partiality, and the one we are concerned with here, is partiality in the specification of denotations for expressions of a for-

---

I would like to thank Richard Crouch for his collaboration on the search for a formal semantics for QLF. The work presented here is an outgrowth of that collaboration. I am indebted to Fernando Pereira, Kees van Deemter and two anonymous referees for many valuable comments on drafts of the paper.

Semantic Ambiguity and Underspecification
Kees van Deemter and Stanley Peters, editors
Copyright © 1995, CSLI Publications

mal or natural language. By this we mean that the association between expressions and denotations may be a relation rather than a function as is normally the case for formal languages. More concretely, we are interested in considering languages for which a truth valuation relation (holding between formulae, models, assignments, and truth values) is defined in such a way that it need not be a function even when only traditional (non-partial) models are considered.

The main motivation behind this is the observation that natural languages exhibit such partiality with respect to quantifier scope, anaphora, underspecified relations, and so on. It would therefore seem reasonable that expressions of formal languages that are meant to capture the meaning of natural language sentences should also exhibit this type of partiality.

The different types of partiality (partiality of models and semantic underspecification) should not be viewed as incompatible alternatives. It seems plausible, and indeed desirable, for them to be present in the same formal system for modeling language and reasoning.

1.2 Our Approach

Here we present two simple first order languages, UL1 and UL2, with a full specification of their model-theoretic semantic definition. Although relatively simple, these languages allow certain kinds of underspecification relevant to natural language, including quantifier scope and simple anaphoric reference, to be expressed in a straightforward way. The two languages are closely related, having the same kinds of underspecification but differing in how they express it. For UL1 this is done with meta-variables, making it suitable for computer implementations using variable bindings. UL2, on the other hand, makes use of 'annotation' operations on strings, and illustrates how it might be possible to provide a direct underspecified semantics for natural language strings. We use the label "UL" to refer generically to UL1 and UL2. Another, more complex, notation for the type of underspecification we are concerned with here is QLF (quasi logical form, Alshawi and Crouch 1992). This has been used in a computational setting to represent a wide variety of phenomena in natural language but because of the complexity of this formalism, only a sketch of its formal semantics was provided by Alshawi and Crouch.

We are also concerned with gradual refinement of meaning. The idea is that interpretations of sentences can start off being vague but can be made more specific as more information becomes available or as interpretation decisions are made. Underspecification is thus identified with having too many possible truth values. At the other end of the spectrum our non-deterministic truth valuation gives rise to uninterpretability, i.e., no possible truth values. A pleasant side effect of the non-deterministic approach to valuation is that we are free to apply the semantic definitions of UL1 and UL2 to *all* strings rather than first defining well-formed formulae. (So UL1 and UL2 are really interpretation schemes rather than formal languages in the traditional sense.)

The approach to defining the valuation relation is closely related to a construction called supervaluation introduced by van Fraassen (1966) for dealing with sentences having 'truth value gaps' arising from the use of non-referring names. We use a different notation for constructing supervaluations, but more significantly, we apply supervaluations to provide truth values to a different class of formulae, ones corresponding to underspecified or partial interpretations of sentences. Familiarity with van Fraassen's treatment of non-referring names is not necessary for understanding our semantic definitions for UL1 and UL2.

Here, then, is a summary of what UL is intended to provide:

- a representation for capturing the kinds of underspecification pervasive in natural language;
- a conservative extension of traditional logic with a formal semantics compatible with traditional logic;
- a representation that is similar to natural language (UL2 succeeds here better than UL1);
- a formal distinction between underspecification and uninterpretability;
- a notion of refinement of interpretation compatible with the formal semantics.

Because of the close relationship between UL1 and UL2, we cover UL2 quickly in section 3 after a longer description of UL1 in section 2. In section 4 we discuss some of the issues involved in basing natural language semantics on the underspecified logics.

2 The Underspecified Logic UL1

2.1 Strings and Valuation

The assignment of truth values to expressions of UL1 will be in terms of a relation V:

$$V(\alpha, m, g, u)$$

where α is a finite string of symbols, m a model, g an assignment and u a 'basic' truth value, i.e., a member of $\{0, 1\}$. The valuation relation V holds when u is a possible basic truth value for α in model m under the assignment g. The relation V is the analogue of the 'usual' truth valuation function $[| \ldots |]$ for which we might have written valuation under m and g as $[\!|\ \alpha\ |\!]^g_m = u$. It will be convenient to write $V(\alpha, m, g, u)$ as $V^g_m(\alpha, u)$.

The model m provides, as usual, an interpretation function I for mapping individual and predicate constants to elements and relations in the domain of discourse. An assignment g maps variables to elements of the domain (among other things, as explained shortly). The functions I and g allow standard atomic formulae to receive truth values in the usual way.

Underspecification in UL1 arises mainly from 'meta-variables', though this is not essential to the partiality aspects as will be illustrated later with the definition of UL2. A string interpreted as a UL1 expression can be semantically underspecified if there are one or more occurrences of meta-variable symbols $X_1, X_2, X_3, \ldots$ in the expression. An assignment function g, as well as mapping object level variables to entities in the domain, also maps meta-variables to UL1 expressions *without* meta-variables. The way we define the valuation relation V, and the notion of truth depending on it, means that this unusual use of assignments will not lead to problems.

In fact, we do not need to go through the usual step taken when defining a formal language of explicitly giving a definition for well-formed formulae of UL1. The reason for this, and for not needing to have meta-variables corresponding to different types of expressions (terms, etc.), is that expressions that are not "well formed" simply turn out to have an empty set of basic truth value possibilities. This is why we stated above that V was a relation between *strings*, models, assignments and values.

However, for a string to receive any basic truth values when viewed as an expression of UL1, it will need to include symbols from the following alphabets, as these are referred to in the definition of V:

constants	$a, a_1, a_2, \ldots$
predicates	$p, p_1, p_2, \ldots$
variables	$x, x_1, x_2, \ldots$
meta-variables	$X, X_1, X_2, \ldots$
indices	$i, i_1, i_2, \ldots$
others	$\wedge, \vee, \neg, \rightarrow, (,), \text{','}, :, \forall, \rightsquigarrow$

Of the 'other' symbols, $\wedge, \vee, \neg, \rightarrow, \text{','}, (,)$, are parallel to their use in 'standard' notation. However, unlike many formal treatments in which parentheses '(' and ')' are treated as meta-language symbols, or just taken for granted, here we treat '(' and ')' as object-language symbols. We will use the term 'variable' on its own to refer to object-level variables, not meta-variables.

A couple of informal remarks about the notation might be make it easier to follow the precise statement of the semantics. The notation for universal quantification and its scope will use the symbols $\forall$ and :. For example, $i_1 : i_2 : \ldots$ will indicate, that a 'restricted quantified term' $\forall^{i_1} p_1(i_1)$ has wider scope than another, $\forall^{i_2} p_2(i_2)$. Expressions $p \leadsto X$ are 'restricted referential terms', analogous to, say, pronouns or perhaps specific indefinite descriptions in natural language (though the semantics of indefinites is somewhat tricky, see Ludlow and Neale 1991). For expressions with such a referential term to get truth values, the meta-variable X will have been assigned to a 'referent' symbol, e.g., a constant a.

2.2 Semantics of UL1

As hinted above, the semantics of UL1 is given in a slightly unconventional way by immediately providing a definition of V for strings of symbols. We will use Greek letters α, β, $\ldots$ to stand for arbitrary finite strings of symbols (i.e., these are meta-variables at the definition level not to be confused with meta-variables $X_1, X_2, \ldots$ of the UL1 language).

For convenience, the definition makes use of a function I_g on constants and variables which is such that

$I_g(\alpha) = I(\alpha)$ if α is a constant,
$I_g(\alpha) = g(\alpha)$ if α is a variable,

otherwise $I_g(\alpha)$ is undefined. In particular, I_g is undefined for meta-variables.

A 4-tuple will be a member of V *only* in accordance with the following rules:

(1) a. $V_m^g(\neg\alpha, 1)$ if $V_m^g(\alpha, 0)$.
   b. $V_m^g(\neg\alpha, 0)$ if $V_m^g(\alpha, 1)$.
   c. $V_m^g(\alpha \vee \beta, 1)$ if $V_m^g(\alpha, 1)$ or $V_m^g(\beta, 1)$.
   d. $V_m^g(\alpha \vee \beta, 0)$ if $V_m^g(\alpha, 0)$ and $V_m^g(\beta, 0)$.
   e. $V_m^g(\alpha \wedge \beta, 1)$ if $V_m^g(\alpha, 1)$ and $V_m^g(\beta, 1)$.
   f. $V_m^g(\alpha \wedge \beta, 0)$ if $V_m^g(\alpha, 0)$ or $V_m^g(\beta, 0)$.
   g. $V_m^g(\alpha \to \beta, 1)$ if $V_m^g(\beta, 1)$ or $V_m^g(\alpha, 0)$.
   h. $V_m^g(\alpha \to \beta, 0)$ if $V_m^g(\alpha, 1)$ and $V_m^g(\beta, 0)$.
   i. $V_m^g((\alpha), u)$ if $V_m^g(\alpha, u)$.
   j. $V_m^g(p(\alpha_1, \ldots, \alpha_n), 1)$ if
      I_g is defined for $\alpha_1, \ldots, \alpha_n$ and $(I_g(\alpha_1), \ldots, I_g(\alpha_n)) \in I(p)$.
   k. $V_m^g(p(\alpha_1, \ldots, \alpha_n), 0)$ if
      I_g is defined for $\alpha_1, \ldots, \alpha_n$ and $(I_g(\alpha_1), \ldots, I_g(\alpha_n)) \notin I(p)$.
   l. $V_m^g(p_2(\alpha_1, p_1 \leadsto \beta, \alpha_2), u)$ if
      β is a constant a or a variable x,
      $V_m^g(p_1(\beta), 1)$, and
      $V_m^g(p_2(\alpha_1, \beta, \alpha_2), u)$.

m. $V_m^g(i : \alpha, 1)$ if
α contains exactly one occurrence of $\forall^i$, preceding a substring
β of α, and $V_m^{g'}(\beta' \to \alpha', 1)$ for all g' like g except possibly at
x, where x is a variable not appearing in α, β' is $\beta[i/x]$, and
α' is $\alpha[\forall^i \beta/x][i/x]$.

n. $V_m^g(i : \alpha, 0)$ if
α contains exactly one occurrence of $\forall^i$, preceding a substring
β of α, and $V_m^{g'}(\beta' \to \alpha', 0)$ for some g' like g except possibly
at x, where x is a variable not appearing in α, β' is $\beta[i/x]$,
and α' is $\alpha[\forall^i \beta/x][i/x]$.

o. $V_m^g(X(\alpha_1, \ldots, \alpha_n), u)$ if
$g(X) = p$ and $V_m^g(p(\alpha_1, \ldots, \alpha_n), u)$.

p. $V_m^g(p_2(\alpha_1, p_1 \rightsquigarrow X, \alpha_2), u)$ if
$\beta = g(X)$ is a constant a or a variable x and
$V_m^g(p_2(\alpha_1, p_1 \rightsquigarrow \beta, \alpha_2), u)$.

q. $V_m^g(X\alpha, u)$ if
$g(X) = i_1 : i_2 : \ldots i_n :$ and $V_m^g(i_1 : i_2 : \ldots i_n : \alpha, u)$
(n can be zero).

Since these rules define V completely, if an assignment maps a meta-variable to the 'wrong' type of expression, in the sense that none of the rules apply, then V will simply not yield a value for the (sub)expression under that assignment.

Rules (1a) to (1h) correspond to the usual ones for sentential connectives. The valuation of a string under a model and assignment may lead to zero, one, or two basic truth values in the V relation, depending on the valuation of substrings. Rule (1i) gives the semantics for matching brackets.

Rules (1j) and (1k) correspond to the standard ones for atomic formulae in first order logic. Such formulae receive a value when $\alpha_1 \ldots \alpha_n$ are term-like expressions. Rule (1o) is for underspecified predicates (cf. compound nominals in English).

Rules (1l) and (1p) give the valuation for 'resolved' and 'unresolved' referential terms. Note that no value arises if the referent (a or $g(X)$) does not satisfy the restriction predicate p. Examples of the interpretation of such expressions, and those for quantification, are given shortly below.

Rules (1m), (1n), and (1q) are for universal quantification (existential quantification can, as usual, arise in combination with $\neg$). Rules (1m) and (1n) give the semantics for an expression α in which the quantified term $\forall^i \beta$ has wide scope over all other quantified terms in α. The semantics is given recursively in terms of the valuation for an expression α', the string resulting from α by substituting x for the quantified term and any occurrences of its index i. The quantificational force of the rules arises from varying the assignment of x in the same way as the valuation rules often given for first order logic. The choice of 'restriction' substring β may be forced by bracketing, or the string α may yield values for different substrings β, the latter situation being similar to an attachment ambiguity in natural language. (1q) allows expressions with underspecified scope to receive values when the meta-variable X is assigned to an appropriate list of indices.

A more virulent form of underspecification could have been used instead of the restricted form of rules (1o), (1p), and (1q). We could have replaced these rules by a single rule (2) for interpreting meta-variables.

(2) $V_m^g(\alpha, u)$ if
       α contains a meta-variable X, $g(X) = \beta$ and
       $V_m^g(\alpha', u)$, where $\alpha' = \alpha[X/\beta]$.

However, the resulting logic would give rise to unpredictable valuations that seem to have little to do with the underspecified expression. For example, the expression $p_2(p_1 \rightsquigarrow X)$, under an assignment g with

$$g(X) = a_1) \vee p_3(a_3$$

so that $\alpha' = p_2(p_1 \rightsquigarrow a_1) \vee p_3(a_3)$ can yield

$$V_m^g(p_2(p_1 \rightsquigarrow X), 1)$$

even if $I(p_2) = \phi$ in m. We therefore prefer, for now, to restrict the assignment of meta-variables to particular kinds of strings, leaving more unrestricted form of underspecification for further research.

2.3   Examples

We now consider a few examples illustrating the truth values that strings can get (under different assignments) when the valuation rules for V are applied to the strings. In the examples, we extend the alphabet of constant symbols p_1, a_1, etc., to also include English words. When we say that an expression of UL corresponds to an English sentence, or a reading of a sentence, this is to be taken as informal explanation. We are not making any claims about linguistic analysis with regard to, say, the appropriateness of an event-based analysis or the adequacy of a first order semantics for natural language.

(3) $saw(female \rightsquigarrow X_1, male \rightsquigarrow X_2)$

Expression (3) corresponds to something like *she saw him*. This will get a valuation under a model and assignment mapping X_1 to a constant a_1 satisfying the predicate *female* and mapping X_2 to a constant a_2 satisfying the predicate *male*. The valuation will be 1 or 0 depending on whether $(a_1, a_2) \in I(saw)$ in the model. No values are produced by meta-variable assignments to constants a_1 and a_2 not satisfying *female* and *male*. Readers interested in the application of this type of underspecification to bound anaphora and strict and sloppy readings may wish to consult Alshawi 1990 or Alshawi and Crouch 1992.

The use of quantification notation with indices is illustrated by (4), which corresponds to *all ducks groom themselves.*

(4) $i : groom(\forall^i duck(i), i)$

This is a fully specified expression equivalent to (5) in standard notation.

(5) $\forall x(duck(x) \rightarrow groom(x, x))$

Expression (4) receives values according to rules (1m) and (1n) with restriction $\beta = duck(i)$ and scope $\alpha = groom(\forall^i duck(i), i)$.

To illustrate underspecified quantifier scope, consider (6)

(6) $X_1 \neg X_2 like(\forall^{i_1} child(i_1), \forall^{i_2} dog(i_2))$

The values for this expression will include all those arising from the expressions (7a), (7b), (7c), and (7d).

(7)   a. $\neg i_1 : i_2 : like(\forall^{i_1} child(i_1), \forall^{i_2} dog(i_2))$
       b. $i_1 : i_2 : \neg like(\forall^{i_1} child(i_1), \forall^{i_2} dog(i_2))$
       c. $i_1 : \neg i_2 : like(\forall^{i_1} child(i_1), \forall^{i_2} dog(i_2))$
       d. $i_2 : \neg i_1 : like(\forall^{i_1} child(i_1), \forall^{i_2} dog(i_2))$

The formula (6) corresponds to a scope-ambiguous *all children don't like all dogs.* Expression (7a) corresponds to a first order formula with widest scope negation and two universal quantifiers (*it is not the case that all children like all dogs*), and (7b) to one with narrow scope negation (*no child likes any dog*). Expression (7c) corresponds to the reading *for all children there's a dog the child doesn't like*, while (7d) corresponds to *for all dogs there's a child that doesn't like it.*

Expression (8) illustrates underspecified predicates.

(8) $X_1 rare(\forall^i X_2(female \rightsquigarrow X_3, i) \wedge duck(i))$

It corresponds to something like *her ducks are rare* in which the relationship between the female and the ducks is not explicit. In a more specific version, we might have *raises* or *studies* instead of X_2.

The string 9a is ambiguous as more than one valuation rule can apply to it (assuming the substrings yield values). It will have the union of truth values for the more disambiguated expressions (9b) and (9c).

(9)   a. $\alpha \vee \beta \wedge \gamma$
       b. $(\alpha \vee \beta) \wedge \gamma$
       c. $\alpha \vee (\beta \wedge \gamma)$

Finally, here is an example comparing disjunction with underspecification arising from a referential term. Let α and β be the strings

$\alpha = (p_2(a_1) \wedge p_1(a_1)) \vee (p_2(a_2) \wedge p_1(a_2))$
$\beta = p_2(p_1 \rightsquigarrow X).$

In the models m_1, m_2, m_3 and m_4 as indicated, with only two individuals $I(a_1)$ and $I(a_2)$, we can get the following sets of possible truth values:

$$m_1 : I(p_1) = \{I(a_1), I(a_2)\}, I(p_2) = \{I(a_1)\}$$
$$\alpha \mapsto \{1\}; \ \beta \mapsto \{1, 0\}$$
$$m_2 : I(p_1) = \{\}, I(p_2) = \{I(a_1), I(a_2)\}$$
$$\alpha \mapsto \{0\}; \ \beta \mapsto \{\}$$
$$m_3 : I(p_1) = \{I(a_1), I(a_2)\}, I(p_2) = \{\}$$
$$\alpha \mapsto \{0\}; \ \beta \mapsto \{0\}$$
$$m_4 : I(p_1) = \{I(a_1), I(a_2)\}, I(p_2) = \{I(a_1), I(a_2)\}$$
$$\alpha \mapsto \{1\}; \ \beta \mapsto \{1\}.$$

2.4 Truth and Monotonicity

With our non-deterministic valuation relation, we need a non-standard definition of truth, in a model, for a string interpreted as a UL1 expression. The definition will be given in terms of the *supervaluation* of an expression with respect to a model, this being a function that collects the possible values allowed by the valuation relation. The supervaluation S_m induced by a model m is defined as follows:

$$S_m(\alpha) = \{u : V(\alpha, m, g, u) \text{ for some } g\}$$

S_m will map a UL1 expression α to one of

- $\{1\}$ (truth),
- $\{0\}$ (falsehood),
- $\{0, 1\}$ (underspecification, or 'truth value gap'), or
- $\{\}$ (uninterpretability).

The special case in which $S_m(\alpha) = \{1\}$ regardless of the model corresponds to the definition of logical validity. Related notions like entailment can be defined analogously.

Although the term 'supervaluation' was introduced by van Fraassen (1966) in his paper on non-referring names, I am also using it for the construction I proposed independently for underspecification because of the close relationship between the two constructions. The third value $\{0, 1\}$ (underspecification) corresponds to what van Fraassen called a 'truth value gap' and is the one assigned to expressions with non-referring names. The fourth value does not arise in his system. A treatment of non-referring constants (i.e., a constant a for which the interpretation function I is not defined) that is consistent with UL would give $\{\}$ (uninterpretable) for predications involving such constants. Informally, then, we would treat such expressions as incomprehensible rather than ambiguous.

We say that a UL1 formula α is "always interpretable" if $S_m(\alpha)$ is non-empty for all m. If we restrict ourselves to formulae which are always interpretable, the above definition of validity coincides with the classical one for standard first order logic using ordinary valuations. (This can be shown with a proof similar to one given by van Fraassen because his system is limited to the case of always interpretable formulae.) So all valid theorems like $\models \alpha \vee \neg\alpha$ and $\models (\alpha \to \beta) \leftrightarrow (\beta \vee \neg\alpha)$ are still valid. An investigation of the appropriate notions to support deduction with strings that are not always interpretable is beyond the scope of the present paper.

It is perhaps worth mentioning that if a fully specified expression with a free variable, for example $p(x)$, gets a supervaluation of $\{1\}$ or $\{0\}$ for a model, then the expression would also be taken as true or false, respectively, under the classical interpretation. However, the supervaluation of an open formula $p(x)$ can be $\{1, 0\}$ for some models where the classical treatment yields false. This seems no less intuitive to me than the classical interpretation.

For UL1 formulae α and α', we say that α *subsumes* α' (and write $\alpha \sqsupseteq \alpha'$) iff α' can be obtained from α by instantiations of meta-variables in α. The basic result relevant to monotonic semantics is 'downwards' monotonicity of basic values: If $\alpha \sqsupseteq \alpha'$ then $S_m(\alpha) \supseteq S_m(\alpha')$ for all models m.

'Upwards monotonicity' of partial truth functions (i.e., increase of certainty with further specification) follows from this: If $\alpha \sqsupseteq \alpha'$ and α' is always interpretable, then $S_m(\alpha') = \{1\}$ (or $\{0\}$) if $S_m(\alpha) = \{1\}$ (respectively $\{0\}$). That is, if an expression is true in a model, then further specification cannot make it false or underspecified; and if it is false, further specification cannot make it true or underspecified.

3 The Underspecified Logic UL2

3.1 Annotations

We now define a logic that is similar to UL1 except that it makes use of annotation (or lack thereof) rather than meta-variables. The idea is that a formula can be further specified by annotations such as referents or indications of scope. The UL1 valuation rules that do not mention meta-variables (i.e., rules 1a to 1n) will be part of the definition of UL2.

In this context, an annotation function is a function f from strings to strings which operates as follows:

$$f : \alpha \longmapsto \alpha_1 \gamma \alpha_2$$
for α_1, α_2 with $\alpha = \alpha_1 \alpha_2$.

In other words, an annotation splices a string γ into a string α.

For the definition of UL2, we restrict annotations to those of the form:

- $\alpha_1 \alpha_2 \longmapsto \alpha_1 p \alpha_2$, for a predicate constant p;

- $\alpha_1 \rightsquigarrow \alpha_2 \longmapsto \alpha_1 \rightsquigarrow \beta\,\alpha_2$, where β is a constant or a variable;
- $\alpha_1\alpha_2 \longmapsto \alpha_1 i : \alpha_2$, for an index i.

$\alpha 1$ and $\alpha 2$ are allowed to be the null string.

These annotation functions correspond to UL1 meta-variable assignments, respectively, in the cases of underspecified predicates (1o), unresolved referential terms (1p), and underspecified quantifier scope (1q). In UL2, predicates, referents, and scope lists can simply be missing from a string. (For scope indices, (1q) corresponds to applying the annotation function n times.) UL2 is thus really the same as UL1 except that an annotation is used instead of an assignment to a meta-variable.

In UL2, the examples (3), (4), (6), and (8) can be expressed by (10a), (10b), (10c), and (10d) respectively:

(10) a. $saw(female \rightsquigarrow, male \rightsquigarrow)$
      b. $groom(\forall^i duck(i), i)$
      c. $\neg like(\forall^{i_1} child(i_1), \forall^{i_2} dog(i_2))$
      d. $rare\forall^i(female \rightsquigarrow, i) \wedge duck(i)$

3.2 Semantics of UL2

We define valuation for UL2 in terms of a relation V' between strings, models, assignments and basic truth values:

$$V'(\alpha, m, g, u).$$

Models, m, and truth values, u, are the same as before. Assignment functions g do not need to be defined for meta-variables, so they are just the same as the ones normally used in the semantics of first order logic. The definition of V' is as follows:

$V'(\alpha, m, g, u)$ holds iff $V(\beta, m, g, u)$ holds according to the rules (1a) to (1n), for some string β obtained from α by a finite number of applications of annotation functions.

The definition of V' for α involves strings longer than α, so the question arises as to whether the definition will lead to an infinite regress. However, it can be seen that V' is indeed well-defined because (i) we will only apply the rules (1a) to (1n) to strings that are a finite number of symbols longer than α, and (ii) we can see by inspection that the recursion on V in (1a) to (1n) is all on strings that are shorter than the string in the consequent of these rules, so the recursion will always terminate (either with the rules of atomic formulae, or when no rules apply).

Supervaluation, truth, *et cetera* for UL2 are then defined as was done for UL1, except V' is used instead of V:

$$S'_m(\alpha) = \{u : V'(\alpha, m, g, u) \text{ for some } g\}$$

Applying annotations to a string can result in a string which does not receive a value according to the valuation rules. This is similar to assigning a meta-variable to an inappropriate expression but in both cases it does not affect the supervaluation of an expression with respect to a model.

4 Underspecified Logic and Natural Language

4.1 UL in Semantic Representation

The definition of UL2 can be seen as a first step to providing a 'direct' semantics for natural language sentences that does not involve translation into a separate formal language. Under such a view, natural language would already be a 'formal language'. Annotations could be added (brackets, quantification indices, referents for anaphora, etc.) turning an input language string into a longer one interpretable with the same rules without destroying the words or their order in the original string. Different annotated versions of the string then correspond to different readings (if they yield values for some model).

Alternatively, we can first translate natural language into expressions of a underspecified logic like UL1, or include meta-variables in our annotations of an NL sentence. This gives us a way of making (contextually motivated) interpretation choices explicit. For this purpose we could have split the assignment g into a 'normal' variable assignment function g' and an assignment function G for meta-variables. Different assignments G then correspond to 'readings', the choice of G being related to the context in which the sentence was uttered.

Other ways of expressing underspecified semantic representations have been proposed, for example the use of meta-statements about the semantic representation expressions (Reyle 1991). However, we hope that the approach taken here will lead to a simpler and more direct view of semantic underspecification.

4.2 Monotonic Semantics

An important measure of the utility of an underspecified meaning representation for natural language is its suitability for modeling gradual refinement of meaning. In particular, we are interested in a 'monotonicity' property whereby elaboration of a meaning representation corresponds to restricting the interpretation possibilities that it allows. We gave a precise definition for monotonicity for UL1. In the general case, it corresponds to defining a relation $\sqsupseteq$ ('less specific' or 'subsumes') between expressions of the language so that if $E_1 \sqsupseteq E_2$ then E_2 has a more constrained denotation than E_1 in the sense of taking fewer values in the valuation relation. Stepwise refinement of an underspecified expression E_1 then corresponds to a series of expressions $E_1 \sqsupseteq E_2 \sqsupseteq E_3 \ldots$

If the representation language is to be convenient for modeling such refinement of meaning, it is desirable that the syntactic relationship between E_1 and E_2 be a simple one, for example for E_2 to include E_1 as a subexpression.

For both UL1 and QLF, $\sqsupseteq$ is defined in terms of instantiation of meta-variables in expressions of these languages, and monotonicity amounts to saying that whenever E_2 is a more instantiated version of E_1 then the truth-value relation for E_2 is a subset of that for E_1. The corresponding monotonicity property in the case of QLF, although never completely formalized, proved to be computationally useful in designing algorithms for natural language interpretation and generation. For example, the algorithms for quantifier scoping and reference resolution both took an underspecified input formula containing meta-variables and simply provided bindings for these meta-variables as scoping and reference resolution decisions were made.

It is not, of course, necessary for a language with underspecified denotations (that is, a non-function denotation relation) to have a syntactic construction for monotonically refining denotations; we are simply claiming that this is a useful property for representations modeling processes involved in natural language interpretation.

4.3 Grammaticality and Uninterpretability

Uninterpretability, and the way meaningful expressions are defined via the semantics rather than through well formed formulae, seems to cause a problem by blurring the distinction between meaningless and ungrammatical strings. It is not clear, as far as truth values are concerned, that this is really a distinction we want to make. As support for this position, consider answers given to yes-no questions. It would seem to me that the correct answer to a yes-no question that is either syntactically illformed or semantically uninterpretable (for example one that violates a referential term restriction) is, in both cases, "that doesn't make sense" (i.e. {}). The alternatives, "yes", "no", or "I don't know", (corresponding roughly to our other supervaluation possibilities {1}, {0} and {0, 1}) seem inappropriate in both cases because they suggest that the question was understood.

Why is it, then, that syntactic gibberish (for example, a sentence permuted to produce 'word salad') seems to carry less content than a sentence with failed presuppositions? Informally, the reason may be that the latter goes further towards reaching an interpretation (in that the valuation rules are largely applicable), only requiring the cost of accepting violations at isolated points in the interpretation process. For word salad, on the other hand, little, if any, of the interpretation process (the application of valuation rules) can take place, requiring a greater leap to assume a reasonable interpretation. This is consistent with the observation that syntactically marginal sentences, appearing for various reasons in non-fluent language, are often just as easy (or easier) to interpret than well formed sentences violating presuppositions. While truth-theoretic semantics, with two or four values, may be appropriate for studying ambiguity and underspecification, it is probably too blunt an instrument to provide a fine grained set of distinctions for classifying failure to understand sentences.

References

Alshawi, H. 1990. Resolving Quasi Logical Forms. *Computational Linguistics* 16:133–144.

Alshawi, H., and R. Crouch. 1992. Monotonic Semantic Interpretation. In *Proceedings of the 30th Annual Meeting of the Association for Computational Linguistics*. Newark, Delaware.

Barwise, J., and J. Perry. 1983. *Situations and Attitudes*. Cambridge, Massachusetts: The MIT Press.

Blamey, S. 1986. Partial Logics. In *The Handbook of Philosophical Logic*, ed. D. Gabbay and F. Guenthner. Dordrecht: Reidel.

Langholm, T. 1988. *Partiality, Truth and Persistence*. CSLI Lecture Notes Number 15. Stanford: CSLI Publications.

Ludlow, P., and S. Neale. 1991. Indefinite Descriptions: In Defense of Russell. *Linguistics and Philosophy* 14:171–202.

Reyle, U. 1991. Dealing with Ambiguities by Underspecification: A First Order Calculus for Unscoped Representations. In *Proceedings of the Eighth Amsterdam Colloquium*. Amsterdam.

van Fraassen, B.C. 1966. Singular Terms, Truth-Value Gaps and Free Logic. *Journal of Philosophy* 63:481–495.

8

Semantic Ambiguity and Perceived Ambiguity

Massimo Poesio

1 The Combinatorial Explosion Puzzle

The alternative syntactic readings of a sentence such as (1) probably number in the hundreds, whereas sentences such as (2) would have hundreds of thousands scopally distinct readings if all permutations of scope-taking sentence constituents were considered admissible readings. Yet, human beings appear able to deal with these sentences effortlessly.

(1)   We should move the engine at Avon, engine E1, to Dansville to pick up the boxcar there, then move it from Dansville to Corning, load some oranges, and then move it on to Bath.

(2)   A politician can fool most voters on most issues most of the time, but no politician can fool all voters on every single issue all of the time.

This COMBINATORIAL EXPLOSION PUZZLE is one of the most fundamental questions to be addressed by a theory of language processing, and a substantial problem for developers of Natural Language Processing (NLP) systems. NLP systems which have to perform non-linguistic actions like booking a flight in response to an user's utterance must

---

I owe the realization of the importance of the phenomenon of deliberate ambiguity to my advisor Len Schubert and to Graeme Hirst. Special thanks to Robin Cooper, Richard Crouch, Kees van Deemter, Howard Kurtzman, David Milward, Manfred Pinkal for many discussions on the topic; and to two anonymous reviewers whose suggestions went well beyond the call of duty. I am also grateful to James Allen, Ariel Cohen, Tim Fernando, Janet Hitzeman, Peter Lasersohn, Barbara Partee, Enric Vallduvi, Sandro Zucchi, and the audiences at the University of Rochester, the University of Edinburgh, ICSI Berkeley, Carnegie-Mellon University, University of Stuttgart, SRI Cambridge, Tilburg University, and University of Saarbruecken. All errors are of course mine. This work was in part supported by the LRE Project 62-051 FraCaS.

Semantic Ambiguity and Underspecification
Kees van Deemter and Stanley Peters, editors
Copyright © 1995, CSLI Publications

arrive at the preferred interpretation of their input in the context of the conversation, if one exists; otherwise, they must realize that their input is ambiguous and request a clarification. Examples such as (1) and (2) indicate that such systems cannot adopt the strategy of generating all the readings of an ambiguous sentence and choosing one of them, because there are too many such readings. In order to develop such systems, a theory of ambiguity processing is needed that is consistent both with linguistic facts and with what is known about the way humans disambiguate.

Work on UNDERSPECIFIED REPRESENTATIONS such as Alshawi 1992, Poesio 1991, Reyle 1993 differs from other work on discourse interpretation (Charniak and Goldman 1988, Hobbs et al. 1990, Pereira and Pollack 1991, Dalrymple et al. 1991, Hwang and Schubert 1993, Kamp and Reyle 1993) because it is explicitly motivated by the Combinatorial Explosion Puzzle, and aims at a unified account of all interpretation processes, including those that occur before the scope of all operators has been determined. The work on underspecified representations holds the promise of yielding a better account of the way interpretive processes such as scope disambiguation and reference resolution affect each other.

The existing theories of underspecification, however, have been motivated almost exclusively by computational considerations. For example, the semantics assigned to underspecified representations is designed so as to support those inferences that are deemed useful for an economical approach to disambiguation, rather than being motivated by an analysis of the phenomenon of ambiguity. In this paper I explore some of the issues that arise when trying to establish a connection between work on underspecification and, on the one side, work on ambiguity in semantics; on the other side, work on ambiguity in the psychological literature. A theory of underspecification is developed 'from first principles', i.e., starting from a definition of what it means for a sentence to be semantically ambiguous and from what we know about the way humans deal with ambiguity. The goal is to arrive at a linguistically and cognitively plausible theory of ambiguity and underspecification that, in addition to computational gains, may provide a better understanding of how humans process language.

Many of the issues discussed in this paper arose from work on the TRAINS project at the University of Rochester, in which the issues of language comprehension, planning, and reasoning encountered in task-oriented natural language conversations are studied (Allen et al. 1995). The theory of ambiguity proposed in this paper is the basis for the implemented surface discourse interpretation system SAD-93, used in the TRAINS-93 demo system. SAD-93 is described in Poesio 1994.

2 Ambiguity in Natural Language

2.1 Ambiguity and Grammar

2.1.1 Meaning, Sense, and Ambiguity

The dictionary definitions of the terms AMBIGUITY and AMBIGUOUS try to capture the intuition that an expression is ambiguous if 'it has multiple meanings'. The need for a more precise definition is seen once one begins to consider the differences between ambiguity and VAGUE-NESS or INDETERMINACY, for example, or to define notions such as HOMONYMY and POLYSEMY.[1]

One problem to be tackled in attempting to make precise the definition of ambiguity is to say what 'meanings' and 'senses' are. In modern semantic theory, the meaning assigned to an expression by a grammar is a function from contexts (or DISCOURSE SITUATIONS) to SENSES. Roughly speaking, the discourse situation provides a value for all context-dependent aspects of the sentence; the sense of a sentence (what we get once we resolve its context-dependent aspects) tells us under which circumstances in the world the sentence is true or false.[2]

Not all notions of 'sense' employed in the literature can serve as the basis for a definition of ambiguity. For example, of the various notions of PROPOSITION (the sense of sentences), the simplest is the one according to which propositions are truth values. But if we were to use this notion of sense, the sentence *Kermit croaked*, ambiguous between a reading in which Kermit utters a frog-like sound and a reading in which he dies, would be classified as unambiguous with respect to all models in which Kermit has both the property of dying and the property of producing a frog-like sound, or he (it) has neither property. In other words, in providing a definition of ambiguity we find the same need for a fine-grained notion of sense that has been observed in connection with the semantics of attitude reports.[3] A model-theoretic definition of ambiguity requires a finer-grained notion of proposition than simply truth values. In most recent semantic theories, senses are intensional objects; the simplest way of achieving intensionality is to use functions

---

[1] A sentence is INDETERMINATE, or UNSPECIFIED, if it is definitely true or false, but could be made more specific. Zwicky and Sadock 1975 bring the example of the sentence *My sister is the Ruritanian secretary of state*, which is indeterminate as to whether "...my sister is older or younger than I am, whether she acceded to her post recently or some time ago, whether the post is hers by birth or by merit," and so forth. The point is that these additional facts do not affect the truth value of the sentence. I will reserve the term UNDERSPECIFIED for sentences which may have different truth values depending on the way the facts are 'filled in' (see below).

[2] For a discussion of these assumptions, see Kaplan 1977, Barwise and Perry 1983, or chapter 2 of Pinkal 1995.

[3] In the case of attitude reports, the problem is to make sure that if *John is tall* and *John is stupid* are both true in a model, *Bill believes that John is tall* does not entail *Bill believes that John is stupid* in that model.

from possible worlds or situations to referents as one finds in Montague Grammar, where, for example, propositions are functions from possible worlds to truth values. This simple form of intensionality will be sufficient for the purposes of the present paper.[4]

2.1.2 A Semantic Theory of Ambiguity

The notions of 'meaning' and 'sense' just discussed are the starting point for the semantic account of the notion of ambiguity and its relation with vagueness developed by Pinkal (1985, translated as Pinkal 1995). Pinkal introduces the notion of INDEFINITENESS to subsume both ambiguity and vagueness. He defines indefiniteness as follows:

Definition 2.1 *A sentence is* SEMANTICALLY INDEFINITE *if and only if in certain situations, despite sufficient knowledge of the relevant facts, neither "true" nor "false" can be clearly assigned as its truth value.*

Pinkal formalizes the notion of indefiniteness in terms of PRECISIFICATION.[5] According to Pinkal, a linguistic expression is semantically indefinite if it has the potential for being made *precise* in distinct ways. For example, the sentence *The Santa Maria is a fast ship* containing the degree adjective *fast* can be 'made precise' (and assigned a definite truth value) either with respect to a context in which 'fast' is interpreted as 'fast for a modern ship', in which case the sentence is false; or with respect to a context in which 'fast' is interpreted as 'fast for a ship of her age', in which case the sentence can be true or false, depending on the class of comparison. Let p and q be two propositions. Proposition p is MORE PRECISE THAN q iff (i) p is true (false) under all states of the world under which q is true (false), and (ii) p is true or false under certain circumstances under which q is indefinite. The notion of PRECISIFICATION is defined as follows:

Definition 2.2 *Expression α in context c* CAN BE PRECISIFIED *to s if and only if (i) s is a sense that α can assume according to its meaning; and (ii) s is more precise than the sense of α in c.*

The connection between indefiniteness and precisification is provided by the following PRECISIFICATION PRINCIPLE:

Precisification Principle : A sentence is of indefinite truth value in a context if and only if it can be precisified alternatively to "true" or to "false".

---

[4]More complex notions of propositions have been introduced in the literature on propositional attitudes, such as those used in Situation Semantics (Barwise and Cooper 1993) or Property Theory (Turner 1992).

[5]A treatment of ambiguity and vagueness in terms of precisifications was proposed early on in Fine 1975.

which Pinkal also reformulates as follows:

Extended Precisification Principle An expression is semantically indefinite in a context iff it can assume different senses in that context.

Pinkal does not equate ambiguity with vagueness. His theory includes, in addition to the notion of precisification, additional criteria to differentiate different forms of ambiguity, as well as differentiating 'pure' ambiguity from 'pure' vagueness. The intuition he is trying to capture is that "...whether an expression is ambiguous or only vague is a question that cannot be cleared once and for all. Indefiniteness is perceived as ambiguity when alternative precisifications are predominant, as vagueness when an unstructured continuum presents itself"

Ambiguity (Pinkal) : If the precisification spectrum of an expression is perceived as discrete, we may call it ambiguous; if it is perceived as continuous, we may call it vague.

Pinkal identifies two fundamental types of ambiguity, according to whether an expression has, or does not have, a 'wider' sense that could be taken as most 'basic'. For example, *ball* does not have a wide sense of 'round object and dancing party', whereas *American* may either mean 'person from the US' or 'person from the American continent'. He classifies expressions like *American* which have a wider sense as having a MULTIPLICITY OF USE, whereas expressions such as *ball* or *green* which do require precisification are called NARROWLY AMBIGUOUS. The cases of ambiguity in the narrow sense are further distinguished in two classes, depending on whether they are subject to the PRECISIFICATION IMPERATIVE. Although the two interpretations of *green* are distinct, it is possible of an object to be both green in the 'ripe' sense and green in the 'color' sense: for example, a green apricot. An object cannot, however, be a 'band' both in the musical group sense and in the piece of tape sense. Pinkal proposes that polysemous expressions behave like *green*, and calls all of these expressions P-TYPE AMBIGUOUS; expressions like *band*, however, are true homonyms, and therefore he calls them H-TYPE AMBIGUOUS. These latter are defined as follows:

Precisification Imperative: An expression is H-type ambiguous iff its base level is inadmissible, i.e., if it requires precisification.

For my purposes, it is not particularly important whether the difference between homonimy and polysemy is completely captured by the Precisification Imperative; what is important is the claim that H-type ambiguous expressions need precisification, and furthermore, that the Precisification Imperative "is a second order phenomenon ...that lies beyond the scope of a strictly truth-conditional approach." (Pinkal 1995, p. 86–87). I will provide independent reasons for including a formalization of reasoning in context in a treatment of ambiguity, and I will argue that such formalization provides the necessary tools to express the Precisification Imperative.

To summarize, a sentence is H-type ambiguous iff the grammar assigns to it distinct precisifications (senses) in a given discourse situation, and if the 'base level' of the expression requires precisification. Thus, the sentence *Kermit croaked* is considered ambiguous since in the 'empty context' that provides all the senses of the expression according to the grammar G for English, that sentence has two senses: the proposition that attributes to Kermit the property of producing the sound that frogs produce, and the proposition that attributes to Kermit the property of dying. (I am assuming here that terms like *Kermit* refer unambiguously.) On the other hand, the sentence *Kermit kissed Miss Piggy* would be considered unambiguous with respect to the same context.

Although Pinkal is only concerned with lexical ambiguity, the precisification approach can also be used to classify as ambiguous sentences which have more than one structural analysis (like the sentence *They saw her duck*) or are scopally ambiguous (cfr. the sentence *Everybody didn't leave*) whenever the grammar assigns to them more than one sense. I will discuss how Pinkal's system can be extended to scopal and referential ambiguity.

2.1.3   The Disjunction Fallacy

It is important to realize that saying that a sentence is ambiguous in a context if it has distinct precisifications is not the same as saying that an ambiguous sentence is equivalent to the disjunction of its distinct precisifications. Intuitively, in uttering S, whose two precisifications are the propositions P and Q, a speaker may have meant P or she may have meant Q, but the following does not hold:

$$[[A \textbf{ means that } P] \lor [A \textbf{ means that } Q]] \equiv [A \textbf{ means that } [P \lor Q]]$$

To treat an ambiguous sentence in such a way would be tantamount to propose that an ambiguous sentence has a single sense in any given discourse situation, namely, the proposition that is true at a situation if either of the distinct interpretations of the sentence is true at that situation; but according to the definition above, an ambiguous sentence is one which has more than one sense at a discourse situation. For example, according to the definition of ambiguity discussed above, the listener of an utterance of *They saw her duck* could either interpret the speaker as saying that the contextually determined set of individuals denoted by the pronoun *they* saw a contextually specified female person lowering herself, or as saying that that set of individuals saw the pet waterfowl of that female person. According to the disjunction theory, instead, the listener would attribute to the speaker of that sentence a single meaning, albeit a disjunctive one; namely, that it was either the case that *they* saw a contextually specified female person lowering herself, or it was the case that *they* saw the pet waterfowl of that female person.[6]

I will refer to the idea that a semantically ambiguous sentence denotes the disjunction of its alternative interpretations as the DISJUNCTION FALLACY. The disjunction fallacy can be found in the literature in two forms. Its 'purest' form is the hypothesis that the interpretation process literally involves generating all of the senses of an expression and putting them together in a disjunction. In this form, the disjunction 'theory' is not simply counterintuitive; it doesn't explain the combinatorial explosion puzzle at all. As far as I know, this 'explicit' form of the theory has only been discussed jokingly. One can find in the literature, however, an 'implicit' form of the disjunction theory, in theories of underspecification that assign to underspecified expressions a semantics that makes them equivalent to the disjunction of their readings. One such proposal is Poesio 1991; the semantics of UDRSs is also disjunctive (Reyle 1993).

2.2 Perceived Ambiguity

As noted by Hirst (1987), the discussions of ambiguity processing in the NLP literature tend to ignore the fact that humans are aware that sentences can be ambiguous, and that they can exploit the ambiguity of sentences for rhetorical effect. Raskin, for example, claims (1985) that humor crucially relies on ambiguity. He discusses examples such as the following (p. 25-26):

(3)   The first thing that strikes a stranger in New York is a big car.

The joke relies on two assumptions about human processing: first, that the clause *the first thing that strikes a stranger in New York* gets interpreted before the end of the sentence, with *strikes* receiving the 'surprise' interpretation; and second, that the reader, upon reading *is a big car*, will go back, produce a second interpretation, and entertain both interpretations simultaneously. The joke could not be understood unless the reader were able to entertain the two interpretations of the sentence simultaneously. These jokes can exploit other forms of ambiguity, e.g., scopal ambiguity, as in *Statistics show that every 11 seconds a man is mugged here in New York City. We are here today to interview him.*

---

[6]A cute example of the problems with the theory is presented in Stallard 1987. If ambiguous sentences were to denote the disjunction of their readings, then the answer to the question *Does the butcher have kidneys?* should always be 'yes'.

The reader's ability to entertain more than one interpretation simultaneously is exploited in poetry, as well (Su 1994). The linguistic articles discussing ambiguity are another literary form that exploits this possibility. Examples such as *They saw her duck* are a clear case of deliberate ambiguity; the whole point of these examples is to show that a sentence can have more than one interpretation.

I will call the situation in which a listener arrives at more than one interpretation for an utterance PERCEIVED AMBIGUITY. A situation in which B perceives an utterance as ambiguous may result in B's appreciating the joke, the poetic phrase, or the point of the linguistic example; if the ambiguity is not perceived as intended, B may say saying something like *This is not very clear,* or perhaps *This sentence is ambiguous.* This situation can be informally characterized as follows:

Definition 2.3 *An utterance U by conversational participant A addressing conversational participant B in a discourse situation D is* PERCEIVED AS AMBIGUOUS IN D *by B if B's processing of U in D results in B obtaining distinct interpretations for U.*

The phenomenon of deliberate ambiguity suggests that the solution to the Combinatorial Explosion Puzzle cannot be that humans either generate only one interpretation at a time by using some clever heuristics, or do not generate any interpretation at all. Humans entertain more than one interpretation at a time, and they may not be able to choose one among them. This conclusion is also supported by psychological results. There is evidence, for example, that during both lexical processing and syntactic processing several hypotheses are generated in parallel, and only later filtered on the basis of contextual information (Swinney 1979, Crain and Steedman 1985, Kurtzman 1985, Schubert 1986, Gibson 1991).[7] Kurtzman and MacDonald (1993) suggest a similar model for scope disambiguation. As far as reference interpretation is concerned, there is some evidence that all pragmatically available referents become active before a referent is identified (see, e.g., Spivey-Knowlton et al. 1994).

These facts are consistent with the view of discourse interpretation taken in Artificial Intelligence, in which processes such as reference resolution or lexical disambiguation are modeled in terms of defeasible inference, which may result in alternative hypotheses. Examples include the theories of the effects of semantic priming on lexical disambiguation, as formalized, e.g., in Hirst's ABSITY system (Hirst 1987) or, more recently, in statistically based terms; the theories about the effects of local focusing on the choice of pronoun antecedents such as Grosz et al. 1983;

---

[7]The results about lexical disambiguation are fairly well established, but there is some controversy about syntactic processing. A constrasting view on syntactic disambiguation is discussed in Frazier and Fodor 1978.

the work on temporal interpretation by Asher, Lascarides, and Oberlander (see, e.g., Lascarides et al. 1992); and work on scopal disambiguation such as Kurtzman and MacDonald 1993, Poesio 1994.

2.3 Semantic Ambiguity versus Perceived Ambiguity

A preliminary and, I hope, uncontroversial conclusion I draw from the discussion on deliberate ambiguity and ambiguity processing is that a theory of ambiguity that aims at explaining the Combinatorial Explosion Puzzle needs to be concerned both with the interpretation that the grammar assigns to a sentence—i.e., what it means for a sentence to be semantically ambiguous—and with the process by which interpretations are generated, i.e., with what it means for an utterance to be perceived as ambiguous. On the one hand, the theory must explain why the disambiguation process will not generate all semantically available interpretations; on the other hand, it must predict that more than one interpretation will be generated. This conclusion is the central idea of this paper, indeed, what gives the paper its title. The inclusion of a theory of disambiguation will also remedy one of the omissions in Pinkal's theory, namely, how to formalize the Precisification Imperative.

The discussion of perceived ambiguity supports a stronger claim, namely, that semantic ambiguity and perceived ambiguity are distinct notions, in the sense that whereas a model of semantic ambiguity has to express the truth-conditional properties of an expression, the reasoning processes involved in disambiguation, and that may lead to a perceived ambiguity, consist of defeasible inferences that are not supported by the semantics of ambiguous expressions.

The distinction I intend to draw, then, is as follows. Semantic ambiguity is part of the specification of the grammar of a language; most, if not all, sentences are semantically ambiguous, but their ambiguity need not be noticed by listeners, and in fact it is typically discovered only by linguistic research. Perceived ambiguity, on the other hand, is a result of the interpretation process, that is defeasible in nature, and may therefore result in more than one interpretation in cases of miscommunication or when the speaker constructs the context appropriately to serve a rhetorical purpose, as in the puns presented above.

Some readers may wonder why the developer of a NLP system should be concerned with perceived ambiguity, i.e., with generating all of the contextually available interpretations of a sentence. The answer is that certain applications need this information. Consider the following example, again from the TRAINS domain. Say that the user utters *move the engine to Avon*, and say that two different engines have been discussed during the elaboration of the current part of the plan. Clearly, we do not want the system to just come out with a plausible guess about which engine was meant: instead, we want it to recognize the ambiguity and ask for clarification. In general, all systems that engage in conversations with their users need to be able to recognize an ambiguity, to ask for clarifications when necessary rather than guess one possible interpretation, and to make their own output unambiguous. (Of course, the theory of contextual disambiguation must be such that no spurious ambiguities are obtained.)

3   The Underspecification Hypothesis

All theories of semantic interpretation based on Montague's general program as exposed in *Universal Grammar* (Montague 1970) assume that the grammar of a language $\mathcal{L}$ specifies two homomorphisms: one between syntactic trees and a DISAMBIGUATED LANGUAGE $\mathcal{DL}$, and a second one between the disambiguated language and objects of the model M (the senses). These two homomorphisms can be composed, thus making the intermediate level of the disambiguated language dispensable. The grammar assigns to an ambiguous expression of $\mathcal{L}$ distinct expressions of $\mathcal{DL}$, each of which has a unique interpretation.

A direct implementation of this strategy in an NLP system would require generating all senses of an ambiguous sentence-string, which would be clearly problematic. Many NLP systems, instead, make use of heuristic methods that generate only one interpretation and ignore the alternatives. These heuristics work fairly well fairly often; such systems, however, won't be able to perceive an ambiguity even when it would be helpful to do so. Other systems therefore split the semantic problem of computing all the interpretations of a sentence from the processing problem of generating these interpretations in context, by making use of an intermediate, UNDERSPECIFIED level of representation. One of the earliest examples of underspecified representations is the 'Logical Form' of Schubert and Pelletier 1982. The representation for (4) proposed by Schubert and Pelletier, shown in (5), is a typical example of these underspecified representations: quantifiers are left in place and the referent for the definite description *the tree* is not specified.

(4)   Every kid climbed the tree.
(5)   [<every kid> climbed <the tree >]

In more recent years, underspecified representations similar to Schubert and Pelletier's have been used by Hobbs and Shieber 1987, Fenstad *et al.* 1987, in Allen's textbook (1987) and, most recently, in the Core Language Engine (Alshawi 1992); the 'uninterpreted conditions' produced during the intermediate steps of the DRT construction algorithm in Kamp and Reyle 1993 can be considered underspecified representations as well.

Underspecified representations were originally conceived as a way to solve a problem in system implementation, namely, separating 'context-independent' from 'context dependent' aspects of the interpretation, thus making either part reusable for different applications. Since the motivation was strictly computational, the underspecified representations used in most NLP systems are little more than data structures, in the sense that they do not have a interpretation other than the one provided by the procedures that interpret them. These representations 'encode' the ambiguity of a sentence in the sense that that sentence has the reading r iff that reading can be generated by repeatedly applying 'construction rules' to the underspecified representation.

In recent years, there has been growing interest for the hypothesis that the ability to encode multiple interpretations in an underspecified language may be (part of) the explanation of the Combinatorial Explosion Puzzle. The idea is that humans, as well, make use of an underspecified language that can encode distinct meanings implicitly, and therefore do not need to generate all of these meanings. A semantically ambiguous sentence, therefore, need not cause processing problems, because it is not necessarily *perceived* as ambiguous in the sense discussed in the previous section. I will call this assumption the UNDERSPECIFICATION HYPOTHESIS:

Underspecification Hypothesis : Human beings represent semantic ambiguity implicitly by means of UNDERSPECIFIED REPRESENTATIONS that leave some aspects of interpretation unresolved.

My goal in the rest of the paper is to spell out the Underspecification Hypothesis both as a theory of grammar and as a theory of discourse interpretation. I assume that the hypothesis is correct, and try to answer questions such as: what kind of language are underspecified representations? What is their semantics? And what kind of inferences are done with them?

The novel aspect of this work is that the answers I give are based on the discussion of semantic ambiguity and perceived ambiguity in the previous section. I hypothesize that underspecified representations are used by humans as the translation of expressions that are indefinite in the sense of Pinkal, and assign them a semantics that reflects this hypothesis. I assume that the disambiguation process consists of defeasible inferences, and examine the characteristics of defeasible reasoning with underspecified representations. Although the same position towards disambiguation and defeasibility has been adopted in the Core Language Engine, most of the issues I discuss have not been mentioned so far in the discussion on underspecified representations.

In the literature on underspecification, one often finds the argument that providing a semantics to underspecified representations is necessary because disambiguation requires inference, and therefore a 'logic of underspecification' is needed (Poesio 1991, Reyle 1993, van Deemter 1991). However, it is not at all clear whether the process of disambiguation involves much semantically justified reasoning; disambiguation seems to consist mostly of defeasible inferences. It is fair to say that the debate on this issue is very open at the moment, as certified by a number of recent panels on the subject. But whatever the final conclusion on this topic will be, it is clear that under the perspective that the grammar of a language $\mathcal{L}$ is a mapping from elements of $\mathcal{L}$ to underspecified representations, the semantics of these underspecified representations becomes a central aspect of the specification of the grammar. Furthermore, the semantics of underspecified representations must be based on an analysis of semantic ambiguity, otherwise we wouldn't even know whether the form of underspecified representation we develop does the job it is supposed to do.

4 An Underspecified Theory of Ambiguity, Part I: Lexical Ambiguity

The simplest way to illustrate my implementation of the Underspecification Hypothesis is to start with lexical ambiguity. In this section, I will present a theory of grammar that makes use of an underspecified language to encode the 'ambiguity potential' of lexically ambiguous expressions, as well as a simple formalization of lexical disambiguation as defeasible inference over underspecified representations. In the next section I will show how to extend the approach presented here to deal with expressions that exhibit other forms of semantic ambiguity.

I start with lexical disambiguation for expository purposes only. Lexical ambiguity is the one case of ambiguity for which a 'generate and test' strategy may well be compatible with the psychological results, and therefore it the one for which the need for underspecified representations is least clear. I will only discuss cases of lexical ambiguity in the narrow sense, which is perhaps the least interesting case of lexical indefiniteness. Discussing lexical disambiguation, however, is the simplest way to explain how underspecified representations can be given a semantics related to Pinkal's proposals about ambiguity, and how to do defeasible reasoning with underspecified representations. In the next sections I will generalize the approach introduced here to cases of ambiguity for which the underspecified approach is much more plausible. Furthermore, at least one theory of lexical disambiguation, Hirst's proposal (1987), makes use of 'Polaroid words' which are essentially underspecified interpretations of lexical items.

4.1 A Lexically Underspecified Grammar

The presentation of a lexically underspecified grammar below is centered on the example of (H-type) lexical ambiguity discussed above, the verb *croak*, which can take two precisifications. Let $\mathcal{L}$ be the language which consists of the single sentence *Kermit croaked*. This sentence is H-type ambiguous because it admits of two precisifications and it is subject to the precisification imperative. A 'Montagovian' grammar MG would map (syntactic analyses of) the sentence into distinct expressions of a 'disambiguated language' $\mathcal{DL}$, each of which denotes a function from discourse situations into intensional objects of the appropriate type (in this case, propositions). A grammar UHG that subscribes to the Underspecification Hypothesis, on the other hand, maps syntactic analyses of expressions of $\mathcal{L}$ into a single expression of a 'lexically underspecified language' $\mathcal{LXUL}$. The semantics of $\mathcal{LXUL}$ is based on the Precisification Principle: expressions of $\mathcal{LXUL}$ denote at each discourse situation a *set* of senses of the type they would be assigned by a Montagovian grammar.[8] The lexically underspecified language $\mathcal{LXUL}$ has the following ingredients:

Terms : the constant k.

Predicates: $\mathbf{croak}_U$, $\mathbf{croak}_1$, and $\mathbf{croak}_2$.

Atomic Formulas: If t is a term and P is a predicate, then $P(t)$ is a formula.

Formulas: If Φ and Ψ are formulas, then $\neg\Phi$ and $\Phi \wedge \Psi$ are formulas.

Note that in addition to two predicates $\mathbf{croak}_1$ and $\mathbf{croak}_2$, corresponding to the disambiguated senses of *croak*, the language includes an 'underspecified' predicate $\mathbf{croak}_U$. The interpretation function for $\mathcal{LXUL}$, $[\![\alpha]\!]^{M,d}$, is defined as follows. Let $M = \langle U, F \rangle$ be a model just like the one that would be used for a disambiguated language $\mathcal{DL}$. The interpretation function $[\![\alpha]\!]^{M,d}$ assigns to an expression α of $\mathcal{LXUL}$ a value with respect to M and a discourse situation d.

- $[\![k]\!]^{M,d} = \{f_k\}$, where f_k : s → the denotation of 'Kermit' in s
- $[\![\mathbf{croak}_1]\!]^{M,d} = \{f_1\}$, where f_1 is a function such that $f_1(s)$ → the set of croaking objects in s
- $[\![\mathbf{croak}_2]\!]^{M,d} = \{f_2\}$, where f_2 is a function such that $f_2(s)$ → the set of dying objects in s}
- $[\![\mathbf{croak}_U]\!]^{M,d} = \{f_1, f_2\}$
- $[\![P(t)]\!]^{M,d} = \{f \mid$ for a $g \in [\![P]\!]^{M,d}$ and an $h \in [\![t]\!]^{M,d}$ $f(s) = g(s)[h(s)] \}$

---

[8]The technique of assigning sets of senses as the denotation of sentences dates back at least to Hamblin (1973), who used it to extend Montague's fragment to questions.

- $\llbracket \Phi \wedge \Psi \rrbracket^{M,d} = \{f \mid \text{for a } g \in \llbracket P \rrbracket^{M,d} \text{ and an } h \in \llbracket t \rrbracket^{M,d}, f(s) = 0$ if $g(s) = 0$ or $h(s) = 0$; $f(s) = 1$ if both $g(s) = 1$ and $h(s) = 1 \}$
- $\llbracket \neg \Phi \rrbracket^{M,d} = \{f \mid \text{for } g \in \llbracket \Phi \rrbracket^{M,d}, f(s) = 1$ if $g(s) = 0$; $f(s) = 0$ if $g(s) = 1 \}$

The language $\mathcal{LXUL}$ has been deliberately kept simple to make it clear that the underspecified languages I propose have two basic properties: (i) the value of an expression at a discourse situation is a set of senses of the type that a sense of that expression would have in a disambiguated language $\mathcal{DL}$; and (ii) expressions can be divided into expressions whose denotation at a discourse situation is a singleton set, such as k or $\mathbf{croak}_1$, and expressions such as $\mathbf{croak}_U$ that denote a non-singleton set. The latter expressions provide the interpretation for ambiguous expressions of $\mathcal{L}$.[9]

The clauses for application and the connectives show how ambiguity 'percolates up' from lexical items. The value of an expression like $\alpha(\beta)$ is obtained by taking the cross-product of the values of α and β, and it includes one function f per distinct pair of functions $\langle \alpha_1, \beta_1 \rangle$ in the denotations of α and β. The value assigned by the function f to the situation $\underline{s}$ is defined by applying a certain operation (in this case, application) to the values assigned to $\underline{s}$ by the functions α_1 and β_1. Thus, if both the denotation of α and the denotation of β are singleton sets, the denotation of $\alpha(\beta)$ is also a singleton set; otherwise, ambiguity 'multiplies,' as it where.[10] The same 'multiplication' technique is also used to define the denotation of connectives.[11]

The following grammar generates an underspecified representation of *Kermit croaked* by mapping the semantically ambiguous predicate *croaked* into an 'ambiguous' predicate of $\mathcal{LXUL}$ as follows:

- S $\rightarrow$ NP VP; VP′(NP′)
- NP $\rightarrow$ Kermit; k

---

[9]A word form can also be ambiguous because it is associated with lexical items of different syntactic categories: for example, *duck* can either be interpreted as a noun or as an verb, as shown by the example *They saw her duck*. I assume a syntactic ambiguity in these cases, i.e., I assume that the grammar assigns two syntactic analyses to *duck*, each of which would then get an interpretation in $\mathcal{LXUL}$.

[10]It is worth emphasizing a difference between the semantics just sketched and virtually all other approaches to underspecification I am aware of. $\mathcal{LXUL}$ does not serve as a 'meta-language' to be given a semantics in terms of the values assigned to the expressions of a 'disambiguated language'; instead, it has a semantics of its own, defined bottom-up, much like the semantics of $\mathcal{DL}$. The approach just sketched does not rely on the assumption that a 'disambiguated language' can be defined, which, in the light of Pinkal's treatment of indefiniteness, appears to be questionable. For example, for Pinkal, an expression is 'purely vague' if no natural precisification exists.

[11]I will ignore the issue of partiality, e.g., what happens when a conjunct has a value other than 0 or 1.

- VP → croaked; **croak**$_U$

The underspecified translation of *Kermit croaked* in $\mathcal{LXUL}$, **croak**$_U(k)$, denotes a set of two propositions at a situation d: the function that assigns 1 to a situation iff Kermit produced a frog-like sound in that situation, and the function that assigns 1 to a situation iff Kermit died in that situation. This makes the sentence indefinite in Pinkal's sense.[12] By contrast, an indeterminate sentence such as *Kermit is the Ruritanian secretary of state* would have a single sense at a given discourse situation.

Pinkal's Precisification Imperative is an attempt at making more precise the observation that human beings don't seem to have good intuitions concerning what follows from a H-type ambiguous sentence. Even when subjects are able to pass judgments about what follows from an ambiguous sentence, it is arguable that they do not give judgments concerning what follows from the underspecified representation: rather, they first generate one interpretation, then decide what follows from that. The conclusion that I would be inclined to draw is that a relation of semantic entailment capturing human intuitions can only be defined, if at all, between expressions whose interpretation is not subject to the Precisification Imperative. So, although it would be possible to define, for example, a 'strong' notion of entailment as what follows from all senses, this definition would be rather artificial. For this reason I will not attempt to define a notion of entailment between expressions of $\mathcal{LXUL}$; the readers interested in the issue are referred to Pinkal's book and to the discussion in van Deemter's dissertation (1991).

4.2 Discourse Interpretation and Perceived Ambiguity

4.2.1 Discourse Interpretation and Defeasible Reasoning

A theory of ambiguity processing solves the Combinatorial Explosion Puzzle if it does not require that all distinct interpretations of a semantically ambiguous sentence are actually generated. A grammar consistent with the Underspecification Hypothesis such as the one just discussed moves us one step towards that goal, since it only imposes the constraint that a single underspecified interpretation be generated.

On the other hand, we can conclude from the discussion of deliberate ambiguity and of the psychological work on ambiguity that a

---

[12]The denotation assigned to an indefinite sentence is a simplification of the denotation assigned to such a sentence in Pinkal 1995, which, in addition to the set of senses associated with a natural language expression, would also include a partial order relation of precisification between them. Such an order relation plays an important role in the meaning of vague sentences such as *Kermit is tall*, which has distinct senses depending on the degree of precision with which the discourse situation is specified, but a less important one in the cases of 'narrow sense' ambiguity with which I am concerned here.

psychologically plausible theory of ambiguity must also predict that more than one interpretation may become available in a given context, although the number of such interpretations will in general be much smaller than the number of possible semantic interpretations.

As discussed above, the view of discourse interpretation that I am going to take is the one typically found in the AI literature, according to which disambiguation involves the generation of (possibly distinct) hypotheses in parallel by means of defeasible inference. This perspective is found, for example, in the work on abductive discourse interpretation by Hobbs and colleagues (Hobbs et al. 1990), in the work on Bayesian disambiguation by, e.g., Charniak and his students (Charniak and Goldman 1988) and in the work on DICE and discourse interpretation by Asher, Lascarides, and Oberlander (Lascarides et al. 1992). Some of the formal models of defeasible reasoning that can be used to formalize the situation in which conflicting hypotheses are generated include Reiter's DEFAULT LOGIC (Reiter 1980), the abductive model (Hobbs et al. 1990), Bayesian Nets, and DICE Lascarides et al. 1992, Asher and Morreau 1991.

4.2.2 Lexical Disambiguation Using Defaults

As a model of defeasible reasoning, I adopt Reiter's Default Logic. In default logic, the process that generates defeasible hypotheses is seen as the computation of the EXTENSIONS of a DEFAULT THEORY (D,W) where D is a set of default inference rules and W is a set of formulas. I will formalize discourse interpretation as the process of generating the extensions of the theory (DI,UF), where DI—the DISCOURSE INTERPRETATION PRINCIPLES—are default inference rules, and UF is a set of expressions of an underspecified language like $\mathcal{LXUL}$. Let us ignore for the moment the fact that the formulas in UF are underspecified representations. The Discourse Interpretation Principles formalize the defeasible inferences that take place in discourse interpretation, such as disambiguating inferences. These rules are operations that map a set of wffs that allow of a certain number of interpretations into a new set of wffs with a more restricted number of interpretations. An example of Discourse Interpretation Principle is the following:

CROAK1-IF-FROG:

$$\frac{\mathbf{croak}_U(x) \wedge \mathbf{frog}(x) : \mathbf{croak}_1(x)}{\mathbf{croak}_1(x)}$$

This inference rule[13] reads: if the set of wffs UF includes the fact that the object x has the property $\mathbf{croak}_U$ and the property $\mathbf{frog}$, and if it is consistent to assume that the interpretation $\mathbf{croak}_1$ of $\mathbf{croak}_U$

---

[13]CROAK1-IF-FROG is an *open* inference rule. Such rules act like inference rule schemas.

was intended, then the inference rule CROAK1-IF-FROG produces a new set of wffs that includes the fact $\mathbf{croak}_1(x)$. The application of CROAK1-IF-HUMAN-LIKE would be blocked by the presence in UF of the wff $\neg\mathbf{croak}_1(k)$. Using Reiter's definition of extension in an 'intuitive' fashion, we can see that the default theory

$$(\{\text{CROAK1-IF-FROG}\}, \{\mathbf{croak}_U(k) \wedge \mathbf{frog}(k)\})$$

has the following (unique) extension:

$$\{\mathbf{croak}_U(k) \wedge \mathbf{frog}(k), \mathbf{croak}_1(k)\}$$

The denotation of a set of wffs $\{\Phi_1 \ldots \Phi_n\}$ will be defined as the denotation of the conjunction $\Phi_1 \wedge \ldots \wedge \Phi_n$ of these wffs. I also assume that the empty set of wffs denotes the function TRUE that is true at every situation. With this definition, and under the assumption that each 'unambiguous' interpretation of *croak* is incompatible with the others (i.e., under the assumption that $\mathbf{croak}_1(x) \vdash \neg\mathbf{croak}_2(x)$), the extension of (DF,UI) admits of only one denotation, the one under which the denotation of k produced a sound like the one frogs produce.[14]

A default theory always has an extension as long as all defaults are normal,[15] but it may have more than one extension if the set of Discourse Interpretation Principles contains two inference rules that both apply but generate a conflict. Consider, for example, the default theory consisting of a set of discourse interpretation principles DI′ that includes, in addition to CROAK1-IF-FROG, a second discourse interpretation principle (let's call it CROAK2-IF-HUMAN-LIKE) stating that the $\mathbf{croak}_2$ interpretation is plausible for human-like beings; and of a set of wffs UF′ including the fact that Kermit is a human-like being.

$$(\{\text{CROAK1-IF-FROG,CROAK2-IF-HUMAN-LIKE}\},$$
$$\{\mathbf{croak}_U(k) \wedge \mathbf{frog}(k), \mathbf{human\text{-}like}(k) \})$$

this theory would have two extensions:

1. $\{\mathbf{croak}_U(k) \wedge \mathbf{frog}(k), \mathbf{human\text{-}like}(k), \mathbf{croak}_1(k)\}$
2. $\{\mathbf{croak}_U(k) \wedge \mathbf{frog}(k), \mathbf{human\text{-}like}(k), \mathbf{croak}_2(k)\}$

Perceived ambiguity can now be redefined more precisely as the state that obtains when the default theory 'encoding' the listener's discourse interpretation processes has more than one extension; and the cases of deliberate ambiguity discussed in section §2 can be formalized as cases in which the speaker has 'reasoned about the other agent's reasoning,' as it were.

---

[14]See the discussion below.
[15]I.e., of the form $\alpha{:}\beta/\ \beta$.

4.2.3 Constraints on Discourse Interpretation and the Anti-Random Hypothesis

Once we start allowing discourse interpretation processes like those just discussed, the Underspecification Hypothesis is not sufficient to explain the Combinatorial Explosion Puzzle anymore. The UH does not rule out a theory of discourse interpretation in which after an underspecified interpretation has been obtained, all possible senses of a sentence are generated. In fact, many NLP systems work this way, and this is also true for such interpretation procedures as Hobbs and Shieber's scoping algorithm (Hobbs and Shieber 1987). In the framework for discourse interpretation just presented, theories of this kind could be formalized by including discourse interpretation principles that generate all the semantically justified interpretations at random. For the case of lexical disambiguation, for example, we could have a theory that includes the two following inference rules:

CROAK1-AT-RANDOM:

$$\frac{\mathbf{croak}_U(x)\colon \mathbf{croak}_1(x)}{\mathbf{croak}_1(x)}$$

CROAK2-AT-RANDOM:

$$\frac{\mathbf{croak}_U(x)\colon \mathbf{croak}_2(x)}{\mathbf{croak}_2(x)}$$

A theory of lexical disambiguation of this kind would simply produce all semantically justified interpretations of a sentence, and the Combinatorial Explosion Puzzle would remain a puzzle. To solve the puzzle, a theory of disambiguation must therefore supplement the Underspecification Hypothesis with constraints on discourse interpretation that ensure that only a few extensions are generated.

The constraints need not be the same for all classes of ambiguity. For certain classes of ambiguity, including perhaps lexical ambiguity,[16] the explanation may simply be that the disambiguation process is *incremental*, i.e., it takes place as the text is processed word by word or constituent by constituent, and each ambiguity is resolved *locally*; in this way, only a small number of alternative hypotheses have to be considered every time. For other classes of ambiguity, however, such as scopal ambiguity and referential ambiguity, incremental processing

---

[16]See however Hirst 1987.

does not seem to be the solution,[17] and different constraints must apply. In Poesio 1994, the following constraint was proposed:

Anti-Random Hypothesis (Informal) Humans do not randomly generate alternative interpretations of an ambiguous sentence; only those few interpretations are obtained that (i) are consistent with syntactic and semantic constraints and (ii) are suggested by the context.

The Anti-Random Hypothesis should be thought of as a 'meta-constraint' on theories of interpretation: if we intend to account for the Combinatorial Explosion Puzzle, we have to develop theories of interpretation (e.g., theories of parsing, or theories of definite description interpretation) that satisfy this constraint, i.e., in which discourse interpretation principles like CROAK1-AT-RANDOM and CROAK2-AT-RANDOM are not allowed.

In order to illustrate more concretely the difference between theories of discourse interpretation that satisfy the Anti-Random Hypothesis, and theories that do not, let us consider how one could formalize a theory of pronominal interpretation. A 'random' theory of pronoun interpretation would go as follows: first, compute all possible antecedents of the pronoun in the discourse. Then, generate an hypothesis for each of them, stating that the pronoun refers to that antecedent. Finally, rank these hypotheses according to their plausibility. A random hypothesis generation process usually leaves the task of choosing one hypothesis to plan recognition; the problem is that most often, the alternatives are equally plausible.

In contrast, CENTERING THEORY (Grosz et al. 1983) is an example of non-random pronoun interpretation theory. According to centering theory, each utterance establishes a 'backward looking center' (Cb), and a pronoun is by default interpreted to refer to the Cb. (I am glossing over a number of complexities here.) Such a theory would generate a single (or a few) hypothesis concerning the antecedent of a pronoun; the other possibilities, although semantically possible, would simply never come up. Examples of theories of definite description interpretation, tense interpretation, the interpretation of modals in discourse, and scope disambiguation that satisfy the Anti-Random Hypothesis are discussed in Poesio 1994.

---

[17]In *John gave a present to each child*, for example, the quantifier *each child* takes wide scope over *a present*. The interpretation of the sentence must therefore either remain partially underspecified until the quantifier is processed, or be revised when it is encountered. Similarly, in the sentence *John always invites MARY to the movies*, whose preferred interpretation is that whenever John goes to the movies, he invites Mary, the restriction of the adverb *always* is only provided by the PP *to the movies*.

The Anti-Random Hypothesis can be made more formal in the framework for discourse interpretation adopted here by introducing a slightly different syntax for default inference rules, one in which the underspecified condition is syntactically separated from additional contextual requirements such as the requirement in CROAK1-IF-FROG that the object in question be a frog:

CROAK1-IF-FROG

$$\frac{\mathbf{croak}_U(x) : \quad \mathbf{frog}(x) : \quad \mathbf{croak}_1(x)}{\mathbf{croak}_1(x)}$$

Except for the fact that one of the prerequisite wffs is 'singled out', an inference rule thus rewritten has the same interpretation as one of Reiter's default rules. We can then require the contextual requirements to be non-trivial (i.e., not satisfied in every situation) as follows:

Anti-Random Hypothesis A discourse interpretation theory (DI,UF) is *Anti-Random* iff for all discourse interpretation principles $\alpha{:}\beta{:}\delta/ \ \gamma$ in DI, β is not satisfied in every situation.

4.2.4 The Condition on Discourse Interpretation

The framework just introduced can also be used to formalize the 'second order' aspects of Pinkal's theory, such as the Precisification Imperative. The Precisification Imperative can be seen as imposing a constraint on the extensions of a discourse interpretation theory, namely, as the requirement that extensions include a 'disambiguating wff' like $\mathbf{croak}_1(k)$ for each H-type ambiguous constituent of the set UF such as $\mathbf{croak}_U(k)$. I will call this constraint CONDITION ON DISCOURSE INTERPRETATION. In first instance, the Condition on Discourse Interpretation might be formulated as follows, for the case of lexical ambiguity:

Condition on Discourse Interpretation (Preliminary): Each extension E of a discourse interpretation theory (DI,UF) must include, for each literal L in UF whose predicate is H-type ambiguous, a distinct DISAMBIGUATING LITERAL, i.e., a literal whose denotation is a single function among those in the denotation of L.

The definition of the Condition on Discourse Interpretation just given is not very general: it depends on the assumption that all cases of H-type ambiguity are originated by predicates. A simpler, and more general, formulation of the Condition on Discourse Interpretation can be obtained by generalizing the format for the discourse interpretation principles once more.

Default inference rules are typically used to augment a set of wffs with additional facts inferred by default: the fact that a particular bird flies, for example. But the purpose of discourse interpretation rules used for disambiguation, like CROAK1-IF-FROG, is to restrict the interpretation by eliminating certain readings. In this perspective, leaving the underspecified wffs around doesn't make much sense. I propose, therefore, to allow discourse interpretation principles to *rewrite* their 'triggering wff' whenever this wff encodes an H-type ambiguity, in addition to adding new wffs to a set. The more general format for discourse interpretation principles is as follows:

$$\frac{\alpha \,:\, \beta \,:\, \delta}{\sigma \,:\, \tau}$$

A rule of this form is an operation from sets of wffs into sets of wffs that, given a set W of wffs containing α and β and not containing $\neg\delta$,[18] produces a set W$'$ of wffs containing τ, and in which α has been replaced by σ. I will call α the TRIGGERING CONDITION. For example, a version of CROAK1-IF-FROG in which the triggering condition $\mathbf{croak}_U(x)$ is rewritten by the consequent $\mathbf{croak}_1(x)$ is as follows:

CROAK1-IF-FROG

$$\frac{\mathbf{croak}_U(x) \,:\quad \mathbf{frog}(x) \;:\; \mathbf{croak}_1(x)}{\mathbf{croak}_1(x) \,:}$$

If all disambiguation rules are rewritten in this format, a completely disambiguated extension can simply be characterized as one which doesn't contain any H-TYPE AMBIGUOUS WFFS. The notion of H-type ambiguous wff can be characterized either syntactically (by identifying certain syntactic constituents as specifying H-type ambiguity, and by classifying as H-type ambiguous a wff that contains one of these constituents)[19] or model-theoretically, e.g., by means of a function ι such that if X is a set of senses, $\iota(X)$ is 1 if the set of senses is admissible, 0 if it is inadmissible in Pinkal's sense. Whatever way we choose to define a H-type ambiguous wff, the Condition on Discourse Interpretation can now be formulated as follows:

Condition on Discourse Interpretation : An extension E of a discourse interpretation theory (DI,UF) cannot contain an H-type ambiguous wff.

---

[18]Strictly speaking, one should check that $\neg\delta$ does not occur in the extension itself, rather than in the intermediate sets of wffs. The cited form makes sense, however, once we adopt a 'syntactic' definition of extension (see below).

[19]Both the treatment of scopal ambiguity and the treatment of referential ambiguity proposed below are such that the constituents that introduce H-type ambiguity can be identified syntactically.

Notice that the statement of the Condition on Discourse Interpretation as a condition on pragmatic reasoning gives it the status of a felicity condition rather than of a hard constraint on interpretation.

4.2.5 Extensions, closure and consistency checking in an underspecified default theory

So far, I've been using the terminology from default logic as if the shift to an underspecified representation had no side effects, but this is not the case. Consider the way in which Reiter defines the notion of extension of a (closed)[20] default theory, for example:

Definition 4.1 *Let* $\Delta = (D, W)$ *be a closed default theory, so that every default of D has the form* $(\alpha:\beta_1,\dots, \beta_m/w)$ *where* $\alpha, \beta_1,\dots,\beta_m, w$ *are all closed wffs of L. For any set of closed wffs* $S \subseteq L$ *let* $\Gamma(S)$ *be the smallest set satisfying the following three properties:*

D1 $W \subseteq \Gamma(S)$

D2 $Th(\Gamma(S)) = \Gamma(S)$

D3 *If* $(\alpha:\beta_1,\dots, \beta_m/w) \in D$ *and* $\alpha \in S$ *and* $\neg\beta_1, \dots, \neg\beta_m \notin S$ *then* $w \in \Gamma(S)$.

A set of closed wffs $E \subseteq L$ *is an* EXTENSION *for* Δ *iff* $\Gamma(E) = E$, *i.e., iff E is a fixed point of the operator* Γ.

This definition crucially relies on the notion of deductive closure $Th(S)$, defined as the set of wffs $\{w \mid S \vdash w\}$; but what was said about semantic entailment holds for provability as well: no clear notion exists of what it means for an expression of an underspecified language to follow from a set of wffs of the same language. Two routes are open to us. One is to define a notion of 'underspecified provability' $\vdash_U$, and to use $\vdash_U$ to define an 'underspecified' notion of closure $Th_U(S)$. For example, we could say that w $\vdash_U$ w' iff for each expression w'' that denotes a single one of the interpretations of w, w'' $\vdash_U$ w'. This route is not very appealing, however, if for no other reason than that it is not clear that any way of defining an underspecified notion of provability will do.

The alternative is to adopt a new notion of extension that does not rely on deductive closure, i.e., one in which an extension is a fixed point of the operator Γ', which does not include condition D2 of the definition of Γ:

- Let $\Gamma'(S)$ be the smallest set satisfying the following two properties:

  D1 $W \subseteq \Gamma'(S)$

---

[20]A closed default theory is one in which no default contains open variables. All really interesting cases of default inference rules include such variables; but Reiter derives the definition of the extension of an 'open' default theory from the definition of extension for closed theories.

D3 If $(\alpha:\beta_1,\ldots,\beta_m/w) \in D$ and $\alpha \in S$ and $\neg\beta_1, \ldots, \neg\beta_m \notin S$
then $w \in \Gamma'(S)$.

Replacing Γ with Γ' in the definition of extension has several consequences. First and foremost, dropping the requirement of deductive
closure makes the test of whether it is consistent to assume $\beta_1, \ldots, \beta_m$
essentially syntactic: it is possible for β_j not to be included in $\Gamma'(S)$
even though it is derivable from $\Gamma'(S)$. (In general, this definition of
extension is a much closer description of the behavior of actual implementations of non-monotonic reasoning than the original definition.)
And therefore, a logic defined in this way does not have the property of
Reiter's logic that a (closed) default theory (D,W) has an inconsistent
extension iff W is inconsistent.

Each extension of a discourse interpretation theory under this new
definition will, in general, be H-type ambiguous, some of the interpretations being inconsistent. However, if we adopt the 'rewriting' version
of disambiguation discussed above, and impose the Condition on Discourse Interpretation, each extension will have a single interpretation,
and therefore its consistency can be checked. I propose therefore to
define the notion of extension of a discourse interpretation theory as
follows:

Extension: A set of closed wffs $E \subseteq L$ is an EXTENSION for the discourse interpretation theory Δ iff E is a fixed point of the operator
Γ' and satisfies the Condition on Discourse Interpretation.

5 Other Forms of Ambiguity

The theory of ambiguity introduced in the previous sections can be
straightforwardly extended to obtain a treatment of two other classes of
semantic ambiguity: scopal ambiguity and referential ambiguity. These
extensions preserve the basic ideas of the theory, semantic ambiguity
as multiplicity of meanings, and perceived ambiguity as multiple extensions of a default theory; what changes is that on the one hand,
a more complex underspecified language is introduced, capable of encoding other forms of ambiguity; on the other hand, more complex
inference rules are used.

5.1 Scopal Ambiguity

I will call the sentence constituents that modify the parameters of
evaluation, and therefore affect the interpretation of other sentence
constituents 'in their scope', OPERATORS. As is well-known, one
cause of semantic ambiguity is that sentences may contain more than
one operator, and their relative scope is not completely determined by
the sentence's syntactic structure. Sentences that have more than one

meaning due to the interaction between operators are called SCOPALLY AMBIGUOUS.[21]

Historically, most underspecified representations have been introduced to deal with scopal ambiguity. Typically, an intermediate step of processing is assumed in which operators are left 'in place,' as well as a subsequent step of processing in which their relative scope is determined by contextual processing. Schubert and Pelletier's underspecified representation of *Every kid climbed a tree* in (5) is an example of underspecified representation in which the operators are left 'in situ'.

These representations are typically justified in terms of ease of processing, and their ability to represent 'intermediate' readings. It is clear, however, that for the purposes of developing a 'principled' theory of ambiguity processing, it would be much better to stick to as few new 'levels of representation' as possible.

---

[21]'Ambiguity elimination' solutions to the combinatorial explosion puzzle, such as Kempson and Cormack's (1981) or Verkuyl's (1992) are attempts at showing that certain cases of 'ambiguity' are in fact cases of indeterminacy. Zwicky and Sadock noted that the identity tests do not classify a sentence as ambiguous if the propositions expressed by the sentence are such that one entails the other. This is the case, for instance, with sentences such as (6) (Lakoff 1970, Zwicky and Sadock 1975, Kempson and Cormack 1981).

(6)   Every kid climbed a tree.

Kempson and Cormack claim that sentences like (7) are not ambiguous, but indeterminate: according to them, such sentences semantically denote the weaker reading. The stronger reading is the result of pragmatic reasoning.

(7)   Every linguistics student has read a book by Chomsky.

Kempson and Cormack propose that all quantified sentences denote a single proposition. This would make the combinatorial explosion puzzle disappear, as far as scopal ambiguity is concerned. However, it is not true in general that a sentence with two quantifiers has two interpretations, one of which entails the other. (8) does not have an interpretation weak enough to be entailed by all others, yet able to capture the truth conditions correctly.

(8)   Few students know many languages.

A second problem with the proposal of Kempson and Cormack is that if one wants to claim that the meaning of a sentences such as (9a) is something like (9b), as Kempson and Cormack do, then one ends up predicting that the meaning of (9c) should be something like (9d), the strongest interpretation of the sentence. In other words, one either has to give up compositionality for sentences like (9b), or to abandon the strategy of letting sentences denote their weakest interpretation (Chierchia and McConnell-Ginet 1990).

(9)   a.   Every kid climbed a tree.
        b. $(\forall x \; \mathbf{kid}(x) \supset (\exists y \; \mathbf{tree}(y) \land \mathbf{climb}(x,y)))$
        c.   It is not the case that every kid climbed a tree.
        d. $\neg(\forall x \; \mathbf{kid}(x) \supset (\exists y \; \mathbf{tree}(y) \land \mathbf{climb}(x,y)))$

It should also be clear that whatever the case for scopal ambiguity, other kinds of ambiguity, such as structural and H-type lexical ambiguity, cannot be reduced to indeterminacy.

In fact, there is no need to introduce a new level of representation. The two requirements on a scopally underspecified representation— that it allow representing the structural information provided by a sentence, and representing the intermediate steps of disambiguation—can be satisfied by using as an underspecified representation the syntactic structure of the sentence, augmented with information about the semantic interpretation of word-forms. In this way we can also maintain semantic translation of lexical items used in Montague grammar, that determine how they combine with other sentence constituents to determine a sentence's meaning.

The 'lexically and scopally underspecified language' $\mathcal{LSUL}$ that I introduce to encode scopal ambiguity generalizes the language $\mathcal{LXUL}$ introduced in the previous section, by allowing for arbitrary functional types. In this way, the lexical item *every* can be given its usual $\langle\langle e,t\rangle,\langle\langle e,t\rangle,t\rangle\rangle$ translation:

$$\lambda P.\ \lambda Q.\ (\forall\ x\colon P(x)\ (Q(x))).$$

The second augmentation to $\mathcal{LXUL}$ is the inclusion of tree-like expressions used to translate syntactic phrases. For example, the NP [NP [Det every] [N dog]] translates into the expression:

$$[\text{NP}\ [\text{Det}\ \lambda P.\,\lambda Q.\ (\forall\ x\colon P(x)\ (Q(x)))]\ [\text{N}\ \mathbf{dog}]]$$

The expression in (10) is the underspecified translation of the sentence *Every dog saw a frog*:

(10)

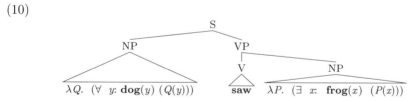

Besides reducing the number of representations floating around, this was of talking about scopal underspecification has two additional advantages over underspecified representations in which all syntactic information except for the position of operators is lost, such as Schubert and Pelletier's underspecified logical forms, Reyle's underspecified DRSs or the Core Language Engine's QLFs. First of all, the semantics of expressions such as (10) —that, for historical reasons, I call LOGICAL FORMS— can be computed in a completely classical fashion using the storage mechanism (Cooper 1983), with the result that syntactic constraints on the available readings, such as the Scope Constraint (May 1985, Heim 1982), can play a role in determining the semantics of these objects, without the need for additional constraints such as the label ordering constraints used in UDRS (Reyle 1993). Secondly, all structural information is preserved, not just information about the relative position of operators. Some of this syntactic information is used as a clue during disambiguation, for example, for interpreting pronouns, but also in certain theories of scopal disambiguation. (See, e.g., Kurtzman and MacDonald 1993 and Poesio 1994 for an account of scope disambiguation which esploits the syntactic information encoded by underspecified expressions such as (10).)

5.1.1 A Lexically and Scopally Underspecified Language

The semantics of the underspecified language $\mathcal{LSUL}$ is classically based on a set T of semantic types, the smallest set such that (i) e and t are types; and (ii) If τ and τ' are types, $\langle \tau, \tau' \rangle$ is a type. The set of meaningful expressions of type α is indicated by ME_α. The set of non-logical constant expressions of type α is indicated as $\mathrm{CE}_\alpha \subseteq \mathrm{ME}_\alpha$.

The semantics of $\mathcal{LSUL}$ is based on the same idea as the semantics of $\mathcal{LXUL}$. Natural language expressions are assigned objects of the same type as in Dowty et al. 1981 (as revised by Partee and Rooth 1983) except that, when I talk about 'meaningful expressions of type τ', I mean expressions that denote sets of functions from the set of situations $\mathcal{S}$ to elements of D_τ (the domain of type τ). Thus, for example, sentences are of type t both in Dowty, Wall and Peters' system, and in the current proposal; but a meaningful expression of type t in $\mathcal{LSUL}$ denotes a (function from a discourse situation to a) set of functions from situations to truth values.

The sets of meaningful expressions of $\mathcal{LSUL}$ include all the expressions in $\mathcal{LXUL}$:

- $\mathrm{CE}_e = \{k\}$.
- $\mathrm{CE}_{\langle e,t \rangle} = \{\mathbf{dog}, \mathbf{frog}, \mathbf{croak}_U, \ \mathbf{croak}_1, \ \mathbf{croak}_2 \}$.
  (The language includes a single underspecified lexical interpretation, $\mathbf{croak}_U$.)
- $\mathrm{CE}_{\langle e,\langle e,t \rangle \rangle} = \{\mathbf{saw}\}$.
- If $\alpha \in \mathrm{ME}_{\langle \tau,\tau' \rangle}$ and $\beta \in \mathrm{ME}_\tau$, $\alpha(\beta) \in \mathrm{ME}_{\tau'}$.
- If α and β are of type t, then $\alpha \wedge \beta$ and $\neg \alpha$ are in ME_t.

The set ME_τ, for any type τ, includes a denumerably infinite set of VARIABLES of type τ. $\mathcal{LSUL}$ also includes lambda-abstracts and quantified expressions, defined below. The language also includes the new syntactic category of LOGICAL FORMS. The sets of logical forms of syntactic category XP, LF_{XP}, are defined as follows:

- $\mathrm{LF}_{\mathrm{Det}} = \{[_{\mathrm{Det}} \ \alpha] \mid \alpha \in \mathrm{ME}_{\langle \langle e,t \rangle, \langle \langle e,t \rangle, t \rangle \rangle} \}$;
- $\mathrm{LF}_{\mathrm{N}} = \{[_{\mathrm{N}} \ \alpha] \mid \alpha \in \mathrm{ME}_{\langle e,t \rangle} \}$;
- $\mathrm{LF}_{\mathrm{PN}} = \{[_{\mathrm{PN}} \ \alpha] \mid \alpha \in \mathrm{CE}_e \}$;

- $\mathrm{LF_{IV}} = \{\, [_{\mathrm{IV}}\ \alpha] \mid \alpha \in \mathrm{ME}_{\langle e,t\rangle} \}$;
- $\mathrm{LF_{TV}} = \{[_{\mathrm{TV}}\ \alpha] \mid \alpha \in \mathrm{ME}_{\langle e,\langle e,t\rangle\rangle} \}$;
- $\mathrm{LF_{NP}} = \{[_{\mathrm{NP}}\ \alpha\ \beta] \mid \alpha \in \mathrm{LF_{Det}}$ and $\beta \in \mathrm{LF_N} \}$
  $\cup \{[_{\mathrm{NP}}\ \alpha] \mid \alpha \in \mathrm{LF_{PN}} \} \cup \{[_{\mathrm{NP}}\ \alpha] \mid \alpha$ a variable of type e $\}$;
- $\mathrm{LF_{VP}} = \{[_{\mathrm{VP}}\ \alpha\ \beta] \mid \alpha \in \mathrm{LF_{TV}}$ and $\beta \in \mathrm{LF_{NP}} \}$
  $\cup \{[_{\mathrm{VP}}\ \alpha] \mid \alpha \in \mathrm{LF_{IV}} \}$;
- $\mathrm{LF_S} = \{[_{\mathrm{S}}\ \alpha\ \beta] \mid \alpha \in \mathrm{LF_{NP}}$ and $\beta \in \mathrm{LF_{VP}} \}$.

Meaningful expressions are assigned a value with respect to a universe $\mathcal{U}$. I will use the notation $\underline{s}$ to indicate that $\underline{a}$ 'stands for' an object in $\mathcal{U}$, i.e., it is part of the meta-language, as opposed to being a meaningful expression of the object language. The models with respect to which a CRT expression is evaluated include a set $\mathcal{S}$ of situations. The only fact about situations I use here is that they have CONSTITUENTS.

The interpretation of types with respect to $\mathcal{U}$ is defined as usual: $\mathrm{D}_{e,U} = \mathcal{U}$; $\mathrm{D}_{t,U} = \{0,1\}$; $\mathrm{D}_{\langle a,b\rangle,U} = \mathrm{D}_b^{D_a}$. In the rest of this paper, I generally drop the indication of the universe (e.g., I write D_e instead of $\mathrm{D}_{e,U}$). The model of interpretation for CRT expressions is the triple $\langle \mathcal{U}, \mathcal{S}, \mathrm{I} \rangle$. The interpretation function 'I' assigns an interpretation to constants of type τ.

The value of meaningful expressions is specified by a function $[\![.]\!]^{\mathrm{M,g,d}}$ that includes an assignment function among its parameters, since the terms of $\mathcal{LSUL}$ include variables. The interpretation of variables is specified by the following clause:

- For α a variable of type τ, $[\![\alpha]\!]^{\mathrm{M,g,d}} =$ the singleton set $\{g(\alpha)\}$, where $g(\alpha)$ is a constant function $\mathrm{f} : \mathcal{S} \to \mathrm{D}_\tau$.

The interpretation of constants, connectives and application is as in $\mathcal{LXUL}$. The denotation of the other expressions is discussed below.

5.1.2 A Scopally and Lexically Underspecified Grammar

The following grammar extends the grammar discussed in section §4 by adding determiners and relations as new lexical items:

- PN $\to$ Kermit; k
- Det $\to$ every; $\lambda P.\ \lambda Q.\ (\forall\ x{:}\ P(x)\ (Q(x)))$
- Det $\to$ a; $\lambda P.\ \lambda Q.\ (\exists\ x{:}\ P(x)\ (Q(x)))$
- N $\to$ dog; **dog**
- N $\to$ frog; **frog**
- IV $\to$ croaked; **croak**$_U$
- TV $\to$ saw; **saw**

and by adding phrase structure rules for NPs and transitive verbs:

- S $\to$ NP VP; $[_{\mathrm{S}}$ NP$'$ VP$']$

- NP → PN; $[_{NP} \, [_{PN} \, PN']]$
- NP → Det N; $[_{NP} \, [_{Det} \, Det'] \, [_N \, N']]$
- VP → IV; $[_{VP} \, [_{IV} \, V']]$
- VP → TV NP; $[_{VP} \, [_{TV} \, V'] \, NP']$

This grammar generates, in addition to lexically ambiguous sentences such as *Kermit croaked*, scopally ambiguous sentences such as *Every dog saw a frog*.

5.1.3 The Denotation of Logical Forms

The denotation of logical forms is specified using the *storage* method, developed by Robin Cooper as a way around a problem with Montague's QUANTIFYING IN technique, namely, the fact that in order to get all the readings of a scopally ambiguous sentence, one has to stipulate that the sentence is syntactically ambiguous (see Dowty et al. 1981).

Cooper proposed that the value of a syntactic tree is a set of SE-QUENCES, each sequence representing a distinct 'order of application' of the operators that may result in a admissible interpretation of a sentence. For example, the quantifier *a frog* can 'enter' the derivation of the VP *saw a frog* in two different ways. The narrow scope reading is obtained by immediately applying the interpretation of the quantifier to the translation of *saw*; but it is also possible to apply the predicate to the variable quantified over, and 'wait' before applying the quantifier, in which case the wide scope reading is obtained. The value of the NP *a frog*, then, is the set of two sequences shown in (11). One sequence consists of a single element, the 'traditional' Montague-style translation of *every frog*. The second sequence consists of two elements: the variable y, and the semantic translation of the quantified NP, put 'in storage'.

(11) $\{\langle \lambda P. \ (\exists \ y\!: \mathbf{frog}(y) \ (P(y)))\rangle,$
         $\langle y, \lambda P. \ (\exists \ y\!: \mathbf{frog}(y) \ (P(y)))\rangle \ \}$

Ambiguity 'propagates up' as follows. The value of the VP *saw a frog* in (12) also consists of two sequences, one obtained by applying the first element of the first sequence in the denotation of *every frog* to the predicate **saw**, the other obtained by applying the predicate **saw** to the first element of the second sequence (the variable y). The result is as in (13).

(12) $[_{VP} \, [_V \, \mathbf{saw}] \, [_{NP} \, \lambda P. \ (\exists \ y\!: \mathbf{frog}(y) \ (P(y)))]]$

(13) $\{\langle \lambda x. \ (\exists \ y\!: \mathbf{frog}(y) \ (\mathbf{saw}(y)(x))) \ \rangle,$
         $\langle \mathbf{saw}(y), \lambda P. \ (\exists \ y\!: \mathbf{frog}(y) \ (P(y))) \ \rangle\}$

Finally, the value of a sentence is obtained by combining the value of the VP with the value of the NP in the usual fashion: the value of $[_S$

Every dog saw a frog] is a set of two sequences, each representing a distinct reading of the sentence.

It is easy to see that Cooper's technique can be used to assign to underspecified representations like (10) a 'multiple sense' denotation like those assigned to lexically ambiguous expressions in the previous section. All that is needed is a function CV that assigns to each expression of the form $[_{XP}\ \alpha]$ its 'Cooper Value'; the denotation of sentence translations like $[_S\ \beta]$ can then be defined in terms of CV as follows:

- If $[_S\ \alpha]$ is a logical form in LE$_S$ then $[_S\ \alpha]$ is a meaningful expression of type t. Let $CV(\alpha)(M,g,d)$ be the set of single-element sequences $\{\langle\{\sigma_{1_1},\ldots,\sigma_{1_j}\}\rangle, \ldots, \langle\{\sigma_{n_1},\ldots,\sigma_{n_k}\}\rangle\}$. Then
  $$[\![_S\ \alpha]\!]^{M,g,d} = \{\sigma_{1_1},\ldots,\sigma_{1_j},\ldots\sigma_{n_1},\ldots,\sigma_{n_k}\}.$$

(An expression of our underspecified language denotes a set of objects, so each scopally disambiguated translation of a sentence will still denote a set of propositions.)

Cooper discusses in detail how semantic and syntactic constraints on scope can be implemented as requirements that the storage be 'discharged' at certain positions—i.e., that no element in storage be 'carried across' syntactic constructions that produce scope islands, such as $\overline{S}$ (Cooper 1983). In this way, no operator in a clause may take scope over operators in an higher clause, or in a sister clause.

The CV function used to define the interpretation of logical forms is based on an implementation of the storage idea less general than Cooper's, but simpler. In order to arrive at a uniform specification of the Cooper Value of all constructs, it is useful to define construct-specific versions of application in which to 'bury' the differences in storage manipulation. These operations are defined as follows:

- $\alpha\{\beta\}_S =$

$$\begin{cases} \alpha(\beta), \text{ if Type}(\alpha) = \langle\langle e,t\rangle,t\rangle \text{ and Type}(\beta) = \langle e,t\rangle, \\ \quad\text{or if Type}(\alpha) = \langle\langle e,t\rangle,\langle e,t\rangle\rangle \text{ and Type}(\beta) = \\ \quad\langle e,t\rangle. \\ \lambda y.\ \lambda x.\ \beta(x)(y)\{\alpha\}_{VP}, \text{ if Type}(\alpha) = \langle\langle e,t\rangle,t\rangle \text{ and} \\ \quad\text{Type}(\beta) = \langle e,\langle e,t\rangle\rangle, \text{ or if Type}(\alpha) = \\ \quad\langle\langle e,t\rangle,\langle e,t\rangle\rangle \text{ and Type}(\beta) = \langle e,\langle e,t\rangle\rangle. \\ \beta(\alpha), \text{ if Type}(\beta) = \langle e,t\rangle \text{ and Type}(\alpha) = e. \\ \text{Undefined otherwise.} \end{cases}$$

- $\alpha\{\beta\}_{\mathrm{VP}} =$

$$\begin{cases} \alpha(\beta), \text{ if } \mathrm{Type}(\alpha) = \langle e,t \rangle \text{ and } \mathrm{Type}(\beta) = e. \\ \lambda w_e. \ \beta(\alpha(w_e)), \text{ if } \mathrm{Type}(\beta) = \langle\langle e,t \rangle,\langle e,t \rangle\rangle \\ \quad \text{and } \mathrm{Type}(\alpha) = \langle e,\langle e,t \rangle\rangle. \\ \lambda w_e. \ \beta(\lambda z. \ \alpha(z)(w_e)), \text{ if } \mathrm{Type}(\beta) = \langle\langle e,t \rangle,t \rangle \\ \quad \text{and } \mathrm{Type}(\alpha) = \langle e,\langle e,t \rangle\rangle. \\ \text{Undefined otherwise.} \end{cases}$$

- $\alpha\{\beta\}_{\mathrm{XP}}$ (where XP is a category other than S or VP) $=$

$$\begin{cases} \alpha(\beta), \text{ if } \mathrm{Type}(\alpha) = \langle \tau,\tau' \rangle \text{ and } \mathrm{Type}(\beta) = \tau. \\ \beta(\alpha), \text{ if } \mathrm{Type}(\beta) = \langle \tau,\tau' \rangle \text{ and } \mathrm{Type}(\alpha) = \tau. \\ \text{Undefined otherwise.} \end{cases}$$

Next, we need an operation that combines two sets of sequences into one. The result of applying this operation to two sets of sequences X and Y is the set of sequences obtained by (typed) applying the first element of a sequence in X to the first element of a sequence in Y and then merging the rest of the sequences, as follows:

- $X \otimes_{\mathrm{YP}} Y$, where X and Y are the sets
  $X = \{\langle x_{11}, x_{12}, \ldots x_{1m}\rangle, \ldots \langle x_{n1}, x_{n2}, \ldots x_{nl}\rangle\}$ and
  $Y = \{\langle y_{11}, y_{12}, \ldots y_{1p}\rangle, \ldots \langle y_{q1}, y_{q2}, \ldots y_{qr}\rangle\}$,
  and YP is any phrase category, is the set:
  $\{\ \langle x_{i1}\{y_{j1}\}_{\mathrm{YP}}, \ y_{j2}, \ldots y_{jp}\rangle, \ x_{i2}, \ldots x_{im} \mid \langle x_{i1}, x_{i2}, \ldots x_{im}\rangle \in X$
  and $\langle y_{j1}, y_{j2}, \ldots y_{jp}\rangle \in Y\ \}$

We also need an operation to put operators into store, and one to 'discharge' them. The **storeaway** operation takes a set consisting of a single single-element sequence and a result, and returns a set that consists of two sequences: the original sequence, and a new sequence consisting of the result and the operator in store.

- **storeaway**(α, X), where $X = \{\langle \beta \rangle\}$, is $\{\langle \beta \rangle, \langle \alpha, \beta \rangle\}$

The **discharge** operation takes a sequence and applies all operators back to obtain a set of sequences with a single element and an empty store. For simplicity, we will assume that all operators are generalised quantifiers, i.e., of type $\langle\langle e,t \rangle,t \rangle$. (No other operators are specified in the grammar above.) **discharge** is defined as follows:

- **discharge**$(\langle x_1, x_2, \ldots, x_m \rangle) = \{x_m\{\ x_{m-1}\{\ldots x_2\{x_1\}_S\}_S\ \}_S\ \}$

  discharge$^*(X)$, where X is a set of sequences, is the union $\bigcup_{x \in X}$ **discharge**(x). We can now specify the Cooper value of logical forms with respect to model M, variable assignment g, and discourse situation d as follows:[22]

---

[22]Strictly speaking, the form $CV(\alpha)(M,g,d)$ should be used. Indices will be omitted.

- $CV([_S [_{NP} \alpha] [_{VP} \beta]]) = \textbf{discharge}^*(CV([_{NP} \alpha]) \otimes_S CV([_{VP} \beta]))$
- $CV([_{NP} [_{PN} \alpha]]) = CV([_{PN} \alpha])$
- $CV([_{NP} [_{Det} \alpha] [_N \beta]]) = \textbf{storeaway}(\lambda Q. \lambda z. Q(z), CV([_{Det} \alpha]) \otimes_{NP} CV([_N \beta]))$
- $CV([_{NP} \alpha]) = \{\langle [\![\alpha]\!]^{M,g,d} \rangle\}$, where α is a variable of type e
- $CV([_{VP} [_{IV} \alpha]]) = CV([_{IV} \alpha])$
- $CV([_{VP} [_{TV} \alpha] [_{NP} \beta]]) = CV([_{TV} \alpha]) \otimes_{VP} CV([_{NP} \beta])$
- $CV([_{PN} PN']) = \{\langle [\![PN']\!]^{M,g,d} \rangle\}$
- $CV([_{Det} Det']) = \{\langle [\![Det']\!]^{M,g,d} \rangle\}$
- $CV([_{IV} IV']) = \{\langle [\![IV']\!]^{M,g,d} \rangle\}$
- $CV([_{TV} TV']) = \{\langle [\![TV']\!]^{M,g,d} \rangle\}$
- $CV([_N N']) = \{\langle [\![N']\!]^{M,g,d} \rangle\}$

There are three tricky aspects to the definition of CV: the discharge operation in the definition of the Cooper Value of a sentence translation, the definition of $CV([_{NP} [_{Det} \alpha] [_N \beta]])$ in which an operator is put in store, and the definition of $CV([_{VP} [_V \alpha] [_{NP} \beta]]$ in which two stores are combined, and that has different results depending on whether the NP is of type e or is a quantifier. I will illustrate these cases by looking at the main steps of the computation of the CV of (10):

1. $CV([_{Det} \lambda P. \lambda Q. (\exists y: P(y) (Q(y)))]) =$
   $\{\langle \lambda P. \lambda Q. (\exists y: P(y) (Q(y)))\rangle\}$
   (In what follows, I will use **a** to indicate the lexical translation of the determiner a.)

2. $CV([_{NP} [_{Det} \textbf{a}] [_N \textbf{frog}]]) =$
   $\textbf{storeaway}(\lambda Q. \lambda z. Q(z), CV([_{Det} \textbf{a}]) \otimes_{NP} CV([_N \textbf{frog}])) =$
   $\{\langle \lambda Q. (\exists y: \textbf{frog}(y) (Q(y)))\rangle,$
   $\langle \lambda Q. \lambda z. Q(z), \lambda Q. (\exists y: \textbf{frog}(y) (Q(y)))\rangle \}$
   (I will use [a frog] to stand for $'\lambda Q. (\exists y: \textbf{frog}(y) (Q(y)))'$.)

3. $CV([_{VP} [_{TV} \textbf{saw}] [_{NP} [_{Det} \textbf{a}] [_N \textbf{frog}]]]) =$
   $CV([_{TV} \textbf{saw}]) \otimes_{VP} CV([_{NP} [_{Det} \textbf{a}] [_N \textbf{frog}]]) =$
   $\{\langle \textbf{saw}\{[a\ frog]\}_{VP}\rangle, \langle \textbf{saw}\{ \lambda Q. \lambda z. Q(z) \}_{VP}, [a\ frog]\rangle \} =$
   $\{\langle \lambda w. (\exists y: \textbf{frog}(y) (\textbf{saw}(y)(w)))\rangle,$
   $\langle \lambda w. \lambda x. \textbf{saw}(w)(x), [a\ frog]\rangle \}$
   (Notice that the first element of the second sequence, in which [a frog] is kept in store, is still of type $\langle e, \langle e, t \rangle \rangle$.) I will use the abbreviations σ and σ' for the first element of the first sequence and the first element of the second sequence, respectively.

4. $CV([_{NP} [_{Det} \textbf{every}] [_N \textbf{dog}]]) =$
   $\{\langle \lambda Q. (\forall x: \textbf{dog}(x) (Q(x)))\rangle,$

$\langle \lambda Q. \ \lambda z. \ Q(z), \lambda Q. \ (\forall \ x: \mathbf{dog}(x) \ (Q(x)))\rangle \}$

(I will use [**every dog**] to stand for $'\lambda Q. \ (\forall \ x: \mathbf{dog}(x) \ (Q(x)))'.$)

5. $\mathrm{CV}([_S \ [_{NP} \ [_{Det} \ \mathbf{every}] \ [_N \ \mathbf{dog}]] \ [_{VP} \ [_V \ \mathbf{saw}] \ [_{NP} \ [_{Det} \ \mathbf{a}] \ [_N \ \mathbf{frog}]]]]) = \mathbf{discharge}^*(\mathrm{CV}([_{NP} \ \alpha]) \otimes_S \mathrm{CV}([_{VP} \ \beta])) =$

$$\mathbf{discharge}^* \left(\begin{array}{l} \{\langle[\mathbf{every\ dog}]\{\sigma\}_S\rangle, \\ \langle[\mathbf{every\ dog}]\{\sigma'\}_S, [\mathbf{a\ frog}]\rangle, \\ \langle \ \lambda Q. \ \lambda z. \ Q(z)\{\sigma\}_S, [\mathbf{every\ dog}]\rangle, \\ \langle \ \lambda Q. \ \lambda z. \ Q(z)\{\sigma'\}_S, [\mathbf{every\ dog}], [\mathbf{a\ frog}]\rangle\} \end{array} \right)$$

$=$

$$\mathbf{discharge}^* \left(\begin{array}{l} \{\langle \ (\forall \ x: \mathbf{dog}(x) \ (\ (\exists \ y: \mathbf{frog}(y) \ (\ \mathbf{saw}(y)(x)))))\rangle, \\ \langle \lambda w. \ (\forall \ x: \mathbf{dog}(x) \ (\mathbf{saw}(w)(x))), [\mathbf{a\ frog}]\rangle, \\ \langle \lambda z. \ (\exists \ y: \mathbf{frog}(y) \ (\ \mathbf{saw}(y)(x))), [\mathbf{every\ dog}]\rangle, \\ \langle \lambda w. \ \lambda z. \ \mathbf{saw}(z)(w), [\mathbf{a\ frog}], [\mathbf{every\ dog}]\rangle \ \} \end{array} \right)$$

$=$

$\{\langle \ (\forall \ x: \mathbf{dog}(x) \ (\ (\exists \ y: \mathbf{frog}(y) \ (\ \mathbf{saw}(y)(x)))))\rangle,$
$\langle \ (\exists \ y: \mathbf{frog}(y) \ (\ (\forall \ x: \mathbf{dog}(x) \ (\ \mathbf{saw}(y)(x)))))\rangle\}$

The Scope Constraint is enforced by requiring a complete discharge at the sentential level, which means no operators can 'move up' outside the sentence in which it occurs, although of course this couldn't occur in this grammar since it doesn't cover relative clauses, sentential complements or coordination. I have assumed that discharge only takes place at sentential level. Allowing operators to take scope over VPs would complicate matters in that a 'partial' discharge operation should be defined.

5.1.4 Lambda Abstracts

Some care is required in the system developed here to get a semantics for lambda-abstraction that preserves properties such as β- and η-reduction. The clause specifying the denotation of lambda-abstraction in Dowty, Wall and Peters's book is the following:

- If α is a variable of type τ and β a meaningful expression of type τ', then $\lambda \alpha.\beta$ is an expression of type $\langle \tau, \tau' \rangle$, and $[\![\lambda \alpha.\beta]\!]^{M,g,w,t}$ is that function h: $D_\tau \to D_{\tau'}$ such that for all objects $\underline{a}$ in D_τ, h($\underline{a}$) is equal to $[\![\beta]\!]^{M,g\{\alpha/\underline{a}\},w,t}$.

If we generalize this clause in the 'obvious' way we get:

- If α is a variable of type τ and β a meaningful expression of type τ', then $\lambda \alpha.\beta$ is an expression of type $\langle \tau, \tau' \rangle$, and $[\![\lambda \alpha.\beta]\!]^{M,g,d}$ is the set $\{f \mid \text{where f: } \mathcal{S} \to (D_\tau \to D_{\tau'}) \text{ and for all situations } \underline{s},$ $f(\underline{s}) = h: D_\tau \to D_{\tau'}, \text{ such that, for all objects } \underline{a} \text{ in } D_\tau, h(\underline{a}) \text{ is}$ equal to $h'(\underline{s})$, for some $h' \in [\![\beta]\!]^{M,g\{\alpha/\underline{a}\},d} \ \}$.

Lambda-abstraction, defined in this way, does not have the required properties. To show that it does not preserve η-reduction,[23] it is sufficient to consider the following example: let $S = \{s_1, s_2\}$, $D_T = \{a, b\}$, and let the expression β of type $\langle \tau, \tau' \rangle$ have the following denotation:

$$\left\{ \left[\begin{array}{l} s_1 \to \left[\begin{array}{l} a \to \alpha_1 \\ b \to \beta_1 \end{array} \right] \\ s_2 \to \left[\begin{array}{l} a \to \alpha_2 \\ b \to \beta_2 \end{array} \right] \end{array} \right], \left[\begin{array}{l} s_1 \to \left[\begin{array}{l} a \to \alpha_3 \\ b \to \beta_3 \end{array} \right] \\ s_2 \to \left[\begin{array}{l} a \to \alpha_4 \\ b \to \beta_4 \end{array} \right] \end{array} \right] \right\}$$

Then $[\![\beta(\alpha)]\!]^{M,g\{\alpha/a\},d}$ is as follows:

$$\left\{ \left[\begin{array}{l} s_1 \to \alpha_1 \\ s_2 \to \alpha_2 \end{array} \right], \left[\begin{array}{l} s_1 \to \alpha_3 \\ s_2 \to \alpha_4 \end{array} \right] \right\}$$

and $[\![\beta(\alpha)]\!]^{M,g\{\alpha/b\},d}$ is as follows:

$$\left\{ \left[\begin{array}{l} s_1 \to \beta_1 \\ s_2 \to \beta_2 \end{array} \right], \left[\begin{array}{l} s_1 \to \beta_3 \\ s_2 \to \beta_4 \end{array} \right] \right\}$$

Then, under the definition above, $[\![\lambda\alpha.\ \beta(\alpha)]\!]^{M,g,d}$ will contain the following function, that is not part of the denotation of β (hence, η-reduction is not a sound inference rule):

$$\left[\begin{array}{l} s_1 \to \left[\begin{array}{l} a \to \alpha_1 \\ b \to \beta_3 \end{array} \right] \\ s_2 \to \left[\begin{array}{l} a \to \alpha_4 \\ b \to \beta_2 \end{array} \right] \end{array} \right]$$

Intuitively, the problem with the definition above is that it does not 'preserve' the functions in the denotation of β. A definition of lambda-abstraction that does preserve these functions, and therefore preserves the soundness of β- and η-reduction, can be obtained as follows.[24]

The denotation function $[\![\alpha]\!]^{M,g,d}$ used so far assigns a value to expression $\alpha \in ME_T$ in model M with respect to the parameters of evaluation g and d, $[\![\alpha]\!]^{M,g,d} \subseteq S \to D_T$. Another way of specifying the value of expressions is to define a function $[\![\alpha]\!]^{M,d}$ that assigns as value to α at discourse situation d a set of functions of type $(\text{Ass} \to (S \to D_T))$, from assignments to functions in $(S \to D_T)$. For example, Dowty, Wall and Peters' clause for lambda abstraction could be rewritten as follows:

- If α is a variable of type τ and β a meaningful expression of type τ', then $\lambda\alpha.\beta$ is an expression of type $\langle \tau, \tau' \rangle$, and $[\![\lambda\alpha.\ \beta]\!]$ $= \Lambda(\alpha, [\![\beta]\!])$, where $\Lambda(\alpha, Y)$ is that function f from Ass $\to (D_T$

---

[23]I.e., that $\lambda\alpha.\ \beta(\alpha) \neq \beta$.
[24]I wish to thank an anonymous reviewer for suggesting this solution to the problem just discussed, much simpler than the solution proposed in Poesio 1994.

$\rightarrow D_{\tau'}$) such that for all $g \in Ass$, $\underline{s} \in \mathcal{S}$, $\underline{a}$ in D_τ, $f(g)(\underline{s})(\underline{a}) = Y(g\{\alpha/\underline{a}\})(\underline{s})$.

This definition can then be generalized as follows:

- If α is a variable of type τ and β a meaningful expression of type τ', then $\lambda\alpha. \beta$ is an expression of type $\langle\tau,\tau'\rangle$, and $[\![\lambda\alpha. \beta]\!]^{M,d} = \Lambda^+(\alpha,[\![\beta]\!])$, where $\Lambda^+(\alpha,Y) = \{\Lambda(\alpha,m)$ for some $m \in Y\} = \{f \in (Ass \rightarrow (\mathcal{S}\rightarrow (D_\tau \rightarrow D_{\tau'})))$ such that for all $g \in Ass$, $\underline{s} \in \mathcal{S}$, $\underline{a}$ in D_τ, and for some $m \in Y$, $f(g)(\underline{s})(\underline{a}) = m(g\{\alpha/\underline{a}\})(\underline{s})$. $\}$

Lambda-abstraction defined this way does support η-reduction.[25] Since this more general way of assigning a value is not needed to provide a semantics for the other constructs of $\mathcal{LSUL}$, I will continue using a function $[\![.]\!]^{M,g,d}$, but the reader should keep in mind that a denotation function of this form is needed to deal with lambda abstraction, hence, with quantification. (The same is true for referential ambiguity, as we will see below.)

5.1.5 Quantification

The treatment of quantifiers in $\mathcal{LSUL}$ is based on Generalized Quantifiers Theory (Barwise and Cooper 1981), i.e., the idea that determiners denote relations between two sets. The 'restricted quantification' notation used in the examples above is defined in terms of the two determiners **every** and **a**, as follows:

- $(\forall \ x: \Phi \ (\Psi)) \equiv_{def}$ **every**$(\lambda x. \ \Phi,\lambda x. \ \Psi)$
- $(\exists \ x: \Phi \ (\Psi)) \equiv_{def}$ **a**$(\lambda x. \ \Phi,\lambda x. \ \Psi)$

A 'single-valued' semantics for **every**$(\lambda\alpha. \ \Phi,\lambda\alpha. \ \Psi)$ could be defined, in first approximation, as in the following clause:

- Let F,G be meaningful expressions of type $\langle e,t\rangle$. Then **every**(F,G) is a meaningful expression of type t, and $[\![\textbf{every}(F,G)]\!]^{M,g,d}$ is the function f such that $f(\underline{s})$ =

$$\begin{cases} \textbf{undefined} \text{ iff either } [\![F]\!]^{M,g,d} \text{ or } [\![G]\!]^{M,g,d} \text{ are} \\ \quad \text{undefined;} \\ \textbf{1} \text{ iff } \{\underline{a} \in \mathcal{U} \text{ such that } [[\![F]\!]^{M,g,d}(\underline{s})](\underline{a}) = 1 \} \subseteq \\ \quad \{\underline{b} \in \mathcal{U} \text{ such that } [[\![G]\!]^{M,g,d}(\underline{s})](\underline{b}) = 1 \}. \\ \textbf{0} \text{ otherwise.} \end{cases}$$

---

[25] The proof is as follows. $[\![\lambda\alpha. \beta(\alpha)]\!]^{M,d} = \{f \in (Ass \rightarrow (\mathcal{S}\rightarrow (D_\tau \rightarrow D_{\tau'})))$ such that for all $g \in Ass$, $\underline{s} \in \mathcal{S}$, $\underline{a}$ in D_τ, and for some $m \in [\![\beta(\alpha)]\!]^M$, $f(g)(\underline{s})(\underline{a}) = m(g\{\alpha/\underline{a}\})(\underline{s})$. $\}$ Because of the definition of $[\![\beta(\alpha)]\!]^{M,d}$, this is the set of functions f such that $f(g)(\underline{s})(\underline{a}) = p(g\{\alpha/\underline{a}\})(\underline{s})[q(g\{\alpha/\underline{a}\})(\underline{s})]$, for some $p \in [\![\beta]\!]^M$ and some q in $[\![\alpha]\!]^M$, i.e., of the functions which occur in $[\![\beta]\!]^M$ since $q(g\{\alpha/\underline{a}\})(\underline{s}) = \underline{a}$.

This definition can be generalized as follows into one that works in the case in which $\llbracket . \rrbracket^{M,g,d}$ is a set:

- $\llbracket \mathbf{every}(F,G) \rrbracket^{M,g,d} =$
  $\{f \mid$ there is an $h \in \llbracket F \rrbracket^{M,g,d}$ and an $h' \in \llbracket G \rrbracket^{M,g,d}$ such that
  $f(\underline{s})$ $=$

  $\begin{cases} \textbf{undefined} & \text{iff } h(\underline{s}) \text{ is undefined or } h'(\underline{s}) \text{ is undefined;} \\ \textbf{1} & \text{iff for every } \underline{a} \text{ such that } [h(\underline{s})](\underline{a}) = 1,\ [h'(\underline{s})](\underline{a}) = 1. \\ \textbf{0} & \text{otherwise.} \end{cases}$

  }

The interpretation of expressions of the form $\mathbf{a}(\lambda\alpha.\ \Phi, \lambda\alpha.\ \Psi)$ is defined in a similar fashion, with the obvious semantics.

5.1.6   Scope Disambiguation by Defeasible Inference

Having extended the language into one that can be used to describe scopal underspecification, the framework for discourse interpretation developed in section §4.2 can also be used to formalize the inferences involved in scope disambiguation. Partially disambiguated interpretations can be represented by expressions which mix logical forms with 'traditional' expressions, as done in DRT. For example, one could formalize Ioup's (1975) Grammatical Function Principle, stating that an NP in subject position by default takes scope over NPs in other position, as follows:

GRAMMATICAL-FUNCTION-PRINCIPLE

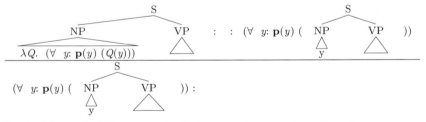

Logical forms in LF_S are sentential expressions, and can therefore serve as triggering condition of discourse interpretation principles. They can also occur embedded in other expressions of $\mathcal{LSUL}$. During the scope disambiguation process, 'less ambiguous' expressions are inferred by deriving expressions such as $(\forall\ y\colon \mathbf{p}(y)\ ([_S\ [_{NP}\ y]\ [_{VP}\ \alpha]]))$ in which some quantifiers have been extracted, by a process similar to the one used in the top-down version of the DRT construction algorithm Kamp and Reyle 1993. 'Partial' scopal disambiguation is thus represented by $\mathcal{LSUL}$ expressions which still contain logical forms.

Some readers may have observed that the GRAMMATICAL-FUNCTION-PRINCIPLE does not satisfy the Anti-Random restriction proposed in §4.2: it does not contain a non-trivial restriction on the contexts in which it can operate. The proposal in Poesio 1994 overcomes this problem by making the activation of scope disambiguation rules dependent on whether the appropriate domain for the quantifier (its RESOURCE SITUATION) has been identified; a presentation of that proposal would, however, require introducing too much additional material.

5.2 Referential Ambiguity

5.2.1 Referential Expressions as Cases of Semantic Ambiguity

Yet another way in which the semantics of sentences is 'underspecified' by their syntax is in the interpretation of anaphoric expressions and other expressions whose interpretation has to be fixed in context. In semantics, referential expressions are traditionally translated as free variables whose interpretation depends on the choice of an assignment function (for the cases of deictic anaphora) or by assigning them the same variable bound by the quantifier that serves as their antecedent (for the cases of bound anaphora). This translation does capture the intuition that the truth conditions of a sentence containing a referential expression can only be evaluated after fixing the value of the referential expressions. It is also clear, however, that distinct propositions are obtained depending on the value assigned to these expressions, much as distinct propositions are obtained depending on the choice of an interpretation for lexical items, or of a scope for operators: in other words, a sentence which includes a referential expression is semantically ambiguous much in the way a sentence containing a lexically ambiguous item is.[26]

A complete discussion of reference interpretation would require introducing a formalization of context, so I will only consider here the issue of providing an underspecified treatment of intra-clausal and deictic anaphora. I propose that referential expressions are cases of semantic ambiguity, and translate into a special kind of underspecified object that I will call PARAMETERS. Semantically, a parameter is a type e

---

[26]Pinkal takes pretty much the same position in Pinkal 1995. He also introduces a distinction between a 'speaker-oriented' versus a 'hearer-oriented' perspective on meaning. A speaker may have a single interpretation in mind, but the hearer may have to recover this interpretation among the many that are possible. This is, of course, true of all kinds of perceived ambiguities, also those which result from pragmatic rather than semantic factors, but in the case of referential ambiguity, the alternative interpretations correspond to distinct propositions in the semantic sense as well.

expression that, in a discourse situation d̲, denotes a set of functions from situations to elements of D_e in d̲. For example, the pronoun *he* would translate into a parameter $\dot{x}$ which, in a discourse situation d̲ with constituents $a_1 \ldots a_n$, and given the set $\mathcal{S}$ of situations, will denote a set of functions $\{f_1, \ldots, f_m, \ldots\}$ from situations in $\mathcal{S}$ to $a_1 \ldots a_n$, including at least the set of all constant functions that map each situation s̲ into a_j if a_j is a constituent of that situation (see below), and the set of all variable denotations. The reader will immediately realize that parameters are the equivalent for type e expressions of 'underspecified predicates' like **croak**$_U$ introduced above.[27]

More formally, I propose to extend the set of terms of $\mathcal{LSUL}$ with a new class of parameters, whose interpretation is defined as follows. First of all, let us reformulate the semantics of variables given before, and make variables functions from assignments to values (rather than the other way around). This involves again using as interpretation function one that maps expressions into functions from assignments to meanings, as done for lambda-abstracts.

- For α a variable of type τ, $[\![\alpha]\!]^{M,d}$ = the singleton set $\{f\}$, where f is a function f : Ass $\to (\mathcal{S} \to D_\tau)$ such that for every assignment g, f(g) is a constant function from $\mathcal{S} \to D_\tau$.

This definition of the meaning of a variable allows us to abstract away from assignments. We can now define the semantics of parameters as follows:

- For α a parameter of type τ, $[\![\alpha]\!]^{M,g,d} = \bigcup_{\beta_\tau} [\![\beta_\tau]\!]^{M,d}$ (the union of the denotation of all variables of type τ) $\bigcup \{f \mid f : \mathcal{S} \to D_\tau$ is a function such that for each s̲, f(s̲) = a̲, where a̲ is an object of τ that is a constituent of a situation s̲' which in turn is a constituent of the discourse situation d, if a̲ is a constituent of s̲; f(s̲) = undefined otherwise.$\}$.

For example, if the subset of D_e in d consists of the two atoms j̲ and b̲, then $[\![\dot{x}_e]\!]^{M,g,d} = \{f_1, f_2, \ldots f_i, \ldots\}$, where f_1, f_2 etc. are the functions that may serve as the denotation of constants and variables—f_1 is the function that maps each situation of which j̲ is a constituent into j̲, f_2 is the function that maps each situation of which b̲ is a constituent into b̲— and the other functions represent all the possible denotations of

---

[27]The term 'parameter' comes from Situation Semantics (e.g., Gawron and Peters 1990), where the lexical items whose interpretation depends on context are called PARAMETRIC, in the sense that their interpretation depends on the value assigned in context to one or more parameters. Parameters are also used in situation theory to translate pronouns and other anaphoric expression. Yet, the parameters I have just introduced are very different from the parameters of situation theory, which are a special sort of objects in the universe, entirely distinct from individuals.

objects that the parameter may be resolved to. Note that the discourse situations plays here the role played by the variable assignment in 'free variable' theories of context dependence.

The grammar presented in the previous section can be straightforwardly extended as follows to generate sentences such as *It croaked*:

- PRO → it; $\dot{x}$
- NP → PRO; [$_{\text{NP}}$ [$_{\text{PRO}}$ PRO']]

The definition of the interpretation of logical forms given above already gives the correct results for these cases.

5.2.2 Parameters and Discourse Interpretation

Referential ambiguity gets 'resolved' by *anchoring* a parameter. A parameter is ANCHORED if only one among the functions in its denotation results in a consistent interpretation of the set of sentences in which the parameter occurs; a parameter can be anchored by means of equality statements of the form [$\dot{x} = a$], where a is not parametric, or is already anchored: such equality statements make all but one of the interpretations of the parameter inadmissible. Once a parameter is anchored, it can be 'replaced' by a term that denotes the one function among those in the interpretation of the parameter that does not result in an inconsistent interpretation, much as in the previous discussion of lexical disambiguation, an H-type ambiguous predicate could be replaced by a disambiguated version. So, the discourse interpretation principles formalizing pronoun disambiguation involve a rewriting operation, just as the discourse interpretation principles formalizing lexical disambiguation.

An apparent disadvantage of the present theory with respect to the 'free variable' theory of context dependence is that we can derive from the latter that the value of referential expressions has to be fixed in order to get the meaning of the sentence in which they occur. A conversation is infelicitous unless the referents of all pronouns and definite descriptions have been identified, the domain of quantification of all quantifiers has been appropriately restricted, and so forth: so much so that listeners appear to be ready to ACCOMODATE new information (e.g., to introduce into the discourse some otherwise unspecified antecedent for a pronoun) rather than leave the interpretation unspecified (Lewis 1979). But this fact about referential expressions also follows if we treat context dependence as a case of (H-type) semantic ambiguity; it is just a corollary of Pinkal's precisification imperative, from which I derived the Condition on Discourse Interpretation in section §4. Accomodation procedures can then be seen as a way of 'precisifying' in lack of sufficient information.

5.3 Syntactic Ambiguity

The one case of ambiguity that requires extending the framework introduced here considerably is syntactic ambiguity, as in *They saw her duck*. Furthermore, I haven't considered the problem of structural disambiguation in any detail. I refer the interested readers to Poesio 1994, Poesio 1995 for a sketchy discussion of how to encode encoding syntactic ambiguity in an underspecified representation.[28]

6 Discussion

I have suggested that to develop a theory of discourse interpretation that is consistent with what we know about the problem of ambiguity, we need to look both at the grammar and at discourse interpretation. I proposed a theory of grammar consistent with what I have called the *Underspecification Hypothesis* and which is not based on the assumption that all natural language expressions can be disambiguated; and a theory of discourse interpretation according to which a perceived ambiguity occurs when defeasible interpretation principles result in conflicting hypothesis. The interpretation process is subject to two constraints: the *Anti-Random Hypothesis* (interpretations are not generated at random) and the *Condition on Discourse Interpretation*, derived from the *Precisification Imperative* (H-type ambiguity has to be resolved). Although treatments of disambiguation based on defeasible reasoning have been proposed elsewhere in the literature (e.g., in Alshawi 1992), I am not aware of any discussion of the characteristics of this inferential process, the consequences of reasoning with an underspecified representation, or the need for constraints on the inference rules.

In the theory, semantic ambiguity is characterized model-theoretically in terms of multiplicity of sense, whereas perceived ambiguity is characterized in terms of inference. One may wonder if the distinction is really necessary; i.e., if it is really the case that the meaning of natural language expressions can be specified *a priori*. Two arguments in favor of a distinction are that it provides for a clean distinction between the role of grammar and the role of discourse interpretation; and that perceived ambiguity may also reflect non-semantic

---

[28]Most systems making use of underspecified representations perform structural disambiguation independently from other forms of disambiguation (Schubert and Pelletier 1982, Allen 1987, Hobbs and Shieber 1987, Alshawi 1992). There is evidence, however, that structural disambiguation interacts at least with reference interpretation (Crain and Steedman 1985, Altmann and Steedman 1988) and a lot of the recent work on statistical parsing relies on the hypothesis that lexical interpretation affects parsing as well. Nothing in the proposal relies on structural disambiguation occurring prior to the other stages of disambiguation.

distinctions, e.g., distinctions in speech act interpretation; this question is not however totally resolved in the paper.

There are two obvious directions in which the present model needs to extended: to provide a model of syntactic ambiguity, and to account for the effect of incrementality in sentence processing. Preliminary work in this direction is discussed in Poesio 1995.

An issue that deserves further inspection is whether the formal similarity between the system used here to assign a denotation to indefinite sentences, and the systems developed by Hamblin for dealing with questions Hamblin 1973 and by Rooth for its alternative semantics Rooth 1985, has some significance. In particular, it would be interesting to explore the consequences of using parameters as the translation of focused elements.

References

Allen, J. F. 1987. *Natural Language Understanding.* Menlo Park, CA: Benjamin Cummings.

Allen, J. F., L. K. Schubert, G. Ferguson, P. Heeman, C. H. Hwang, T. Kato, M. Light, N. Martin, B. Miller, M. Poesio, and D. R. Traum. 1995. The TRAINS project: a case study in building a conversational planning agent. *Journal of Experimental and Theoretical AI.* To Appear.

Alshawi, H. (ed.). 1992. *The Core Language Engine.* The MIT Press.

Altmann, G. T. M., and M. Steedman. 1988. Interaction with Context during Human Sentence Processing. *Cognition* 30:191–238.

Asher, N., and M. Morreau. 1991. Common Sense Entailment: A Modal Theory of Commonsense Reasoning. In *Proc. 12th IJCAI.*

Barwise, J., and R. Cooper. 1981. Generalized Quantifiers and Natural Language. *Linguistics and Philosophy* 4(2):159–219.

Barwise, J., and R. Cooper. 1993. Extended Kamp Notation. In *Situation Theory and its Applications, v.3*, ed. P. Aczel, D. Israel, Y. Katagiri, and S. Peters. Chap. 2, 29–54. CSLI.

Barwise, J., and J. Perry. 1983. *Situations and Attitudes.* Cambridge, MA: MIT Press, Cambridge Mass.

Charniak, E., and R. P. Goldman. 1988. A Logic for Semantic Interpretation. In *Proc. ACL-88*, 87–94. Buffalo, NY.

Chierchia, G., and S. McConnell-Ginet. 1990. *Meaning and Grammar: An Introduction to Semantics.* Cambridge, MA: The MIT Press.

Cooper, R. 1983. *Quantification and Syntactic Theory.* Dordrecht, Holland: D. Reidel Publishing Company.

Crain, S., and M. Steedman. 1985. On not being led up the garden path: the use of context by the psychological syntax processor. In *Natural Language Parsing: Psychological, Computational and Theoretical perspectives*, ed. D. R. Dowty, L. Karttunen, and A. M. Zwicky. 320–358. New York: Cambridge University Press.

Dalrymple, M., S. M. Shieber, and F. C. N. Pereira. 1991. Ellipsis and Higher-Order Unification. *Linguistics and Philosophy* 14(4):399–452.

Dowty, D. R., R. E. Wall, and S. Peters. 1981. *Introduction to Montague Semantics.* Dordrecht, Holland: D. Reidel.

Fenstad, J.E., P.K. Halvorsen, T. Langholm, and J. van Benthem. 1987. *Situations, Language and Logic.* Dordrecht: D.Reidel.

Fine, K. 1975. Vagueness, Truth, and Logic. *Synthese* 30:265–300.

Frazier, L., and J. D. Fodor. 1978. The sausage machine: A new two-stage parsing model. *Cognition* 6:291–295.

Gawron, J. M., and S. Peters. 1990. *Anaphora and Quantification in Situation Semantics.* Lecture Notes, Vol. 19. CSLI.

Gibson, E. 1991. *A Computational Theory of human linguistic processing: memory limitations and processing breakdown.* Doctoral dissertation, Carnegie Mellon University, Pittsburgh.

Grosz, B.J., A.K. Joshi, and S. Weinstein. 1983. Providing a Unified Account of Definite Noun Phrases in Discourse. In *Proc. ACL-83*, 44–50.

Hamblin, C. 1973. Questions in Montague English. *Foundations of Language* 10:41–53.

Heim, I. 1982. *The Semantics of Definite and Indefinite Noun Phrases.* Doctoral dissertation, University of Massachusetts at Amherst.

Hirst, G. 1987. *Semantic Interpretation and the Resolution of Ambiguity.* Studies in Natural Language Processing. Cambridge, UK: Cambridge University Press.

Hobbs, J. R., and S. M. Shieber. 1987. An Algorithm for Generating Quantifier Scopings. *Computational Linguistics* 13(1-2):47–63.

Hobbs, J. R., M. Stickel, P. Martin, and D. Edwards. 1990. Interpretation as Abduction. Technical Note 499. Menlo Park, CA: SRI International, December.

Hwang, C. H., and L. K. Schubert. 1993. Episodic Logic: A Situational Logic for Natural Language Processing. In *Situation Theory and its Applications, v.3*, ed. P. Aczel, D. Israel, Y. Katagiri, and S. Peters. 303–338. CSLI.

Ioup, G. 1975. Some Universals for Quantifier Scope. In *Syntax and Semantics 4*, ed. J. Kimball. 37–58. New York: Academic Press.

Kamp, H., and U. Reyle. 1993. *From Discourse to Logic.* Dordrecht: D. Reidel.

Kaplan, D. 1977. Demonstratives. An Essay on the Semantics, Logic, Metaphysics and Epistemology of Demonstratives and Other indexicals. Unpublished manuscript, University of California, Los Angeles.

Kempson, R., and A. Cormack. 1981. Ambiguity and Quantification. *Linguistics and Philosophy* 4(2):259–310.

Kurtzman, H. 1985. *Studies in Syntactic Ambiguity Resolution.* Doctoral dissertation, MIT, Cambridge, MA.

Kurtzman, H. S., and M. C. MacDonald. 1993. Resolution of Quantifier Scope Ambiguities. *Cognition* 48:243–279.

Lakoff, G. P. 1970. A note on vagueness and ambiguity. *Linguistic Inquiry* 1(3):357–359.

Lascarides, A., N. Asher, and J. Oberlander. 1992. Inferring Discourse Relations in Context. In *Proc. ACL-92*, 1–8. University of Delaware.

Lewis, D. K. 1979. Scorekeeping in a language game. *Journal of Philosophical Logic* 8:339–359.

May, R. 1985. *Logical Form in Natural Language*. The MIT Press.

Montague, R. 1970. Universal Grammar. *Theoria* 36:373–398. Reprinted in Thomason 1974.

Partee, B. H., and M. Rooth. 1983. Generalized Conjunction and Type Ambiguity. In *Meaning, Use and Interpretation of Language*, ed. R. Bauerle, C. Schwarze, and A. von Stechow. Berlin, West Germany: Walter de Gruyter.

Pereira, F. C. N., and M. E. Pollack. 1991. Incremental Interpretation. *Artificial Intelligence* 50:37–82.

Pinkal, M. 1985. *Logik und Lexikon: Die Semantik des Unbestimmten*. Berlin: de Gruyter.

Pinkal, M. 1995. *Logic and Lexicon*. Oxford.

Poesio, M. 1991. Relational Semantics and Scope Ambiguity. In *Situation Semantics and its Applications, vol.2*, ed. J. Barwise, J. M. Gawron, G. Plotkin, and S. Tutiya. Chap. 20, 469–497. Stanford, CA: CSLI.

Poesio, M. 1994. *Discourse Interpretation and the Scope of Operators*. Doctoral dissertation, University of Rochester, Department of Computer Science, Rochester, NY.

Poesio, M. 1995. A Model of Conversation Processing Based on Micro Conversational Events. In *Proceedings of the Annual Meeting of the Cognitive Science Society*. Pittsburgh.

Raskin, V. 1985. *Semantic Mechanisms of Humor*. Dordrecht and Boston: D. Reidel.

Reiter, R. 1980. A Logic for Default Reasoning. *Artificial Intelligence* 13(1–2):81–132.

Reyle, U. 1993. Dealing with ambiguities by underspecification: Construction, Representation and Deduction. *Journal of Semantics* 3.

Rooth, M. 1985. *Association with Focus*. Doctoral dissertation, University of Massachusetts, Amherst.

Schubert, L. K. 1986. Are There Preference Trade-Offs in Attachment Decisions. In *Proceedings of the Fifth National Conference on Artificial Intelligence*, 601–605. Philadelphia, Pennsylvania, August.

Schubert, L. K., and F. J. Pelletier. 1982. From English to Logic: Context-Free Computation of 'Conventional' Logical Translations. *American Journal of Computational Linguistics* 10:165–176.

Spivey-Knowlton, M., J. Sedivy, K. Eberhard, and M. Tanenhaus. 1994. Psycholinguistic Study of the Interaction between Language and Vision. In *Proceedings of 12th National Conference on Artificial Intelligence*. Seattle.

Stallard, D. 1987. The Logical Analysis of Lexical Ambiguity. In *Proceedings of the 25th Meeting of the ACL*, 179–185.

Su, S. P. 1994. *Lexical Ambiguity in Poetry*. London: Longman.

Swinney, D. A. 1979. Lexical Access During Sentence Comprehension: (Re)consideration of Context Effects. *Journal of Verbal Learning and Verbal Behavior* 18:545–567.

Thomason, R. H. (ed.). 1974. *Formal Philosophy: Selected Papers of Richard Montague*. New York: Yale University Press.

Turner, R. 1992. Properties, propositions and semantic theory. In *Computational Linguistics and Formal Semantics*, ed. M. Rosner and R. Johnson. CUP, Cambridge.

van Deemter, K. 1991. *On the Composition of Meaning*. Doctoral dissertation, University of Amsterdam.

Verkuyl, H. J. 1992. Some Issues in the Analysis of Multiple Quantification with Plural NPs. OTS Working Papers OTS-WP-TL-92-005. The Netherlands: University of Utrecht, Research Institute for Language and Speech.

Zwicky, A., and J. Sadock. 1975. Ambiguity Tests and How to Fail Them. In *Syntax and Semantics 4*, ed. J. Kimball. 1–36. New York: Academic Press.

9

Towards a Logic of Ambiguous Expressions

Kees van Deemter

1 Coping with Ambiguous Information

Ambiguity has more than once been identified as the main single obstacle for various natural language processing tasks (e.g., Bar-Hillel 1960, Carbonel and Hayes 1987). Surprisingly, however, the logical properties of ambiguous expressions have not been studied in much depth. The reason is, presumably, that ambiguity is not a real phenomenon, but rather what you see when you look at a real phenomenon (namely: an utterance) with insufficient knowledge about it (that is: disregarding its linguistic or nonlinguistic context). This view is represented in a pure form by Barwise and Perry, who claim that although sentences can be ambiguous, utterances cannot (Barwise and Perry 1983). Each particular utterance of an expression is an utterance of it in a certain "way" that removes all ambiguity. In accordance with this idea, if ambiguity is treated in practical systems, it is usually treated in the same manner in which an illness is treated: to get rid of it. This is called the resolution of ambiguity. The result of resolution is a formula from which all ambiguity has been removed and which does its job (database query, or whatever) in standard ways.

However, complete ambiguity resolution is not always possible. It

I am indebted to Johan van Benthem for inspiration during the time when I worked on van Deemter (1991), which contains the oldest ancestor of the present paper. Thanks are due to two anonymous reviewers for valuable comments. Thanks are also due to the members of the Semantics Workshop at CSLI, Stanford University, and more specifically to Cleo Condoravdi, Mary Dalrymple, Mark Gawron, Yasunari Harada, David Israel, Megumi Kameyama, Stanley Peters and Henriette de Swart, for many useful discussions on the topic of ambiguity and underspecification. I am obliged to the Netherlands Organization for Scientific Research (NWO), whose grant made possible my stay at CSLI from September 1992 till October 1993.

Semantic Ambiguity and Underspecification
Kees van Deemter and Stanley Peters, editors
Copyright © 1995, CSLI Publications

is of little use to ask whether an utterance situation must, *in principle*, always contain enough information to afford complete disambiguation. What counts is that *in practice*, often not enough information is available to an interpreter. This holds whether the interpreter is a person or a computer. Various authors have argued that semantic theories attribute so many interpretations to sentences, that to assume that interpreters can always retrieve the intended meaning amounts to believing in miracles.[1] In addition, a human interpreter may perceive an utterance incompletely, or lack some of the background knowledge required to retrieve the intended meaning. When the interpreter is a computer, the interpretive problems are even greater. For example, the computational difficulties involved in the use of background knowledge to discard impossible or unlikely readings are notorious, since this requires storage of, and reasoning with a vast body of encyclopaedic knowledge.

Under the circumstances it is natural to ask whether disambiguation is always necessary. Communication does not always require absolute clarity: partial understanding is often enough for making the inferences that a hearer is most interested in. For example, when a speaker cries: 'Watch out! He's dangerous!', the hearer may infer that he or she is in danger and rush into hiding before disambiguating the deiktic pronoun 'he'. The same holds for the translation of the sentence into a language with a similar pronominal system.[2] This easy-going idea may be extrapolated to other linguistic tasks. For instance, suppose the task is question answering and consider the situation of a reading ϕ_1 and a *weaker* reading ϕ_2 of a given question ϕ. If ϕ_1 happens to be true, or if ϕ_2 happens to be false, then no choice between the two readings has to be made to determine the answer. This situation is very common, since the interpretations of a given sentence are often logically related.[3]

These examples show that some important information-processing activities can often cope with ambiguous information. Consequently, *modeling* the processing of ambiguous information is a potentially important field of research. Now since inference is such a vital component

---

[1] This includes older work, such as van Lehn (1978), Bobrow and Webber (1980), and Hobbs (1983). Hobbs, for example, claimed that people can understand, and yet not fully disambiguate a sentence like *In most democratic countries most politicians can fool most of the people on almost every issue most of the time*, given all the 120 different scope orders that its NPs can have (Hobbs 1983).

[2] The observation that translation does not always require complete resolution of all ambiguities in the input sentence is an old one. See, e.g., McCord 1986.

[3] For example, if a sentence contains n quantifiers, each of which is either an *existential* or a *universal* quantifier, then the corresponding interpretations can be ordered linearly according to logical strength. (Thanks are due to Jaap van der Does, pers.com., for this observation.)

of information processing, the logical behaviour of ambiguous expressions is a natural object of study. This includes reasoning from ambiguous expressions to ambiguous conclusions, but also, as important boundary cases, reasoning from unambiguous premisses to ambiguous conclusions, and the other way round. Disambiguation of an ambiguous expression by means of background information is a special case of this program. For example, one would like to be able to make inferences reflecting pragmatic rules of the following kind:

Disambiguation as reasoning: Let S be ambiguous between two interpretations. Then, if a speaker says S, while one of the two interpretations is known to be false, then this utterance of S should be treated as having the other interpretation.

So far, we have been using the words 'meaning', 'reading', and 'interpretation' without explanation. We assume a logical grammar of the kind proposed in Montague 1973, where (disambiguated) sentences are translated into logical formulas. Each logical formula ϕ has a model-theoretic meaning denoted $\|\phi\|$, and we will assume that this meaning is a function from possible worlds, or models, to truth values. Given the translation between sentences of the natural language and logical formulas, the meaning of ϕ can also be viewed as the meaning of the sentence, say S, that ϕ translates. We will speak of ϕ as one of the infinitely many formulas *representing* the meaning of S, and we will sometimes be sloppy enough to speak of ϕ as *being* the meaning, interpretation, or reading of S.

The scenario for the rest of this paper is as follows: in section 2 the possibility of a disjunctive approach to the meaning of ambiguous expressions will be discussed. Section 3 will sketch how the approach of this paper compares with other recent work on ambiguity. Sections 4 and 5 will present the semantics of a logical language containing ambiguous constants. Section 6 evaluates the resulting logics, and section 7 takes up some loose ends.

2 Against a Disjunctive Theory of Ambiguity

The notion of ambiguity has given rise to different explications. Some writers have taken a syntactic view and have defined an expression to be ambiguous whenever it has different derivations (Montague 1973b). Others have taken a semantic stance and have considered an expression ambiguous only if it can have nonequivalent meanings. [4] It seems

---

[4]Yet others get caught up in contradictions: Hirst (1987) proposes a syntactic definition of ambiguity, but in practice has a semantic perspective on ambiguity. Gillon (1990) proposes a semantic definition for ambiguity, but from the fact that a sentence has denumerably many *derivations* he concludes that it must be ambiguous between denumerably many readings (*Definition 1*, on p.477, and *note 3*, on p.479).

clear that for most NLP applications a semantic definition is required. For example, what counts in question-answering is whether a question must be answered as true or false with respect to a certain domain of discourse. If the question can be analysed in different ways, all of which must always lead to the same answers, then the question does not count as ambiguous. Thus, a definition along the following lines is assumed, where the word *grammar* refers to the entire mechanism that maps sentences onto meanings:

Ambiguity: Given a grammar G for a language $\mathcal{L}$, an expression α of $\mathcal{L}$ is *ambiguous* if G attributes different meanings to α.

Note that this definition does not decide the empirical issue of which natural language expressions *ought* to be designated as ambiguous, that is, which expressions should be attributed more than one meaning. This difficult issue will be taken up in section 5.1. We will now define another notion, namely that of an unambiguous paraphrase, or briefly a *paraphrase*, which will prove useful in relation to ambiguous expressions in natural language as well as in logic:

Paraphrase: Let an expression α of language $\mathcal{L}$ be ambiguous given a grammar G. Then if G attributes exactly one of the meanings of α to an expression α_i of $\mathcal{L}$, then α_i is called an (unambiguous) *paraphrase* of α with respect to $\mathcal{L}$ and G.

The reference to $\mathcal{L}$ and G will be dropped whenever confusion about the language and the grammar are unlikely to arise. An ambiguous expression is, by definition, less informative than any of its paraphrases. In principle, the viewpoint of incomplete information can be exploited for the analysis of ambiguity in many different ways. For example, if a sentence S is ambiguous between interpretations ϕ and ψ, one might be tempted to represent the meaning of S by a formula χ that is verified by any model that verifies either ϕ or ψ. In classical logic, the *disjunction* of all the possible interpretations (in this case the disjunction $\phi \vee \psi$) plays the role of χ, hence the name 'disjunction theory'. If this intuitively plausible theory, which is implicit in much informal discourse about language, were correct, no special logic for ambiguity would be required, since reasoning under ambiguity would simply amount to reasoning with disjunctions.[5] However, in what follows we will argue against the disjunctive approach to ambiguity.

---

[5]The version of logical consequence that corresponds with the disjunctive view (i.e., $\models_{\vee\exists}$, cf., section 4.2) does not itself lead to problems with compositionality, provided a notion of meaning is chosen that keeps all the different interpretations of an ambiguous expression apart. It is only when connections between interpretative choices (see below), are taken into account that compositionality becomes more difficult to uphold. See van Deemter 1991 for a brief discussion.

My first argument against disjunctive theories of ambiguity is that there are important semantic distinctions that they are unable to make. The argument is best illustrated using the situation that was mentioned earlier, in which a sentence S has a number of paraphrases, including S_1 and S_2, one of which is logically stronger than the other. Suppose S_1 is translated as ϕ_1 and S_2 as ϕ_2, where $\phi_1 \models \phi_2$. Then if S is translated as $\phi_1 \vee \phi_2$, the meaning of S equals $\|\phi_2\|$, because ϕ_1 is stronger than ϕ_2. The disjunctive theory fails to distinguish between the ambiguous sentence S and an unambiguous sentence, S_2. Note that this conflation of S and S_2 also causes a breakdown of compositionality. This can be seen from an operator such as *It is not the case that*, which, we will assume, corresponds logically with wide-scope negation. If S and S_2 have the same meaning, then compositionality of meaning implies that the same is true for

It is not the case that S, and
It is not the case that S_2.

Hence, the meaning of *It is not the case that S* equals $\|\neg\phi_2\|$. But on the disjunction theory, the meaning of an ambiguous sentence equals the disjunction of its possible interpretations. So, on the plausible assumption that $\neg S_1$ and $\neg S_2$ are the possible interpretations of *It is not the case that S*, the meaning of *It is not the case that S* must equal $\|\neg\phi_1 \vee \neg\phi_2\|$, and this equals $\|\neg\phi_1\|$ rather than $\|\neg\phi_2\|$. Thus, a contradiction has been derived.

The disjunctive theory of ambiguity confuses the scope of the disjunction with the scope of another, pragmatic operator 'The speaker means to say that', here denoted as 'Mean'. The disjunctive theory asserts (**a**), which is false, instead of (**b**), which is true:

(**a**) S is ambiguous between S_1 and S_2 $\Leftrightarrow$ Mean $(S_1 \vee S_2)$.
(**b**) S is ambiguous between S_1 and S_2 $\Leftrightarrow$
Mean(S_1) $\vee$ Mean(S_2).

Clause (**b**) does not run into the difficulties noted above. Moreover, (**b**) avoids a pragmatic problem with (**a**): On a Gricean theory of communication, the disjunction in (**a**) implies that the speaker does not know which disjunct is true. This is clearly at odds with the facts about uttering an ambiguous sentence. Clause (**b**) does not share this problem. What the Gricean maxim of Quantity implies for (**b**) is simply that the interpreter does not know whether the speaker intended to assert S_1 or S_2, and that seems just right.

There is one final argument against the disjunctive theory of ambiguity that we want to add because of its relevance to what is to come: the disjunctive theory is unable to reflect **connections between interpretive choices** in a natural way. More precisely, if the set of meanings that an ambiguous expression may have is subject to a connection constraint, then this set of meanings cannot be determined compositionally.

For example, suppose the sentence e is ambiguous between logical translations e' and e'', while a connection constraint requires that all occurrences of e must be interpreted equally. Suppose, further, that the sentence f can also mean either e' or e'', while there is no connection constraint that is applicable to f. Then consider a sentence S_{ee} containing 2 occurrences of e as subsentences. Although each occurrence has two possible meanings, leading to 4 possible combinations, the connection constraint requires the meaning of S_{ee} to be a disjunction of only 2 disjuncts:

$$(... \; e' \; ... \; e' \; ...) \vee (... \; e'' \; ... \; e'' \; ...) \; .$$

Now let S_{fe} be the sentence that results from S_{ee} when the *first* occurrence of e in S_{ee} is replaced by f. Then compositionality requires that S_{fe} and S_{ee} have the same meaning, since both e and f have meanings representable as $e' \vee e''$. But this would stretch the connection constraint to also cover the sentence S_{fe}, to which it should not apply.

Note that this argument has little to do with the operation of *disjunction* itself. Rather, what one can learn from it is that the meaning of an ambiguous expression is not determined by the set of its possible interpretations. Like the disjunction theorist, we will assume that the proper analysis of an ambiguous expression must, at some level, appeal to notions that are non-ambiguous, but we will use the individual meanings themselves (i.e., the meanings that an ambiguous expression *can* have) as the centrepiece of our account, and we will do this in such a way that one can keep track, for each ambiguous subexpression of a sentence, of the possible interpretations of that subexpression.

3   Ambiguous Representations in Earlier Proposals

Traditional NLP systems map natural language expressions to unambiguous representations of some sort or other. If a system uses a version of compositionality, there is of course the problem that an ambiguous expression must be mapped to more than one such representation, but this problem is usually solved (see e.g., Montague 1973) by postulating a syntactic difference to match the different interpretations. For example, different quantifier scope orders motivate the postulation of different derivations. Likewise, if an ambiguous word like *pitcher* is treated in a system of this kind, two different words are postulated which happen to have the same form, and these two words are attributed different interpretations.

Since the early eighties, this treatment of ambiguity has given way to a more flexible account, in which the system makes use of a level of representation that uses expressions that are themselves ambiguous. An early example is Philips' Phliqa system (see e.g., Bronnenberg et al. 1979), in which this strategy was applied mainly to cope with lexical ambiguities. An invented example is the ambiguity of the word *American*, which can mean

$\lambda x : Country(DeparturePlace(x)) = USA$ (for a flight),
$\lambda x : Country(Manufacturer(x)) = USA$ (for an airplane),
$\lambda x : Country(PlaceOfBirth(x)) = USA$ (for a person),

and so on. In Phliqa, the word *American* would be mapped onto an ambiguous constant *American*, which is later mapped to one of the unambiguous paraphrases $American_1$, $American_2$, etc., each of which had one of the interpretations listed above. Something similar was done for the interpretation of ambiguous prepositions.

Later, a similar approach was taken by others, most notably several authors at SRI (see e.g., Moran 1988), to deal with scope ambiguities. These authors, and many others following up on their work, make use of so-called quasi-logical formulas, in which scope ambiguities are left unresolved. The advantage of doing this is considerable: the syntax is not burdened by what most syntacticians feel are purely semantic considerations, and the computational load on the system, for storing and processing the meaning of a formula at a stage at which has not yet been resolved, is reduced considerably. On the other hand, these approaches are conservative, logically speaking. The ambiguous representations were never evaluated as to their truth, and they were not subjected to logical inference. They only serve for storage. No 'functionally' interesting operations were defined on ambiguous representations.[6]

In the last few years, however, a growing number of researchers have looked into semantic questions that involve ambiguous representations (Poesio 1991, van Deemter 1991, Reyle 1992). Reyle, for example, has come up with a proposal in which Discourse Representation Structures can leave scope undefined, and in which a relation of inference is proposed between these scope-ambiguous formulas. Most of the work has focused on rather complex ambiguities, mostly involving quantifier scope. The empirical questions in that area are far from resolved, and the ambiguities involved are considerably harder to handle than, say, lexical ambiguities. As a result, some of this work is difficult to understand. Secondly, fundamental questions about the relation of logical consequence that fits the new, ambiguous setting, have seldom been

---

[6]A partial exception is Westerståhl et al. 1993, in which certain ambiguities are resolved by means of a reasoning component that makes use of ambiguous formulas. The possibility of reasoning with formulas that are ambiguous with respect to the scope of quantifiers and/or the resolution of anaphors was indicated, but not actually pursued in Fenstad et al. 1987.

asked. Instead, research has tended to move straight to proposals for deductive systems. The present paper, which is a much revised and expanded version of a chapter of van Deemter 1991, will argue that there are some nontrivial semantic questions that ought to be answered before questions of deduction can be handled with the success they deserve.

4   Simple Logics for a Lexically Ambiguous Language

4.1   Interpretation and Truth

This section will present a model theory for a language with ambiguous constants. A simplifying assumption will be made, namely that there are no *connection* constraints (cf., section 2) in place. In other words, each occurrence of an ambiguous constant is evaluated without regard for the way in which other occurrences of ambiguous constants happen to be disambiguated. This assumption is abandoned in section 5.

First, let the unambiguous language $\mathcal{L}$ be a many-sorted version of first order predicate logic. Sorted domains are essential for modeling the disambiguating effect that context may have on interpretation, as will become clear later on. Let us assume that the language $\mathcal{L}$ has individual constants as well as variables of types $e_1, ..., e_n$, all of which have disjoint domains, namely $D_{e_1}, ..., D_{e_n}$. There are predicates of types $\langle e_1, t \rangle, ..., \langle e_n, t \rangle$ with corresponding functional domains, where D_t is the set of truth values. Now let $\mathcal{L}(A)$ be an extension of $\mathcal{L}$ that contains ambiguous constants. A given ambiguous constant can live in more than one domain. Accordingly, constants of $\mathcal{L}(A)$ are attributed *sets* of types rather than one single type. The domain that is associated with a given set of types equals the union of the domains that are associated with A's elements. Formally:

> The set **N-type** of nonambiguous types contains the type t (*Domain:* $\{1, 0\}$) and the individual types $e_1, ..., e_n$ (*Domains:* $D_{e_1}, ..., D_{e_n}$), and functional types of the form $\langle \alpha, \beta \rangle$ where α and β are N-types (*Domain:* $D_\beta^{D_\alpha}$).

Each expression of $\mathcal{L}$ has an element of *N-type* as its type. Each expression of $\mathcal{L}(\mathbf{A})$, however, has a nonempty subset of *N-type* as its type. The resulting set of types will be denoted *Types*:

$$Types =_{Def} \mathcal{P}(\textit{N-type}) - \{\phi\}.$$

Each element $A \in Types$ is associated with a domain D_A that is the union of the domains that are associated with the elements of A:

$$D_A = \bigcup_{\alpha \in A} D_\alpha$$

For example, a constant e that is ambiguous as to whether it denotes an element of D_{e_1} or one of D_{e_2} is associated with the type $\{e_1, e_2\}$, and its domain equals $D_{e_1} \cup D_{e_2}$. If a constant happens to be ambiguous between interpretations that live in the same domain D_e, then it has the type $\{e\}$, and its domain is just D_e. Application of a predicate F with type α to an argument a of type β is well-formed iff at least one element of α has the form $\langle \gamma, t \rangle$ such that $\gamma \in \beta$.

For an interpretation function to be suitable for interpreting ambiguous constants, it must be allowed to have different values for different occurrences of a constant. One way to look at the situation is to imagine an enumeration of all the occurrences of formulas of $\mathcal{L}(A)$ that will ever be formulated, and to attach the superscript i to the i-th occurrence of a constant α. Thus, any two occurrences α^i, α^j become different expressions of the language, as the superscripts indicate. However, superscripts are suppressed unless confusion is possible.

If we call a model in the new style a *mode*, then a mode must contain a sorted domain D and a new-style interpretation $\Im$. $\Im$ interprets occurrences of constants, under the constraint that occurrences of unambiguous constants are sent to the same object. Even if a predication $F(a)$, where F and/or a are ambiguous, is well-formed, F and a may be interpreted in such a way that $\Im(a)$ does or does not live in the domain from which $\Im(F)$ takes its arguments. If it does, then F (or also $\Im(F)$) is said to be *Applicable* to a (or also to $\Im(a)$). If it is not, it is *Inapplicable* and a *type conflict* is said to have arisen. *Truth* with respect to a mode is basically a classical notion, except for the fact that the clause for an atomic formula must allow different interpretations for different occurrences of constants. We will use $m \models R^k(a_1^i, ..., a_n^j)$ as short for '$R^k(a_1^i, ..., a_n^j)$ is true with respect to m', and it is assumed that $m = \langle D, \Im \rangle$.

$$m \models R^k(a_1^i, ..., a_n^j) \Leftrightarrow \langle \Im(a_1^i), ..., \Im(a_n^j) \rangle \in \Im(R^k).$$

The set of interpretations that are possible for a given ambiguous constant is constrained by special Meaning Postulates. Each ambiguous constant α has a Meaning Postulate Set MPS_α associated with it that has at least two formulas of $\mathcal{L}(A)$ as its elements. Each of these is a biconditional spelling out one particular interpretation that α may have. For example, if α is a predicate, then the elements of MPS_α have the following form:

$$\forall \overrightarrow{x} \, ((\alpha(\overrightarrow{x}) \leftrightarrow \phi(\overrightarrow{x})),$$

where ϕ is a formula of $\mathcal{L}$, and hence unambiguous, and $\overrightarrow{x}$ is a tuple of variables. For instance, the set $\text{MPS}_{pitcher}$ contains the following biconditionals:

$\forall x(Pitcher(x) \leftrightarrow Jug(x))$,
$\forall x(Pitcher(x) \leftrightarrow Baseballplayer(x))$.

Each occurrence $pitcher^i$ of the word *pitcher* must correspond to one of the two, either meaning the same as *jug*, or the same as, roughly, *baseball player*.[7]

If D_p is the set of people and D_u is the set of utensils, with corresponding types e_p and e_u, then the ambiguous constant *pitcher* is of type $\{\langle e_p, t\rangle, \langle e_u, t\rangle\}$ and has domain $D_{\langle e_p, t\rangle} \cup D_{\langle e_u, t\rangle}$. Conventional Meaning Postulates are to spell out the relationships between nonambiguous constants. For instance, $\forall x(Jug(x) \rightarrow Inanimate(x))$ expresses that, in a mode with interpretation $\Im$, all occurrences jug^i and $inanimate^j$ of the words *jug* and *inanimate* must be interpreted in such a way that $\Im(\text{jug}^i) \subseteq \Im(\text{inanimate}^j)$. The set of these conventional Meaning Postulates is denoted **MP**. We define

A mode $m = \langle D, \Im \rangle$ is *admissible* if m verifies all elements of **MP**, while, for each occurrence of an ambiguous constant α, m verifies one element of MPS_α.

Thus, for a mode to be admissible, it must obey the meaning postulates in its interpretation of any occurrence of any constant in any text.[8] Below, **M** denotes the set of admissible modes. Assume that we are dealing with a text τ and a classical model $M = \langle D, I \rangle$. When ambiguous constants enter the picture we say that a new-style interpretation $\Im$ *extends* (is an extension of) a classical interpretation I if it treats all occurrences of unambiguous constants in accordance with I:

$\Im$ *extends* I if, for all occurrences α^i of unambiguous constants α, $\Im(\alpha^i) = I(\alpha)$.

The key to a formalization of a 'way to interpret' ambiguous constants lies in the dependence of the denotation of ambiguous constants on that of unambiguous ones. To model this dependence, the notion of a disambiguation function μ is used that takes a model as its argument and a *mode* as its value. The set **Dis** of possible disambiguations is defined as follows:

Dis is the set of functions μ that have a model $M = \langle D, I \rangle$ as argument and a mode $\mu(M)$ as value, and such that, for all M, it holds that $\mu(M) = \langle D, \Im \rangle$, for a certain $\Im$ that *extends* I.

However, not just any element of **Dis** can pass for a realistic disam-

---

[7]In the current example, the right-hand side of the biconditional happens to be an atomic formula. This may not always be possible, in which case a complex predicate must take its place. – To simplify presentation, we pretend that *baseball player* is a suitable predicate, even though the actual English word *pitcher* is not synonym with *baseball player* on any of its interpretations.

[8]Recall the perspective on occurrences that triggered the introduction of superscrips. A weaker version of admissibility, in which a *text* is a parameter of the definition, can easily be formulated.

biguation unless it chooses the same interpretation, no matter to what model it is applied. This property, which will be called **model independence**, can be formalized as follows. Note that c is a variable over *occurrences* of ambiguous constants and **c** is the constant of which c is an occurrence. We will sometimes write $\mu \in Indep$ to say that μ is model independent.

μ is **model independent** $\Leftrightarrow_{Def}$
$\forall c \exists \phi \in \text{MPS}_{\mathbf{c}} \forall M : \mu(M) \models \phi.$

In other words, something must hold for all occurrences of constants α: the mode that results when μ is applied to a model must always verify the same 'choice' ϕ from amongst the possible interpretations MPS_{α}. Intuitively, μ can be identified with this choice. Note that model independence of a disambiguation μ implies that μ must always lead to *admissible* modes:

Fact: If $\mu \in Indep$ then $\forall M : \mu(M)$ is admissible.

There are several plausible options for truth and falsity with respect to a *model*, since models are incomplete when it comes to dealing with an ambiguous constant. On the assumption that truth/falsity of an ambiguous formula in a model depends on the truth of the formula in extensions of the model, different notions of truth (of the ambiguous formula) arise through different ways of quantifying over extensions that verify the formula:

ϕ is true with respect to a model M $\Leftrightarrow$
ϕ is true in Q admissible modes that extend M,

where Q is any generalized quantifier. In principle, many different values for Q could be defended, as long as Q is monotone increasing. Falsity is defined analogously, except that then Q has to be monotone decreasing. If standard logical practice is followed and attention is restricted to the four 'logical' quantifiers, we are left with the following options:[9]

Strong: ϕ is true (false) with respect to a model M $\Leftrightarrow$
ϕ is true (false) in all admissible modes that extend M,

Weak: ϕ is true (false) with respect to a model M $\Leftrightarrow$
ϕ is true (false) in some admissible modes that extend M.

Note that if truth and falsity are defined in the weak sense, then a sentence may be both true and false, while conversely, if truth and falsity are defined in the strong sense, a sentence may fail to be true

---

[9]Note that this leaves out some interesting possibilities, such as the case where Q_1 is the quantifier *most*. For a mathematical characterization of the four logical quantifiers, cf., van Benthem 1986.

and fail to be false. Both options make sense in their own way. This is the first sign that in an ambiguous setting, logical concepts (truth, falsity, logical consequence) become ambiguous themselves.

4.2 Reasoning under Lexical Ambiguity

Now that versions of truth and falsity have been defined, the next step is logical consequence. There are several ways of doing this. One *a priori* class of possibilities arises when the principle is applied that logical consequence should *preserve truth*. Consider an inference of the form $\phi \models^a \psi$ (the notation $\models^a$ refers to a hitherto unspecified relation of 'ambiguous' logical consequence), where both ϕ and ψ may be ambiguous. Then a direct application of the principle says that

$\phi \models^a \psi \Leftrightarrow_{Def}$ For all models M, if ϕ is true with respect to M then ψ is true with respect to M,

which has 4 different interpretations, depending on the way in which *true* is defined (see section 4.1). However, it seems that none of the resulting notions of ambiguous consequence is very natural. Consider the most cautious of the four variants:

$\phi \models^a \psi \Leftrightarrow_{Def}$ For all models M, if ϕ is strongly true with respect to M then ψ is (at least) weakly true with respect to M.

Consider ϕ having two incompatible interpretations, such as

Pitcher(j).

Baseball-player(j) and *Jug(j)* are incompatible in the sense that no admissible model can verify both formulas, provided the Meaning Postulates forbid that something is both a baseball player and a jug. Thus, the antecedent of the definiens (ϕ is strongly true w.r.t. M) is false for any M. But then it follows that the argument

Pitcher(j) $\models^a \psi$

is valid for arbitrary ψ. This is clearly undesirable. Analogous objections apply to the other three notions of ambiguous consequence that result from a direct application of the principle that logical consequence consists in the preservation of truth.

More natural notions of ambiguous consequence result if we stick to the idea of quantifying over possible interpretations, while abandoning the idea that premises and conclusion must be judged independently of each other. For example, one may define, informally,

$\phi_1, ..., \phi_n \models^a \psi \Leftrightarrow_{Def}$ For *each* way of interpreting $\phi_1, ..., \phi_n$, there *is* a way of interpreting ψ that makes the argument classically valid.

Before moving on to more precise semantic versions of ambiguous consequence, let us take a syntactic view. Let us move the notion of a *paraphrase* (cf., section 2) from the domain of natural language into that of logic. Thus, a paraphrase of an ambiguous expression α is any unambiguous formula that has as its *only* interpretation what α has on *one* of its interpretations. An important special case of a logical paraphrase is that of a *canonical* paraphrase, in which the paraphrase results by replacing ambiguous constants by their counterparts in the relevant meaning postulate. For example, if the relevant meaning postulate is the biconditional $\forall \overrightarrow{x} \, ((\alpha(\overrightarrow{x}) \leftrightarrow \phi(\overrightarrow{x})))$, then if an ambiguous expression β contains α as its only ambiguous constant, then the canonical paraphrase of β results from replacing α by ϕ, throughout β. The notion of a canonical paraphrase will be useful later on.

Returning to the notion of a paraphrase, each 'way of interpreting' an ambiguous formula corresponds with a set of paraphrases, all of which are logically equivalent. Using this viewpoint, the just-cited definition instantiates the following schema:

$$\phi_1, ..., \phi_n \models^a \psi \Leftrightarrow_{Def} Q_1\chi \in A \; Q_2\eta \in B : \chi \models \eta$$

where A is the set of paraphrases of $\phi_1 \& ... \& \phi_n$ and B is the set of paraphrases of ψ. In this particular instantiation, Q_1 is identified as the universal quantifier, and Q_2 as the existential quantifier. This notion of logical consequence is equivalent to what one gets if both the premises and the conclusion are represented by means of the disjunction of their interpretations.[10] Other instantiations lead to different relations between premises and conclusion.

Which of all these possible relations between A and B are *bona fide* notions of ambiguous consequence? To obtain a partial answer to this question, let us replace the relation $\models$ by a variable R and make the relation of ambiguous consequence dependent on the choice of R:

$$\phi_1, ..., \phi_n \models^a_R \psi \Leftrightarrow_{Def} Q_1\chi \in A \; Q_2\eta \in B : \langle \chi, \eta \rangle \in R.$$

A natural requirement for the relation of ambiguous consequence is monotonicity in R:

If $R \subseteq R'$ then $\models^a_R \subseteq \models^a_{R'}$.

In other words, if the underlying relation of unambiguous logical consequence is relaxed (for example by the addition of a meaning postulate to R), then the corresponding relation of ambiguous consequence is also relaxed. Let Q_1 and Q_2, once more (cf., section 4.1), be logical

---

[10]See section 2. If the set A consists of $A_1, .., A_n$, each of which corresponds to a way of disambiguating all the premises, while the set B consists of $B_1, ..., B_m$, each of which corresponds to a way of disambiguating the conclusion, then this instantiation can also be written as $\phi_1, ..., \phi_n \models^a \psi \Leftrightarrow_{Def} (A_1 \vee .... \vee A_n \models B_1 \vee ... \vee B_m)$, where $\models$ denotes classical logical consequence.

quantifiers. Then the following Fact can be proven by inspecting all 16 possible combinations of quantifiers:

Fact: $\models_R^a$ is monotonic in R iff Q_1 and Q_2 have equal monotonicity, i.e., iff both are $(-\uparrow)$ or both are $(-\downarrow)$.

For example, if $Q_1 = Q_2$ is the existential quantifier (i.e., *some*), then ambiguous consequence requires that premises and conclusion *have paraphrases* that stand in the relation R. If this is true, then ambiguous consequence (i.e., $\models_R^a$) is clearly monotonic in R. The Fact that was just cited leaves us with only 4 possible combinations:

1. $Q_1 = Q_2 = some$
2. $Q_1 = Q_2 = all$
3. $Q_1 = some$, $Q_2 = all$
4. $Q_1 = all$, $Q_2 = some$

Once more, each of the resulting definitions is perfectly legitimate. The instantiation (1) says that the argument can be made valid by a properly chosen disambiguation, whereas (2) says that the relation *cannot* be *in*validated by such a disambiguation. Likewise, (3) says that the premises can be disambiguated in such a way that the conclusion cannot be disambiguated in such a way that it fails to follow; (4) expresses that no matter how the premises are disambiguated, a validating disambiguation of the conclusion can be found. Below, instantiation (1) will be denoted as $\models_{\exists\exists}$, (2) as $\models_{\forall\forall}$, (3) as $\models_{\exists\forall}$, and (4) as $\models_{\forall\exists}$. The various meta-logical properties of the different notions of ambiguous consequence will be taken up in section 6.

The different possible notions of ambiguous consequence can be formalized in the framework of the present section. We will write $m \models \phi$ for "ϕ is true with respect to m". A is a formula and τ is a text, that is, a sequence of formulas. Note that if μ is a disambiguation and M is a model, then $\mu(M)$ is a mode:

$\tau \models_{\forall\forall} A \Leftrightarrow_{Def}$
$\forall\mu\forall M \ (\mu(M) \in \mathbf{M} \ \& \ \mu(M)$ does not lead to type conflict in $\tau \cup \{A\}$
$\Rightarrow (\mu(M) \models \tau \ \Rightarrow \ \mu(M) \models A))$.

$\tau \models_{\exists\exists} A \Leftrightarrow_{Def}$
$\exists\mu\forall M \ (\mu(M) \in \mathbf{M} \ \& \ \mu(M)$ does not lead to type conflict in $\tau \cup \{A\}$
$\Rightarrow (\mu(M) \models \tau \ \Rightarrow \ \mu(M) \models A))$.

$\tau \models_{\forall\exists} A \Leftrightarrow_{Def}$
$\forall\mu\forall M((\mu(M) \in \mathbf{M} \ \& \ \mu(M)$ does not lead to type conflict in $\tau \cup$
$\{A\} \ \& \ \mu(M) \models \tau)$
$\Rightarrow (\exists\mu' : \mu'(M) \in \mathbf{M} \ \& \ \mu'(M) \models A))$.

$\tau \models_{\exists\forall} A \Leftrightarrow_{Def}$

$\exists \mu (\forall M ((\mu(M) \in \mathbf{M} \ \& \ \mu(M)$ does not lead to type conflict in $\tau \cup \{A\}$
$\& \ \mu(M) \models \tau)$
$\Rightarrow (\forall \mu' : \mu'(M) \in \mathbf{M} \Rightarrow \mu'(M) \models A)))$

The intuitive idea of the first definition is simple: the relation $\models_{\forall \forall}$ holds if it is true for each admissible mode that does not lead to type conflict in either τ or A that if it verifies τ then it verifies A. In the second definition, a real separation between disambiguations and models becomes necessary. The reason is that the disambiguation must appear existentially quantified, while logical consequence requires the models to appear universally quantified: $\models_{\exists \exists}$ holds in case a disambiguation μ can be found such that each mode that is based on μ and that avoids type conflicts and verifies τ must also verify A. The other two definitions follow a similar pattern.

In these definitions, the restriction that $\mu(M) \in \mathbf{M}$ may be replaced by the condition that μ itself is model independent. For example, $\models_{\forall \exists}$ can equivalently be formulated as follows:

$\tau \models_{\forall \exists} A \Leftrightarrow_{Def}$
$\forall \mu \in Indep \ \forall M ((\mu(M) \models \tau) \ \& \mu(M)$ does not lead to type conflict
in $\tau \cup \{A\} \Rightarrow (\exists \mu' \in Indep : \mu'(M) \models A))$.

A more crucial use of *Indep* is made in the next section.

In section 6, some of the notions of ambiguous consequence that have come up so far will be compared, but first a number of interpretive principles will be studied that will lead to yet different varieties of ambiguous consequence.

5   Constraints on Interpretation

5.1   Some Constraints and their Applications

In section 2, we briefly hinted at the existence of certain constraints on the interpretation of occurrences of ambiguous expressions which can lead to connections between different occurrences of a given ambiguous expression. Imagine that *no* such constraints are in place, other than the obvious requirements deriving from type correctness. For example, let F be ambiguous between interpretations $\|F_1\|$ and $\|F_2\|$, both of which are applicable to the argument $\|a\|$, while the Meaning Postulates allow that there are models in which $F_1(a)$ is true and $F_2(a)$ is false. Then two of the relations of logical consequence that were mentioned in section 4 do not support this instance of reflexivity:

$F(a) \not\models_{\forall \forall} F(a)$
$F(a) \not\models_{\exists \forall} F(a)$.

However, there is considerable evidence that in actual natural language interpretation, several interpretative principles are active beyond mere type correctness. Two plausible candidates for such principles will be discussed, namely a principle of coherence and a principle of charitable interpretation.

First, there is **coherence**. There is a tendency towards *equal* interpretation of different occurrences of a given expression throughout a 'discourse'.[11] "Coherence" effects of this kind have been reported in corpus-based research, where it was found that an extremely high percentage of occurrences of ambiguous words taken from one and the same discourse are interpreted as having the same sense [12] (Gale et al. 1992, Gale et al. 1992b). Experiments in the psycholinguistic literature suggest a partial explanation of this phenomenon, through what might be called 'interpretive slowness': Experiments by Simpson and Kellas reported a remarkable persistence in subjects' interpretation of ambiguous words offered in isolation, that is, without the context of a discourse or even a sentence (Simpson and Kellas 1989). Thus, it seems plausible that well-written texts are written in such a way that this interpretive tendency is rewarded. Needless to say, principles of coherence can take different forms, leading to different predictions. For now, let me observe that if a notion of ambiguous consequence somehow incorporates a coherence constraint that requires the two occurrences of F in the argument '$F(a)$, therefore $F(a)$' to be interpreted in the same way, then the argument must become valid. In other words, reflexivity would be saved.

Secondly, there is the principle of **charity**. Consider the constants F and a that were also invoked in our discussion of coherence, and consider the discourse

$F(a) \ \& \ \neg F(a).$

Coherence alone would make the discourse inconsistent. Instead of coherence – or as a qualification of coherence – one might assume there to be a principle of Charity, which requires one to interpret a discourse in a consistent (and non-trivial) way whenever this is possible. This principle underlies what is written by working linguists when they explain the absence of a certain interpretation of an expression by the fact that it would lead to an implausible interpretation.

Before we come to a formalization of some of these ideas, let me stress how useful the principles of coherence and charity can be. If it is assumed that an interpreter uses the two principles (in some com-

---

[11] No precise definition of 'discourse' will be attempted here, but it will be assumed that a logical argument constitutes a discourse.

[12] The discourses were taken from New Grolier's Electronic Encyclopedia. Interpretation of polysemous words (e.g., *sentence*) was judged by 5 independent judges and an occurrence of a word was counted as having a given sense if a majority of judges attributed that sense to it. The outcome was that 96.9% of the word occurrences that were taken from the same text were judged to have the same sense.

bination) as a filter for all the interpretations that he considers, this accounts for a very interesting class of disambiguations.

A very different application of these principles is to explain some of the empirical tests that linguists have proposed for distinguishing ambiguity from non-specificity. Why, for instance, is *person* not ambiguous between, say, *man* and *woman*? We have seen in section 2 that there is a difference between not making a distinction and being ambiguous as to the distinction, but how does one decide which of the two applies in a specific case? Two tests for recognizing ambiguity are often cited: Lakoff's conjunction test (Lakoff 1970) and Margalit's 'pragmatic' tests (Margalit 1983).

The **first test** takes the expression that is at stake, and puts it in a VP that is followed by VP ellipsis:

(a) x is a pitcher and y too.
(b) x is a person and y too.

Lakoff observed that in (b), the first conjunct may refer to a woman and the second to a man, whereas in (a), either both conjuncts refer to jugs, or both refer to baseball players. Lakoff attributes this difference to a highly specific semantic constraint on the transformational rule of VP Deletion that derives (a) from (a′) and (b) from (b′), respectively:

(a′) x is a pitcher and y is a pitcher too.
(b′) x is a person and y is a person too.

The constraint says that VP Deletion can only delete one of two occurrences of a VP if both have the same meaning.

This test may lead to the right results, but authors like Atlas have rightly asked for an explanation (Atlas 1984). Our own answer is that an explanation can be obtained through the concept of *coherence*. Lakoff misses a generalization, since he makes no predictions as to the meaning of unreduced conjunctions, such as (a′) and (b′). After all, (b′) can felicitously (and truly) be uttered if x is a man and y is a woman, but an utterance of (a′) in a situation in which x is a jug and y a baseball player can only be felicitous as a joke. Unlike Lakoff's otherwise unmotivated constraint on VP deletion, a principle of coherent interpretation will automatically explain the facts about (a′) and (b′). The facts about the elliptical forms (a) and (b) follow immediately if these are derived via VP Deletion.

The **second test**, proposed by Margalit, seeks to exploit more directly that ambiguous expressions can be used in one and the same sentence and yet result in different truth values (cf., Quine 1960). Take the expression α that is at stake and put it in a contrastive context, such as (if α is a Common Noun)

This is no α! This is an α.

If a speaker can get away with saying this, then α is ambiguous, and otherwise it is not. As in the case of Lakoff's test, one may agree with Margalit's proposal and yet be unsatisfied. After all, wouldn't the principle of coherence predict that both occurrences of α should have the same meaning? How then is it possible that this rule is violated?

The answer that we want to suggest is that the facts that Margalit exploits are predicted if coherence is modified to reflect the principle of *charity*. Charity requires an interpreter to choose an interpretation that avoids logical inconsistency. Obviously, the principle of coherence cannot require *absolute* coherence, since type restrictions may force different occurrences of an ambiguous expression to have different meanings, as in

The pitcher was drinking wine from a pitcher.

In a case like this, suitably chosen type constraints may do the job. Type constraints overrule 'absolute' coherence, as it were. But coherence may also be overruled by logical considerations. For example, in

I am not so green as to eat green bananas (Landsbergen and Scha 1979),

type definitions cannot do the job, since it is possible for a person to assume a greenish colour. Thus, coherence should be formulated carefully, so as to become active only after all logically defective interpretations have been filtered out. Formulated in this way, the combined principle of Coherence/Charity will also predict Margalit's schema to be perfectly felicitous in case α is ambiguous.

This concludes our defence of the interpretive principles of Coherence and Charity. In the next section a formalization will be attempted.

5.2 A Possible Formalization of the Constraints

Given that *complete* coherence is sometimes impossible in an ambiguous setting, the question is how much coherence is required? Should the interpretation of a given expression be required to be coherent with both past and future bits of discourse? How far away can an interpretive 'antecedent' be from the expression that is to be interpreted? Should an ambiguous constant be coherent with other occurrences of the same ambiguous constant only, or also with unambiguous constants, as when *pitcher* is juxtaposed with *jug* (making it more likely to also be interpreted as *jug* too)? And should only synonymy of interpretations be taken into account, or also subsumption of interpretations, as when *star* is juxtaposed with *movie* (which might make it less likely to be interpreted as a heavenly body)?

Rather than try to determine which variety of coherence is empirically most accurate, we will formulate one possible version, which is, in its general implications, representative of other options.[13] The entire discourse will be taken into account for the interpretation of a given ambiguous constant, but only in as far as occurrences of the same constant are concerned. As many occurrences of constants as possible are interpreted equally. First, a variant of coherence will formulated that does not take the principle of Charity into account. Charity will be added later.

We will build on the proposal in section 4, in which such notions as a new-style interpretation, a *mode* of interpretation, and a *disambiguation function* were defined. At least initially, Coherence is defined as a property of either a mode or an interpretation, relative to a text and a set of Meaning Postulates. This is done by requiring of the interpretation $\Im$ that it contains a minimum of exceptions. To do this, let the *agreement number* of a new-style interpretation, relative to a text, denote the number of occurrences of constants in that text that are interpreted in the same way as some other occurrence of the same constant in that text:

$\Im$'s *agreement number*, relative to a text τ, equals

$| \{\alpha^i : \alpha^i$ occurs in τ and there occurs α^j in τ such that $i \neq j$ and $\Im(\alpha^i) = \Im(\alpha^j)\} |$.

If $m = \langle D, \Im \rangle$, $\Im$'s agreement number will also be called m's agreement number. *Coherence* can now be defined as a property of a mode:

Let M be a model $\langle D, I \rangle$. Then a mode $m = \langle D, \Im \rangle$, where $\Im$ extends I is *coherent* with respect to a text τ iff
— **(i)** m is admissible,
— **(ii)** $\Im$ does not lead to type conflict in τ.
— **(iii)** there is no extension $\Im'$ of I such that $m' = \langle D, \Im' \rangle$ fulfills (i) and (ii) and has a higher Agreement Number, relative to τ, than $\Im$.

An *interpretation* is called coherent with respect to a text if it is contained in a coherent mode for that text. A mode m is said to *extend* a model M if the interpretation function contained in m extends the one contained in M. A coherent notion of logical consequence must restrict quantification to coherent modes. In the following, coherence is required with respect to the argument as a whole.[14]

$\tau \models_{\vee\vee}^{Coh} A \Leftrightarrow_{Def}$

---

[13] In particular, the behaviour with respect to most structural rules (cf., section 6.2) remains largely unaffected by the details of the coherence principle.
[14] Alternatively, interpretations of the *premisses* could be required to be coherent with respect to the premisses, and interpretations of the *conclusion* could be required to be coherent with respect to the conclusion.

$\forall\mu\forall M\,(\mu(M)$ coherent w.r.t. $\tau\cup A \;\Rightarrow\; (\mu(M)\models\tau \;\Rightarrow\; \mu(M)\models A)).$

$\tau \models^{Coh}_{\exists\exists} A \;\Leftrightarrow_{Def}$
$\exists\mu\forall M\,(\mu(M)$ coherent w.r.t. $\tau\cup A \;\Rightarrow\; (\mu(M)\models\tau \;\Rightarrow\; \mu(M)\models A)).$

$\tau \models^{Coh}_{\forall\exists} A \;\Leftrightarrow_{Def}$
$\forall\mu\forall M((\mu(M)$ coherent w.r.t. $\tau\cup A\;\&\;\mu(M)\models\tau) \Rightarrow$
$(\exists\mu' : \mu'(M)$ coherent w.r.t. $\tau\cup A\;\&\;\mu'(M)\models A)).$

$\tau \models^{Coh}_{\exists\forall} A \;\Leftrightarrow_{Def}$
$\exists\mu(\forall M((\mu(M)$ coherent w.r.t. $\tau\cup A\;\&\;\mu(M)\models\tau) \Rightarrow$
$(\forall\mu' : \mu'(M)$ coherent w.r.t. $\tau\cup A \Rightarrow \mu'(M)\models A)))$

Suppose the constant a behaves like the English noun *integration*, in that it has two interpretations, one of which (a_m) lives in a mathematical domain D_m and the other (a_s) in a social domain D_s. The first of the two is of type e_s and denotes the social process of integration; the second is of type e_m and denotes the mathematical function of integration. The set of Meaning Postulates MPS_a contains at least the options $a = a_m$ and $a = a_s$. Suppose there are disambiguating predicates A of type $\langle e_m, t\rangle$ and G of type $\langle e_s, t\rangle$. For example, A could be *Applied in calculations*, and G *Good for society*. Suppose the equality relation has no type constraints, so $a = b$ is true if a and b denote the same object, and false in any other case, regardless of the types of a and b. Then consider the following three bits of discourse.

$\tau := (a = a_s)$
$\tau' := (G(a) \rightarrow a = a_s)$
$\tau'' := (A(a) \rightarrow a = a_s)$

Which interpretations are coherent with respect to each of these? For τ, any admissible interpretation – that is, any interpretation that interprets a as either a_s or a_m – is fine. Some of these verify $a = a_s$, others falsify it. For τ', the situation is different, because the predicate G forces its argument a to be interpreted as a_s, or else a type conflict results. But then the Agreement Number of an interpretation will only be maximized if the second occurrence of a in τ' is also interpreted as a_s. Consequently, a coherent interpretation must verify the consequent of τ', and therefore also τ' itself. In other words,

$\models^{Coh}_{\exists\exists} \tau$, and $\models^{Coh}_{\exists\exists} \tau'$.
$\not\models^{Coh}_{\forall\forall} \tau$, but $\models^{Coh}_{\forall\forall} \tau'$. [15]

---

[15] The only relevant difference between the two notions of ambiguous consequence in this particular case is, of course, in the quantification over the interpretations of the conclusion, since the set of premises is empty. Therefore, $\models_{\exists\exists}$ and $\models^{Coh}_{\exists\exists}$ behave exactly like $\models_{\forall\exists}$ and $\models^{Coh}_{\forall\exists}$, respectively; and $\models_{\forall\forall}$ and $\models^{Coh}_{\forall\forall}$ behave like $\models_{\exists\forall}$ and $\models^{Coh}_{\exists\forall}$.

The situation for τ'' is different again, since no coherent interpretations whatsoever can verify it:

$$\not\models^{Coh}_{\exists\exists} \tau'', \text{ and } \not\models^{Coh}_{\forall\forall} \tau''.$$

So far, Charity was not taken into account. Note that the concept of Charity is closely related to that of logical consistency. Consistency has to do with being true in *at least one* mode. Therefore, a slight change of perspective is needed, in which Coherence is no longer defined as a property of a mode, but of a disambiguation. Now suppose a disambiguation μ is model independent. Then the question of whether $\mu(M)$ leads to type conflict does not depend on M. But unfortunately, the agreement number of $\mu(M)$ *can* depend on M. After all, a model M may 'accidentally' make occurrences α^1 and α^2 coextensive, even though two different elements (i.e., meaning postulates having the form of a biconditional) of MPS_α are chosen for them.[16] However, such accidental identifications cannot happen in all models, since this would cause the two elements of MPS_α to collapse. In other words, the minimal number of identifications equals the number of non-accidental identifications. Let us define

> The Lowest Agreement Number of μ, given a set $\mathbf{S}$ of models and a text τ (notation: $\text{LAN}(\mu, \mathbf{S}, \tau)$) equals the minimum of the set of agreement numbers, relative to τ, of all the modes $\mu(M)$, where $M \in \mathbf{S}$.

Now we can redefine coherence as a property of disambiguations, making use of the set $\mathbf{M}$ of admissible modes:

> A model independent disambiguation μ is *coherent* with respect to a text τ iff
> — **(i)** μ does not lead to type conflict in τ,
> — **(ii)** there is no model independent disambiguation μ' that fulfills (i) and such that $\text{LAN}(\mu', \mathbf{M}, \tau) > \text{LAN}(\mu, \mathbf{M}, \tau)$.

The following definition applies this idea to Coherence/Charity. Clause (ii) contains the requirement of Charity:

> A model independent disambiguation μ is Coherent/Charitable with respect to a text τ iff
> — **(i)** μ does not lead to type conflict in τ,
> — **(ii)** $\exists M' : \mu(M') \models \tau$,
> — **(iii)** there is no model independent disambiguation μ' that fulfills (i) and (ii), and such that $\text{LAN}(\mu', \mathbf{M}, \tau) > \text{LAN}(\mu, \mathbf{M}, \tau)$.

By substituting Coherence/Charity for Coherence in the definitions of

---

[16] For example, this is true when *pitcher* is ambiguous between *baseball-player* and *jug*, while these two predicates happen to be coextensive in M. This possibility was pointed out to me by an anonymous reviewer.

truth and ambiguous consequence, new relations of ambiguous consequence are obtained. For example, still assuming all disambiguations to be model independent,

$$\tau \models_{\forall\forall}^{Coh/Char} A \Leftrightarrow_{Def} \forall M \forall \mu \forall m \ (m = \mu(M) \Rightarrow$$
$$((\mu \text{ is coherent/charitable w.r.t. } \tau \cup \{A\} \Rightarrow$$
$$(m \models \tau \Rightarrow m \models A))).$$

A somewhat artificial example of a logical argument that is validated by this notion of ambiguous consequence but not by its 'merely coherent' counterpart is the following. Assume that the predicate F is ambiguous between paraphrases F_1 and F_2, and assume that $F_1(a)$ is true, but $F_2(a)$ is false. Then

$$F_1(a)\&\neg F_2(a) \models_{\forall\forall}^{Coh/Char} F(a)\&\neg F(a),$$

because the quantification is restricted to disambiguations that force the first occurrence of F to mean F_1 and the second to mean F_2. A natural language analogon would be something like

> *This is a jug, and no baseball player. Therefore, it is both a pitcher and not a pitcher.*

The example becomes more natural if the information in the premisse is given the status of a background assumption, rather than of an overt premisse.

6   An Evaluation of some Ambiguous Logics

So far, a rather large number of possibilities have been sketched for a logic with ambiguous constants. They will now be compared. As it turns out, *all* display non-classical behaviour, and this will raise the question in how far classical logical behaviour is a virtue.

Because of the peculiarities of the Coherence principle, it will prove fruitful to look at the logics from two different perspectives: [17] an 'internal' perspective, in which the strength of the relation of logical consequence will be investigated (cf., section 6.1); and an 'external' perspective, in which it will be investigated how logical arguments are combined into new ones (cf., section 6.2). The discussion in 6.1 will be relatively sketchy in comparison with the more thorough treatment in 6.2, which will also summarize some of the main results of 6.1.

6.1   The Strengths of the Logics

The logics of the previous sections are very different in terms of the set of logical inferences that they validate. At one end of the scale there are the notions of ambiguous consequence that involve some sort of existential quantification over interpretations: $\exists\exists$, $\exists\forall$ and $\forall\exists$. Let us call

---

[17] This idea is due to Johan van Benthem.

these the *weak* varieties. The remaining ones, which involve universal quantification over all interpretations ($\forall\forall$) are called the strong ones.

First, the **weak** notions of ambiguous consequence. Perhaps the most striking deviation from classical logic lies in a form of syntactic inconsistency that these logics display. Let us call a notion of logical consequence $\models$ *strongly inconsistent* if ϕ can be found such that $\models \phi \& \neg\phi$. Further, $\models$ is *weakly inconsistent* if ϕ can be found such that $\models \phi$ and $\models \neg\phi$. Finally, $\models$ is *conditionally inconsistent* if ψ and noncontradictory ϕ can be found such that $\phi \models \psi$ and $\phi \models \neg\psi$. Each of the *weak* notions of ambiguous consequence that were defined in earlier sections involve some sort of inconsistency:

$\models_{\exists\exists}$ and $\models_{\forall\exists}$ are conditionally, weakly, and strongly inconsistent.

$\models_{\exists\exists}^{Coh}$ and $\models_{\forall\exists}^{Coh}$ are conditionally and weakly inconsistent.

$\models_{\exists\forall}$ and $\models_{\exists\forall}^{Coh}$ are conditionally inconsistent.

This can be illustrated as follows. Suppose F is ambiguous between a property that is true of all appropriate arguments of a certain type (informally, $\lambda x(x = x)$) and one that is false of all arguments of the same type (i.e., $\lambda x(x \neq x)$). Let a be such that both interpretations of F are applicable to it. Then $\models_{\exists\exists} F(a)\&\neg F(a)$. Note that if $\models_{\exists\exists}$ is replaced by $\models_{\exists\exists}^{Coh}$, the formula $F(a)\&\neg F(a)$ is no theorem anymore, since coherence forces the two occurrences of F to be interpreted in the same way. However, if the two subformulas $F(a)$ and $\neg F(a)$ are distributed over different logical arguments, coherence does not affect them. Consequently, $\models_{\exists\exists}^{Coh}$ is weakly inconsistent, because $\models_{\exists\exists}^{Coh} F(a)$ and $\models_{\exists\exists}^{Coh} \neg F(a)$. Note that inconsistency is not a straightforward argument against these logics, since it may be argued that ϕ and $\neg\phi$ are only syntactic contradictories, to be resolved by an interpreter by chosing different interpretations for the two occurrences of ϕ. The 'coherent-and-charitable' notion of ambiguous consequence formalizes this strategy.

Strong consequence is quite a different story. Again, there is a marked difference between the *noncoherent* version ($\models_{\forall\forall}$) and its coherent kin ($\models_{\forall\forall}^{Coh}$). The noncoherent version leads to an extremely weak logic. Of course, all classical theorems are also theorems of $\models_{\forall\forall}$, since they do not contain ambiguous material:

$$\models \; \subseteq \; \models_{\forall\forall}.$$

In addition, there are inferences that contain ambiguous constants and nevertheless hold on purely classical grounds.[18] But when ambiguous

---

[18] For example, this holds for the inference $G(a) \models_{\forall\forall} G(a) \vee F(a)$, where G and a are unambiguous constants. This inference is valid, no matter whether F is ambiguous or not.

material enters the picture in a more essential way, inference in $\models_{\vee\vee}$ often breaks down. For example, it does not even hold generally that $\phi \models_{\vee\vee} \phi$, since an occurrence of an ambiguous constant in the premiss can be interpreted differently from an occurrence in the conclusion. Yet, $\models_{\vee\vee}$ also contains some truly nonclassical theorems. For example if F is ambiguous between F_1 and F_2, only the first of which is applicable to a, then $F(a) \models_{\vee\vee} F_1(a)$, which is not a classical theorem. Actually, of course, it is not even well-formed in a classical logic, since F is ambiguous. To formulate a connection between $\models_{\vee\vee}$ and classical $\models$, even though they are defined on different classes of formulas, the notion of a paraphrase is once more useful. This time, the notions of a paraphrase and a canonical paraphrase will be applied to a text as a whole, rather than to individual formulas. In particular (and with disregard for coherence), if τ' and ϕ' are paraphrases of τ and ϕ, respectively, then the inference $\tau' \models \phi'$ is a paraphrase of $\tau \models \phi$. Now we can formulate the following Fact:

Fact: $\tau \models_{\vee\vee} \phi \Leftrightarrow$ each paraphrase of $\tau \models \phi$ is classically valid.

Outline of proof: It is sufficient to prove a version of the Fact in which only *canonical* paraphrases are taken into account. This version can be proven along the following lines: ($\Rightarrow$) Suppose there is a canonical paraphrase $\tau' \models \phi'$ of $\tau \models \phi$ that is not classically valid due to a model M that verifies τ', while falsifying ϕ'. This model can be 'translated' into a mode that verifies τ, while falsifying ϕ. Conversely ($\Leftarrow$), suppose $\tau \not\models_{\vee\vee} \phi$, due to a mode m that verifies τ, while falsifying ϕ. Then m can be used to find canonical paraphrases τ' and ϕ', and a model M such that M verifies τ', while falsifying ϕ'. Consequently, $\tau' \not\models \phi'$ is a canonical paraphrase of $\tau \models \phi$ that is not classically valid.

The *Coherent* version of strong consequence bears a closer resemblance to classical logical consequence. Evidently, all theorems of $\models_{\vee\vee}$ are also theorems of $\models_{\vee\vee}^{Coh}$, since the latter quantifies over fewer modes:

$$\models \subseteq \models_{\vee\vee} \subseteq \models_{\vee\vee}^{Coh}.$$

But $\models_{\vee\vee}^{Coh}$ contains some other theorems as well. For instance, reflexivity is restored:

$$\phi \models_{\vee\vee}^{Coh} \phi,$$

since coherence forces matching occurrences (i.e., occurrences in the same place) of the same constant in the two occurrences of ϕ to be interpreted equally. Relating $\models_{\vee\vee}^{Coh}$ to classical logic is difficult, since the effects of Coherence are hard to capture. Here we will only formulate, without proof, the following modest proposition:

Fact: $\tau \models_{\vee\vee}^{Coh} \phi \Rightarrow$ at least one paraphrase of $\tau \models \phi$ is classically valid,

and we will leave a more precise characterization for future work.

To conclude, let us take a very brief look at Coherent-and-Charitable notions of strong consequence. Note that $\models_{\forall\forall}^{Coh}$ $\not\subseteq \models_{\forall\forall}^{Coh/Char}$, since the set of modes that are quantified over in $\models_{\forall\forall}^{Coh/Char}$ is no subset of the set of modes that are quantified over in $\models_{\forall\forall}^{Coh}$.[19] An important consequence of adding considerations of charity is that the logics become weakly inconsistent in the presence of some (admittedly rather unusual) ambiguities. For example, assume that F is ambiguous between the interpretations $F_1 = (\lambda x : x = x)$ and $F_2 = (\lambda x : x \neq x)$. Then both

$$\models_{\forall\forall}^{Coh/Char} F(a)\&\neg F(a), \text{ and}$$
$$\models_{\forall\forall}^{Coh/Char} \neg(F(a)\&\neg F(a)).$$

In the same way, even strong inconsistency can be exemplified. Thus, $\models_{\forall\forall}^{Coh/Char}$ shares one of the most striking properties of the weak varieties of ambiguous consequence.

This may suffice for a sketch of the strengths of the logics. A comparison from a different point of view will be undertaken in the next section.

6.2 Structural Rules

Ambiguous logics are not just extensionally different from classical logic. They are also more radically different from it. The cause is always the same: an ambiguous constant may be interpreted differently on its different occurrences in a logical argument. The Coherence principle removes *some* of this freedom,[20] but in return it adds contextual effects on interpretation, as will soon become clear.

The characteristics we are talking about are most apparent when logical arguments are combined, and this is reflected in violations of the so-called *structural rules* of logic. These rules do not concern the formal properties of specific operators of a language, they govern the way in which old results can be used and combined to yield new ones. A case in point is monotonicity, which expresses that the addition of new premises to an argument does not jeopardize the inference. Monotonicity is one of the rules that prove to be violated by various of the logical systems that were presented in the previous section.

Violation of structural rules is a trend in current logical and linguistic research. In logical research, the best-know example is linear logic

---

[19]For example, consider the inference $F(a)\&\neg F(a) \models^a$ FALSE, in which F is ambiguous between a predicate that is true of all appropriate arguments and one that is false of all appropriate arguments. This inference is a theorem of $\models_{\forall\forall}^{Coh}$ but not of $\models_{\forall\forall}^{Coh/Char}$.

[20]Removing *all* freedom, and returning to complete coherence, is impossible in an ambiguous setting, given that type restrictions may force different occurrences of a constant to be interpreted differently.

(e.g., Troelstra 1992). In linguistics, structural rules have been used to characterize the logical properties of *categorial grammars* (van Benthem 1986). In this section, the validity of the structural rules will be tested with respect to some of the systems of ambiguous consequence that were discussed earlier. Coherent-and-Charitable consequence will not be discussed separately, since the results are very similar to those for merely coherent consequence. Here is a list of the relevant structural rules.

— **permutation invariance:** $\eta, \chi, \psi, \kappa \models \phi \Rightarrow \eta, \psi, \chi, \kappa \models \phi$
— **reflexivity:** $\eta \models \eta$
— **monotonicity:** $\eta \models \psi \Rightarrow \eta, \chi \models \psi$
— **contraction:** $\eta, \chi, \chi \models \psi \Rightarrow \eta, \chi \models \psi$
— **expansion:** $\eta, \chi \models \psi \Rightarrow \eta, \chi, \chi \models \psi$
— **cut:** $\eta \models \psi$ and $\psi, \chi \models \phi \Rightarrow \eta, \chi \models \phi$

First, let us consider notions of ambiguous consequence that take all admissible modes into account, without considerations of coherence. Most structural rules are validated by these notions, as one may easily verify. Take the version with the doubly-existential quantification. *Reflexivity* holds for $\models_{\exists\exists}$, since any disambiguation μ that happens to attribute the same values to corresponding occurrences of ambiguous constants must satisfy the clause for $\eta \models_{\exists\exists} \eta$. Similarly, *monotonicity* is validated by $\models_{\exists\exists}$: If there is a disambiguation μ that satisfies the clause for $\eta \models_{\exists\exists} \psi$, then it is easy to see that μ must also satisfy the clause for $\eta, \chi \models_{\exists\exists} \psi$. The only rule to fail for $\models_{\exists\exists}$ is the *cut rule*.

Consider the following counterexample: F is ambiguous between F_1 and F_2, G is ambiguous between $G_1 = F_1$ and G_2, while H is ambiguous between $H_1 = G_2$ and H_2. Now

$$F(a) \models_{\exists\exists} G(a) \text{ and } G(a) \models_{\exists\exists} H(a), \text{ but } F(a) \not\models_{\exists\exists} H(a),$$

since G can be "unified" with F and with H, while F itself cannot be unified with H.

Thus, transitivity, a special case of the cut rule, is invalidated by the fact that *different* interpretations may be attached to different occurrences of a constant within a larger argument.

Similar results are obtained for the other non-coherent notions of ambiguous consequence. The $\models_{\exists\forall}$ version, for example, obeys all the structural rules except *Reflexivity*.

On to the more interesting, *coherent* versions of ambiguous consequence. Let us first consider the strong version. One effect of coherence is that the relation is *reflexive*. For, whenever a premiss contains a constant that also occurs in the conclusion, the agreement number of the argument is maximized if the two occurrences are interpreted in the same way. Also, of course, *permutations* of the premisses do not affect interpretation. But none of the other structural rules holds. For instance, the calculus is *nonmonotonic*, since addition of premises can destroy validity. Our formalization of Coherence causes even the number of occurrences of a given premiss to be significant, and therefore even *expansion* (and, for analogous reasons, *contraction*) fails to hold:

> Suppose, F is ambiguous between F_1 and $F_2 = G$. Assume that the reading F_1 is inapplicable to a, but applicable to b and c, while the reading $F_2 = G$ is inapplicable to c but applicable to a and b. Then
>
> $F(a), F(a), F(b), F(c) \models^{Coh}_{\forall\forall} G(b)$, but
> $F(a), F(a), F(b), F(c), F(c) \not\models^{Coh}_{\forall\forall} G(b)$,
>
> because coherence forces the occurrences of F in the first inference to mean $F_2 = G$, but in the second inference, there is as much pressure on F to mean F_1 as there is for it to mean G. As a result, the occurrence of F in the premiss $F(b)$ becomes free to mean either F_2 (which can be unified with G) or F_2, which cannot be unified with G.

A counterexample against the *cut rule* can be construed as follows:

> Suppose a is ambiguous between a_1 and a_2, and assume that a_1 is a contant that occurs in the language; furthermore, assume that G is ambiguous between G_1, a reading that is inapplicable to a_1, and $G_2 = F$, a reading that is inapplicable to a_2 but applicable to a_1. Then
>
> $F(a_1) \models^{Coh}_{\forall\forall} F(a)$, and
> $F(a) \models^{Coh}_{\forall\forall} G(a)$, but
> $F(a_1) \not\models^{Coh}_{\forall\forall} G(a)$.
>
> This can be seen as follows: the occurrence $F(a)$ in the second premiss forces the reading a_1 upon a. But since only the reading F of G is applicable to a_1, $F(a) \models^{Coh}_{\forall\forall} G(a)$ really 'means' $F(a) \models F(a)$, which is true. But this constraint on the meanings of G and a does not extend to the conclusion $F(a_1) \models^{Coh}_{\forall\forall} G(a)$. Consequently, the conclusion contains a formula that can be invalidated by choosing an appropriate interpretation.

As can be easily seen, the invalidity of all these structural rules is caused by the Coherence Principle, which enforces a maximization of the Agreement Number. Note that the Agreement Number does not distinguish between occurrences to the left and to the right of a given constant. Thus, the order in which the premises are presented has become immaterial. If this version of coherence were to be replaced by a unidirectional 'backward looking only' version, then coherent versions of ambiguous consequence would also violate *permutation invariance*, but in the bidirectional version that was tentatively adopted here, this never happens.

As it happens, weak varieties of the coherent calculus behave in the same way as the strong variety, as far as the structural rules are concerned. For instance, the $\models^{Coh}_{\exists\exists}$ calculus violates *monotonicity*, *expansion* and *contraction*, since by adding or dropping a premiss, previously coherent interpretations may become obsolete, as the following counterexample against Expansion illustrates. As before, different occurrences of the constant a are numbered consecutively for further reference:

Suppose H is ambiguous between H_1 and $H_2=G$, while a is ambiguous between a_1 and a_2. Further, assume that H_1 is applicable to both of these readings of a, while G is only applicable to a_2, and F can only be applied to a_1. Then
$$F(a^1), F(a^2), G(a^3), G(a^4) \models^{Coh}_{\exists\exists} H(a^5), \text{ but}$$
$$F(a^6), F(a^7), F(a^8), G(a^9) \not\models^{Coh}_{\exists\exists} H(a^{10}).$$

The occurrence a^5 is still ambiguous between a_1 and a_2, since there are equal amounts of pressure on a^5 to mean a_1 and a_2. Consequently, there is a disambiguation that validates the first argument. (Namely the disambiguation in which a^5 means a_2, and H means the same as G.) However, the occurrence a^{10} can only be interpreted as a_1, since that interpretation is enforced by the majority of occurrences of a in the second argument. As a result, the second argument cannot be validated, as H and G cannot be unified.

A counterexample against the *cut rule* can be construed as follows:

Let a be ambiguous between a_1 and a_2 again, while F is ambiguous between F_1 and F_2, and G is ambiguous between G_1 and $G_2 = F_2$. Then the following is a counterexample against Modus Ponens:
$$\models^{Coh}_{\exists\exists} F(a_1) \rightarrow G(a), \text{ and}$$
$$(F(a_1) \rightarrow G(a)) \models^{Coh}_{\exists\exists} (F(a_1) \rightarrow G(a_2)), \text{ but}$$
$$\not\models^{Coh}_{\exists\exists} F(a_1) \rightarrow G(a_2).$$

The second premiss can only be validated by interpreting $G(a)$ as $G(a_2)$, an interpretation that does not validate the first premiss. The conclusion is false, as can easily be seen.

Proofs for the other systems are mostly omitted to avoid repetitiveness. Here is one example, showing why $\models^{Coh}_{\forall\exists}$ does not obey the *cut rule*:

Let the individual constant a be ambiguous between a_1 and a_2. Let F be ambiguous between H, which is applicable to a_1 but inapplicable t a_2, and S, for which the reverse holds. The predicate L is ambiguous between H (again) and K, which is applicable to both a_1 and a_2. Then
$$F(a) \models^{Coh}_{\forall\exists} H(a)\&L(a), \text{ and}$$
$$H(a)\&L(a) \models^{Coh}_{\forall\exists} L(a), \text{ but}$$
$$F(a) \not\models^{Coh}_{\forall\exists} L(a),$$

because the interpretation in which F is interpreted as S is excluded in $F(a) \models^{Coh}_{\forall\exists} H(a)\&L(a)$, but not in the conclusion $F(a) \not\models^{Coh}_{\forall\exists} L(a)$.

The following schema summarizes our findings for the structural behaviour of ambiguous logics. In addition, some of the results of the previous section are summarized under the heading 'Cons'. 'Cons' stands for the property of being strongly consistent, weakly consistent, *and* conditionally consistent. $\forall\exists$ stands for the relation $\models_{\forall\exists}$, and so on:

	Refl.	Monot.	Perm.	Contrac.	Expan.	Cut	Cons.
∀∀	no	yes	yes	yes	yes	yes	yes
∃∃	yes	yes	yes	yes	yes	no	no
∀∀(Coh)	yes	no	yes	no	no	no	yes
∃∃(Coh)	yes	no	yes	no	no	no	no
∀∃	yes	yes	yes	yes	yes	yes	no
∃∀	no	yes	yes	yes	yes	yes	no
∀∃(Coh)	yes	no	yes	no	no	no	no
∃∀(Coh)	yes	no	yes	no	no	no	no

All varieties of ambiguous consequence show nonclassical behaviour, in terms of both structural rules and logical strength. Of course, weakened versions of the structural rules may be formulated,[21] but they are weakenings, not the real thing. So, what should one conclude? Should all these logics be rejected because of nonclassical behaviour, should they all be accepted as equally defensible, or should one choose the logic that is closest to classical behaviour, whichever that is?[22]

If these notions of ambiguous consequence are rejected because of their nonclassical behaviour, repair is an option. In particular, a more sweeping version of Coherence may be formulated, requiring that an argument as a whole must show some form of coherence, over and above the coherence of its individual steps. If this is done, the resulting notion of $\models_{\forall\forall}^{Coh}$ validates the *cut rule*, for example, because now the same disambiguation must be employed for ambiguous constants in the premises *and* in the conclusion.

Looking for strengthenings of Coherence is a possible strategy, but it is not necessarily the best approach if one tries to model actually occurring processes of interpretation and reasoning. If actual interpretation obeys principles that lead to non-classical behaviour, then the logic must mirror this behaviour. In fact, as was mentioned before, actual interpretation is probably even less classical than we have assumed, since the order in which constants occur is probably relevant, and this tends to lead to violations of *Permutation* by all coherent varieties of ambiguous logic.

It is important to distinguish between the two main reasons why different notions of ambiguous consequence had to be formulated. One source of divergence is whether or not ambiguous consequence should be Coherent, and if so, in what precise sense. This is an empirical issue,

---

[21] For instance, a weakened form of *monotonicity*, in which premises that are added to an established argument may not contain ambiguous constants that occur in the old argument, can still be upheld.

[22] Even if closeness to classical logic is what counts, it is unclear which of the notions of ambiguous consequence should be favoured. For example, $\models_{\forall\exists}$ is the only notion that is Reflexive, Transitive and Monotonic, whereas $\models_{\forall\forall}^{Coh}$ is the only one that is Consistent and Reflexive.

as was just noted. The other source is the question of how to quantify over the possible interpretations of the premisses and the conclusion of a logical argument. As was argued in section 4, this seems to be a matter of 'logical ideology'. Consider an argument which is valid on one interpretation of its conclusion, but invalid on another. The logical purist may answer that this argument is not valid, since it is possible for the premisses to be true while the conclusion is false. The logical relativist can counter that it all depends on what is counted as true: if truth is defined as *weak* truth, the conclusion cannot fail to be true.

My own inclination is to say that, in an ambiguous setting, logical consequence becomes an ambiguous notion. A speaker who claims that some ambiguous statement 'follows from' another has yet to make clear in which sense of 'follows' this is. Which notion of ambiguous consequence is most useful has more to do with pragmatic factors (the goals of the interaction, the possible consequences of drawing a false conclusion) than with logic. If this is correct, it seems possible to apply the principles of this paper to the notion of ambiguous inference ($\models^a$) itself: If logical consequence is ambiguous, then it may be subject to Coherence and Charity. The consequences of this move are intriguing. Suppose a speaker presents an argument that is valid on some notions of ambiguous consequence and invalid on others. Then Charity forces the hearer to choose an interpretation of the inference that makes it valid. One way of doing this is by choosing a charitable interpretation of the nonlogical constants. Another possibility is to choose a charitable interpretation of $\models^a$. However, the idea of treating logical consequence itself as an ambiguous constant will not be pursued any further here. Instead, we will take up some loose ends.

7 Loose Ends

This concludes a survey of possible notions of logical consequence for an ambiguous language. Much further study is needed to complete our understanding of all the issues. In the present section, we want to say a little bit about nonlexical ambiguities; introduce a non-standard logical connective; sketch the possibility of using ambiguous reasoning as a tool in the disambiguation process; and mention some other applications.

1. Non-lexical ambiguities. Clearly, the motivation for the work that has been described in this paper (cf., section 1) is not restricted to *lexical* ambiguities. Without going into any detail, let me indicate how the approach of the present paper might be applied to some other kinds of ambiguities.

An important *contextual ambiguity* arises when the domain of discourse that governs a given quantifier is unclear. For example, when it is said that *Everyone knows that Plato was a Greek philosopher*, the context may sometimes fail to make clear precisely what set of people is being quantified over. A simple way of modeling such an ambiguity is by using an ambiguous constant denoting the domain of discourse:

$\forall x \in DoD(\text{Person } (x) \rightarrow \text{K}(x))$

The constant DoD is then stipulated to be ambiguous between the relevant possible domains of discourse. For all the naivity of this approach, it could be used to highlight the sensitivity of contextual ambiguities to a principle of Coherence. Consider the following argument:

```
Everyone knows that Plato was a Greek philosopher
------------------------------------------------- therefore
Everyone knows that Plato was a philosopher
```

The argument is validated by means of a coherence assumption that forces the two implicit occurrences of DoD in the respective logical translations of the two sentences to be interpreted equally, so the two occurrences of *Everyone* must quantify over the same domain.

Many ambiguities can in principle be modeled by postulating a hidden constant in the fashion of this example.[23] If such analyses are used, all these ambiguities are, in principle, amenable to an analysis along the lines of the present paper. *Derivational ambiguities* are a harder nut to crack. There does seem to be evidence that they are subject to a coherence constraint. For example, the argument

```
All old plants and trees were green
------------------------------------- therefore
All very old plants and trees were green
```

would not be valid without some sort of coherence assumption. On the other hand, it is intuitively valid, because if *old* applies to the entire CN *plants and trees* in the premiss, then so must *very old* in the conclusion, but if it applies to *plants* only, then the same holds for *very old*. We will not go into the question of how a Coherence principle for derivational ambiguities could be formally modeled, but will only note that it is possible in principle,[24] and that it might be desirable for empirical reasons.

2. The disjunction theory revisited. Non-standard logics tend to give rise to non-standard connectives. In the present case one might think of such modal operators as 'being true in some/all interpretations', for example. Another new connective is a so-called ambiguity operator, or 'meta-or'. The meta-level disjunction is a binary connective '|' that creates an expression that is ambiguous between its

---

[23] See, for example, Bunt 1985 for a treatment of distributive/collective interpretations of predication along these lines.

[24] A simple way of doing this would be to minimize the number of different grammar rules that are applied in the derivation of a text.

two arguments. For illustrative purposes, we will focus on ambiguous predicates, but other categories (individual constants, formulas) can be treated analogously.

Syntax: If α and β are predicates then $(\alpha \mid \beta)$ is a predicate.
Semantics: For all α and β and for all $\Im$, $\Im(\alpha^i \mid \beta^j) = \Im(\alpha^i)$ or $\Im(\alpha^i \mid \beta^j) = \Im(\beta^j)$.

From this it follows that

If $\Im(F^i \mid G^j) = \Im(F^i)$ then
$\langle D, \Im \rangle \models (F^i \mid G^j)(a) \iff \Im(a) \in \Im(F^i)$, and

If $\Im(F^i \mid G^j) = \Im(G^j)$ then
$\langle D, \Im \rangle \models (F^i \mid G^j)(a) \iff \Im(a) \in \Im(G^j)$.

Note the similarities, but also the differences with ordinary, object-level disjunction (cf., section 2). Suppose the information that a formula conveys is captured by its effect on the set of worlds, or models that are compatible with the hearer's knowledge, then $(F \mid G)(a)$ and $F(a) \vee G(a)$ convey the following bits of information, respectively:

$W := \{\langle D, \Im \rangle \in W : (\Im(F \mid G) = \Im(F) \text{ and } \Im(a) \in \Im(F)) \text{ or } (\Im(F \mid G) = \Im(G) \text{ and } \Im(a) \in \Im(G))\}$.

$W := \{\langle D, \Im \rangle \in W : \Im(a) \in \Im(F) \text{ or } \Im(a) \in \Im(G)\}$.

The two updates are equal except for the bit about $\Im(F \mid G)$, which says something about the language (namely, the interpretation that happens to chosen for $F \mid G$), rather than about the world. Consequently, if only information about the world is taken into account, $(F \mid G)(a)$ and $F(a) \vee G(a)$ can count as 'informationally equivalent'. Yet, $(F \mid G)$ is not always, in this sense, informationally equivalent with $\lambda x(F(x) \vee G(x))$. For example, $\neg((F \mid G)(a))$ and $\neg(F(a) \vee G(a))$ lead to the following information updates:

$W := \{\langle D, \Im \rangle \in W : (\Im(F \mid G) = \Im(F) \text{ and } \Im(a) \notin \Im(F)) \text{ or } (\Im(F \mid G) = \Im(G) \text{ and } \Im(a) \notin \Im(G))\}$.

$W := \{\langle D, \Im \rangle \in W : \Im(a) \notin \Im(F) \text{ and } \Im(a) \notin \Im(G)\}$,

the latter of which conveys much more information about the world than the first.

3. Disambiguation by reasoning. In the introductory section of this paper it was argued that disambiguation should, optimally, be conducted by an inference engine that is robust enough to use ambiguous premises. Given the material of section 5, suitable notions of inference are at our disposal. Suppose a hearer is given an ambiguous premisse while knowing that all but one interpretations of it are incompatible with mutual knowledge. Then a *charitable* variety of ambiguous reasoning allows him or her to infer that the only remaining interpretation of the premisse is the intended one. For example, when we use the meta-or of the previous paragraph, and an arbitrary version of the Coherent/Charitable variety of ambiguous consequence, we get

$$(F_1 \mid F_2)(a), \neg F_2(a) \models^a F_1(a).$$

Even though this does not capture the epistemic aspect of disambiguation, it seems to be an admissible simplification. Note that the reasoning is exactly analogous if a constant $((F_1 \mid (F_2 \mid F_3))$, for example) has three or more interpretations, leading to *incomplete* disambiguation. Thus, disambiguation has become a special case of reasoning, and complete disambiguation is a special case of disambiguation.

4. Other applications. Principles such as Coherence and Charity can be applied outside the realm of logical inference. For example, they can be applied directly in interpretation, to reduce the set of interpretations that an expression may have. In addition, they can explain a number of empirical tests that have been proposed for recognizing ambiguity, as was pointed out in section 5.1. But perhaps the most fruitful possible application of *reasoning* with ambiguous expressions is in meaning-oriented NLP tasks such as database query. Consider a database Γ of non-ambiguous facts, and a yes-no question that is ambiguous between interpretations ϕ and ψ, neither of which can be discarded on grounds of Coherence or Charity. Then the yes-no question can be rephrased as the question of whether $\Gamma \models^a (\phi \mid \psi)$, where $\models^a$ is some appropriate calculus of ambiguous logic. Note that since Γ consists of unambiguous material only, quantification over interpretations of the premises is immaterial. Consequently, there are only 3 possible situations: **(1)** the inference happens to hold for both $\Gamma \models \phi$ and $\Gamma \models \psi$ (hence $\Gamma \models_{\forall\forall} (\phi \mid \psi)$), **(2)** it holds for neither of the two (hence $\Gamma \models_{\forall\forall} \neg(\phi \mid \psi)$), or **(3)** it holds for exactly one of the two (hence $\Gamma \not\models_{\forall\forall} (\phi \mid \psi)$ and $\Gamma \not\models_{\forall\forall} \neg(\phi \mid \psi)$). The first case allows the system to answer in the affirmative, the second allows it to answer in the negative, and the third situation should trigger a warning to the effect that no answer can be given since the question is crucially ambiguous.

References

Atlas, Jay. 1984. Grammatical Non-specification: The Mistaken Disjunction 'Theory'. In *Linguistics and Philosophy* 7, 1984.

Bar Hillel, Yehoshua. 1960. The Present Status of automatic translation of languages. In *Advances in Computers* 1, pp.91-163.

Barwise, Jon and Perry, John. 1983. *Situations and Attitudes*, The MIT Press/Bradford.

van Benthem, Johan. 1986. *Logical Semantics*. Reidel Publ., Dordrecht and Boston.

van Benthem, Johan. 1990. *Language in Action. Categories, Lambdas and Dynamic Logic.* North Holland, Amsterdam, Studies in Logic.

Bobrow, R. and B.Webber, eds. 1980. PSI-CLONE: Parsing and semantic interpretation in the BBN natural language understanding system. In *Proc., Third National Conf. of Canadian Soc. for Comp. Studies of Intelligence,* pp.131-142. Victoria, British Columbia.

Bronnenberg, W., H.C. Bunt, S.P.J.Landsbergen, R. Scha, W.Schoenmakers, and E.van Utteren. 1979. The Question Answering System PHLIQA1. In *Natural Communication with Computers, Vol. II,* ed. L.Bolc. Carl Hanser Verlag, Muenchen & Wien.

Bunt, Harry. 1985. *Mass terms and model-theoretic semantics.* Cambridge Studies in Linguistics, Cambridge Univ. Press, Cambridge (U.K.).

Carbonel, Jaime. and Patrick Hayes. 1987. Natural Language Processing. In *Encyclopedia of Artificial Intelligence,* ed. S.Shapiro, D.Eckroth and G.Vallasi. Wiley & Sons, New York.

van Deemter, Kees. 1991. *On the composition of meaning; four variations on the theme of compositionality in natural language processing.* Ph.D.thesis Amsterdam University, March 1991.

van der Does, Jaap, and Verkuyl, Henk. 1990. The semantics of

Fenstad, J.E., P.Halvorsen, T.Langholm, and J.van Benthem. 1987. *Situations, Language and Logic,* Reidel Publ. Comp., Dordrecht, The Netherlands.

Gale, William, Kenneth W.,Church, and David Yarowsky. 1992. One sense per discourse. In *Proc. of Darpa Speech and Natural Language Workshop.*

Gale, William, Kenneth W.,Church, and David Yarowsky. 1992. Estimating upper and lower bounds on the performance of word-sense disambiguation programs. In *Proc. of ACL 1992.*

Gillon. 1987. The Readings of Plural Noun Phrases in English,

Gillon, Brendan. 1990. Plural Noun Phrases and their readings: A reply to Lasersohn. In *Linguistics and Philosophy* 13, pp.477-485.

Hirst, Graeme. 1987. *Semantic Interpretation and the Resolution of Ambiguity.* Cambridge Univ. Press, Cambridge, Mass.

Hobbs, Jerry. 1983. An improper treatment of quantification in ordinary English. In *Proc. ACL 1983.*

McCord, Michael C. 1986. Design of a Prolog-Based Machine Translation System. In *Proc. of the Third Int. Conf. on Logic Programming,* ed. E.Shapiro. Springer.

Lakoff, George. 1970. A Note on Vagueness and Ambiguity. In *Linguistic Inquiry* 1, 1970.

Landsbergen, Jan, and Remko Scha. 1979. Formal Languages for Semantic Representation. In *Aspects of Automatized Text Processing* ed. Allen,S. and J.S.Petofi. Helmut Buske Verlag, Hamburg.

van Lehn, Kurt. 1987. Determining the scope of English quantifiers. MIT Artificial Intelligence Lab. Technical Report AI-TR-483.

Margalit, Avishai. 1983. Review of: 'Israel Scheffler, *Beyond the Letter: A Philosophical Inquiry into Ambiguity, Vagueness, and Metaphor in Lan-*

guage (Routledge and Kegan Paul, Boston, 1979)'. In *The Journal of Philosophy* 80, pp.129-138.

Montague, Richard (ed.). 1973. The Proper Treatment of Quantification in Ordinary English. In *Formal Philosophy*, Yale University Press, New Haven and London.

Montague, Richard. 1973. Universal Grammar, in *Formal Philosophy*, ed. R.H.Thomason. Yale Univ. Press, New Haven and London.

Moran, D.B. 1988. Quantifier Scoping in the SRI Core Language Engine. SRI Report.

Poesio, Massimo. 1991. Relational semantics and scope ambiguity. In *Situation semantics and its applications, Vol. 2.*, ed. J.Barwise, J.M.Gawron, G.Plotkin and S.Tutiya. CSLI Lecture Notes, Stanford, Ca.

Quine, Willard V.O. 1960. *Word and Object*. The MIT Press, Cambridge, Mass.

Reyle, Uwe. 1992. Dealing with Ambiguities by underspecification: a first order calculus for unscoped representations. In: *Proc. Amsterdam Colloquium Dec. 1991*.

Simpson and Kellas. 1989. Dynamic contextual processes and lexical access. In *Resolving Semantic Ambiguity*, ed. D.S.Gorfein. Springer-Verlag, New York.

Thomason, Richard. 1973. *Formal Philosophy*, Yale University

Troelstra, Anne. 1992. *Lectures on Linear Logic*. CSLI Lecture Notes. Stanford, Ca.

Westerståhl, D., B.Haglund, and T.Lager. 1993. A situation-theoretic representation of text meaning: Anaphora, quantification and negation. In *Situation Theory and its Applications*, Volume 3, ed. P. Aczel, D. Israel, Y. Katagiri, and S. Peters. CSLI Lecture Notes No. 37. 1993. pp. 375-408.

10

Co-Indexing Labeled DRSs to Represent and Reason with Ambiguities

UWE REYLE

1 Introduction

Whenever humans process natural language sentences or texts, they build up mental representations that leave some aspects of their meanings underspecified. In particular, this is true for all kinds of ambiguities, especially scope ambiguities of quantifiers and ambiguities that arise from the distributive/collective distinction of plural NPs. The mental representations we build up when we hear, or read ambiguous sentences cannot characterise the described situations more precisely than the sentences themselves. Only if additional information is available can such underspecified representations be refined towards partially (or even completely) disambiguated ones. But in almost all of the cases there is not enough information available to identify exactly one reading. (It is not even clear that the speaker of the sentence had exactly one reading in mind.) But nevertheless, we may accept such sentences as true and will, therefore, use the underspecified representations as premises for our arguments. It is thus not enough to say what the underspecified representations look like and how they may be disambiguated. We also must be able to define a suitable consequence relation and to formulate inference rules for them.

The problem of reasoning with ambiguities is addressed

The first ideas of this paper where circulated as 'Monotonic Disambiguation and Plural Pronoun Resolution', DYANA-Report R.2.2.B, Oktober 1994. I am particulary grateful to Anette Frank, Esther König, Hans Kamp, Peter Krause, Larry Moss, and one anonymous reviewer, who gave comments on this report and on earlier versions of the present paper.

Semantic Ambiguity and Underspecification
Kees van Deemter and Stanley Peters, editors
Copyright © 1995, CSLI Publications

in Poesio 1991, van Deemter 1991, Reyle 1993, and Reyle 1995. van Deemter 1991 considers lexical ambiguities and investigates structural properties of a number of consequence relations based on an abstract notion of coherency. He correctly rejects the idea of analysing ambiguous expressions as the disjunction of their disambiguations. Poesio 1991, Reyle 1993, and Reyle 1995 focus on quantifier scope ambiguities. Poesio 1991's inference schemata yield a very weak logic only; and Reyle 1993's deductive component is too strong. A systematic discussion of how to derive the consequence relation that holds for reasoning with ambiguities on the basis of empirically valid arguments is given in Reyle 1995. The consequence relation and the inference rules in Reyle 1995 reflect the fact that any occurrence of an ambiguous expression may/must be interpreted as dependent on some previous occurrence. This can be seen as coherency requirement, and thus is a point of contact with Van Deemter's work. This dependency of interpretation will also play a crucial role in the present paper.

Note that inferences do not only play a role in arguments. There are inferences that come into play already during the interpretation process.

(1) These five boys are terrible. At Hannah's and Lena's birthday they ate five cakes. They didn't do that at Kevin's birthday again.

Arguably the second sentence of (1) has some 20 readings. Nevertheless the (repetitive use of) **again** in the third sentence allows us to directly derive that the relevant birthday of Kevin's was after the mentioned birthdays of Hannah and Lena without explicitly considering all cases that correspond to different disambiguations. Another case of a lexically triggered inference is given in (2).

(2) Fünf Softwarefirmen kauften dreizehn Computer. Anschließend liehen sie sie aus.
   Five software companies bought thirteen computers. Then they lent them out.

The German verb **ausleihen** is ambiguous. It can either mean **borrow** or **lend**. Assuming **ausleihen** to mean **borrow** leads to an inconsistency in the interpretation of (2), if the resultive state of the buying event, namely 'having x', is identified with the preconditions of **borrow**, that is, 'not having x'. Detecting this inconsistency is again an inferential process that is independent of any particular disambiguation of (2). We will discuss this in detail in Section 6.

Let us further note that the verb **ausleihen** may not only be disambiguated without knowing in exactly which situations (2) is meant to be true, but also that the anaphoric links between the pronouns and their antecedent NPs are already established at this stage of interpretation.

This poses a further constraint on the underspecified representations. They must be able to establish an anaphoric link between a plural pronoun and its antecedent NP already at a stage where syntactic and semantic plurality of the pronoun may still diverge. This is better explained by (3).

(3)   The lawyers hired a secretary they liked.

Sentence (3) has a reading according to which each of the lawyers hired a secretary he liked. In this case the pronoun **they** is interpreted as semantically singular. Its syntactic plurality is licensed by the plurality of its grammatical antecedent. Semantically it is interpreted as individual variable bound by the distribution over the set of lawyers. We now claim that any link that is established between a pronoun and its grammatical antecedent should obey the monotonicity requirement, according to which the transition from an underspecified representation r_1 to a less underspecified (or even fully specified) representation r_2 is achieved only by *adding* information. I.e. the underspecified representations we are going to develop must provide some means to specify the impact of possible disambiguations of the antecedent phrase (in our example: the fact that the subject NP is interpreted distributively, or not) to the set of readings of the phrase containing the pronoun.

In the next section, we give three reasons for labelling DRSs, that are related to the construction and representation of ambiguities. We then briefly show how scope ambiguities of quantifiers are dealt with in the theory of Underspecified Discourse Representation Structures (UDRSs). A new definition of the semantics for UDRSs is given in Section 3. This definition allows for a direct formulation of the consequence relation that respects aspects of coherence. In other words, it may treat different occurrences of ambiguous phrases to mean the same thing (in each possible disambiguation of the text containing them). It also allows for the representation of dependent readings. This will be shown when the theory is extended to deal with collective/distributive ambiguities of plural NPs as well as with generic and cumulative readings they may license. Section 4 provides the basics of this extension. Sections 5 and 6 deal with the problem to link a plural pronoun to its antecedent phrase such that the property of monotonic disambiguation is preserved. Section 5 considers intra-sentential anaphoric relationships and inter-sentential links between a plural pronoun and a group of entities that is built by abstraction. Section 6 concentrates on dependent readings.

2   A Short Introduction to UDRSs

Before presenting the formalism of UDRSs, I will state three requirements that a language of underspecified meanings should meet. As the language of UDRSs directly implements these requirements it presents an approach to underspecification that is not only natural but also has advantages over approaches that do not fulfill them.

The first requirement states that we must be able to represent any partial order of scoping relations. Consider the sentences in (4). Because the scope of generalised quantifiers is clause bounded, [Everybody]$_1$ has wide scope with respect to [many a problem about the environment]$_2$ and [every politician]$_3$, while the relative scope of the latter two quantifiers is not determined in (4.a). In (4.b), only [most politicians]$_2$ must have narrow scope with respect to [Everybody]$_1$. In contrast to in (4.a) the interpretation of the third NP (i.e., the indefinite [a book on economics]$_3$) is not restricted to the clause in which it occurs.

(4)   a.   [Everybody]$_1$ believed that [many a problem about the environment]$_2$ preoccupied [every politician]$_3$.

       b.   [Everybody]$_1$ believed that [most politicians]$_2$ had read [a book on economics]$_3$.

This shows that we need a representation language that is able to directly represent and manipulate *partial orders* of quantifier scope. The strategy to achieve an underspecified representation of quantifier scopings by partially instantiating the final order of scoping relations[1] is not suited to deal with sentences like (4.a) and (4.b). Such an approach would fix the relative scope of Q_1 and Q_2 in (4.b) by partially instantiating the final sequence of quantifier scope to $\langle Q_1, Q_2 \rangle$ and leave Q_3 'in store' until there is enough information available to add it to the list. But note that inserting Q_3 amounts to imposing a linear order between Q_1, Q_2 and Q_3. There is thus no possibility to implement a weaker requirement saying that Q_3 has wide scope over Q_2. To be able to represent and monotonically disambiguate partial orders of scoping relations we must, therefore, give up the idea of dealing with scope ambiguities by such a kind of storage mechanism. We must directly talk about the partial relations, i.e. about pairs of quantifiers and not about a (set of) quantifier(s) and a (partially intstantiated) sequence. Saying that Q_3 has scope over Q_2 in our example, but enters no scoping relation with respect to Q_1, would then amount to extending the set $\{\langle Q_1, Q_2 \rangle\}$ to $\{\langle Q_1, Q_2 \rangle, \langle Q_3, Q_2 \rangle\}$. This requirement is fulfilled by the language of UDRSs and their construction procedure.

The second requirement concerns the representation of indefinite NPs. Within DRT indefinite NPs introduce discourse referents that may be bound by sentence constituents unrelated to the introducing

---

[1]This is essentially the idea in Alshawi and Crouch 1992 and HPSG (Pollard and Sag 1994).

phrase. This feature allows for a simple treatment of donkey sentences, like (5).

(5)   Every student who owns a book on semantics reads it.

The semantic contribution of **a book on semantics** is a partial DRS of the form 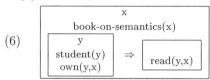 . The quantificational force of the introduced discourse referent **x** is then determined by its position within the structure that represents the meaning of the whole sentence. If the indefinite is interpreted specifically then it ends up in the top DRS as in (6).

(6)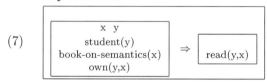

The universal interpretation of **a book on semantics** is shown in (7), where the discourse referent **x** is bound by the universally quantified NP **every student**.

(7)

As the translations of (6) and (7) into predicate logic use two different types of quantifiers ($\exists x(...\wedge ...)$ in the case of (6) and $\forall x(... \rightarrow ...)$ in the case of (6)) there is no direct way of representing the meaning set of (5) in a single formula of some underspecified predicate logical language. In the Core Language Engine,[2] for example, so-called unresolved quantifiers are used to represent (5) by a quasi-logical form (QLF). QLFs do, however, not admit model-theoretic interpretation. In order to be interpretable the QLF for (5) must be resolved, i.e. translated into the two fully specified representations of standard predicate logic.

The third requirement states that the binding relations between NP meanings (i.e. between quantifiers, or discourse referents declared in some universe of a DRS) and their occurrences in subformulas should be preserved under any disambiguation. Algorithms that create all possible scoping relations between quantifiers (and operators) occurring in a single unscoped representation typically do not meet this requirement. To compensate this they use some meta-level constraint to rule out 'ill-formed' output. Consider (8)

(8)   Every professor who works with an industrial partner has at least two beautiful secretaries.

---

[2]See Alshawi 1992

and the possible output (9)

(9) $\forall x(professor(x) \land work\text{-}with(x,y) \rightarrow$
$\exists^{\geq 2} z(b.secretary(z) \quad \land \quad \exists y(ind.partner(y) \quad \land$
$has(x,z))))$

of an algorithm that assigns the NP **an industrial partner** narrow scope with respect to **at least two beautiful secretaries** which in turn has narrow scope with respect to **every professor**. Then the so-called 'free-variable-constraint' (Pereira 1990, Hobbs and Shieber 1987) rules out (9) as a possible interpretation of (8) because the occurrence of y in $work\text{-}with(x,y)$ is free in (9). The need for such a meta-level constraint results from the fact that neither the unscoped representations themselves nor the disambiguation algorithm are subject to a corresponding demand on wellformedness. As a consequence, the free-variable-constraint is not directly applicable to *partial* disambiguations. If we are to decide whether a partial disambiguation step is permitted, we must check whether the free-variable-constraint holds for each of the total disambiguations compatible with this step.

Let us try to do better: Suppose we had some means to express in the object language that the formula $work\text{-}with(x,y)$ (that we assume to be part of the unscoped representation for (8)) is a 'subformula of the second conjunct' of both, the translation $\lambda Q \exists y(ind.partner(y) \land Q(y))$ of **an industrial partner** and the translation $\lambda Q \forall x(professor(x) \rightarrow Q(x))$ of **every professor** – meaning that after λ-conversion for Q (y and x) the second conjunct in $\lambda Q \exists y(ind.partner(y) \land Q(y))$ and $\lambda Q \forall x(professor(x) \rightarrow Q(x))$ will turn into a formula that contains $work\text{-}with(x,y)$ as a subformula. As these conjuncts correspond to the 'nuclear scope' of the quantification over x and y let us refer to them with the terms $scope(x)$ and $scope(y)$, respectively. We then express the subordination relation by $work\text{-}with(x,y) \leq scope(x)$ and $work\text{-}with(x,y) \leq scope(y)$. Similarly we get $has(x,z) \leq scope(x)$, and $has(x,z) \leq scope(z)$, where $\lambda Q \exists^{\geq 2} z(b.secretary(z) \land Q(z))$ is the translation of **at least two beautiful secretaries**. Furthermore, we know from the syntactic analysis that $work\text{-}with(x,y)$ modifies the restrictor of **every professor**, which we express by $work\text{-}with(x,y) \leq res(x)$, where $res(x)$ denotes the antecedent of the implication in $\lambda Q \forall x(professor(x) \rightarrow Q(x))$.

Note that adding $\lambda Q \exists y(ind.partner(y) \land Q(y)) \leq res(x)$ would already correspond to a disambiguation step, because it forces the indefinite to have narrow scope with respect to the universal quantification. Similarly, the set of readings with **every professor** having wide scope over **at least two beautiful secretaries** is selected by demanding $\lambda Q \exists^{\geq 2} z(b.secretary(z) \land Q(z)) \leq scope(x)$. But note that we cannot add $\lambda Q \exists y(ind.partner(y) \land Q(y)) \leq scope(x)$, because this would imply that $work\text{-}with(x,y)$ is a subformula of $scope(x)$, which is not possible since we already have $work\text{-}with(x,y) \leq res(x)$.[3] Besides the axioms for partial orders, $\leq$ must, therefore, fulfil a further constraint guaranteeing that a subformula A of B can only be a subformula of C in case C is a subformula of B, or B is a subformula of C (in some disambiguation).[4] This constraint will be part of the definition of UDRSs below. The disambiguation procedure for UDRSs can, thus, be formulated such that it automatically guarantees wellformed output for any disambiguation step (without the need to go all the way to the set of total disambiguations this step allows).[5]

We now introduce the language of UDRSs. It follows from the discussion above that the relation, $\leq$, of being a subformula will play a pivotal role. With respect to DRSs $\leq$ matches with the subordination relation between DRSs (and DRS conditions). Let us consider the DRSs (13) and (14) representing the two readings of (12).

(12)   Everybody didn't pay attention.

(13)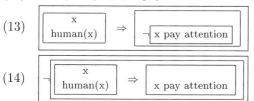

(14)

The following representations make the subordination relation – which is read ¿from bottom to top – more explicit.

---

[3]We use the fact that for generalized quantifiers we always have $scope(x) \not\leq res(x)$ and $res(x) \not\leq scope(x)$.

[4]We do not consider branching quantification here.

[5]It also guarantees a proper treatment of the related example (10).

(10)   A manager of every company has a beautiful secretary.

And for examples involving pronouns, like

(11)   Every man saw a friend of his.

where the universally quantified noun phrase must have scope over the indefinite if the pronoun is assumed to be bound by the universal quantifier, the free-variable-constraint is implemented by the general principle saying that a bound pronoun must be bound within the scope of its binder. This principle can be expressed by a simple constraint of the form $l_\pi \leq l_\alpha$, where l_π represents the meaning of the pronoun and l_α the scope of its antecedent. (For more details see Section 5.)

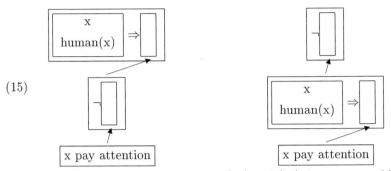

The structure that is common to both, (13) and (14), is represented by (16),

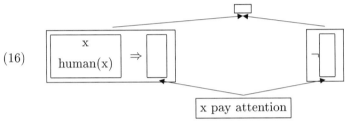

which is a graphical representation of the UDRS that represents (12) with scope relationships left unresolved. We call the nodes of such graphs UDRS-*components*. It is convenient to give each such component (in fact each sub-DRS occurring in a UDRS) a name, called its *label*. We furthermore define for every UDRS two functions, *scope* and *res*, which map labels of UDRS-components to the labels of their scope and restrictor, respectively. A UDRS consists of UDRS-components together with a partial order ORD of its labels. An example is given in (17).

(17) $l_\top : \langle\langle l_1 : \boxed{l_{11} : \boxed{\begin{array}{c} x \\ \text{human(x)} \end{array}} \Rightarrow l_{12} : \boxed{}}, \; l_2 : \boxed{\neg l_{11} : \boxed{}}, \; l_0 : \boxed{\text{x pay att.}}\rangle, ORD\rangle$

If ORD in (17) is given as $\{l_2 \leq scope(l_1), l_0 \leq scope(l_2)\}$ then (17) is equivalent to (13), and in case ORD is $\{l_1 \leq scope(l_2), l_0 \leq scope(l_1)\}$ we get a description of (14). If ORD is $\{l_0 \leq scope(l_1), l_0 \leq scope(l_2)\}$ then (17) represents (16), because it only contains the information common to both, (13) and (14).

In any case ORD lists only the subordination relations that are neither implicitly contained in the partial order nor determined by complex UDRS-conditions. This means that (17) implicitly contains the information that, for example, $res(l_2) \leq l_\top$, and also that $res(l_2) \leq l_2$, $res(l_1) \leq l_\top$, $scope(l_1) \leq l_\top$, and that neither $scope(l_1) \leq res l_1$ nor $res(l_1) \leq scope l_1$. We define

(18) $l < l'$ iff $l \leq l'$ and not $l' \leq l$
       $l \sim l'$ iff $l \leq l'$ and $l' \leq l$

It is clear that disambiguation of UDRSs is a monotonic process. If we add $l_2 \leq l_{12}$ to (16) we get a representation equivalent to (13). There is thus no need to restructure (parts of) a semantic representation if more information about scope restriction has become available. This process of enrichment is characteristic for the construction of UDRSs: Information from different sources (syntactic[6] and semantic knowledge as well as knowledge about the world) may be incorporated in the structure by elaborating it in the sense just described.

The construction algorithm for UDRSs will associate meaning components of verbs with the lowest node of a UDRS-clause, sentence boundaries with its highest node and NP-meanings with the other nodes of the clause. For relative clauses the upper bound label l' is identified with the label l of its head noun (i.e., the restrictor of the NP containing the relative) by $l' \sim l$ (see clause (i.c.β) of the following definition). In the case of conditionals the upper bound label of subordinate clauses is set equal to the label of the antecedent/consequent of the implicative condition. The ordering of the set of labels of a UDRS builds an upper-semilattice with one-element $l_\top$. We assume that databases are constructed out of sequences S_1, ..., S_n of sentences. Having a unique one-element $l_\top^i$ associated with each UDRS representing a sentence S_i is to prevent any quantifier of S_i to have scope over (parts of) any other sentence. The UDRS for (8) is given in (19).

(19)

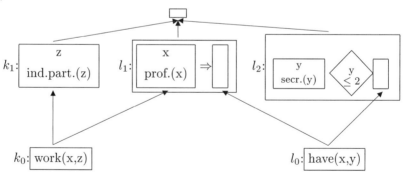

We see that adding $k_1 \leq scope(l_2)$ and $l_2 \leq scope(l_1)$ results in $k_0 \leq res(l_1)$ and $k_0 \leq scope(l_1)$, which – as discussed above – is a structure that doesn't correspond to a DRS in a natural way. (Recall that $\leq$ means nestedness of boxes.)

---

[6] An HPSG grammar for a fragment of German that realises these principles is presented in Frank and Reyle and Frank and Reyle 1995. Frank and Reyle focusses on scope ambiguities triggered by scrambling and/or movement.

In clause (i.c.β) of the following definition we constrain the partial order of labels of a UDRS such that for implicative conditions and generalized quantifiers the set $\{res(l), scope(l)\}$ cannot have a lower bound. The definition of UDRSs furthermore ensures that

(i) the verb is in the scope of each of its arguments, (clause (ii.b)),

(ii) the scope of proper quantifiers is clause bounded, (clause (ii.c))

(iii) indefinite descriptions may take arbitrarily wide scope, (clause (ii.c) and (iii)).

Definition 1: Underspecified Discourse Representation Structures

(i) A quadruple $l:\langle\langle U_K, C'_K \cup C''_K\rangle, res(l), scope(l), ORD_l\rangle$ is a *UDRS-component* if the following conditions are satisfied:

(a) $\langle U_K, C'_K\rangle$ is a DRS containing standard DRS-conditions only, and

(b) C''_K may contain at most one of the following conditions.

(α) a UDRS-clause $k{:}\gamma$ (defined under (ii) below),

(β) $l_1{:}K_1 \Rightarrow l_2{:}K_2$,

(γ) $l_1{:}K_1\langle Qx\rangle l_2{:}\langle\{\},\{\}\rangle$

(δ) $\neg l_1{:}\langle\{\},\{\}\rangle$

where K_1 and K_2 are standard DRSs that may contain a UDRS-clause $k{:}\gamma$.

The conditions in (β)-(δ) are called *distinguished* conditions of the UDRS-component, referred to by $l{:}\gamma$. UDRS-components with distinguished conditions are called *scope-bearing*.

(c) *res* and *scope* are functions on the set of labels, and ORD_l is a partial order of labels such that

(α) if $k{:}\gamma \in C''_K$, then
$k \sim l \in ORD_l$ and $ORD_k{\subset}ORD_l$;

(β) if $l_1{:}K_1 \Rightarrow l_2{:}K_2 \in C''_K$, or $l_1{:}K_1\langle Qx\rangle l_2{:}\langle\{\},\{\}\rangle$, then $res(l) = l_1$, $scope(l) = l_2$, and $l_1{<}l$, $l_2{<}l$, $l_1{\not\leq}l_2$, $l_2{\not\leq}l_1 \in ORD_l$;
and there is no l_0 such that $l_0 \leq l_1 \in ORD_l$ and $l_0 \leq l_2 \in ORD_l$;
if in addition if $k{:}\gamma \in C_{K_1}$, then $k \sim l \in ORD_l$ and $ORD_k{\subset}ORD_l$;

(γ) if $\neg l_1{:}K_1 \in C''_K$, then $res(l) = scope(l) = l_1$ and $l_1{<}l \in ORD_l$.

(δ) Otherwise $res(l) = scope(l) = l$.

(ii) A *UDRS-clause* is a pair of the form $l{:}\langle\langle\gamma_0, ..., \gamma_n\rangle, ORD_l\rangle$, where $\gamma_i = l_i{:}\langle K_i, res(l_i), scope(l_i), ORD_{l_i}\rangle$, $0 \leq i \leq n$, are UDRS components, and

(a) $ORD_{l_i} \subset ORD_l$, for all i, $0 \leq i \leq n$

(b) $l_0 \leq scope(l_i) \in ORD_l$ for all i, $1 \leq i \leq n$

(c) $l_i \leq l \in ORD_l$ for all i, $1 \leq i \leq n$, for which $l_i{:}\gamma$ is a generalised quantifier.

For each i, $1 \leq i \leq n$, l_i is called a *node*. l is called *upper bound* and l_0 *lower bound* of the UDRS-clause. Lower bounds neither have distinguished conditions nor is there an l' such that $l' < l$.

(iii) A UDRS-clause $l_\top{:}\langle \Gamma, ORD_{l_\top} \rangle$ is a *UDRS* if $ORD_{l_\top}$ is an upper semi-lattice with one-element $l_\top$.[7]

(iv) A *UDRS-database* is a set of UDRSs $\{l_\top^i{:}\langle \Gamma, ORD_{l_\top^i} \rangle\}_i$.
A *UDRS-goal* is a UDRS.

For the fragment without plurals UDRS-components that contain distinguished conditions do not contain anything else. That is, they consist of labelled DRSs K for which $U_K = C_K' = \{\}$ if $C_K'' \neq \{\}$.

The dynamic aspects of indefinite NPs can be accounted for by a suitable extension of the definition of accessibility to UDRSs and UDRS databases. Note that although the definition of accessibility for DRSs is given in terms of subordination (i.e., $\leq$) it yields a weaker notion if it is applied to UDRSs. Take, for example, a sentence with two indefinites. With respect to accessibility on DRSs the discourse referent introduced by the first indefinite is accessible from the second, and vice versa. But if we apply the same definition to UDRSs neither the first one is accessible from the second nor the second from the first. This of course presupposes that the only NPs occurring in the sentence are the two indefinites. If, in addition, any quantified NP (or a negation) is present, then mutual accessibility between the two indefinites requires that they both have wide scope over the quantifier (or the negation). We will call the relation we get when applying the definition of accessibility to UDRSs *weak accessibility*. And we will us the term accessibility for the appropriate extension of this notion.

3 Truth and Consequences of UDRSs

To define an underspecified representation to be *true* if one of its readings is true may be defensible – but is certainly not sufficient as a basis for a suitable definition of logical consequence. Consider (20),

(20) If the students get £100 then they buy books. The students get £100. $\models$ The students buy books.

which shows that sentences in a discourse are often disambiguated in tandem, with the effect that the same disambiguating option is taken

---

[7]This means that for all nodes k without a 'path' to $l_\top$ a condition $k \leq l_\top$ is added to $ORD_{l_\top}$.

for them. Thus the meaning of the premise of (20) is given by (21b) not by (21a), where a_1 represents the first and a_2 the second reading of the second sentence of (20).

(21) a. $((a_1 \to b) \lor (a_2 \to b)) \land (a_1 \lor a_2)$

  b. $((a_1 \to b) \land a_1) \lor ((a_2 \to b) \land a_2)$

We will call sentence representations that have to be disambiguated similarly *correlated ambiguities*. And we will express such correlations by co-indexing. The types of ambiguities we will consider are lexical ambiguities, ambiguities triggered by plural noun phrases and quantifier scope ambiguities. Lexical ambiguities will be represented by ambiguous atomic DRS-conditions, quantifier scope ambiguities by the partial order of labels, and ambiguities triggered by plural noun phrases by a combination of both. If two occurrences of atomic DRS-conditions γ and γ' are coindexed then they express the same lexical meaning. This is straightforward. But what does it mean for UDRS-components and UDRS-clauses to be co-indexed, and under which circumstances is it possible to co-index them? Suppose $l{:}\gamma$ and $k{:}\delta$ are UDRS-clauses. And let us assume that coindexing is done with respect to their labels, that is, $l^i{:}\gamma$ and $k^i{:}\delta$. As UDRS-clauses express scope ambiguities in terms of the partial orders of their labels the co-indexing should imply a certain isomorphism between the orders. This isomorphism must in addition map the labels of the grammatically corresponding nodes onto each other. Recall that we defined UDRS-clauses in terms of a list of UDRS-components (and not a set). Let us assume that the order of the elements in this list is canonical (for each verb). Then we can say that two UDRS-clauses may be co-indexed if the isomorphism between ORD_l and ORD_k also respects the canonical order of the arguments of the verb. As ORD_l contains also the labels of UDRS-clauses contained in components of $l{:}\gamma$ it seems reasonable to require in addition that the embedded UDRS-clauses of $l^i{:}\gamma$ and $k^i{:}\delta$ must also be co-indexed.[8]

We will, therefore, assume that co-indexing is inherited from UDRS-clauses to URDS-components and from URDS-components to the conditions they contain.

---

[8]Consider the following variants of (20). If we assume that the pronoun **they** does not refer to the set of all students but to a subset of five of them, then the example shows that this notion of coindexing is too strong.

(22)   Five of my students will buy books if they get £100.

$$\left\{ \begin{array}{l} \text{Five of my students} \\ \text{The students} \\ \text{They} \end{array} \right\} \text{get £100.} \models \text{They buy books.}$$

For the purposes of the present section it will, however, be sufficient. There are several directions in which the notion must be refined. One possible refinement will be discussed in a later section.

An isomorphism ω between ORD_l and ORD_k that respects all canonical orders of sub-clauses of $l^i{:}\gamma$ and $k^i{:}\delta$ is called an *isomorphism between UDRS-clauses* $l{:}\gamma$ and $k{:}\delta$. Let $\overline{ORD}_l$ be the set of linear orders that extend ORD_l such that $l{:}\langle\gamma, \overline{ORD}_l\rangle$ is a UDRS-clause; and let c_l be a choice function on $\overline{ORD}_l$. Similarly for ORD_k. We then say that the choice function $c = c_l \cup c_k$ *respects the index* i of the two UDRS-clauses $l^i{:}\gamma$ and $k^i{:}\delta$ (in symbols c^i), if the isomorphism between their orders is preserved. Let I be a set of indices, and c a choice function that respects all $i \in I$ (in symbols c^I). If $c^I(\Gamma)$ denotes the disambiguation of Γ triggered by c^I, then the consequence relation we assume underlies ambiguous reasoning is given in (23).

(23) $\quad \forall c^I (c^I(\Gamma) \models c^I(\gamma))$

We now give the definition of truth for UDRS-databases. We will use $M, f \models K$ to mean that the embedding function f verifies the DRS K in model M according to the standard truth conditions of DRSs. $FV(\underline{l})$ is the set of discourse referents x that occur *free* in at least one labelled DRS $k{:}K$ with $k < l$, and such that $x \notin U_{K'}$ for all labelled DRSs $k'{:}K'$ that are accessible ¿from K and for which $k' < l$ holds. Finally, let $\mathcal{E}$ be the set of sets e of embedding functions of a certain K in a certain model M. We interpret labels by means of elements of $\mathcal{E}$. Λ denotes the empty function.

Definition 2: Let l be a label, M a model, f an embedding function defined on the set of discourse referents declared in DRSs K' labelled by a label k such that $l < k$, and c a choice function on $\overline{ORD}_l$.

  (i) Suppose l is the label of a lower bound, or occurs in a distinguished condition of some UDRS-clause. Let K be the DRS labelled by l. Then $\|l\|^c_{f,M} = \{g \mid dom(g) = dom(f) \cup U_K \cup FV(\underline{l})$ and for all $\gamma \in C_K \; M, g \models^c_e \gamma\}$.

 (ii) Suppose l is the label of a UDRS-component that is neither a lower nor an upper bound. Let K be the DRS labelled by l. Then
 $\|l\|^c_{f,M} \in \mathcal{E}^{\mathcal{E}}$ such that $\|l\|^c_{f,M}(e) =$
 $\{g \mid dom(f) \cup U_K \subseteq dom(g) \subseteq dom(f) \cup U_K \cup FV(\underline{l})$
 $\qquad\qquad\qquad\qquad$ and for all $\gamma \in C_K \; M, g \models^c_e \gamma\}$,
 where $\models^c_e$ is defined as follows.
   (a) $M, g \models^c_e \gamma$ iff $g \in e$ and $M, g \models \gamma$
       if γ is a standard DRS-condition
   (b) $M, g \models^c_e l_1{:}K_1 \Rightarrow l_2{:}K_2$ iff
       $\forall h \;(\; \text{if } h \in \|l_1\|^c_{g,M}, \text{ then } \|l_2\|^c_{h,M} \cap e \neq \{\})$
   (c) $M, g \models^c_e \neg l_1{:}K_1$ iff $\|l_1\|^c_{g,M} \cap e = \{\}$
   (d) $M, g \models^c_e l_1{:}\gamma$ iff $\|l_1\|^c_{g,M} \neq \{\}$ for upper bounds l_1

(iii) Suppose l is an upper bound, i.e. l labels a UDRS-clause
$l{:}\langle\langle l_0{:}\gamma_0, ..., l_n{:}\gamma_n\rangle, \mathrm{ORD}_l\rangle$. Let $\langle l_{j_0}, ..., l_{j_n}\rangle$ be the linear order of
$\{l_0, ..., l_n\}$ that is induced by $c(\overline{ORD_l})$. Let c_j be the restriction
of c to $\overline{ORD}_{l_j}$, for $j \in \{j_0, ..., j_n\}$. Then

$$\|l\|^c_{f,M} = \|l_{j_1}\|^{c_{j_1}}_{f,M}(...(\|l_{j_n}\|^{c_{j_n}}_{f,M}(\|l_0\|^{c_{j_0}}_{f,M}))..)$$

We refer to $\|l_{j_{r+1}}\|^{c_{j_1}}_{f,M}(...(\|l_{j_n}\|^{c_{j_n}}_{f,M}(\|l_0\|^{c_{j_0}}_{f,M}))..)$ by $e^c_{l_{j_r}}$, $1 \le r \le$
n.

Applying this definition to the UDRS in (17) gives the following denotations for its labels. (We omit explicit reference to the model M,
writing $\|.\|^\Lambda_\Lambda$ instead of $\|.\|^\Lambda_{\Lambda,M}$.)

$\|l_0\|^\Lambda_\Lambda = \{g \mid dom(g) = \{x\}$ and $g \models x\ pay\ attention\}$
$\|l_2\|^\Lambda_\Lambda(e) = \{g \mid dom(g) \subseteq \{x\}$ and $\|l_{21}\|^\Lambda_g \cap e = \{\}\}$
$\|l_{21}\|^\Lambda_\Lambda(e) = \{g \mid dom(g) \subseteq \{x\}$ and $g \in e\}$
$\|l_1\|^\Lambda_\Lambda(e) = \{g \mid dom(g) = \{\}$ and $\forall h($ if $h \in \|l_{11}\|_g$, then $\|l_{12}\|_h \cap e \ne$
$\{\})\}$
$\|l_{11}\|^\Lambda_\Lambda(e) = \{g \mid dom(g) = \{x\}$ and $g \models human(x)\}$

Definition 3: Let I be the set of indices i, $\{i_r\}_r$ be the set of oc-
currences of index i in a *UDRS-database* $\mathcal{K} = \{\langle l^i_\top{:}\Gamma, ORD_{l^i_\top}\rangle\}_i$,
$\{c_j\}_j$ a set of choice functions.
  (i) $\mathcal{K}$ is *true* in a model $\mathcal{M}$ with respect to $\{c_j\}_j$ if
    (a) there is an isomorphism ω_i between coindexed clauses
      that respects i for all $i \in I$, and
    (b) $\bigcap_j \|l^j_\top\|^{c_j}_{\Lambda,M} \ne \{\}$.
  (ii) $\mathcal{K}'$ *follows from* $\mathcal{K}$, $\mathcal{K} \models \mathcal{K}'$, iff for all $\{c_j\}_j$ if $\mathcal{K}$ is true in $\mathcal{M}$
    with respect to $\{c_j\}_j$, then $\mathcal{K} \cup \mathcal{K}'$ is true in $\mathcal{M}$ with respect
    to $\{c_j\}_j$.

As the disjunctions in (24.a) cannot be represented by co-indexed
UDRSs, (24.a) is not a tautology, because not all of its readings are
true. And as the sentences in (24.b) also lack a common index the
inference in (24.b) does not hold, because **Everybody was awake**
does not follow from both readings of the premise.

(24)   a. $\models$ Everybody slept or everybody didn't sleep.
     b. Everybody didn't sleep. $\models$ Everybody was awake.

This means that ambiguities in the data are interpreted by the disjunction of their readings and ambiguities in the goal by their conjunction
– if there are no indices which correlate them. Therefore (25) holds
only if the UDRSs that interpret the two occurrences of **Everybody
didn't sleep** are co-indexed.

(25)   Everybody didn't sleep. $\models$ Everybody didn't sleep.

Co-indexing different occurrences of ambiguities amounts to saying that they mean the same thing. This is especially the case if they are uttered in the same context of interpretation. But suppose that the first occurrence of, e.g., **The students get £ 100** in (20) is interpreted with respect to a context that is different from the context relevant to interpret its second occurrence (e.g. because there are 100 pages of text in between the two occurrences), then there is the possibility that they actually mean different things. In this case the interpreter does not establish a correlation between them.

4 Ambiguities Triggered by Plural NPs

Plural NPs bear a high potential for creating ambiguities. For one thing, many of them can be understood either as denoting a collection of individuals or quantifying over the members of that collection and thus give rise to the well-known collective/distributive ambiguity. But there are further possibilities for interpreting sentences with plural NPs. (26.a) and (26.b) are examples of so-called generic and shared responsibility readings, respectively.

(26)   a. The children in this city thrive.

        b. The guys in 5b have been cheating on the exam again.

These readings differ from the distributive reading in that they can be accepted as true even if not all members of the set denoted by the subject NP are in the extension of the predicate expressed by the VP (when it is interpreted as a predicate of individuals). To see that they differ from the collective reading for a similar reason consider (27).

(27)   The girls gathered in the garden.

(27) has only a collective reading. This means that a predicate P is true of a group X, if every member of X contributes in some way or other to the fact that P is true of X. In (27) the contribution is the same for each girl and consists of having the property of going to the garden (eventually with the intention to meet the others). The generic and shared responsibility readings of (26) differ from the collective readings because they can be accepted as true even if not all members of the set denoted by the subject NP are in the extension of predicates that stand in such a relation to the VP. To specify the relevant relations is the task of lexical theory (and part of the specification of world knowledge). The task of UDRT is to provide an underspecified representation which subsumes all these readings.

Collective and distributive uses of a verb γ are determined by the type of discourse referents γ takes. The UDRS in (29), for example, represents the collective reading of (28). (Discourse referents of type group are represented by capital letters.)

(28) The lawyers hired a secretary.

(29)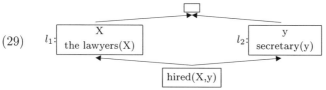

And its distributive reading is given in (30), where the quantification over the individual lawyers introduces a discourse referent, x, of type individual.

(30)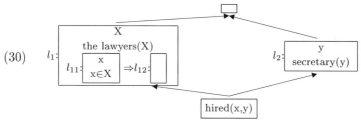

Let us note that while (29) is not ambiguous any more, the choice of the distributive reading (30) for (28) leaves leeway for a further ambiguity. This ambiguity is due to the fact that the node representing the subject NP has been turned into a scope-bearing node by applying distribution to **the lawyers(X)**. Thus the indefinite can be interpreted as being within the scope of the distribution, or not. In (29) the NP-node is not scope-bearing, and, therefore, the UDRS is equivalent to the DRS that results by taking the union/merge of all sub-DRSs of (29).

In order to come to a representation that is underspecified with respect to the choice of possible readings of (28), we first mark UDRS-components to which a distribution might still be applied as *potentially* scope-bearing, and second, leave it open whether the corresponding argument slot of the verb is instantiated by the plural discourse referent (in case the collective reading is chosen), or by the singular discourse referent that is bound by the distributive, generic or cumulative interpretation. To this end we simply use terms of the form $\alpha(\mathbf{X})$ to specify which NP occupies which argument slot of the verb. To indicate that the argument slot is filled by a plural individual we will add the condition $\alpha(\mathbf{X}) = \mathbf{X}$, and for the singular case we add $\alpha(\mathbf{X}) = \mathbf{x}$. To define the notion of potentially scope bearing, we modify the definition of UDRS-components such that *res* and *scope* are allowed to be partial functions. Thus clause (i.c.δ) of Definition 1 must be restricted to labels l for which *scope* and *res* are defined. It now reads: Otherwise $res(l) = scope(l) = l$, if $l \in dom(scope) \cap dom(res)$. And clause (ii.b) of Definition 1 is replaced by the following two clauses.

(1.ii.b′) $l_0 \leq scope(l_i) \in ORD_l$ for all i, $1 \leq i \leq n$, if $scope(l_i)$ is defined.

(1.ii.b″) $l_0 \leq l_i \in ORD_l$ for all i, $1 \leq i \leq n$, if $scope(l_i)$ is not defined.

Definition 4: Let l label a UDRS-component. Then

    (i) l is *scope bearing* if $scope(l) \neq l$.

    (ii) l is *not scope bearing* if $scope(l) = res(l) = l$.

    (iii) if *res*, or *scope*, are not defined for l, then l is called *potentially scope bearing*.

Using this definition the underspecified representation (31) of (28) has exactly the shape of (29), but the argument DRSs l_1 is still marked as potentially scope bearing, i.e. *scope* and *res* are not yet defined for l_1.

(31)   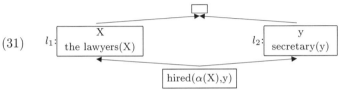

To disambiguate (31) we must not only add a condition of the form $\alpha(\mathbf{X}) = \mathbf{X}$, or $\alpha(\mathbf{X}) = \mathbf{x}$ (accompanied with $l_{11}\!: \boxed{\begin{array}{c} x \\ x \in X \end{array}} \Rightarrow l_{12}\!: \boxed{}$), but also define *res* and *scope* for l_1. In case of the collective reading this will turn l_1 into a node that is not scope bearing. We thus define $res(l_1) := l_1$ and $scope(l_1) := l_1$. And in case the distributive reading is chosen we take $res(l_1) := l_{11}$ and $scope(l_1) := l_{12}$.

    In a similar way, the choice of a generic or shared responsibility reading can be dealt with. Both introduce a quantificational structure turning the node of the subject NP into a scope bearing one. The generic reading, e.g., for (26.a) may be represented by (32), in which GEN denotes the generic quantifier.

(32)   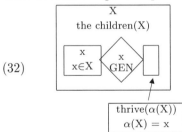

    This method applies also to cumulative readings which are available when a verb is accompanied with two plural NPs, as in (33).

(33)   Three breweries supplied five inns.

    Under the cumulative reading (33) can be accepted as true if for each of the three breweries there is at least one inn the brewery supplies, and each inn is supplied by at least one brewery. To represent this reading let us introduce a straightforward extension of (monadic) duplex conditions to "polyadic" ones. The restrictor of the polyadic duplex condition in (34) consists of the pair of DRSs associated with the nouns, and the diamond is not only equipped with the quantifications over the corresponding variables, but also marks the polyadic quantification to be cumulative by means of the superscript *cum*.

(34)

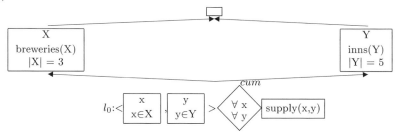

The verification conditions of the polyadic duplex condition in (34) are equivalent to those of the condition set in (35).

$$(35)\{ \quad \boxed{\begin{array}{c} x \\ \hline x \in X \end{array}} \Rightarrow \boxed{\begin{array}{c} y \\ \hline y \in Y \\ \text{supplied}(\alpha(X),\beta(Y)) \\ \alpha(X) = x \\ \beta(Y) = y \end{array}} \;,\; \boxed{\begin{array}{c} y \\ \hline y \in Y \end{array}} \Rightarrow \boxed{\begin{array}{c} x \\ \hline x \in X \\ \text{supplied}(\alpha(X),\beta(Y)) \\ \alpha(X) = x \\ \beta(Y) = y \end{array}}$$
$$\}$$

We now extend the verification conditions to intransitive and transitive verbs with underspecified argument types. We assume that the embedding function f has X (and Y) as well as x (and y) in its domain.

(36) - $f \models P(\alpha(X))$ iff $f \models P(X)$ or $f \models P(x)$
  - $f \models P(\alpha(X), \beta(Y))$ iff
    $\qquad f \models P(X,Y)$, or
    $\qquad f \models P(x,Y)$, or, $f \models P(X,y)$, or $f \models P(x,y)$, or

$$f \models \left\langle \boxed{\begin{array}{c} x \\ \hline x \in X \end{array}} , \boxed{\begin{array}{c} y \\ \hline y \in Y \end{array}} \right\rangle \; \bowtie^{cum} \begin{array}{c} \forall x \\ \forall y \end{array} \boxed{\text{supply(x,y)}} .$$

For UDRS-components introduced by plural NPs we assume that clause (ii) of Definition 2 applies only to labels l for which *scope* is defined. We add the following clause to capture potentially scope bearing components.

(ii') Suppose l is neither a lower nor an upper bound, and $scope(l)$ is not defined. Let X be the distinguished discourse referent[9] of U_K. Then
$\|l\|_f^c \in \mathcal{E}^{\mathcal{E}}$ such that $\|l\|_f^c(e) =$
$\{g \restriction dom(f) \cup U_K \cup \{x\} \subseteq dom(g) \subseteq dom(f) \cup U_K \cup FV(l)$ and

---

[9] This is the discourse referent that represents the group described by the NP.

$$(g \quad\models^c_e \quad \boxed{} \quad C_K \quad \text{or} \quad (g \quad\models^c$$

$$C_K \text{ and } \{g \models^c_e \boxed{\begin{array}{c} x \\ \hline x \in X \end{array}} \Rightarrow \boxed{}\}))\}.$$

For standard DRS-conditions $\models^c$ is the same as $\models$. Only for UDRS-clauses, i.e., upper bound labels, $\models^c$ is defined as $\models^c_e$ in Definition (2.ii.d). This accommodates relative clauses. Note that $g \models^c C_K$ does not entail $g \models^c_e C_K$: Because in the absence of the implicative condition the parameter e constrains g itself. And if the implicative condition is there, then e constrains the scope of this condition.

Note furthermore that this clause does not affect the interpretation of indices associated with UDRS-clauses. To impose a constraint that co-indexed clauses must be interpreted in parallel we must guarantee that we choose embedding functions that enter the stage through the same disjunct in (36) above. The simplest way to achieve this is to interpret lower bound labels l_0 not as sets of embedding functions but as sets of pairs $\langle e, r \rangle$, where e is a set of embedding functions that contains exactly those functions that verify the conditions of l_0 on the basis of one particular disjunct in (36) and r says which disjunct this is We will assume that r takes one of the forms c, d, $\langle c, c \rangle$, $\langle d, c \rangle$, $\langle c, d \rangle$, $\langle d, d \rangle$, for the non-cumulative readings. And for cumulative readings we define $r = l_{02}$, where l_{02} labels the scope of the polyadic duplex condition. The choice function that linearises ORD to compute the denotation of the upper bound label will then in addition to selecting a particular linearisation choose one element out of this set and record r as particular choice associated with l_0.

What we have done for verbs may be extended to all lexical ambiguities. We, therefore, generalise clause (i) of Definition 2.

(2.i) Suppose l is a lower bound, or occurs in a distinguished condition of some UDRS-clause. That is, l labels a standard DRS K. Suppose further that γ is a lexically ambiguous expression in K, and that $\{K_1, ..., K_n\}$ is the set of meanings that results from γ's ambiguity in K. Then $\|l\|^\Lambda_f = \langle \{g \mid dom(g) = dom(f) \cup U_{K_r} \text{ and } g \models C_{K_r}\}, r \rangle$, where $1 \leq r \leq n$.

We will assume that the output of the choice function is a pair $\langle lin, R \rangle$, where lin is the particular linearisation chosen, and R contains the information about the choices of particular lexical meanings for occurrences of ambiguous lexical expressions. This requires a straightforward modification of the definition of truth for UDRSs to guarantee that if several occurrences of an ambiguous lexical expression are co-indexed, then the isomorphism will also respect this kind of correlation by being the identity function on R.

5 The Antecedents of 'They'

Plural pronouns are plural NPs and therefore share their ambiguity potential. In addition plural pronouns may be interpreted as 'individual variables', as shown by (37).

(37) Few lawyers hired a secretary they liked.

The NP **few lawyers** in (37) binds the **they** in the embedded clause. Being a quantifying NP, it does not introduce a plural discourse referent as possible antecedent for **they** and, therefore, has only one reading. This situation changes drastically if we replace the subject by a plural non-quantifying NP, as in (38).

(38) The lawyers hired a secretary they liked.

If we ignore the cases where **a secretary** is interpreted specifically, then (38) has the five readings listed in (39).

(39)   a. $\exists X(lawyer(X) \land \exists y(secretary(y) \land hire(X,y) \land like(X,y)))$
   b. $\exists X(lawyer(X) \land \exists y(secretary(y) \land hire(X,y) \land \forall x(x \in X \to like(x,y))))$
   c. $\exists X(lawyer(X) \land \forall x(x \in X \to \exists y(secretary(y) \land hire(x,y) \land like(X,y))))$
   d. $\exists X(lawyer(X) \land \forall x(x \in X \to \exists y(secretary(y) \land hire(x,y) \land$
$\forall z(z \in X \to like(z,y)))))$
   e. $\exists X(lawyer(X) \land \forall x(x \in X \to \exists y(secretary(y) \land hire(x,y) \land like(x,y))))$

In (39.a) to (39.d) the pronoun is bound by the group variable X irrespective of the choice whether or not to quantify over the members of this group as in (39.c) and (39.d). Only in (39.e) this quantification binds the pronoun. It is interpreted as a singular bound variable, to which no further distribution is possible.

The previous section suggests (40) as underspecified representation of this set of five readings.

(40)

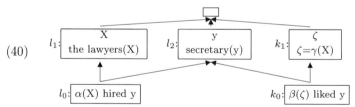

ζ is a neutral discourse referent, so it ranges over singular as well as plural entities. The anaphoric linkage between plural pronouns and their antecedent NPs is expressed by an equation of the form $\zeta=\gamma(X)$, where X is the discourse referent introduced by the antecedent NP and ζ the one introduced by the pronoun. The equation $\zeta=\gamma(X)$ leaves the choice to add $\gamma(X)=x$, or $\gamma(X)=X$.

The structure (40) does, however, not automatically guarantee that all linearisations are proper, i.e., that the open variable problem doesn't occur. Take, for example, a variant of (38) in which **a secretary** is replaced by the quantifier **at least two secretaries**. Then it would be possible to linearise such that $l_1 < scope(l_2) < k_1$. We thus proceed as follows. The UDRS-components introduced by singular and plural pronouns are l': $\boxed{\begin{array}{c} y \\ \hline y=? \end{array}}$ and l': $\boxed{\begin{array}{c} \zeta \\ \hline \zeta=\alpha(?) \end{array}}$, respectively. When resolving the pronoun we (i) instantiate '?', and (ii) add $l' < l$ to ORD, where l is the label of ?'s value. This means that we have (41) instead of (40).

$$(41)$$

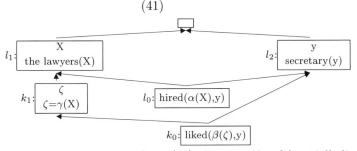

There are several ways to transform (41) via a couple of (partial) disambiguation steps into one of the fully specified readings given in (39). One possibility is to interpret **they** as referring to the group $\mathbf{X}$ of lawyers. This leaves the possibility of distribution open both with respect to **liked** and to **hired**. The different choices give us representations for (39.a) to (39.d). If we choose the collective reading of **hired**, then $\alpha(\mathbf{X})=\mathbf{X}$ is added to l_0 in (41). We thus have deprived the subject UDRS of its scope bearing potential, because with $\alpha(\mathbf{X})=\mathbf{X}$ also $scope(l_1) = l_1$ becomes part of the description of the UDRS. This blocks distribution with respect to $\mathbf{X}$. Consequently, only $\gamma(\mathbf{X})=\mathbf{X}$ can appear in k_1, and the only possibility for further disambiguating is to fix the interpretation of **liked**. Because ζ is set equal to a group discourse referent it is possible to distribute over it. This yields (42) (= (39.b)).[10]

---

[10]Without further syntactic information, (42) allows a disambiguation according to which the indefinite **a secretary** is within the scope of the distribution w.r.t. the verb **liked**. The problem of having more syntactic information available in order to restrict the disambiguation algorithm for UDRSs appropriately also shows up in the singular fragment and is discussed in Reyle 1993.

(42)

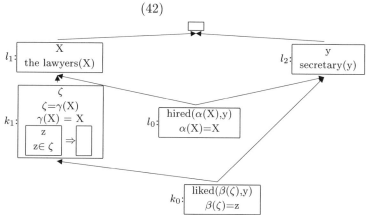

If the subject of **liked** is a collection, then no quantificational condition is introduced in k_1. We only add $\beta(\zeta)=\zeta$ to k_0 and get the reading (39.a).

If we start by choosing the distributive reading of **hired**, (43) gets transformed into (41).

(43)

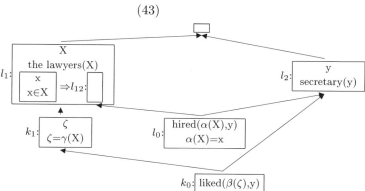

As the equation $\zeta=\gamma(X)$ still leaves open whether ζ is to be identified with **x** or **X** we now have the option to interpret **they** as bound by **x**. In this case we must add $k_1 < l_{12}$ to ORD and get (44), which represents the reading in (39.e).

(44)

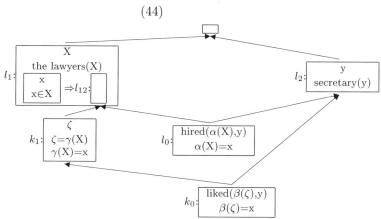

There are cases where no plural discourse referent has been introduced and the antecedent for **they** must be generated by Abstraction. Abstraction creates plural discourse referents by building the sum of discourse referents of DRSs that are created out of duplex conditions. This is done by, first, building the union K of the left hand and right hand side boxes of the duplex condition, and second, adding a condition of the form $\Sigma\eta$:K to the DRS in which the duplex condition occurs. To construct the antecedent of the **they** in (45), for example, we abstract over the discourse referent **x** in the DRS of the first sentence of (45) as shown in (46).

(45)   Every teacher showed a picture to some child (in the class). They were bored.

(46)

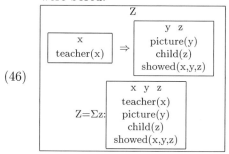

The discourse referent **Z** representing the group of children that have been shown a picture may now be picked up as antecedent for the pronoun. Note, however, that (46) represents only one reading of the first sentence of (45). There is also the reading where the indefinite **a picture** is interpreted specifically, as shown in (47).

(47)

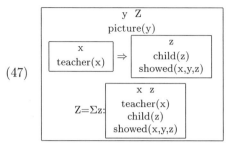

As **a picture** has wide scope over the universal quantifier its content doesn't show up in the DRS K used for Abstraction. This ambiguity has to be preserved when Abstraction is applied to UDRSs. Consider the UDRS (48).

(48)

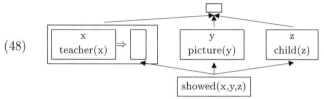

It not only represents the two readings (46) and (47) of (45), but also two other readings which we get out of (46) and (47) when we interpret **a child** specifically. Of course, these readings are ruled out once we apply Abstraction to create a group of children. To establish the anaphoric link between the plural pronoun **they** in (45) and the NP **some child**, therefore, has disambiguating force. To implement this we must require that,

> whenever a plural pronoun is linked to an indefinite singular NP, then the link can only be established if there is some duplex condition occurring in the same clause as this NP. Furthermore, the label of the indefinite NP must be set equal to the scope of one such duplex condition (whereas the label of the duplex condition should be accessible from the label of the pronoun).

We will call the duplex condition that supports the abstraction operation *licensing condition*. The link itself will be represented by a condition of the form $\zeta = \Sigma z{:}l$, where z is the singular discourse referent introduced by the antecedent NP, and l labels the licensing condition. This gives us the following as representation for (45).

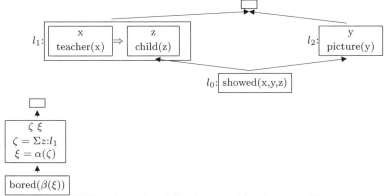

Standard DRT gives the following verification condition to equations of the form $Z = \Sigma z{:}K$ (see Kamp and Reyle 1993, p. 426).

(49) $f \models^c_e Z = \Sigma z{:}K$ iff $f(Z) = \oplus\{b \mid f \cup \{\langle z, b \rangle\} \models K\}$

Suppose the consequent of the licensing condition in (46) is labelled l_{12}. Then the set of embedding functions that verify the union of its restrictor and nuclear scope is equal to $\|l_{12}\|^c_g$. We thus define the verification condition for implicit Abstraction as follows.

Definition 5: Suppose x is declared in a UDRS-component labelled l_j belonging to some clause $l_{T_i}{:}\langle\langle \gamma_0, ..., \gamma_n\rangle, \mathrm{ORD}_i\rangle$, whose UDRS-components are labelled by $l_0, ..., l_n$. Suppose further that the licensing condition for $\xi = \Sigma z{:}l$ is $l_i{:}l_{i1} \Rightarrow l_{i2}$. Let c_i be a linearisation of ORD_i. Then

$f \models^c_e \zeta = \Sigma z{:}l_i$ iff $\forall e^{c_i}_{\underline{l_i}} f(\zeta) = \oplus\{b \mid f \cup \{\langle z, b\rangle\} \in \|l_{i2}\|^{c_i}_g(e^{c_i}_{\underline{l_i}})\}^{11}$

This definition does, however, not cover so-called dependent uses of plural pronouns. Sentence (50) has a reading according to which **them** is interpreted as dependent on **they**, i.e. each child copied the picture that was shown to him.

(50)   Every teacher showed a picture to some child. They copied them.

To get this reading we cannot apply distribution with respect to both arguments of **copied** in the UDRS for the second sentence of (50). This would require far too many copyings of pictures by children. We must distribute over the subject and then interpret the object as dependent on the subject, in almost the same way we did in (44). The only difference is that in (44) the pronoun is *directly* bound by the quantification over the set of lawyers, whereas in the case of (50), it is not the discourse referent introduced by distributing over the subject **they** which binds the object. Here the object **them** is bound *implicitly* in the following sense: Distribution over the subject not only amounts

---

[11]$e^{c_i}_{\underline{l_i}}$ is defined in Definition 2.iii.

to considering all embedding functions g that satisfy $\boxed{\begin{array}{c} \text{w} \\ \hline \text{w} \in \zeta \end{array}}$. It re-

ally amounts to considering the functions g satisfying $\boxed{\begin{array}{c} \text{x} \quad \text{y} \quad \text{z} \\ \hline \text{teacher(x)} \\ \text{picture(y)} \\ \text{child(z)} \\ \text{z} = \text{w} \end{array}}$. In

Kamp and Reyle 1993 this reinterpretation is achieved syntactically by accommodating the content of the DRS used for Abstraction within the restrictor of the duplex condition introduced by Distribution. We will not generalize this syntactic approach to the case under discussion. We will instead present a semantic solution.

6 Dependent Readings

The reading for (50) just discussed is a particular instance of *dependent* interpretations of verb meanings. Interpreting **copied** as dependent on **showed** in (50) means that the children-picture-pairs in the extension of **showed** are also in the extension of **copied**. Another case of dependent verb interpretation is (2) already mentioned in the Introduction, here repeated as (51).

(51)   Fünf Softwarefirmen kauften dreizehn Computer. Anschließend liehen sie sie aus.

We said that one cannot understand **ausleihen** in (51) to mean **borrow**. The reason being that the resultative state of the buying event cannot be consistently identified with the preconditions of **borrow**. Any justification of this relies on the fact that the interpretation of the second sentence of (51) is dependent on that of the first. To see this let us assume, for example, that a group of five software companies collectively bought thirteen computers. Then the second sentence of (51) can only mean that the group as such lent them out. It definitely cannot mean that each company borrowed the computers from the consortium (of which it is a member). Although this would not result in a contradiction, because each company does not possess any one of the computers on its own and, therefore, fulfills the preconditions of a borrowing event.[12]   To exclude such independent interpretations we will mark the label k_0 of the second verb as dependent on the label of the first, i.e. $k_0^{dep(l_0)}$. This is to guarantee that in the case just described

---

[12]Intuitions might differ from ours for those who accept the sentences in (52).
(52)   Five software companies bought thirteen computers.
$\left\{\begin{array}{l} \text{Subsequently they borrowed them from the consortium.} \\ \text{Subsequently each of them borrowed one (from the consortium).} \end{array}\right\}$
But even if the sentences in (52) are acceptable they are marginal, and the dependent interpretation of (51) is definitely preferred over the non-dependent one. Note that one may use **zurück/back** to force dependent interpretations. Like in **They immediately gave them back.**

the collective reading of **kaufen** forces a collective reading of **ausleihen** (with respect to the subject NP). But note that the choice of the "same type" of reading is not sufficient. As the dependent reading on (50) showed we must interpret the coindexation as a constraint on the chosen sets of embedding functions[13] of the coindexed verbs (and not only as constraint on the choice itself). In the case of (50) we could have put the constraint into the verfication condition for the equation introduced by Abstraction. But consider (53), where no Abstraction is needed and the same dependent reading is possible. (We treat **didn't have any contract with** as transitive verb.)

(53) Three breweries supplied$_{l_0}$ five inns. They [didn't have any contract with]$_{k_0^{dep(l_0)}}$ them.

As the second verb is marked dependent on the first,[14] we will use this marking to constrain its extensions. As long as we don't know what the first sentence is supposed to mean, this constraint must apply for any possible disambiguation. So in case the first sentence is interpreted distributively with respect to both arguments, the second should be interpreted in the same way. And in case the first has a cumulative interpretation, the supply-relation must be included in the [didn't have any contract with]-relation. We have seen that, whereas in the former case it is sufficient to say that the verb of the second sentence also has the distributive-distributive reading, a correct interpretation is not ensured in the latter case simply by requiring a cumulative reading also for the second sentence. Here, dependency marking must achieve more. It must make sure that any embedding function f that verifies the nuclear scope of the polyadic duplex condition representing the cumulative reading of the first verb must also verify the scope of the condition for the second verb.

We proceed as follows. Suppose l_0 and k_0 are lower bound labels, such that k_0 is marked dependent on l_0 (i.e., $k_0^{dep(l_0)}$). Let $FV(l)$ denote the set of discourse referents that occur (free or bound) in (some sub-DRS of the DRS labelled) l. We then restrict the set of embeddings that verify k_0 by those verifying l_0 as follows. Recall that $\|l_0\|$ is defined as sets of pairs on page 257.

---

[13]Recall that the denotation of a verb with underspecified arguments was a set of sets of embedding functions according to the modifiction (2.i) of Definition 2 on page 257.

[14]We claim that situations like this occur very often in the interpretation process. Disambiguation requires a choice to be made among different concepts, lexicalized by some verb. In complex sentences, or texts, more than one verb occurs and each of them will be subject to this choice. More often than not, however, we cannot disambiguate. Nevertheless we are forced to either choose a specific concept type for all of these verbs simultaneously, or to allow a free choice to be made for each of them.

Definition 6:

Suppose $\|l_0\| = \{\langle e_{l_0}, r_{l_0}\rangle\}_{r_{l_0}}$, $\|k_0\| = \{\langle e_{k_0}, r_{k_0}\rangle\}_{r_{k_0}}$, $\pi : FV(k_0) \mapsto FV(l_0)$. Then the restriction of $\|k_0\|$ to $\|l_0\|$ induced by π, short $\|k_0^{\pi:dep(l_0)}\|$, is $\{\langle e_{k_0}^\pi, r_{k_0}^\pi\rangle\}_{r_{k_0}}$, where

(i) $f \in e_{k_0}^\pi$ iff $f(x_i) = g(\pi(x_i))$ for some $g \in e_{l_0}^\pi$ and all $x_i \in FV(k_0)$

(ii) $r_{k_0}^\pi = r_{l_0}^\pi$, in case $r_{k_0}^\pi \in \{c, d, \langle c, c\rangle, \langle d, c\rangle, \langle c, d\rangle, \langle d, d\rangle\}$

(iii) $f \in \|r_{k_0}^\pi\|$ iff $f(x) = g(\pi(x))$ for some $g \in r_{l_0}^\pi$, in case $r_{k_0}^\pi$ labels the nuclear scope of k_0's polyadic duplex condition.

To apply this to (51) let us assume that

(i) the resultative state of a buying event **e:kaufen(x,y)** is s_r^e:**Have(x,y)**,

(ii) the preconditions of a lending event **e** require s_p^e:**Have(x,y)**, whereas the preconditions of a borrowing event require s_p^e:¬**Have(x,y)**,

(iii) the meaning of **anschließend** triggers the identification of the resultative state of **kaufen** with the preconditions of **ausleihen**.

Then we get (54) as representation of the first sentence of (51).

(54)

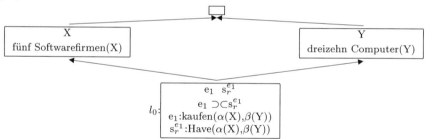

Without having disambiguated **ausleihen** the second sentence may be represented as in (55).

(55)

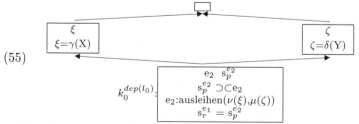

Now let us assume that **ausleihen** is meant in the sense of **borrow**, and that $\pi^{-1}(\alpha(X)) = \nu(\xi)$ and $\pi^{-1}(\beta(Y)) = \mu(\zeta)$. Then it follows from Definition 6 that

$$(56) \quad f \in \|k_0^{dep(l_0)}\| \quad \text{gdw} \quad f \models \begin{array}{|c|} \hline e_1 \quad s_r^{e_1} \quad e_2 \quad s_p^{e_2} \\ e_1 \supset \subset s_r^{e_1} \\ s_p^{e_2} \supset \subset e_2 \\ e_1{:}\text{kaufen}(\nu(\xi),\mu(\zeta)) \\ s_r^{e_1}{:}\text{Have}(\nu(\xi),\mu(\zeta)) \\ e_2{:}\text{ausleihen}_{borrow}(\nu(\xi),\mu(\zeta)) \\ s_p^{e_2}{:}\neg\text{Have}(\nu(\xi),\mu(\zeta)) \\ s_r^{e_1} = s_p^{e_2} \\ \hline \end{array}$$

But this DRS cannot be verified at all, and therefore, **ausleihen** cannot mean **borrow** in (51). Note that we found the inconsistency in (56) (i) without having decided upon a particular interpretation of the first (and thus the second) sentence, and (ii) without considering the logical contribution of the arguments of **ausleihen**. Exactly the same reasoning will thus be applicable if we replace the object pronoun **sie** of (51) by **die meisten von ihnen** (meaning 'most of them').

7 Conclusion

We have presented an extension of the formalism of underspecified DRSs to deal with ambiguities triggered by plural NPs. We emphasized the fact that the representation language must be able to correlate different occurrences of ambiguous phrases, in the sense that any particular disambiguation chosen for one occurrence triggers the same disambiguation of all correlated occurrences. An even stronger requirement is given by dependent readings of verbs whose argument phrases contain plural pronouns. Here, it is not only the same type of disambiguation that must apply to correlated verbs. The arguments of the dependent verb must be interpreted as bound by those of the one it is dependent on.

We introduced co-indexation and dependency marking to represent these types of correlated interpretations. And we have defined a semantics for them that does not presuppose any kind of accommodation to prepare the ground for dependent readings.

As a matter of fact indexation and dependency marking is also neccessary in order to control reconstruction procedures for elliptical phrases, especially in cases of gapping (Fiengo and May 1994, Kamp). As a matter of fact, the restrictions on reconstructing elliptical phrases and the restrictions on the disambiguation of dependent ambiguities are very similar. Results from the literature on ellipsis may, therefore, be used to refine the co-indexing mechanism used here. And the semantics given in the present paper may be generalised to apply to elliptical phrases. These are important questions for further research on underspecification.

References

Alshawi, Hiyan (ed.). 1992. *The Core Language Engine*. ACL-MIT Press

Series in Natural Languages Processing. Cambridge, Mass.: MIT Press.

Alshawi, Hiyan, and Richard Crouch. 1992. Monotonic Semantic Interpretation. In *Proceedings of ACL*, 32–39. Newark, Delaware.

Fiengo, Robert, and Robert May. 1994. *Indices and Identity*. Cambridge, Mass.: MIT Press.

Frank, Anette, and Uwe Reyle. n.d. Principle Based Semantics for HPSG (long version). Technical report.

Frank, Anette, and Uwe Reyle. 1995. Principle Based Semantics for HPSG (short version). In *Proceedings of EACL 95, Dublin*.

Hobbs, Jerry, and Stuart M. Shieber. 1987. An Algorithm for Generating Quantifier Scopings. *Computational Linguistics* 13:47–63.

Kamp, Hans. n.d. Technical report.

Kamp, Hans, and Uwe Reyle. 1993. *From Discourse to Logic. Introduction to Modeltheoretic Semantics of Natural Language, Formal Logic and Discourse Representation Theory*. Studies in Linguistics and Philosophy 42. Dordrecht, The Netherlands: Kluwer Academic Publishers.

Pereira, Fernando C.N. 1990. Categorial Semantics and Scoping. *Computational Linguistics* 16(1):1–10.

Poesio, Massimo. 1991. Scope Ambiguity and Inference. Technical report. University of Rochester, N.Y.

Pollard, Carl, and Ivan A. Sag. 1994. *Head Driven Phrase Structure Grammar*. Chicago: University of Chicago Press.

Reyle, Uwe. 1993. Dealing with Ambiguities by Underspecification: Construction, Representation, and Deduction. *Journal of Semantics* 10(2).

Reyle, Uwe. 1995. On Reasoning with Ambiguities. In *Proceedings of EACL 95, Dublin*.

van Deemter, Kees. 1991. *On the Composition of Meaning*. Doctoral dissertation, University of Amsterdam.

Index